THE CONTINUUM
ENCYCLOPEDIA OF
SYMBOLS

FOR REFERENCE

Do Not Take From This Room

DPLC

THE CONTINUUM ENCYCLOPEDIA OF SYMBOLS

UDO BECKER

Translated by Lance W. Garmer

With 16 color plates
and more than 800 ilustrations

CONTINUUM

NEW YORK | LONDON

2000
The Continuum International Publishing Group Inc
370 Lexington Avenue, New York, N Y 10017

The Continuum International Publishing Group Ltd
Wellington House, 125 Strand, London WC2R 0BB

German Edition Copyright © 1992
by Verlag Herder Freiburg im Breisgau
English Language Edition Copyright © 1994
by The Continuum Publishing Company, New York

Printed in Spain

Library of Congress Cataloging-in-Publication Data

Becker, Udo
    [Lexicon der Symbole, English]
    The Continuum encyclopedia of symbols /
    Udo Becker : translated by Lance W. Garmer.
        p.   cm.
    Includes bibliographical references.
    ISBN 0-8264-1221-1 (paperback)
1. Signs and symbols - Dictionaries.   I. Title.   II. Title:
Encyclopedia of symbols.
AZ108.B4313   2000
302.2 2203-dc20   94-11000
                                               CIP

FOREWORD

Upon hearing, reading or seeing the word "symbol," one inevitably forms a chain of associations whose links are certainly not rooted in the realm of the commonplace: allegory, attribute, metaphor, image, emblem, archetype, good luck charms and signs, hieroglyphics, signs of the elements—each individual idea can belong to an elite multi-disciplinary area of research. Perhaps this also explains many people's attraction to and interest in being involved with symbols, most of which are derived from antiquity: that one might reflect on one's roots in an age that—as it is said—has become increasingly devoid of orientation. If one then pursues the stream of these traditions to their sources, it becomes clearer with each step how manifold, entangled, contradictory and often inextricable symbolic expressions can be.

How can this be explained? The word *symbol* is based on the Greek verb *symballein*, which means "to toss together" or "to join together"; the nominal form is *symbolon*. This word "symbolon" is first found on an ancient Egyptian lead token like those used in antiquity as a sort of identification stamp made of various materials and called *tesserae* in Latin. The *tessera* was originally regarded as a symbolon. Only later did the concept apply to the sign and to the pictorial reference of the tesserae.

At the same time, however, the verb *symballein* was used in manners of speech that suggested a gathering together, a hiding or a veiling. The sign, having become a symbol, therefore encoded or camouflaged the apparent meaning of an expression or that which was represented: the uninitiated observer could no longer understand the statement so encoded.

Aside from this, *symbolum* also referred to those articles of faith of a religious community that were summarized in a few basic statements and always surrounded by something mysterious, by an *arcanum*.

Aside from symbols, one also distinguishes among *attributes*, *allegories*, *emblems*, and *logograms*, which are similar and whose differentiations are often tricky and difficult to grasp. Considered unto itself, however, the symbol—and this quality is part of its essence—can and will always yield a self-contained statement: this is the difference from allegory, from attribute, and from metaphor, and it is not always easy to outline clearly the differences among them.

Amidst the inestimable number of symbols or symbolic signs, a selection is always a *personal* one made consciously or unconsciously by the editor. There neither can be nor will be absolute completeness, especially when one considers a geographical and temporal factor that often exists amidst centuries of change and extends over continents: the migration of symbols and their meanings has become one of the most exciting and stimulating areas of research within modern interdisciplinary studies.

That which is true of textual (verbal) statements is, of course, especially applicable to visual presentation. Modern semiotics has produced so many new insights and viewpoints that symbol research is being placed on an increasingly secure foundation. In that sense, the archaic symbols in this encyclopedia (prehistoric rock drawings, for example) as well as numerous examples from the 19th century (such as those easily recognized in the ornamentation of churches or of sacred art of that time) mark the grand trajectory of the symbol's history (some of the pictorial representations in our lexicon are from A. Schmid's "Musterbuch [BOOK OF PATTERNS], for use by Christian artists," published in Freiburg in 1909).

In our age of inundation by optical stimuli, there is a great danger that man's own capacity for pictorial thought will continue to languish. Working with symbols can help us find means and ways to see *behind* things and to tie together visual and verbal manifestations of a world so wonderfully varied and multi-layered.

Udo Becker

ABRAHAM: Isaac's "sacrifice"
(Alsatian miniature, 12th century).
ABRAHAM: Abraham's Bosom;
miniature from the 12th century.

A **and** Ω - See ALPHA AND OMEGA.

Aaron's Rod - A plant with a club-shaped inflorescence and a whitish, lily-like bract; during the Middle Ages, it was an attribute of Mary. Since the plant also refers to the budding rod of Aaron, it, like the latter, is also associated with the symbolism of resurrection.

Abracadabra - Already present in late Greek writings as an evocation and probably connected with ABRAXAS. It was used as an amulet inscription, mostly in a DISAPPEARING PATTERN, in order to make diseases "disappear."

Abraham - The Biblical patriarch. Often thought of as a symbolic figure of a new race of humans. He represents the man chosen by God who is blessed with fulfilled prophecies (wealth, progeny); he is also regarded as a primeval image of unconditional, obedient faith and unquestioning readiness to sacrifice. The "sacrifice" of his son Isaac has been variously interpreted as the symbolic precursor of Christ's Passion.—Representations of Abraham's bosom are a symbol of the protection of the faithful in God. Considered in the New Testament to be favored in heaven, Abraham carries in his bosom a group of chosen persons gathered together in a cloth; Lazarus also appears occasionally in Abraham's bosom (with respect to the image of the poor Lazarus).

Abraham's Bosom - See ABRAHAM.

Abraxas - A magical spell. The name of the god of the year in Greek gnosticism. The word is probably comprised of the first letters of the Hebrew names for God. The 7 letters of the name have a numerical value of 365 (a = 1, b = 2, r = 100, x = 60, s = 200). The word is found in Hellenistic magic papyri as a magical sign and symbol of totality (probably with respect to the number SEVEN). It is also found on ancient and medieval amulet stones, mostly together with a human trunk having a rooster's head, human arms and snakes as legs. It has recently been interpreted as an ancient Jewish symbol for God; the actual name is Iao.

Abyss - That which is without foundation or base, symbolizes conditions that have not (yet) assumed form or are unimaginable from the standpoint of ordinary consciousness. It thus symbolizes the origins

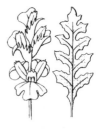

ABRAXAS: Abraxas gem.
ACANTHUS: Above, flower and leaf;
  below, acanthus on a capital.

of the world, which are shrouded in darkness, as well as the end of the world, the indeterminacy of earliest childhood and the dissolution of the individual in death. Yet it also symbolizes the process of becoming one with the absolute in unio mystica. C.G. Jung sees the symbol of the abyss in connection with the archetype (see ARCHETYPES) of the loving, yet simultaneously terrible mother and with the powers of the unconscious.

Acacia - A tree frequently identified as a locust tree or a MIMOSA tree. The wood of a genuine acacia is very durable and was thus regarded as a symbol of immutability. Especially among the Freemasons, it is a symbol of purity, immortality and initiation.

Acanthus - A thistle-like plant found in warmer climates. The scalloped leaves of the two varieties of acanthus in the Mediterranean were the pattern for leaved ornaments, especially those on Corinthian capitals; they were also used as decorative surface garland. The symbolic significance of acanthus is probably based on its thorns; it indicates that a difficult problem has been completely solved.

Acedia (Sloth) - The female personification of one of the seven deadly sins; rides on an ass. Symbolized by, among other things, an ostrich with its head in the sand.

Actaeon - An important hunter. He was raised and instructed in hunting by the centaur Chiron. As Actaeon saw Artemis bathing naked, the goddess transformed him into a stag; he was then ripped apart by his dogs, which did not recognize him. A symbolic warning to persons who approach the sphere of the gods curiously and irreverently.

Adam - In the Biblical account of creation, Adam represents the first human, i.e., humanity itself. In art, he is rarely represented without EVE (see ADAM AND EVE). According to legend, Adam's burial place was at Golgotha, represented by Adam's skull, which is frequently encountered beneath the cross in depictions of the Crucifixion and occasionally also with the rib from which Eve was begotten, or with the entire skeleton: symbolic reference to Christ as the new Adam.—In alchemy, Adam often represents *materia prima*.—For Jung, Adam symbolizes "cosmic man," the original entirety of all psychological forces, appearing (among other things) in the form of the old, wise man.

Adam and Eve - According to the biblical

ADAM AND EVE: Eve giving Adam the apple. Reims Cathedral, 13th century.

ADAM AND EVE: Expulsion from Eden with the flaming sword; from *Speculum Humanae Salvationis*, a Dutch block-book.

account of creation, Adam and Eve embody the first, or prototypical, pair of humans. Most frequent depiction: the temptation by the SERPENT in Eden, often together with the first instance of shame and the expulsion from Eden. Adam and Eve are also found depicted at both sides of the cross of Christ, representing all persons who, following Christ, will find salvation. Not infrequently, symbolic signs are found with Adam and Eve. A LAMB at Eve's feet refers to Christ, one of her descendents. Sheep, sheaves and tools refer to the work that Adam and Eve must do outside Eden.

Adder - The VIPER in PHYSIOLOGUS.

Adonia - Privately held mourning ceremonies in honor of ADONIS that were celebrated at various times in the Orient and in Greece. Important aspects of the cult were the mock burial of the god and the tiny ADONIS GARDENS.

Adonis - The symbolic figure in Greek mythology of a beautiful youth who was loved by Aphrodite (VENUS) and killed while on a hunt. Aphrodite bade Persephone to allow Adonis to live on the earth six months of the year.—Adonis is probably a fertility god that originated in the Orient or in Phoenicia ("Adon" is Phoenician for "lord"), representing continually sprouting and withering vegetation. The ADONIA held in his honor enjoyed great popularity.

Adonis Gardens - The pots, pitchers and baskets filled with the quickly growing and quickly withering plants and flowers for the Feast of Adonis. See ADONIA.

Adorant - From the Latin. A worshipper at the feet of Christ or the Madonna. See ORANT.

Advent Wreath - See WREATH.

Adyton (Also Abaton) - Both from the Greek, meaning "that which may not be trespassed." A holy place, especially the holy of holies in a temple, that is off-limits to all or certain persons at all or certain times.

Aegis - The shield of Zeus, forged by Hephaestus and bearing the head of Gorgon in its middle (see GORGONEION). Due to etymological misinterpretations, the shield in post-Homeric stories was thought to be covered with the skin of the GOAT Amalthea. Zeus loaned it to Athena, among others. It was a sym-

ALCHEMISTIC WORK

The *Alchemistic Work*, also called the *Opus*, consists of a "practical part," called the *Operatio*, and a "theoretical part," called the *Amplificatio*. The *Alchemistic Work* is subdivided into twelve epochs whose twelve "works" are correlated with the signs of the zodiac, thereby reflecting the circular flow of time. Older than this twelve-part division is the seven-part division, comprising the operations of calcination, sublimation, solution, putrefaction, distillation, congelation and tinctura. Personifications of the seven metals of the planets accompany the work on the outside of the mountain; within the mountain, PHOENIX has the work completed. (See illustration, taken from St. Michelspacher's *Cabala*, Augsburg, 1615.)

ALCHEMISTIC WORK: The *Alchemistic Work*, the Mountain of Adepts with the Philosopher's Temple inside. The personified planets stand upon the mountain, which is bordered by the zodiac as a symbol of time. The four elements in the corners refer to the entirety of the "work". Only the adept at the left, who is looking at the rabbit, knows "into which hole the rabbit races"; the other adept with the blindfold is vainly groping around in front of the seven steps that could lead him to the perfection of his art within the mountain where the "chemical wedding" is taking place.

ALEXANDER THE GREAT: Image,
with the horns of Ammon, on a coin.

bol of the gods' protection; from this comes the expression, still used today, "to stand under the aegis of someone."—The interpretation of the aegis as a symbol of storms and storm clouds is controversial.

Agate - Since antiquity, agates have been highly valued gem stones and were regarded as a remedy and an aphrodisiac as well as a protection against violent storms, snake bites, the evil eye, and other things.—PHYSIOLOGUS reports that pearl-fishers found PEARLS by sinking into the water an agate that was tied to a line. The agate sought a pearl and hovered above it so that the fishers could easily find it. Agates are thus compared to John, as he showed us the spiritual pearl with his words, "Behold, this is the Lamb of God."

Agave - See ALOE.

Age - A divisional category of early human history encompassing broad expanses of time, often envisioned as a succession of typified, symbolic sets of circumstances. The idea of (usually) four of five successive ages, particularly a Golden Age, exists in many cultures, such as in antiquity, where it first appeared in Hesiod: during the Golden Age, people

lived long and carefree, without distress, work and laws. The people of the Silver Age were godless and were destroyed by Zeus; during the subsequent Bronze Age, people killed one another and no longer lived after their death; the Heroic Age, in which wars for Troy and Thebes occurred, brought a new upturn in human virtue, yet inaugurated the Iron Age, which was thought (at that time) to be continuing up to the present and which brought complete downfall.

Agla - A secret Hebrew sign composed of the first letters of Psalms 89:52 ("Blessed be the Lord for evermore. Amen, and Amen.").

Agrarian Fertility Rites - Symbolic ritual ceremonies that were supposed to influence the growth of plants. The desired height of grain, for example, was symbolized by equally high leaps; the fertility or fertilization of the earth was symbolized by sprinkling a maiden with water, etc.

Agrimony - A rose plant with yellow, erect flower clusters; it is an ancient medicinal and magical plant. Dug up with a nonferrous (see IRON) tool on Good Friday, the agrimony is supposed to provide one with the affection and love of women.—

ALPHA AND OMEGA: The Book of
Life with A and W entered in it.
From Schmid's *Musterbuch*.

ALTAR: Slaughtering of a calf on
sacrificial altar; based on a
miniature in an Evangeliar,
Auersbach, 12th century.

It is sometimes encountered next to Mary as a salvation symbol in medieval panel paintings.

Ahasverus - The symbolic figure of the "Eternal Jew" who, according to legend, must wander restlessly upon the earth until the Last Judgment. According to legend, Ahasverus is supposed to have hit Jesus at the interrogation before Caiaphas or to have insulted Jesus while He was carrying the cross. See FLYING DUTCHMAN.

Air - Along with EARTH, WATER and FIRE, air is one of the four ELEMENTS in the cosmologies of many peoples; like fire, it is thought to be lively, active and masculine, in contrast to the feminine, passive elements of water and earth. Air is closely related symbolically to BREATH and WIND; it was often thought to be a fine material intermediary realm between the earthly and spiritual realms; it was sometimes seen as a symbol of spirit, which is invisible to the eye, yet noticeable in its effects.—In astrology, air became associated with the signs of the ZODIAC Gemini, Libra and Aquarius.—In alchemy, air is frequently represented by the sign ⌀.

Air Bubble - See BUBBLE.

Alchemy - The theoretical and experimental analysis of chemical materials that probably arose mainly in Egypt and blossomed from the Middle Ages into early modernity. Alchemy was a high point of symbolic thought and represents a limited breakthrough of early scientific, religious and psychological ideas. It also was closely connected with the astrology and medicine of its time (see MICROCOSM-MACROCOSM). Practitioners of alchemy primarily sought a refinement of materials and a mystical union of microcosm and macrocosm as well as a concommitant purification of the soul. The alchemists recognized not only the four elements of Greek natural philosophy (FIRE, WATER, AIR and EARTH), but also the "philosophical elements" of SALT, SULPHUR and QUICKSILVER (See MERCURY).

Alcohol - Also called "fire water." Symbolizes the unification of the opposing elements of FIRE and WATER. It is therefore a symbol of vitality as well.

Alexander the Great - Symbolic figure of the bold army leader and ruler, King of Macedonia, and founder of the world empire (336 - 323 B.C.) that was partitioned upon his death. See I Maccabees 1:1 cf.; Daniel 8:5 cf. where he is referred

AMULET: 1: astrological sickness amulet; 2: defensive amulet against the "evil eye", made of buffalo horn; 3: bird amulet of the Tungus (Siberia); 4: Finger amulet (gesture of envy or insult), especially common in southern lands; 5: medallion amulet with Druid's foot.

AMULET: Tiki, ancestral father of man.

---

to as a "goat"; and in Daniel 11:3, where he is referred to as a "mighty king." He visited the shrine of Zeus Ammon (Jupiter Ammon) at Memphis, which probably accounts for the attribute of the horn (Ammon horns) on coins and in many legendary fictional works.

Allegory - From the Greek. The conscious transposition of a conceptual context into a pictorial representation with determinate meanings of the individual pictorial motives; especially common as personification (which differs from symbol), for example, the representation of the battle between virtues and vices. In Greek art of the 2nd and 3rd centuries B.C., allergory replaced the old mythology. In the Middle Ages, theological (dogmatic and moral) allegory and political allegory (the virtues of the political system) predominate. During the Renaissance and the Baroque period, allegory for sacred and secular life was at times extravagant, often having mythological motives.

Almond - As a sweet fruit in a hard shell, the almond is a symbol of the essential or the spiritual, of that which lies hidden behind the surface. It is a symbol of Christ because His human nature hides His divine nature; it is also a symbol of His in-

carnation. Because of its protected, hidden kernel, the almond, like the nut, was regarded in antiquity as a symbol of pregnancy and fertility and was thus tossed about at weddings. It was also a symbol of patience, since one first had to extract the tasty kernel from the shell. Among the Greeks, the oil extracted from the almond had phallic significance and was regarded as the seed of Zeus.

Almond Tree - Blooms in Mediterranean lands as early as in January; it thus became a symbol of vigilance (because it "awakens" early) and of rebirth.

Aloe - The aloe mentioned in the Bible is a tall tree whose wood yielded a very valuable, bitter, and aromatic oil, which was frequently used in conjunction with MYRRH. Aloe and its oil are regarded as symbols of repentance and abstinence. Because it is mentioned in connection with the burial of Christ (its oil having been used for His embalming), it is often a symbol of Christ's death. The long-lived agave (also called "100-year aloe") grows a single tall stalk with many flowers and then dies. In the Middle Ages, it was regarded as a symbol of the virgin birth given by Mary.

Alpha - The first letter of the Greek alpha-

ALTAR

ALTAR: 1: Egyptian altar (circa 2400 B.C.); 2: horned altar from Israel (9th century B.C.); 3: step altar from Jordan (4th century B.C.); 4: Greek voluted altar (end of the 3rd century A.D.); 5: altar of Zeus from Pergamon (180-160 B.C.); 6: Jewish altar for burnt sacrifices (7th century B.C.); 7: altar with five pillars (Romanesque, 12th century); 8: chest altar; 9: block altar; 10: sarcophagal altar (Baroque, 18th century); 11: Ciborium altar; 12: reverse altar (Gothic, 13th century); 13: winged altar (Late Gothic, 16th century); 14: pulpit altar (Baroque, 18th century).

ANCHOR: Anchor with a cross and monogram of Christ (from Schmid's *Musterbuch*).

ANCHOR: Anchor with fish (the faithful), based on a representation in catacombs (from Schmid's *Musterbuch*).

bet and of the word "arche," meaning "beginning." In the Bible as well as in Christian art and literature, it symbolizes the primeval beginning. See ALPHA AND OMEGA; OMEGA; and TAU.

Alphabet - See LETTERS.

Alpha and Omega - A and W, the first and last letters of the Greek alphabet, "encompass" all other letters. They are thus a symbol for the Comprehensive, the Totality, for God, and especially Christ as the Beginning and the End. They are frequently a secondary motif of Christ's monogram, appearing on grave stones, coffins, coins, rings and other objects. They are also an apocalyptic symbol for Christ. See ALPHA; OMEGA; and TAU.

Altar - A raised area (altus) within a house of worship that, in nearly all religions, is used for sacrifice and other sacred activities. The rise symbolizes the lifting of the sacrifice to the gods or to God. The altar was occasionally conceived of as the spiritual center of the world and stands in close connection with the symbolic meaning of the mountain and of the tree. In Christianity, it symbolizes the holy table of the Last Supper of Christ or the body of Christ itself (in which case, the white altar cloth symbolizes the burial shroud). Since the 4th century, the altar has also been regarded as a place of protection and of sanctuary: even the worst criminals could not be arrested in a church, and especially at the altar.

Amazon - A warlike nation of women of Greek legend led by a queen; said to have come from the northeastern part of Asia Minor and to have fought against various heroes (Heracles, Theseus, Achilles and others). Being utterly hostile toward men, the Amazons had sexual intercourse with them only once each year and raised only girls. An Amazon's right breast was either burned off or cut off so that it would not be an obstacle to drawing a bow. For this reason, the Greeks also called Amazons "breastless."—Today, the idea of an Amazon is used as a symbol (or synonym) for women who are "emancipated" or athletically very active.

Amber - A popular material made from the fossilized resin of coniferous trees and used since antiquity for making amulets, jewelry and medicaments.

Ambrosia - In antiquity, ambrosia, along with nectar, was frequently mentioned as a food of the gods, giving immortality.—

ANGELICA: Angelica.
ANKH: Worship of the falcon-headed
   Horus, who has an ankh sign on his
   knees and a sun disk; from the
   papyrus of Ani.

In Christian literature, the Word of God and the Eucharist are occasionally symbolically called ambrosia.

Amen - An acclamatory, affirmatory word in Jewish synagogue services, in the New Testament, in all Christian liturgies, and in Islam. In the Book of Revelation, Christ is symbolically called "the Amen."—As an efficacious word, it is related to the meditative syllable OM. See NINETY-NINE (under NINE).

Amethyst - A popular ornamental stone (see JEWELS) considered in antiquity to be a remedy for poison and drunkenness ("amethysios" being a Greek word meaning "not drunk").—In the language of Christian symbolism, it is a symbol of humility because it is the color of the modest violet plant and symbolically refers to the Passion of Christ (see VIOLET). This explains its popular use as a material for rosaries. The amethyst was also thought to be one of the cornerstones of Holy Jerusalem (see JERUSALEM, HOLY).

Amulet - A small object usually worn on one's body. In the world view of magic, an amulet is used by humans as a protective charm (against ghosts, the evil eye, bad luck, illness) and as a good luck charm, whereby the rarity or specific form of the object was probably thought to be a symbolic expression of the coercion of particular powers of fate. Prevalent types of amulets include: the HORN, reptiles, SPIDERS, clover leaves (see CLOVER), obscene gestures, precious and semi-precious stones, names or LETTERS, conspicuous natural formations (see MANDRAKE), images of saints (see ENCOLPION). The wearing of jewelry probably has to do with the original use of amulets. Amulets were already common in prehistoric times and were especially widespread in the ancient Orient and in China. In Egypt, mummies were protected from "death" by amulets. The use of amulets survives to some extent even today. See ABRACADABRA; ABRAXAS; PENTAGRAM; SATOR-AREPO FORMULA.

Analogy, Magic Of - Magical, imitative actions that are supposed to produce a corresponding (analogous) effect in beings that are conjured up. IMAGE MAGIC is an example of this.

Analogy, Principle Of - A principle and logical method of occultism based on induction and on the assumption that identical conditions will produce identical re-

ANKH: The goddess Nut, with an ankh on each wrist, carrying the sun; painting from grave #2 Khabekhet; 20th Dynasty.

APE: Baboon from a scene in the Underworld; grave of Tutankhamen, 18th Dynasty.

sults. The principle of analogy is not a strict proof. Goethe says of the principle of analogy that "in observing nature, we must consider one and all: nothing is inside, nothing is outside: for what is inside, is outside." See MICROCOSM-MACROCOSM.

Anastasius, Cross Of - In sarcophagal art, this is a symbolical representation of the death (a cross bearing Christ's monogram but not his body) and resurrection of Christ (sleeping guards, cross of victory).

Ancestors - All persons from whom one is descended.

Anchor - Attribute of various sea gods.— Because the anchor symbolizes a ship's only stability during a storm, it is a symbol of hope, especially in Christian symbolism (appearing frequently on grave stones and coffins), and a symbol of consistency and fidelity. It was used as a secret symbol (anchor cross) in early Christianity by the addition of the crossbar.

Androgyne - An individual having a mixture of masculine and feminine characteristics, as the conception of those characteristics has been determined by ideas throughout history. Also, as pertains to the physical and the psychological, an androgyne is a man or woman who has characteristics and sensibilities of the opposite sex. Androgynes are to be distinguished from HERMAPHRODITES, which represent a somatic dual sexuality; however, these two names are often erroneously used as synonyms.

Anemone - In antiquity, the anemone was a symbol of disease and death, and of impermanence in general, as it did not live long ("anemos" is Greek for "wind"). The flower of Adonis, who was transformed by Venus into a purple anemone.—In Christian symbolism, anemones (as well as roses and marguerites) signify the blood spilled by saints.

Angelica - Umbelliferous plant growing in the northern hemisphere; one of the oldest symbolic plants in Christianity. In art, it is a symbol of the Trinity and of the Holy Spirit because the stem grows out from between two cuticles that wrap around one another. It was considered the primary remedy for the plague, having, according to legend, been brought to a monk by an angel.

Angel Prince Of Persia - The idea of heavenly guardian angels for nations derives

APE: Capital of the Church of Saint-
Jouin-de-Marnes.

ARK: Noah's ark; based on an
illustration in Queen Mary's
Psalms, 14th century.

from the idea that the gods worshipped by nations are not "nothings," but rather powerful beings, albeit ones inferior to the God of Israel.

Angel Princes - The idea of a heavenly princely court, a council of the God of Israel, can be found in older texts of the Old Testament. In late and post-Old Testament apocalyptic writings, these heavenly beings are accorded an important mediatory role between earthly empires and the kingdom of God: God acts and appears through angel princes; the final victory of the kingdom of God will be announced by angel princes.

Angels - During the late and post-Old Testament period, various levels of heavenly beings in God's presence are distinguished. The angels standing around God's throne occupy the highest spot (Revelation 8:2-6). According to Tobias 12:15, there are seven angels at the throne and according to other, non-Biblical texts, there are four: Michael, Gabriel and Raphael are among them. Their appearance on the earth is a sign of the imminent coming of God's dominion.

Animalism - Religious-like reverence of animals as protective spirits, ancestors, and the like, especially in hunting cultures. See TOTEMISM.

Animals - Animals often symbolically represent supernatural divine and cosmic powers as well as powers of the subconscious and of instinct. Representations of animals in ROCK PAINTINGS are probably closely related with mythic religious ideas and ceremonies.—Among many peoples, gods were depicted in the form of animals or with animal heads (such as in Egypt and India); even in Christianity, the Holy Spirit is represented by an animal, the DOVE. Among primitive peoples, animals often played a role as the human "alter ego." In the symbolic languages of many cultures, animals, including fabulous animals, appear as symbols of human traits. Animal-human hybrid creatures often symbolize humans' dual spiritual-corporeal nature. See EVANGELISTS, SYMBOLS OF; MINOTAUR; SACRIFICE; ZODIAC; CENTAUR.

Animatism - See ANIMISM.

Animism - From the Latin word "anima," meaning "soul." 1) The belief in the animation of natural things. Distinguished from animatism, a belief in the universal animation of objects that is sometimes

ARK: Noah's ark in the form of a chest, corresponding to an ancient myth (from Schmid's *Musterbuch*).

considered a precursor of animism. 2) Occultism: a trance that admits of a medium's extraordinary spiritual powers, but not of the intercession of "spirits" (such as deceased persons).

Ankh - An Egyptian looped cross symbolizing life as well as the fertilization of the earth by the sun. Appears frequently in Egyptian art, often in the hands of gods and kings. In depictions of burial, it is often lifted high and held by the side of the loop (perhaps symbolizing a key that opens the realm of the dead). The Christian Egyptians (called "Coptics") appropriated the sign as a symbol of the life-giving power of the cross of Christ.

Anointing - See OILS; CHRISM.

Ant - The ant, like the BEE, is a symbol of diligence and organized communal life. Because of its abundantly stocked winter provisions, it is also a symbol of prudent foresight, as mentioned in Job or Proverbs 6:6-8 and 30:25. These character traits are cited in PHYSIOLOGUS: "Shun animals as nourishment and partake of the grain that is set aside."—In India, the ant, due to its restless activity, is a symbol of the futility of all earthly activities. — Among African peoples, the anthill is often asso-

ciated with cosmogonic imagery; it is occasionally also associated with female fertility, which it is supposed to impart to women who sit on it.

Anthill - See ANT.

Antelope - Perhaps an antelope that appears in PHYSIOLOGUS with two large horns symbolizing the Old and New Testaments.

Anthropomorphization - The practice of using human forms and behavior to describe non-human beings. For example, a spring becomes a nymph or a storm cloud becomes thundering Zeus. Anthropomorphization also plays a large role in how symbols come to be.

Ant-Lion - A hybrid creature having the upper body of a lion and the lower body of an ant that PHYSIOLOGUS takes from Job 4:11 and interprets as meaning that every doubter is unsteady in all his ways because he walks on two paths with a divided and sinful heart.

Anvil - Frequently interpreted as the symbolic counterpart to the active, masculine HAMMER. The anvil also occasionally appears as an attribute of the cardinal virtue of bravery (fortitudo).

ARK OF THE COVENANT: Symbolic
representation made of wood and
gold (from Schmid's *Musterbuch*).
ARM: Dancing Shiva with four arms;
bronze, circa 1400 A.D.

Ape - Common symbolic animal, due mostly to its agility and intelligence, but also due to its cunning and lasciviousness as well as its tendency to imitate and its quarrelsome greediness.—In the Far East, it is frequently a symbol of wisdom. The three apes of the "Holy Stall" in Nikko became famous, the one ape closing its eyes, the second its ears and the third its mouth. Today, the ape is often interpreted as a popular symbol of a life full of wisdom (and thus of happiness) and especially of social intercourse: See no evil, hear no evil, and speak no evil. Apes originally played a role as messengers who were supposed to report to the gods about human affairs, and were therefore portrayed as deaf, dumb and blind.—The baboon was worshipped in Egypt as a divine being. Being large, white, stooping, and having an erect penis and frequently a disk of the moon on its head, the baboon was the incarnation of the moon god Thoth, the protective patron of scholars and scribes who also often appears as a divine messenger and as a guide of souls. In the hereafter, the soul is received not only by good apes, but also by demonic ones that threaten to catch it in a net.—In India, apes are often holy and inviolable even to this day.—In Christian art and literature, the ape is usually considered in a negative vein. Frequently with a MIRROR in its hand, it represents the person who has been brought down by his vices, especially by the deadly sins of greed, lust and vanity. Tied up by a chain, it usually protrays Satan's having been conquered.—Psychoanalytic dream interpretation frequently views the ape as a symbol of audacity, of internal tumult or, because of its similarity to man, as the animalist caricature of the personality.—The ape is the ninth sign of the Chinese zodiac, corresponding to Sagittarius.

Apophis - See SERPENT.

Apostles, Attributes of the - In Christian art, the apostles have been differentiated by their divine attributes since the 13th century.

Apotropaic Figures - Apotropaic figures are grotesque heads, such as the GORGONEION, whose horrifying expression have served to ward off hostile influences since time immemorial; by means of their repulsive appearance, they symbolize the gesture of rejection and banishment.—The Egyptian BES, for example, which is portrayed as having a mask instead of a face, fulfilled a similar function.

ARM: The arm of God with a Lamb (Christ) and dove (Holy Spirit); symbol of the Trinity; based on an illustration by R. Seewald.

ARROW AND BOW: Ceramic painting, Djuwi.

Apple - An ancient symbol of fertility and, especially in the case of the red apple, of love. Because of its spherical shape, it was occasionally interpreted as a symbol of eternity. The apple is also frequently encountered as a symbol of spiritual knowledge, especially in the Celtic tradition. The golden apples of the Hesperides were regarded as symbols of immortality. The apples of Iduna gave the Ases eternal youth.—The apple's spherical shape is also interpreted in Christian symbolism and elsewhere as a symbol of the earth or, due to its beautiful shape and sweetness, as a symbol of the temptations of this world. The apple is thus a common symbol of the initial Fall from grace (instead of a FIG or a QUINCE). With respect to this, an apple in the hand of Christ symbolizes the salvation from Original Sin that came about from the Fall. Apples on a CHRISTMAS TREE symbolize the return of humanity to Eden brought about by Christ. The apple should be interpreted in the same vein as an attribute of Mary, the new Eve (see POMEGRANATE). The imperial orb, symbol of the globe, is a symbol of world domination. In antiquity, it appears in various forms in depictions of Nike, the goddess of victory, and is shown, usually topped with a cross, with Christian rulers. The apple acquired sym-bolic significance because it is one of the oldest fruits gathered by man.

Apron - Ritual clothing of the Freemasons; usually WHITE; a symbol of work and innocence.

Aquarius - The constellation of the WATERBEARER.

Arbor Philosophica - Also called the Arbor Dianae, Philosopher's Tree, or silver tree. A phenomenon of crystalization that occurs when quick silver is added to a silver-nitrate solution, resulting in crystals shaped like small trees with branches. The alchemists considered this as a symbol and proof of the "plant-like sprouting nature" of metals.—The concept also signifies the "alchemistic operations," of which there are usually twelve: Calcinatio, Solutio, Elementorum separatio, Coniunctio, Putrefactio, Coagulatio, Cibatio, Sublimatio, Fermentatio, Exaltatio, Augmentatio, Proiectio. Their interrelationships were frequently represented visually in the form of a branched tree.

Arcanum - The secretive, mysterious or secluded. The concept was probably derived from an ancient, mysterious lan-

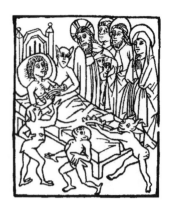

ARROW AND BOW: Mounted Death with arrow and bow as a hunter of people; detail from Johannes von Tepl's *Der Ackermann aus Böhmen*, 1461.

ARS MORIENDI: Woodcut (probably from Ulm, circa 1470).

guage and used to impart the secret, ineffable content of secret teachings. In alchemy, the arcana were secret preparations of such great effect that they were to be kept strictly secret (see PHILOSOPHERS' STONE). Paracelsus thought arcana to be the hidden forces of nature.

Archetypes - According to the philosophy of late antiquity, archetypes are primeval images or ideas that exist in the spiritual/mental world. C.G. Jung used the concept to designate symbols, figures and images that were common to humanity and that could be found in dreams as well as in myths, fairy tales, etc. He termed this the "collective unconscious" and maintained that these symbols, figures, and images could lead humans by visual means to insight into constantly recurring basic structures of personal development.

Archetypization - Hyperbolic treatment of a historical event that elevates the event to heroic, mythic status. An example is the presumed inception of heroic Germanic sagas from the cult of the hero. Another example is Siegfried's fight with the dragon as a symbol for the battle in the Teutoburg Forest, with particular symbolism involving a deer.

Architectural Symbolism - The symbolic meaning of a building or its parts, often read into it post facto (such as by ritual use or theoretical interpretation). Architectural symbolism already played an important role in ancient Oriental architecture (for example, the grave cupola as maternal covering of earth), also decisively determining how medieval Christian churches were constructed (for example, the Byzantine cupola church as a replica of the cosmos, the shape of the basilica as a SHIP, etc.). Secondary architectural symbolism results from the construction of individual parts of buildings for particular functions, such as the BAPTISTERY.

Ariadne's Thread - See THREAD.

Aries - The constellation of the RAM.

Ark - In the Bible, Noah's ark is the SHIP (see CHEST) on which Noah, his family and the chosen animals escaped the Flood. Noah's ark is seen as an exemplary instance of salvation by baptism. It is also a symbol of the Church. In addition, it also symbolizes the entire corpus of holy knowledge that cannot be destroyed.—C.G. Jung speaks of the ark as a symbol of the maternal womb. —The Ark of the

ASCENSION: The Ascension of Christ.

ASCENSION: The Ascension of Christ; H.L. Schaeufelein; detail of woodcut (note the footprints).

Covenant is the name the Israelites gave to the chest bearing the Ten Commandments. As an intermediary of salvation, the Mother of God is also called an ark.

Ark Of The Covenant - A gilded wooden chest in the tabernacle in which the tablets bearing the Ten Commandments, the vessel with manna, and Aaron's staff are contained; two golden Cherubim stand to the side; from here, God spoke with Moses and the priests; in medieval symbolism, the Ark is a symbol of Mary because Mary carried Christ, the New Covenant, within her. With its boxed shape, the Ark is closely related with the symbolism of the CHEST (and thus with the symbolism of Noah's ARK).

Arm - A symbol of force and power. An outstretched arm is also frequently a symbol of judicial power.—Various Indian divinities have more than two arms as a sign of their omnipotence.—In Christian liturgy, for example, raised arms signify the opening of the soul and the request for mercy. In Christian painting of the Middle Ages, an arm (or HAND) that reaches from heaven into the scene is a symbol of God.—A defeated person raising his arms as a gesture signifies the relinquishment of all defense.

Arma Christi - See PASSION, IMPLEMENTS OF THE

Arnica - A plant of the Compositae family having yellow, fragrant flowers. It was already in use as a medicinal plant among the ancient Germans. It was originally sacred to the Germanic mother goddess Freya, then to Mary. It was also thought to offer protection from lightning, witches, and sorcerers.

Arrow - See ARROW AND BOW.

Arrow And Bow - A symbol of war and power.—The bow frequently refers to vigor and vitality; the arrow is a symbol of celerity as well as of quickly approaching death (for example, it is sometimes a symbol of the plague!); it frequently symbolizes a movement that extends over set boundaries; it sometimes also symbolizes the rays of the sun (for example, the arrows of Apollo); as a symbol of light, it is also a symbol of knowledge; in addition, it can also have phallic significance; in medieval, and especially Romanesque, art, the archer is thus frequently associated with sensuality and lust (and, on rare occasion, with the vengeful God); as an arrow-shooting CENTAUR, it has similar significance. Amor (Cupid) is often por-

ASCLEPIUS, STAFF OF: Staff with a sacred snake as the trademark of Asclepius.

ASS: Human-animal hybrid creature with an ass's head, symbol of crudity and narrowness; from U. Aldrovandi's *Monstrorum historiae*, 1642.

trayed with arrows, bows and quivers, shooting arrows at lovers.—In Hinduism and Buddhism, the syllable OM signifies an arrow that proceeds from man, who is conceived of as a bow, goes through ignorance and reaches true and highest being; on the other hand, Om can also signify the bow from which the arrow of the ego flies in the direction of the absolute (Brahma) with which it wants to merge.— The unintentional aiming of an arrow and bow at a target is a well-known Japanese meditation technique (*Kyudo*) that effects the letting go of one's own, ego-oriented will. Similar practices exist in Islam.

Ars Moriendi - From the Latin, meaning "the art of dying." A short book from the late Middle Ages used for preparation for the hour of death. The oldest illustrated edition is a Dutch block-print book from about 1430/1440. It contains a series of pictures that deal with the struggle between heaven and hell for the soul of the dying person and his peaceful death. The book was also known as a series of copperplate engravings by the master E.S.

Artes Liberales - See ARTS.

Ascension - A representation of a figure rising toward the sky, frequently having outstretched or raised arms. The ascension symbolizes either the soul after death (see EAGLE) or an initiation, a spiritual calling, or a unification with God.

Asceticism - From the Greek word "askesis," meaning practice or pursuit. As abstention and torture, asceticism is known to all religions in various forms and with varying emphases. Magical asceticism seeks to attain magic power in order to reach a profane goal; religious asceticism seeks to attain mystical union with the divinity through ritual death (as in the case of INITIATION). Magical asceticism and religious-ritualistic asceticism are frequently intertwined, as in the case of dualistic systems (Zoroastrianism, Gnosticism, Neo-Platonism, etc. See DUALISM), where asceticism aids one in breaking away from the (evil) corporeal and attaining spiritualization. Such asceticism was foreign to the Old Testament.

Asclepius, Staff Of - A staff with a SERPENT wound around it. It is the attribute of Asclepius (the ancient god of healing), a symbol of the physician's profession and, when appearing aside a bowl, the sign of a pharmacist. In this regard, the serpent, which sheds its skin each year, is a symbol of the renewal of life, at the same

ASS AND OX: The birth of Christ. In this miniature from Herrad von Landsberg's *Hortus Delicaiarum* (12th century), corresponding to the iconographic tradition of the Eastern Orthodox Church, Mary is on a bed, the child is lying in a stone crib, an ass and ox next to Him.

time symbolizing the use of its venom for healing. See KERYKEION.

Ash - The symbolic meaning of ash has to do with its dust-like quality and with the fact that it is the cold, purified incinerated material left over once fire has been put out. In many cultures, it is therefore considered a symbol of death, of impermanence, of repentance and atonement, as well as of purification and resurrection.—Among Greeks, Egyptians, Jews, Arabs and, occasionally even today, primitive peoples, rubbing one's head with or rolling around in ashes was regarded as an expression of mourning.—As a sign of their renunciation of the world, Indian yogis cover their bodies with ashes.—In Judaism and other faiths, the holy ashes of burned sacrificial animals were thought to be purifying.—In Christianity, ashes are used in rituals as a symbol of atonement and purification, such as on Ash Wednesday and at the consecration of a church.

Ash Tree - The ash tree plays an important role in Nordic mythology; the evergreen, immutable world tree Yggdrasil, for example, is an ash (see WORLD AXIS).—According to the Greeks, the ash tree, and particularly its wood, was a sym-

bol of firm stability; it was occasionally attributed with the ability to drive away SERPENTS.

Asp - A type of SERPENT or DRAGON (or sometimes a type of quadruped). In architectural sculpture and book art of the Middle Ages, it often appeared together with the basilisk, the LION and the DRAGON. It occasionally appears with one ear to the ground and the other stopped up with its tail. It is a symbol of evil and callousness.

Aspen - See POPLAR.

Asphodel - A plant of the lily family indigenous to the Mediterranean region that has white, loosely branched flower clusters and a fleshy, sugary root. Among the Greeks and Romans, it was thought to be a death plant (and was, therefore, sacred to Hades and Persephone). The roots were thought to be the food of the deceased, who were sometimes imagined (by Homer, for example) as wandering around on the Plain of Asphodel. The asphodel plant was also regarded as a defense against evil spirits.—During the Middle Ages, the plant was associated with the planet Saturn.

ARTS

Also known as the "liberal arts," the "seven liberal arts," and "artes liberales." They give a picture of the manner in which knowledge was organized at the advent of the modern age, and are full of symbolism. - Education and bodies of knowledge necessary for education were divided into a more or less rigid system that had its origin in the ancient notion of the encyclopedia: *Philosophia divina* stands sublimely at the center of the system of *Philosophia rerum humanarum*, which is comprised of *Philosophia naturalis*, *rationalis* and *moralis*. The indispensible Seven Liberal Arts are united under the wings of philosophy: grammar, rhetoric and logic (dialectic) constitute the so-called Trivium, and music, arithmetic, geometry and astronomy constitute the so-called Quadrivium, all of which are also part of many pictorial depictions. - In the famous depiction of the wheel in Landsberg's *Hortus Deliciarum* (right), the wheel-shaped circular system is

portrayed as resting on the encyclopedia, which is the circle of knowledge. In the equally famous 1503 depiction in *Margaria Philosophica*, done by the Carthusian prior Gregor Reisch of Freiburg, this depiction in circular form is maintained only to some extent. The philosophers Aristotle and Seneca and the church fathers (Augustine, Ambrosius, Gregory the Great and Hieronymus) with Gregor Reisch, the philosophers Socrates and Plato, as well as heathen writers and "Magi" (visible by the blackbirds on their shoulders, symbolizing the devil's whisperings) are part of the depiction of the wheel.—The images associated with the sciences that are to be taught are not images of knowledge; rather, they are instructional, allegorical images bearing reference to the authorities. Thus, they present the organization of knowledge.

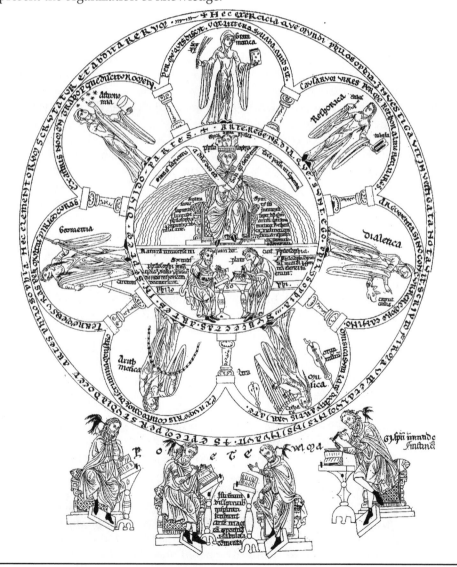

ASP: Illustration based on an English miniature

ATHANOR: One of the most important objects of alchemistic work (H. Barlet, 1653)

Ass - An animal having starkly contrasting symbolic meanings: in Egypt, the red jackass was thought to be a dangerous creature that the soul met after death.—In India, the jackass appears as the steed of deities who bring misfortune.—Antiquity saw the jackass as a dumb, stubborn animal on the one hand, yet, on the other hand, it was brought to Delphi as a sacrifice; Dionysus and his followers ride on jackasses; the Romans associated the jackass with the fertility god Priapus.—In the Bible, the jackass sometimes appears as a symbol of unchastity, but it is also mentioned in various positive contexts: thus, for example, Bileam's talking jenny represents the creature that sometimes can understand more about God's will than man. Jackasses and oxen at the Nativity possibly allude to the fulfillment of the prophecy of the prophet Isaiah, who said, "The ox knoweth his owner, And the ass his master's crib." One also sometimes comes upon an interpretation of the jackass as a symbol of the heathens and an interpretation of the ox as a symbol of the Jewish people. The animal being ridden when Christ entered Jerusalem was a jenny filly, which is usually interpreted as a symbol for gentleness and humility (on the other hand, though,

jackass colts, especially white ones, were sometimes considered at that time as a sign of high rank).—Especially in Roman art, jackasses frequently appear as symbols of lewdness, laziness and stupidity. Jackasses reading Mass often refer to the famous festival of the jackass of the Middle Ages. See ONAGER.

Astral Mythology - Or "star mythology." From the Greek. The corpus of myths in which stars play a role, particularly as divinities or gods in astral configuration. Astral mythology is more comprehensive than ASTRAL WORSHIP, since only some astral myths have a religious character. In agrarian and especially in highly advanced cultures (such as Babylon, Egypt, Mexico), astral mythologies arose surrounding the sun, the moon, planets, and individual groups of stars. A pure astral religion never existed.

Astral Worship - Also called "star worship" or "astrolatry." It is the religious worship of the sun, the moon, and certain planets.

Athanor - An alchemist's furnace in which physical, mystical and moral transformations take place. It was occasionally compared with the WOMB or world EGG.

ASTROLOGY

Astrology deals with the spiritual meaning that works within the stars, and therefore assumes—even though this is largely unknown today—the existence of *astral spirits*. According to this, people believed that immaterial and material beings unite in the heavenly bodies. The basic assumptions of astrology are the conviction that time is not uniform, but rather qualitatively different (from which follows the necessity of the creation of a calendar science and the concomitantly necessary observations of the cycles of the stars, rules pertaining to the rising and setting of stars) and the conviction that a qualitative relationship between things of different categories exists. In MICROCOSM-MACROCOSM thought, all earthly things are brought into relation with the heavenly temporal signs in a complicated manner.—Astrology and ALCHEMY are closely related to one another and make use of each other's conceptual and symbolic systems. See ELEMENTS; CORRELATIVE; DOCTRINE OF SIGNS; and ZODIAC.

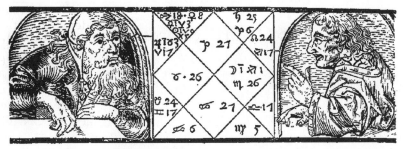

ASTROLOGY: Typical Renaissance horoscope with readers

ASTROLOGY: The system of planets in its astrological form. The correlative system of the planets in is the center — week days with the aspects and signs of the zodiac, surrounded by the seven planets with their houses and simplified depictions of the children of the planets and sayings concerning iatromathematics. Woodcut from the end of the 15th century (1480-1490)

AUREOLE: Resurrection of Christ
(detail from a mural), A. da Firenze,
1366.

ATTRIBUTES OF THE SAINTS (SELECTION):

Eagle
   John the Evangelist
Anchor
   Nicolas
Axe
   Boniface, Joseph
Beehive
   Ambrosia, Bernhard ofClairvaux
Bread
   Elizabeth of Thuringia, Nicolas
Book
   Apostles, Evangelists, Church Fathers,
   Theresa of Avila
Dragon
   George, Margaret, Michael
Angel
   Matthew the Evangelist
Heart
   Augustine, Bridget, Francis of Sales,
   Theresa of Avila
Stag (Cross in Antlers)
   Eustace, Hubert
Baby Jesus
   Anthony of Padua, Christopher
Cardinal's Hat
   Church Fathers
Chalice
   Barbara, John the Evangelist, Norbert,
   Thomas Aquinas
Cross
   John the Baptist, Andrew, Bridget, Helen
Lamb
   Agnes, John the Baptist

Lance
   George, Apostle Thomas
Lion
   Jerome, Mark
Cloak (being shared)
   Martin of Tours
Mitre
   Bishops and abbots
Orgen
   Cecilia
Palm
   Martyrs
Arrow
   Sebastian, Ursula
Wheel
   Catherine of Alexandria
Gridiron
   Lawrence
Ship
   Adelaide, Nicolas,
   Ursula
Serpent
   John the Evangelist
Sword
   martyrs
Steer
   Luke
Dove
   Gregory the Great
Tower
   Barbara
Pincers
   Agatha

AXE: The axe as an attribute (symbol) of Shiva; Pallava, 7th century A.D.; Calukya, 6th century A.D.

AXE: Late Minoan double-axe symbol made of gold and having a cult loop.

Atlantis - According to Plato, Atlantis was a fabled empire in the Atlantic Ocean and was swallowed up by the sea. It is a symbol of paradise lost and of the Golden Age.

Atman - See BREATH

Attribute - From the Latin, meaning "that which is accorded." An attribute is a sign by which portrayed persons can be recognized. The most important types of attributes are: official attributes (such as a sovereign's insignia); historical or legendary attributes (such as those of saints); mythological attributes (such as the eagle as a divine bird); and allegorical attributes (such as the scales of justice).

Attributes Of The Saints - Objects or symbols that characterize a specific saint (individual attribute) or assign a saint to a particular category of saints (general attributes of saints, such as a scroll or book for the apostles or the church fathers, or a palm branch for the martyrs). The individual attributes of the saints are associated with the lives, martyrdom or legends of the saints. For an example, see CROSS OF ANTHONY.

Aureole - Appearing mostly in Christian art, the aureole is a bright light or wreath of light rays around an entire figure, symbolizing the divine light. In Christian art, it contrasts with the nimbus (see HALO), which is usually reserved for Christ and Mary. For its appearance in the shape of an almond, see MANDORLA.

Avaritia (Greed) - Feminine personification of one of the seven deadly sins, usually riding on a toad, a badger or a wolf.

Axe - A symbol of war and destruction as well as of work, similar to the HAMMER.—As an instrument for slaughtering sacrificial animals, the axe is also a ritual symbol as well as a symbol of power and a sign of rank (especially the double-axe).—It is occasionally interpreted as having a symbolic connection with LIGHTNING.—In the Bible, the axe that has already struck the roots of a tree is a symbol of the Last Judgment.—An axe atop a pyramid or atop a cube that is balanced on one of its corners occasionally appears in older documents of Freemasonry; this presumably has to do with an initiation symbol that refers to the courageous act of exposing a hidden secret. The symbolic significance of the axe is closely related to that of the CLUB.

Axis - See WORLD AXIS

BABYLON: The Whore of Babylon on the beast of the Apocalypse; from Dürer (Apocalypse).

BABYLON: "Unveiled" Babylonian goddess, perhaps the "Whore of Babylon" (Syrian seal, 17th-16th century B.C.)

Baal - 1) In everyday usage, the name means "possessor" or "husband"; in the sense of "lord," however, it is also a term of address for God and was sometimes used as an address for Yahweh up until the early Age of Kings in biblical history. 2) The name of a Canaanite fertility god. An epic in the Syrian Ugarit (14th century B.C.) portrays Baal as a storm god, victor over "sea" or "current." Vanqui-shed by Mot (a name meaning "death"), he is brought to life by his sister Anat. Anat and he are married in royal matrimony and she bears a bull—a prototype of sacred prostitution. Personal names from the northern Syrian settlement of Ebla dating from as early as 2500 B.C. mention a god named or entitled Baal. —In the late Age of Kings, Prophets (such as Elijah or Hosea) fought syncretism, which worshipped Yahweh as the fertility god Baal.

Babylon - The etymology that maintains the word is derived from the Babylonian "Babilu," meaning "divine gate," is uncertain and controversial, yet the word is associated in the Bible with the concept "confusion." A city on the river Euphrates.

Nebuchadnezzar II robbed the Jews of their national autonomy and led a large proportion of them into Babylonian captivity; this is the reason for Babylon's negative connotation for Jews, as Babylon is an antithesis of Holy Jerusalem. In the Book of Revelation, Babylon is the seat of all anti-Christian forces, a place of godless life, of opulence (the "Hanging Gardens of Semiramis"), and of whoring ("Sins of Babylon" being a familiar term still used today). John describes the vision of the "Whore of Babylon," a woman clothed in scarlet and purple and holding a golden cup filled with filth. According to the New Testament, however, Babylon is in this case a code word for Rome, the power hostile to Christianity; the reference to Rome is also made clear by the "seven hills."

Badger - In Japan, the badger is a symbol of cunning in a positive sense; the fat-bellied badger is also regarded as a symbol of self-satisfaction. —In Christian art, it is the steed signifying covetousness.

Bamboo - In eastern Asia, it is thought to bring good luck. It is frequently portrayed as an object of meditatively understood painting. In Buddhism and Taoism, the plant's knots, individual sections and straightness symbolize the Way and

BAPTISM: Baptism of Jesus, relief from the christening font of the Cathedral of Hildesheim, circa 1220.

the individual steps of spiritual development.

Banana Tree - A giant bush with a soft stem, often having wind-torn leaves. Buddha regarded it as a symbol of the impermanence of all earthly things. In Chinese painting, it often appears with a wise man, who is sitting under it and meditating on the nothingness of the world.

Bandage - See BLINDFOLD; RIBBON.

Banquet - In many cultures, a ritual banquet is a symbol of participation in a community and thus often of participation in a spiritually distinguished situation.

Baptism - The ritual washing with, submerging, in or spraying with WATER in the sense of spiritual cleansing; baptism is common in many cultures, primarily in conjunction with birth rites, death rites or INITIATIONS. Spiritually cleansing bathing in sacred rivers (such as the Euphrates or the Ganges) is often a part of Eastern religions. —In the cults of Attis and Mithra, baptism with steer's blood was common. —In contrast to the repeated washings of cleansing rites, Christian baptism, originally a type of bath, is an act that is performed only once and that marks one's admission into the Christian church. The baptism of Christ also signifies spiritual cleansing and the descent of the Holy Spirit. According to St. Paul, Christian baptism by immersion is a symbol of death and resurrection in Christ. See WASHING OF HANDS AND FEET.

Baptismal Chapel - See BAPTISTERY.

Baptismal Font - A wooden, stone or metal vessel used for administering the sacrament of baptism and containing consecrated baptismal water; beginning in the 8th century, it slowly replaced the baptismal fountain, which was still used for immersion baptism up to the 15th century, and was usually in the shape of a cauldron, goblet, cup or vat with figured or ornamental decoration. See BAPTISTERY.

Baptistery - From the Greek and Latin. Originally a bathing basin in antiquity, the term "baptistery" later referred to the christening font or the structure in which baptisms took place and which was usually consecrated in the name of John the Baptist. Since the 3rd century A.D., baptisteries have been constructed as a separate or auxiliary building of a bishop's church or other important church. The primary building, supplemented by

BABEL

Babel is the Hebrew name for Babylon and has been considered since Genesis 11:1–9 as a symbol of humanity's arrogant, unbridled failed attempt to build a tower that would exceed bounds set by God. The confusion of tongues, which is the punishment that God imposed for this violation, and the resultant failure to build the tower have their New Testament correlate in the descent of the Holy Spirit at Pentecost and the resultant speaking in tongues. According to tradition that lasted into the Middle Ages, seventy-two languages were created by the confusion of tongues; the fact that exactly seventy-two languages were created, has played an important role in the discussion about the number of languages of the world's peoples.

The Tower of Babylon was patterned after a high temple of the ziggurat type; within the illustrations, one sees the two most common scenes from the account of the building of the tower: the building of the tower by people who were still speaking in the same tongue, as depicted in the 12th century in Herrad von Landsberg's *Hortus Deliciarum*, and the collapse of the tower (based on a 1547 etching by C. Anthonisz). Frequently encountered "designs" of the tower, especially in representations from the Middle Ages, that show it as having a snail-shaped, rising ramp, are not derived from representations of ziggurats, but probably depict the tower of the mosque of Samarra.

Bibliography: E. Unger. *Babylon: Die heilige Stadt*. (Re-edited by B. Hrouda), 1990. A. Borst. *Der Turmbau von Babel*, 1958.

BAPTISM: Baptism of Christ; miniature from Herrad von Landsberg's *Hortus Deliciarum*, 12th century

niches, side paths or side rooms, bears a symbolic connection with the baths or mausoleums of antiquity. The christening font was usually situated in the middle, a place later occupied by the baptismal font. In the course of the Middle Ages, it was usually placed in the church itself. Christening fonts and baptistries were often octagonal, symbolizing new life after baptism. See EIGHT.

Barrow - See MEGALITHIC GRAVES.

Basilisk - A fabulous animal that is supposedly hatched from a deformed chicken's or hen's egg by snakes or toads or out of dung. In the symbolism of late antiquity, it is described as a snake (see ASP), in the Middle Ages as a fantastic hybrid (such as a cock with a snake's tail, a cross between a cock and a toad, and the like), whose breath and gaze have deadly power. It is a symbol for death, the devil, the Antichrist, or sin and is often depicted at the feet of a victorious Christ.

Basket - A symbol of the maternal womb; when it is filled with fruit, it is sometimes an attribute of fertility goddesses, as in the case of Artemis of Ephesus.

Bas-Reliefs - Relief representations on steep, sometimes inaccessible walls of rock, particularly common from the 3rd to 7th centuries A.D. in the ancient Orient and made to glorify the deeds of the ruler (such as the rock relief of Commagene) or to depict religious/cult themes. Significant bas-reliefs are at Yazilikaya, Behistun, Naksh-i-Rustam, the area near Firuzabad, and elsewhere. —The only bas-reliefs in Europe are the "horseman of Mandara" in Bulgaria and the Extern Stones.

Bat - A symbolic animal with many different meanings. In the Far East, it is regarded as a symbol of good luck because the words for bat and luck (fu) are homonyms. Because it lives in caves (see CAVE), the supposed entrances to the hereafter, the bat itself was thought to be immortal and thus became a symbol of immortality. —The bat, which, like the vampire, does not wake up until night, is also associated with sexual symbolism; in Europe, demons and ghosts, which supposedly slept with women at night, were sometimes thought of as bats. —Its sure orientation in darkness made the bat a symbol of intelligence (among black African peoples, for instance); in a different context, though, the bat was thought to be an enemy of LIGHT. Yet, as an animal that sleeps upside down, it can also appear as an enemy of the natural order. —

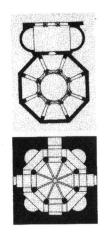

BAPTISTERY: Above: floor plan of the baptistery in Riez (southeastern France, 6th century); below: floor plan of the baptistery in the Lateran on the Piazza San Giovanni, Rome

BASILISK: Engraving on the shrine of St. Elizabeth in Marburg

The Bible counts the bat among the impure animals. —During the Middle Ages, the bat was regarded as a malevolent animal that, for instance, sucked the blood from sleeping children; the devil was frequently represented as having a bat's wings. —As a nocturnal animal, the bat is also an emblem of melancholia. —A bat's wings sometimes refer to death. —Because the bat flies under cover of darkness, it is also a symbol of envy (especially in German visual arts), which does not show itself in the open. —As a cross between a bird and a mammal, the bat played a role in alchemy as a symbol for ambiguities, such as the HERMAPHRODITE.

Bath - Positive connotations: place of cleansing, renewal, and rebirth as well as a place (in alchemy) of mystical unions. Negative connotations: a warm bath, in particular, is an indication of softening and opulence and a place of unchaste sensual pleasure. In many cultures, the bath is closely associated with ritual, particularly the ritual washing away of all sins (see BAPTISM). In antiquity, even statues of gods were bathed as a sign of the renewal of the relationship between gods and humans, such as Hera and Aphrodite. —In the view of psychoanalysis, bathing is an expression of an unconscious attempt to return to the womb. See WASHING OF HANDS AND FEET.

Battle - Ritual battles existed among various peoples, symbolizing the battle between order and chaos and ultimately the victory of the former over the latter. During the spring, battles between the sexes were waged at some locations according to certain rules; they symbolized, and were supposed to bring about magically, the victory of fertility and life over death and the stagnancy of winter.

Battle Axe - The club (skull breaker) of the Indians in eastern and central North America. See TOMAHAWK; PEACE PIPE; CALUMET.

Baubo - In Asia Minor, the baubo was originally a symbol of female fertility, yet was later thought of in ancient Greece as signifying an obscene gesture used as a magical defense. It is depicted as a female demon or demigoddess who has her head on her legs or who has no head.

Beans - As seeds of an abundant, useful plant, beans promise good fortune and fertility, particularly in Japan. They are also thought to offer defense against evil

BAS-RELIEF: Drawing of the stone relief of the lion at Commagene with meticulously written names of the planets; this is the monumental horoscope made for the occasion of the coronation of King Antiochus I of Commagene (69-34 B.C.)

spirits, disease and lightning. See FODDER BEAN.

Bear - As shown by rock drawings and bone findings, bears played an important role in pre-historic rituals. They were worshipped as human-like, powerful beings by the Nordic peoples in particular and were sometimes regarded as mediators between heaven (see SKY) and EARTH; many peoples thought them to be the ancestors of humans. See BEAR CULT. In the Northern European tradition, the bear, rather than the LION, is king of the animals. Among the Celts, bears were closely connected with warriors and the martial arts. In Siberia and Alaska, the bear was associated with the MOON, because, as an animal that hibernates, it regularly "comes and goes." —With respect to its hibernation, the bear is also an occasional symbol in medieval art for a person's old age and death. —In China, the bear was regarded as the masculine principle, being closely associated with Yang (see YIN AND YANG). —The alchemists regarded the bear as a symbol of darkness and of the mystery of prima materia. —In Greek mythology, the bear is the companion or incarnation of Artemis. —In Christian symbolism, it usually appears as a dangerous animal, occasionally representing the devil; sometimes it is also a symbol of the deathly sin of gluttony and of vice in general. Sometimes, however, one finds a female bear as a symbol of virgin birth, since she supposedly gives her cubs their shape by licking them. —C.G. Jung sees bears as a symbol for the dangerous aspects of the sub-consciousness.

Bear Cult - The corpus of ceremonies, rituals and taboos having to do with the hunting, killing and eating of bears. The bear's bones and skull are buried so that the bear can rise from the dead. The ceremony is based on the anxiety and fear that the bear will avenge its soul and on the desire for reconciliation with the dead bear. Bear cults are found among hunting peoples of northern Asia and North America.

Beard - A symbol of masculinity and strength; a long beard is often a symbol of wisdom. Gods, sovereigns, and heroes were usually depicted as having beards (such as Indra, Zeus, Hephaistos, Poseidon, and the god of the Jews and Christians). Even female Egyptian sovereigns were given beards as a symbol of their power. Dwarfs of lore, in particular, have long beards that have grown grey with age. In antiquity, philosophers and rheto-

BAT: St. Anthony, tempted by devils and bats and lifted into the air; detail from work by M. Schongauer
BAUBO

ricians had beards as a sign of their high position. In contrast, Christ is depicted as beardless (that is, as a youth) until the 6th century. —In some cultures, it was considered a grievous insult if one's beard were cut off by an enemy; on the other hand, one sometimes cut off one's own beard as a sign of mourning.

Bear Fat - A symbol of healing, since it supposedly revitalizes.

Beaver - In PHYSIOLOGUS, the beaver is a symbolic animal that calls upon humans to cast off all that is impure and thereby to fend off the devil's threat. This is based on a fable according to which the beaver, while being chased, bites off its testicles, which have medicinal value to the hunter; thus mutilated, the beaver is uninteresting as a game prize.

Bed - A symbol of regeneration through sleep, the place of marital community, of birth and of death. In antiquity, though, it was once the place where one ate and received visitors.

Bee - The bee is a symbolic animal having relation to various traits, particularly diligence, social organization, and cleanliness (since it avoids uncleanliness and lives from the "fragrance" of flowers). —In Chaldea and imperial France, it was a regal symbol (people long considered the queen bee a king); the fleur-de-lis of the House of Bourbon presumably developed from the bee symbol. —In Egypt, the bee was associated with the sun and regarded as a symbol of the soul. —In Greece, it was regarded as a priestly animal (the priestesses of Eleusis and Ephesus were called bees, probably with reference to the "virginity" of the worker bees). The bee, which seems to die in the winter and return in the spring, is also occasionally encountered as a symbol for death and resurrection (e.g., Persephone, Christ). In Christianity, its tireless work also led it to become a symbol of hope. For Bernhard von Clairvaux, it was a symbol of the Holy Spirit. Its association with HONEY and stingers was an additional reason for the bee's becoming a symbol of Christ: honey represents Christ's gentleness and compassion, whereas the stinger represents Christ as judge of the world. —Since, according to ancient tradition, bees do not produce their own offspring, but rather gather from blossoms, they were regarded during the Middle Ages as a symbol of the Immaculate Conception. —Finally, the bee was also regarded as a symbol of honey-sweet rhetoric, intelligence, and poetry.

Beehive - In Christian art of the Middle

BEAR: The Celtic goddess Artio with her symbolic animal
BEAR: The black bear as the steed of a horned demonic creature; from an illustration in Jean Wier's *Pseudomonarchia daemonum*

Ages, the beehive is a symbol for Mary, who bore within herself "all sweetness," that is, Jesus. See BEE.

Beelzebub - See FLY.

Bell - Frequently a symbol of the connection between heaven and earth; bells call one to prayer and remind one of obedience toward God's laws. The sound of the bell frequently symbolizes (in China, for example) the cosmic harmonies. In Islam as in Christianity, the sound of the bell is regarded as the echo of divine omnipotence, the "voice of God" that, when heard, leads the soul beyond the confines of the mundane. —It is a very common notion that bells ward off misfortune. During the late Middle Ages, magic bells played a particular role in conjuring up good spirits (white magic) of the planetary realm.

Bell (Tiny) - According to Exodus 28:33 ff., a golden bell that is to be attached alternately with pomegranates to the robe of priests and that must ring when the priest enters the temple.

Bellows - The bellows is closely related symbolically to BREATH. In Taoism, it plays a role as a symbol for the relationship between heaven (see SKY) and EARTH, whereby the upper part of the bellows represents heaven and the under part represents the earth.

Belly - A symbol of maternal warmth and maternal protection (see WOMB) as well as of horrible devourment. —The emphasis on the belly as the seat of the stomach is also a symbolic reference to gluttony and a materialistic attitude toward life. — In Buddhist visual arts, especially in Japan, male figures having bare, corpulent bellies, such as good luck gods, symbolize friendliness, calm, and well-being.

Belly Face - A type of HYBRID CREATURE, portrayed as headless or with a second face on its belly. Found in Indian civilization as well as in medieval books on nature.

Belt - Because of its circular shape and its fastening function, it is a symbol of strength, power, initiation, fidelity (association with a person, group or endeavor), protection and chastity. Thus, to rob someone of his belt means to take away his ties and his strength and sometimes his dignity as well. —In India, having a belt put on by the guru is a substantial part of spiritual initiation. —In the Bible, the belt is also mentioned as a symbol of readiness (girded loins and shod feet). —Among the Indians,

BEE: Two bees with honeycomb; jewelry pendant, early Minoan, circa 2000 B.C.

BEE: Hieroglyphs from the royal titulature, the rush and the bee, King of Upper and Lower Egypt

BEEHIVE: Bee and beehive as a Christian symbol (from Schmid's "Musterbuch")

Greeks and Romans, it was a custom at weddings for the groom to loosen the belt. —The girdle of Venus was thought to be irresistably magical. Yet a belt in the erotic area also had a dividing and hiding function as well: the first belt of which the Bible speaks, is the belt of fig leaves with which Adam and Eve cover their nakedness. The angels were thought to be girded as a sign of their strength and control of their libido; the belts of hermits, monks and priests at mass have the same meaning. During the Middle Ages, prostitutes were allowed to wear neither veils nor belts. —The belts of various saints were attributed with the power of easing birth.

Benedict Root - See CARNATION ROOT.

Benefactors of Mankind - Also "benefactors of civilization," "cultural heroes." Beings, partly animal, partly human, that are regarded as creators or bearers of useful plants and animals or as founders of human institutions. They are often appropriated as mythic ancestors, for example, in the genealogy of a clan.

Bes - A dwarf-like, ancient Egyptian protective spirit with a mask/grimace, usually with its tongue sticking out. It is supposed to protect one from bad influences and to bring cheerfulness. It is a symbol of sexual potency, comparable to APOTROPAIC FIGURES.

Bestiarium - A later type of books on animals that is based mostly on PHYSIOLOGUS and that greatly increases the number of real and imaginary animals.

Bianchi Girari - A ribbon decoration in a braided pattern. Used in the Near East since the 3rd century B.C. and in Europe since the Early Iron Age. It was used in antiquity as a building ornament and as a final piece of moulding in mosaics. Its golden age was in the Middle Ages, especially in illuminated manuscripts as well as in architecture. It is probably a common symbol for the stirrings of growth.

Billows - See WAVES.

Birch Tree - A symbol of spring and young girls, especially in Russia.

Bird, Migratory - A rarely used symbol of resurrection in medieval images.

Bird of Paradise - Since the Baroque period, the bird of paradise has been a symbol of agility and of God's closeness and distance; it is also a symbol of Mary.

BELL: Magic bell as a means for
conjuring up spirits
BELLY FACE: Calukya, 6th century
A.D.

Birds - Because of their flight, birds have been regarded since time immemorial as related to the SKY, as mediators between heaven and earth, and as embodiments of the immaterial, namely, of the soul. —In Taoism, for example, the immortals were thought to be in the form of birds. —There was a common notion that the soul left one's physical body as a bird after death. —In a great many religions, there are heavenly beings that have wings or are in the form of birds, such as angels (see CHERUB; SERAPH) or cupids. —The Koran speaks of birds in a symbolic context relating to fate as well as to immortality. —In various mythologies of the Occident as well as of India, birds dwell in the world TREE as intermediate spiritual beings or as the souls of the deceased. The Upanishads, for example, speak in this context of two birds: one, a symbol of the active soul of the individual, that eats the fruits of the world tree, and one, a symbol of absolute spirit and pure knowledge, that does not eat, but only watches. The idea that birds have a close connection with divine powers is the reason why the flight of a bird was attributed with prophetic import, as was the case in Rome. —In Africa, birds are often encountered as symbols of vitality, and occasionally in battle with a SERPENT, which symbolizes death or ruinous powers. —In the art of early Christianity, birds appear as symbols of saved souls. —According to the psychoanalytic interpretation of dreams, the bird is often a symbol of a dreaming individual's person. See CHICKEN; COCK; DOVE; DUCK; EAGLE; GOLDEN ORIOLE; HAWK; HEN; HERON; IBIS; KINGFISHER; KITE; MAGPIE; NIGHTINGALE; PARROT; PARTRIDGE; PEACOCK; PELICAN; PHEASANT; PHOENIX; QUAIL; RAVEN; SPARROW HAWK; STORK; SWALLOW; SWAN; WOODPECKER.

Black - As a non-colored hue, black is symbolically analogous to WHITE and, like white, corresponds to the absolute and can therefore symbolize an abundance of life as well as a complete lack of it. With respect to the undifferentiated and the abysmal, it frequently appears as a designation for darkness, primeval chaos, and death. As a color of mourning, it is closely related to quiet suffering and stands in contrast to brightly hued white, which signals hope. —As the color of night, it shares in the symbolic complex of mother-fertility-mystery-death, and is thus also frequently the color of fertility and mother goddesses and their priestesses; in this respect, it is occasionally re-

BELT: Part of a Franconian belt buckle with crosses, 7th century

BELT: Two parts of a belt buckle from Obervorschütz in Hesse. The individual body parts of the animals represented are so clearly distinguished from one another that the animal appears to be made of a series of independent details

lated symbolically to the color of blood, RED. In China, black is the color of the feminine principle Yin (see YIN AND YANG) and stands opposed not to white (as in the Occident) but to YELLOW (and sometimes to RED). —Black is encountered as the color of evil in black magic, for example. —At the Spanish court, black was long the color of stern dignity. —In the view of psychoanalysis, black animals and humans appearing in dreams frequently symbolize impulsive tendencies of the subconscious.

Black Amber - See JET.

Blackbird - Similar to the RAVEN, yet additionally endowed with the gift of seductive song, a symbol of the devil's temptations.

Black Sun - See SUN.

Blessing - A transmittal of energy or an evocation of divine grace tied to symbolic gestures (such as laying one's hands on someone, making the sign of the cross) and thought to have actual efficacy. See HAND; RIGHT AND LEFT.

Blindfold - A symbol of "not seeing." In positive terms: Blind JUSTITIA, who judges without regard for the personage. In negative terms: Blind FORTUNA, who distributes her gifts indiscriminately (occasionally appearing with gouged eyes); and the blindfold of the synagogue that, in contrast to the CHURCH, remains spiritually blind.

Blindness - Blind old men frequently symbolize wisdom, the inner light, and visionary sight; seers (Teiresias, for example) are thus often blind. At the same time, blindness can be the divine punishment (also for seers) for the unpermitted viewing of something divine; in the Bible, it is also (next to insanity) punishment for disobedience to God. —Christ's healings of the blind are sometimes thought to be actions that symbolize enlightenment amidst spiritual darkness, and are thus at the same time a symbol for enlightenment through baptism as well. —Synagogues are usually represented with bound eyes, a symbol of their spiritual blindness or delusion. See BLINDFOLD.

Blond - As a light hair color, blond shares in the symbolic significance of GOLD. The Greeks therefore liked to imagine their gods as being blond.

Blood - Among most peoples, blood is

BES

BIANCHI GIRARI: From a
Romanesque capital

regarded as something mysterious. According to myth, blood is identified with the life force (see LIVER), FIRE, the SUN, and especially with the SOUL. Through human and animal sacrifice, these forces are supposed to be set free. Blood was frequently used in blood magic. —The Greeks poured blood into the graves of the deceased in order to give vitality to the shades in the hereafter. —Among various peoples, seers drank blood in order to be transported into a state of esctasy (see BLOOD RITUALS). —In the cults of Cybele and Mithra, initiates were baptized with the blood of sacrificed steers (see SACRIFICE), which was thought to purify and to give strength. —However, it is also a common notion that blood defiles; thus, especially among primitive peoples, women who menstruate or have born a child are subject to certain rites of segregation and cleansing. —In the blood of Christ, Christianity sees a reconciliatory and redeeming force; as symbols, the ANEMONE, the STRAWBERRY, LION'S TOOTH, the DAISY, and the GRAPE (see WINE) are to be understood in this vein.

Blood Brotherhood - A practice, especially common among primitive peoples, having a symbolic character, in which men ally themselves with one another in life and death by mixing and drinking their blood. The general concept of blood superstition often constitutes the primary motif of legends and fictional stories (such as Poor Henry or Hirlanda's Saga).

Blood Rituals - The use of human blood (usually of children and virgins) in ritual and magical acts.

Blossom - See FLOWER.

Blue - The color of the SKY, things far away, and WATER, usually perceived as being transparent, pure, immaterial, and cool. The color of the divine, of truth and, in the sense of maintaining truth and with respect to the fixed firmament of heaven, of fidelity. —It is also the color of the unreal and the fantastic (see BLUE FLOWER), occasionally in a negative sense as well (for example, "to be blue" means to be sad in English while in German it means to be so drunk as to lose one's mind). —Egyptian gods and kings frequently have blue beards and wigs. —The Hindu divinities Shiva and Krishna are usually portrayed as being blue or bluish-white. —Zeus and Yahweh are enthroned over an azure sky. —In Christian panel paintings of the Middle Ages, the struggle between heaven (see SKY) and EARTH is

BIRDS: Winged Eros; Myrina, Hellenistic age

BIRDS: The soul of the deceased person leaving the body in the form of a bird with a human head; from an ancient Egyptian funerary papyrus

frequently symbolized by the opposition of blue and WHITE against RED and GREEN (such as St. George's fight against the dragon). As a symbol of purity, blue is also the color of Mary's robe. —In the Orient, particularly in Islam, blue is even today thought to offer protection against the evil eye.

Blue Flower - A symbol of poetry in Novalis's novel *Heinrich von Ofterdingen*. It is thus a general symbol of romantic longing for the infinite as well as of romantic literature in toto.

Boar - In Celtic imagery, the boar is a symbol of battle strength and is frequently depicted on coins. There is no evidence indicating that boar worship occurred. In contrast to the PIG, the boar is almost always a positive symbol, even though it is occasionally thought of as a symbol of the devil (such as the boar that destroys the Lord's vineyard in Psalms 80:13).

Boat Man - A HYBRID CREATURE with a boat for a body, already existent in the early dynastic age of Mesopotamia.

Bodhi Tree - The fig tree under which Buddha achieved Enlightenment (bodhi). A symbol of Buddha.

Body Painting - A custom practiced by most primitive peoples; originally, it probably served only as decoration or to heighten war-like appearance, yet it later acquired great ritual or symbolic significance (frequently at weddings, ceremonies involving a person's passage into puberty, and religious dances). Black, white and red, as well as ocher, were preferred; blackening one's face was regarded as a sign of mourning. Body painting is also sometimes a sign of age and rank; in India, for example, painting on one's forehead was an indication of one's sect and caste. Among some African peoples, the purpose of painting is to deceive evil spirits as to the identity of the painted person. The American Indians place great value on painting as war decoration. Here and there, it is supposedly also used as protection against inclement weather and insects.

Bog - See SWAMP.

Bones - As a relatively hard and unchanging part of more highly evolved living creatures, bones were thought to be the seat of a creature's being or of its life force, especially among hunting peoples. The practice of returning the bones of a killed animal to nature (i.e., to the earth, water

BLACKBIRD: A blackbird at the head of a "poet or magician"; symbol of the devil's whisperings. Detail from a depiction of the Seven Liberal Arts from Herrad von Landsberg's *Hortus Deliciarum*.

BLINDNESS: Christ healing the blind, Bernward Column, Hildesheim, circa 1029.

or fire) after it had been eaten, was a custom commonly practiced in order to maintain the continued existence of the species.

Book - A symbol of wisdom and knowledge as well as of the totality of the universe (insofar as a book is a unity composed of many individual pages and markings). One sometimes encounters the notion of a *Liber Mundi* (Book of the World) that lists all laws that served the divine intelligence when the world was created. —Islam sometimes still distinguishes between a macrocosmic and a microcosmic aspect of this book symbolism: corresponding to the Liber Mundi is the book of every single individuality in its entirety. —The notion of a book in which the destinies of all persons are written, can be traced all the way back to the Oriental belief in divine tablets of fate. —In the Bible, the phrase "book of life" indicates all those who are chosen. The book with the seven seals in the Book of Revelation is a symbol of esoteric secret knowledge. The eating of a book or scroll signifies the reception of the word of God in one's heart. —A closed book in the visual arts sometimes refers to possibilities not yet actualized or to mysteries; in Christian art, it also refers to Mary's virginity, while an open book in connection with Mary refers to the fulfillment of the promise of the Old Testament. —The book appears as an attribute of evangelists, apostles, church fathers, and others.

Book of Hours - "Horarium" in Latin, "Livre d'heures" in French. The prayer book for the noble laity that came into use during the High Middle Ages and that had texts for specific time periods; from the outset of the 15th century on, they were richly decorated with miniatures in those areas influenced by Dutch and French art; an example is the "Très riches Heures" of the brothers von Limburg for the Duke of Berry and the Breviarium frimani. —In all cases, a calendar, which marks the days of high feasts and of the saints and is usually illustrated by CALENDRICAL PROGRAMS, is at the beginning. They often appear with the corresponding constellation of the ZODIAC and thereby demonstrate the intertwinement of cosmic and earthly occurrences.

BOOK OF HOURS: Scheme of a typical book of hours:
Calendar
Sequences
Prayer: Obsecro te
Prayer: O intermerata
Hourly prayer in honor of the Virgin Mary
Hourly prayer in veneration of the Cross

BOOK: Lion with tablet; Salzburg, 1st third of 13th century

BOOK: Esdras, the Jewish Torah scholar, restoring holy books. Florence, 7th century, Biblioteca Laurenziana

Hourly prayer to the Holy Spirit

Psalm of Penitence

Litany

Remembrance of the Dead

Intercessionary prayers to the saints

BOOK OF HOURS: Typical series of pictures depicting monthly activities in a book of hours:

January: Banquet table (Aquarius/Capricorn)

February: Warming at a fire (Pisces/Aquarius)

March: Arboriculture (Aries/Pisces)

April : Scenes in a garden (Taurus/Aries)

May: Falcon hunting, musicians (Gemini/Taurus)

June: Hay harvest (Cancer/Gemini)

July: Grain harvest (Leo/Cancer)

August: Grain harvest, threshing (Virgo/Leo)

September: Grape harvest, pressing grapes (Virgo/Libra)

October: Ploughing, sowing (Scorpio/Libra)

November: Mast for swine (Sagittarius/Scorpio)

December: Pig slaughtering, bread baking, wild boar hunt(Capricorn/Sagittarius)

Borage - This plant was long believed to dispel gloomy thoughts. Because it is coarse and bristled, yet is also a tasty seasoning, it is a symbol of excellent quali-ties that lie hidden behind humbleness, especially the outward simplicity of the Virgin Mary.

Bosom - See WOMB; ABRAHAM.

Bottom - See DEPTH.

Bouquet - Also "flower bouquet." As a combination of many, often different and variously colored flowers, the bouquet is a symbol of unity in multiplicity.

Bow - Next to the sling, the bow is the oldest and most common weapon for hunting and war. It consists of the bow frame and a taut string and is especially used to shoot arrows. The bow already existed in pre-historic times and is still used today among many primitive peoples. See ARROW AND BOW.

Box - The box is sometimes a symbol of protection, the maternal womb, or a hidden secret. Closed boxes and chests (frequently three in number) containing good and bad occasionally appear at turning points in fairy tales as symbols of truths that are not obvious.

Box Tree - In antiquity, the box tree was sacred to Haden and Cybele. Even today,

BOW: Archer, Sumerian, 3rd millenium B.C.

BRACTEATE: North German bracteate in the form of a Bucephalos with a rider's head from which a swastika protrudes

it is a death plant as well as a symbol of immortality, as it always remains green. As a leathery, tough plant, it is also a symbol of stamina and stability; for that reason, its wood was used as a material for the symbolic Freemasons' hammer.

Bracteate - Good luck charm that was worn as a pendant; a gold foil stamped on one side with the image of a ruler (a horse, Bucephalus or rider's head); these are copies of ancient coins, often bearing runic inscriptions that are supposed to bring good luck.

Brahma - The four-headed god of creation in Hinduism, usually represented as sitting on a lotus flower or with a swan (or goose) as a symbolic animal or steed. The attributes of Brahma are a book and a water vessel.

Branch Cross - Like the TREE CROSS, the branch cross grows out of the Tree of Knowledge, whereas Christ grows in the Tree of Knowledge.

Branches - Green branches, in particular (and, less frequently, a golden branch), symbolizes honor, fame and immortality. In folk customs, branches of different trees and bushes were thought to bring good

fortune and protection. See CHERRY BLOSSOM; OLIVE TREE; PALM TREE; WILLOW.

Brazen Sea - The bronze basin on the porch of Solomon's temple. According to 1 Kings 7:23 ff. and 2 Chronicles 4:2 ff., it was used for cleansing the priests. The basin stood on twelve sculptures of oxen that became symbols of the twelve tribes of Israel and later of the Twelve Apostles. The brazen sea is sometimes closely associated with a cosmic symbolism (the cosmic or heavenly ocean as a symbol of the "higher" waters).

Brazen Serpent - An image of a SERPENT (Numbers 21:4 ff.) used for healing and built by Moses at God's command. It was later placed in the temple (II Kings 18:4). According to John 3:14, it is a symbol of the Crucified.

Bread - As one of the most important means of physical nourishment, it is also a symbol of spiritual nourishment. Among the offerings of the Old Testament were the Twelve Showbreads, symbols of the bread of life. In the New Testament, Christ is the "living bread that has come down from heaven." In the Eucharistic transubstantiation, bread, along with WINE,

BRAHMA: Illustration from the 5th/
   6th century A.D.
BRANCH: The archangel Gabriel
   appearing to Maria with a branch

acquires its holiest significance in Christianity. In early Christian illustrations, four bread loaves with cross-shaped notches are a reference to the Eucharist. See SALT.

Breast Cross - Also called a "pectoral." Usually a golden cross with relics, it has been worn since the 13th century by the pope, cardinals, bishops, and abbots; developed from the ENCOLPION.

Breath - A symbol for cosmic, animating forces, also occasionally for the spirit, particularly the creating spirits present at the beginning of the world. Thus, in Taoism, for example, there is the idea of nine different primeval streams of breath whose eventual confluence created physical space, which is the precondition for everything that exists. —In India, the notion of a breath that permeates everything and binds together various levels of existence, plays a large role. *Atman*, the individual spiritual-eternal Self that is united with Brahma, the divine Self, at the end of spiritual development, was originally thought of as breath; in addition, the psycho-physical entirety of man unfolds into five different streams of breath that bear a strong connection with the kundalini SERPENT. —In the Book of Genesis, God awakens

with His breath the man He created; breath here symbolizes the spirit of the creator.

Breeze - See WIND.

Bridal Veil - See VEIL.

Bridge - A connection between two spatially separate areas; in this sense, it is a widespread symbol of contact and mediation. Many peoples have the idea of a bridge connecting the SKY and the EARTH, often in the form of a RAINBOW; a bridge is frequently the path that the souls of deceased persons have to take after death. In Islam, for example, the bridge is narrower than a hair and more slippery than the blade of a sword such that the damned fall into hell while the chosen arrive by it in paradise more or less quickly, depending on their merit.

Bronze Age - See AGE.

Broom - The broom is not only a secular object, but a ritual one as well, and is occasionally used for the symbolic cleansing of the temple. —In a negative sense: An object on which witches are depicted as riding (A phallic symbol? Or a symbol for the powers that the broom could not

BRAZEN SERPENT: Brazen serpent as illustrated in Schmid's "Musterbuch"

BREATH: The Creator God breathing the breath of life into Adam; from a mosaic, Cathedral of Monreale; 12th century.

dispel and that then take control of the broom?).

Brown - The color of the earth and of fall. In antiquity and the Middle Ages, brown was a color of mourning; since the late Middle Ages, brown has also had erotic significance in folk songs and poems.

Bubble - Or "air bubble." A symbol for empty, unrealistic plans and wishes. In a moral and religious context, especially in Buddhism and Taoism, the bubble is a symbol of the vanity and impermanence of the world.

Buckle of Daniel - Burgundian buckles discovered in western Switzerland bearing an image of "Daniel in the lion's den" as an apotropaic sign (defensive magic) and depicting a figure between wild animals; it is supposed to represent Daniel's invulnerability. This is a parallel to many pictorial representations that arose from the time of the Mesopotamian cylinder seals used for the glorification of Gilgamesh and the "lord of the animals." In this respect, Daniel is a prefiguration of Christ.

Buddhist Symbols - The wheel of the Dharma, the BODHI TREE, the empty throne, and FOOTPRINTS appear as symbols of Buddha. Representations of Buddha himself, standing or, more frequently, sitting, arose from the 1st century A.D. onward in the mixed Hellenic-Indian culture of the northern Indian region of Gandhara and afterwards in Mathura. Graphic representations of Buddha achieve their final form during the Gupta era in the 4th to 7th centuries A.D.

Buffalo - See OX.

Bull Roarer - A cult object used mostly in Australia, Africa, among American Indians and Eskimos, and only by men (women are usually forbidden even to look at it): a lancet-shaped piece of wood with a hole at one end through which a string is drawn; the bull roarer is swung in a circle by the string and produces a droning sound that is usually thought to be the voice of spirits or of THUNDER or an expression of masculine virility. It is used in rain and fertility rites, and other ceremonies such as INITIATIONS. In Greece, it was sometimes associated with expressly sexual rites.

Bustard - A crane that often moves by walking. The male is often accompanied by several females; the bustard is thus regarded among black African peoples as a

BROOM: Imitated Witches' Ride; from *The History of Mother Shipton*; 18th century woodcut

BUCKLE OF DANIEL: Motive of the buckle of Daniel in Daillens (Switzerland); a figure raising its arms between two wild animals is shown; it is named after Daniel because the image is reminiscent of "Daniel in the lion's den"

symbol of polygamous marriage. Because of its attachment to the earth, the bird is also seen as a symbol of children who do not want to separate from their mothers.

Butter - Especially in India, butter is regarded as a vessel of cosmic energies. See MILK and WHIP.

Butterfly - Because of its lightness and colorful beauty, it was a symbol of women in Japan; two butterflies symbolize marital happiness. —The essential symbolic meaning of the butterfly, however, is based upon its metamorphosis from an EGG to a CATERPILLAR and a pupa encapsuled in state of rigor mortis to a radiantly colorful winged insect that enjoys sunlight. Thus,

even in antiquity, it was a symbol of the soul, which cannot be destroyed by physical death (its Greek name is *psyché*); in later times, though, the butterfly's pleasant nature, its flighty, wandering character, and its relation to Eros, the god of love, were emphasized. —In Christian symbolism, the butterfly is sometimes a symbol of resurrection and immortality, but also a symbol of empty vanity and nothingness, due to its short lifespan and ephemeral beauty. — In the psychoanalytical interpretation of dreams, the butterfly is sometimes encountered as a symbol of liberation and new beginning. See MOTH.

Butterfly Pupa - See PUPA.

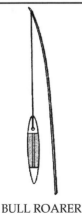

BULL ROARER

BUTTER: Krishna as a child, playing with a butter ball; small bronze sculpture

BUTTERFLY: Eros with a plough drawn by butterflies; cameo, 18th century

CANDLESTICK: The seven-armed candlestick as a symbol of the Old Testament; from an Alsatian miniature, 12th century

CANDLESTICK: Tree-like candlestick from the synagogue at Dura Europos and a stone relief from Kfar Tamra

Caduceus - See KERYKEION.

Calamus - An Aaron's staff plant that grows on river banks in Asia and Europe. Oils for consecration and medicinal agents were derived from the plant, which is why it sometimes appeared during the Middle Ages as a Marian plant.

Calendrical Programs - Cycles of representations of typical agricultural labors and amusements of the nobility during individual months or individual signs of the zodiac; initially on mosaic floors of late antiquity, they were later an important element in the calendars of prayer books, having already been in iconographs (see ICONOGRAPHY) of churches and in folkish (peasant) calendars. Calendrical Programs and zodiac signs on medieval churches are symbols of the course of the year and of the flight of earthly time, referring to Christ, the ruler over time and eternity.

Calf - As an animal that is slaughtered, the calf is a symbol of sacrifice. As such, it also occasionally appears in place of the steer as an attribute of Luke the Evangelist (see EVANGELISTS, SYMBOLS OF). See GOLDEN CALF.

Calumet - The sacred or PEACE PIPE of North American Indians.

Camel - In North Africa, the camel is a symbol of sobriety, willfulness and arrogance. —In the Old Testament, it is occasionally mentioned as being a impure animal. —In the writings and art of Christianity, it is a symbol of humility and obedience (insofar as it is a beast of burden); on the other hand, though, it is also a symbol of anger, sluggishness and narrowness.

Camomile - A plant variety of the Compositae family having a piquant fragrance. Since time immemorial, it has been used as an effective medicinal plant (especially for gynecological ailments during the Middle Ages, which accounts for its Latin name "Matricaria") and is therefore also a symbol of Mary. The simple, useful plant is also regarded as a symbol of modesty coupled with strength, such that, according to one proverb, no virgin may pass by it without making a curtsy.

Cancer - The constellation of the CRAB.

Candied Lemon Tree - In the Far East, it

CAT: The Egyptian goddess Bastet; bronze statuette of the Late Period

CAULDRON: Sacrificial cauldron of Peckatel (Mecklenburg)

is called the "hand of the Buddha"; it is a symbol of long life. Because of its many seeds, the candied lemon is also a fertility symbol.

Candle - A symbol of light, a symbol of the individual soul, a symbol of the relation between spirit and matter (the FLAME that burns wax). In fairy tales, the personification of death has power over burning candles, each of which represents a human life. —Even in their time, the Romans used candles during worship. In Christianity (especially in the Catholic liturgy), candles play a large role as symbols of light and faith during masses and funerals, at festivals and during processions. See TORCH; LAMP.

Candlestick - A symbol of (spiritual) light and salvation. The Jewish candlestick (see MENORAH), made of GOLD and having SEVEN branches, is probably based in part on the Babylonian tree of lights; it is also associated with cosmic symbolism (the seven planets and the seven heavens). —In Christian art of the Middle Ages, the seven-branched candlestick frequently symbolized Judaism.

Canopy - Originally a portable protective and honorary covering made of valuable silk materials from Baghdad (called "baldacco" in Italian), a canopy as a "heaven" over thrones, altars, graves, christening fonts, etc., signifies the location's sanctity. The concept also extends to canopies over medieval statues. As architectonic structures of a church or a city, they can be thought of as symbols of Holy Jerusalem: the saints standing there have whisked off to Holy Jerusalem.

Capricorn - The constellation of the IBEX.

Cardinal Virtues - FORTITUDO (fortitude), JUSTITIA (justice), PRUDENTIA (prudence), TEMPERANTIA (temperance).
Caritas - A symbolic figure of the theological virtue of love; attributes of Caritas are the LAMB, the TORCH, the flaming HEART, children, and beggars (due to the secondary meaning of caring love of one's neighbor).

Carnation - A bush with pointed, grass-like leaves. The shape of the leaf and the flower caused Germans to see it as a nail (thus it is also called "little nail" or "tack" in German). The carnation thus became a symbol of the Passion of Christ. The plant frequently appears in representations of the Madonna with the child. —In addition, it is also found on many representa-

CAULDRON: Two witches presiding over transformations in a witch's cauldron; woodcut, Ulm, circa 1490

CEREBUS: Heracles retrieving Cerebus from the Underworld; illustration on an Attic amphora

tions of betrothals from the late Middle Ages and the Renaissance, probably as a love and fertility symbol. —Later, the carnation (primarily the red one) became a symbolic flower of May Day, the Socialist holiday.

Carnation Root - Also called "Benedict Root." Common rose plant with yellowish blossoms and roots that smell like carnations. A medicinal plant, it is an attribute of Mary; when associated with Christ, it alludes to him as the "salvation of the world."

Carp - Primarily due to its longevity, it is a symbol of good fortune in Japan and China, where it is also regarded as the animal ridden by immortals. Because it supposedly swims upstream, it was also thought to be a symbol of courage and stamina.

Castle - A common fairy tale motif; often stands in the middle of enchanted forests or on bewitched mountains; usually symbolizes (especially when described as being bright and shining) the sum and fulfillment of all wishes for things positive. —A dark and empty castle can also be a symbol of loss and of hopelessness.

Cat - An ambivalent symbolic animal. —In Japan, the sight of a cat is regarded as an evil omen. —In the Cabala and in Buddhism, the cat is closely related symbolically to the SERPENT. —In Egypt, the cat, domestic, agile and useful, was revered as a sacred animal of the goddess Bast, the protectoress of the house. —During the Middle Ages, cats (especially black ones) were considered to be witches' animals, and the black male cat, in particular, was a symbol of the devil; superstition thus sees the black cat as a bringer of misfortune. —The cat is the fourth sign of the Chinese ZODIAC and corresponds to CANCER.

Caterpillar - As a crawling larva (corresponding to the WORM), the caterpillar is sometimes a symbol of lowliness and ugliness. —In India, it is also a symbol of the transmigration of souls (because it becomes a butterfly after passing through the cocoon stage).

Cattle - See COW; OX; STEER.

Cat Weed - See VALERIAN.

Cauldron - Particularly in Indo-European areas, magical and mystic transformations take place in cauldrons in fairy tales and during alchemistic and ritual practices. It

CHAIN: Satan bound in chains; from an Alsatian miniature of the 17th century

CHAOS: Chaos of the elements. From Roberto Fludd's *Utriusque Cosmi Historia*, Oppenheim, 1916.

is thus a symbol of change, renewal, initiation, and resurrection (see GRAIL). As a container with burbling, boiling substances, it can also be a symbol of abundance and surplus. In China, it is a symbol of good fortune and prosperity.

Cave - Even in prehistoric times, caves served as settings for cult ceremonies (see ROCK PAINTINGS). The symbolic significance of the cave has to do as much with the realm of death (the dark space) as with that of birth (the maternal womb). Caves were thus often revered as the sites where gods, heroes, spirits, demons, and the deceased stayed or were born; they were often seen as the entrance to the realm of the dead. —The Sumerians imagined the realm of the dead as being in a cave in the world MOUNTAIN. —The Egyptians believed that the life-giving water of the Nile had its source in a cave. —Caves played an important role in initiation rites (*regressus ad uterum?*), such as in the Eleusinian Mysteries or in the oracle rites of the fertility god Trophonius. — Plato's allegory of the cave is a symbolic representation of man's epistemological situation in the world of mere images and appearance; man's task is to get out of this "cave" and finally to attain sight of the realm of Ideas. —In the art of the Eastern Orthodox Church, Christ's birth is almost always depicted as having taken place in a cave (which, in Palestine, usually served as a stall); the portrayal of this cave as a crack in the earth sometimes symbolizes the womb, with reference to the symbolism of the fertilization of the EARTH by the SKY.

Cave Art - Evidence of prehistoric artistic creation, probably for cult purposes, handed down from the Lower, Middle, and Upper Paleolithic periods in the form of ROCK PAINTINGS, rock drawings, rock scratchings and rock engravings, rock reliefs, small sculptures of animals, etchings and relief decorations or tools made of bone, ivory and stone. There are large reliefs of animals, and less frequently of women, particularly from the Aurignacian and Magdalenian periods, usually in grotto-like, open caves, as well as individual discoveries of large, sculptured animal figures. Examples of cave art exist in Eurasia, Africa, America and Australia.

Cave Paintings - See ROCK PAINTINGS.

Cave Temple - Temples carved out in natural caves or cliffs, particularly numerous in India (such as those at Adshanta, Elephanta, and Karli) and China; they are

CHARIOT: Elijiah's ride across the sky on a chariot of fire; from an early Christian mural in the cemetery of Lucina, Rome

CHARIOTEER: Greek racing chariot with charioteer and warrior; relief dedicated to an Olympic victory; end of the 5th century

also in Egypt (Abu Simbel), the Mediterranean region (Petra) and Anatolia.

Cedar Tree - The Lebanese cedar is frequently mentioned in the Bible. Because of its size, it was regarded as a symbol of the lofty and the sublime; because of its durable wood, it was regarded as a symbol of strength and stamina. Like all conifers, the cedar tree is also a symbol of immortality. —During the Middle Ages, it was associated with Mary.

Celandine - A type of poppy plant having yellowish milk; used as a multipurpose medicinal plant; the alchemists attempted to make gold from its goldish-yellow sap. The name of the plant is derived from the Greek word for the SWALLOW, *chelidonios*, since, according to folk belief during antiquity, swallows used the sap of the celandine plant to enable their young to see. The celandine therefore has the symbolic meaning of "enabling one to see," of healing spiritual blindness, of being a bringer of light; in medieval art, it thus often refers to Christ. —Folk belief also saw the plant as a symbol of contentment, since it supposedly granted to anyone who carried it the power to settle disagreements.

Centaur - A wild, fabulous creature of Greek mythology having the upper body of a man and lower body of a horse. Centaurs (except Chiron) were regarded as being coarse and irrational and are usually interpreted as a symbol of the animalistic side of humans (in contrast to the HORSEMAN who controls animalistic forces). The centaur is also a symbol of humans' dual mind-body nature. —In art of the Middle Ages, centaurs were usually depicted on friezes and capitals, often with an ARROW AND BOW. They were usually regarded as symbols of vice and sin, heresy and the devil, such as in PHYSIOLOGUS, where the centaur (specifically, the ass-centaur) is interpreted in conjunction with the SIRENS. The fleeing centaur, shooting behind himself, can also be a symbol of man at battle with evil, though. In the art of the 19th and 20th centuries, the centaur often has erotic significance. See MINOTAUR.

Cerberus - The hell hound in Greek mythology that guards the entrance to Hades; wagging his tail, he greeted every deceased person in a friendly manner, yet normally permitted no living person to enter and no dead person to leave. Usually represented as having two or three heads and a snake as a tail; symbolizes the horrors of death and the irrevocability of

CHERUB: Cherub from the Mauritius
shrine in Church of St. Pantaleon,
Cologne (circa 1170)
CHESS: Miniature of the Manessian
manuscript of Heidelberg

life lost; today, Cerberus is a term used colloquially as a personification in an extended sense.

Cernunnos - A Celtic god who was worshipped primarily in the northern and eastern parts of Gaul. Characteristic for representations of him are antlers, about which there is much uncertainty. The famous image on the Gundestrup cauldron shows him seated in Buddha-position, which is typical; in the one hand, he is holding a ring, in the other, the head of a snake.

Chain - A general symbol of connection and attachment; frequently a symbol of the relations between heaven and earth. For the Neo-Platonists, the chain symbolized the uninterrupted emanation of the One into individual beings and things; correlate ideas that see each person as being tied to God by a golden chain, also exist in Christianity; prayer is also occasionally compared with a golden chain. —In Christian art, the conquered devil (sometimes in the form of an APE) appears bound with a chain on Judgment Day.

Chalice - See CUP.

Chamber - See ROOM.

Chameleon - Because of its ability to change color, it is regarded as a symbol of instability and falsehood. In Africa, it is a sun-like, divine animal.

Chaos - In antiquity, the biblical account of creation (Tohu va bohu), and elsewhere, chaos is a symbol for the state of the world before the inception of all existence; the Germanic notion of GINNUNGAGAP corresponds to the Greek concept of Chaos. —According to ancient Egyptian thought, chaos existed in the form of the primeval ocean Nun before the creation of the world and surrounded the world since creation as a permanent source of energy and renewal. For the alchemists, chaos was a term for *prima materia*. —In psychoanalysis, it is frequently a symbol of complete passivity. See ABYSS.

Charadrius - A bird mentioned in PHYSIOLOGUS, probably the golden plover. It is supposed to mark the passing of an illness and ascends in flight in order to proclaim recovery; this trait was extended to Christ: "...and he took away our sins and bore our illness and was raised to the cross...."

CHESS: Woodcut from the *Golden Game*. Printed by Günther Bainer in Augsburg in 1472

Chariot - The chariot is closely associated with the symbolic significance of the WHEEL and thus of the SUN; it is therefore also associated with the cults of sun or plant deities (Apollo, Attis, Cybele, Mithra). —A chariot riding through the sky with a deafening roar is a symbol of Zeus, the "lover of lightning" and the "thunderer on high." In many religions, good and evil deities were thought to come to the world on chariots. The animals that drew the various chariots of the gods modified the symbolic meaning of the chariot, such as the EAGLES of Zeus's chariot and the SWANS or DOVES of Aphrodite's chariot. The fiery chariot that ascends into the sky occasionally symbolizes the spiritual elevation of a person (Elijiah, St. Francis of Assisi). —The chariot can also represent the various components of the human personality that are controlled by the CHARIOTEER. —The sun chariot of Sol invictus (see SUN) is of particular importance.

Charioteer - In antiquity, the charioteer was a symbol of control over the passions and desires and thus a symbol of reason. See CHARIOT.

Cherry - In Japan, the cherry is a symbol of self-discovery and self-sacrifice, par-ticularly of the Samurai's sacrifice of blood and life in war. —In Christian artistic representations of the Middle Ages, the cherry, like the APPLE, can sometimes signify the forbidden fruit.

Cherry Blossom - A symbol of purity, beauty and good fortune in Japan; a cherry blossom carried away by the wind is a symbol of ideal death. Since cherry blossoms bloom for only a short time and quickly fade, they were a symbol for the Samurai, who were always ready to die for their lords. —In Central Europe, cherry branches that were cut and that bloomed in the nights before Christmas (especially on the name days of Barbara, which is December 4, and Lucia, which is December 13) were regarded as a good luck symbol and a reference to an imminent wedding.

Cherub - The plural form is cherubim. The cherub is a half animal, half human-like hybrid of the higher spiritual hierarchy and frequently appears in the graphic symbolic language of the Near East. In the Old Testament, cherubim and SERAPHIM are spiritual beings attending to God as keepers of Eden, bearers of the divine throne, and protectors of the Ark of the Covenant. In Christian art, they are usually portrayed as having many wings and

CHIMERA: Etruscan bronze; 5th
    century B.C.
CHURCH CONSTRUCTION:
    Cruciform church with cupola; floor
    plan of the Apostolic Church in
    Constantinople

being covered with eyes: a symbol of the omnipresence and omniscience of the higher spiritual worlds. They are frequently depicted as TETRAMORPHS or as having a head and four or six wings. Its attribute is the WHEEL.

Chess - A symbol of battle of two opposing parties, usually associated with the basic oppositions of masculine-feminine, death-life, light-dark, good-evil, and heaven-earth. In India, for example, chess, as a forum of operation for calculating intelligence, is regarded as a symbol of cosmic reason and order. In India, China, Japan and Europe, chess has been correspondingly modified by the respective culture. Indian chess represents the Indian ideal of government, the preservation of norms and the caste society; it was only slightly dynamic. Chinese chess divides space into hierarchies; it is non-dynamic; the world is conceived of as a closed universe; the player of the ruler, who organizes the world, lies in the center. Japanese chess, like Chinese chess, also sub-divides the board into three territories; the playing figures are not defined autonomously, but rather are determined by their de-centralized and indeterminate surroundings. European chess is altogether courtly; new rules (such as an in-crease in the movement radius allowed of the rook, queen and knight, and the possibility of castling) make time and space dynamic.

Chest - In antiquity and the early Middle Ages, a form of container (box) inspired by the world view of antiquity; it is the prototype of Noah's ark (which is not a ship!) found in nearly all existing ancient iconographic models; adapted in early Christendom and identified with the protective bosom of the mother church. See CUBE.

Chestnut tree - In China, the edible chestnut was associated with the Orient and autumn. Because its fruit was gathered in the autumn and provided nourishment during the winter, it was a symbol of wise foresight.

Chicken - In Africa, parts of South America (the Makumba cult), and the Caribbean (the Voodoo cult), the chicken is a guide of souls in initiation rites and a cult animal in ecstatic, magical-religious ceremonies. Chicken sacrifices made in order to establish contact with the dead have to do with a belief in a relation between the—frequently black—chicken and the dead. —The chicken is the tenth sign of the Chinese ZODIAC; it corre-

CIRCLE: Magic circle; from Francis Barrett's *The Magus*, London, 1901

CIRCLE: Magic circle with hexagram and cross

sponds to CAPRICORN. —See COCK, and HEN.

Child - A symbol of naiveté and innocence; this is the sense meant in the Gospels, for example ("that you become as children…"); the child is also a symbol of the beginning and of a wealth of possibilities.

Chimera - A fire-spewing HYBRID CREATURE of Greek mythology, frequently depicted with a lion's head, a goat's body and a dragon's or snake's tail; each of the three parts can also have its own head. It is a creature that gave rise to various symbolic interpretations, all of which have to do with the realm of the dark, the uncontrolled, and the impulsive. The chimera

was killed by Bellerophon, who rode upon the winged horse PEGASUS (parallel to St. George, the dragon slayer). —In modern parlance, it frequently denotes a vague flight of the imagination.

Chimney - See FIREPLACE

Chisel - Like the PLOUGH, the chisel is a symbol of the active, masculine principle that works and shapes passive, feminine matter.

Chrism - An anointing oil used in the Catholic Church; a mixture of olive oil and spices, it symbolizes the unity of Christ's dual divine and human nature.

Christ Monogram - A sign existing in various forms and comprised of the ini-

CHRIST MONOGRAM: Three different forms

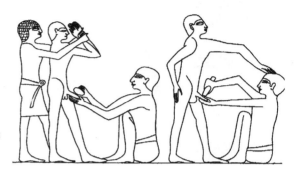

CIRCUMCISION: Circumcision scene; wall drawing in an Egyptian grave

tial Greek letters of the name of Christ, X (chi) and P (rho), or (as was earlier the case) from the initial letters of Jesus Christ (J and X); the sign has been used symbolically since the time of Constantine the Great for Christ as well as Christianity in general. Both letters are often bounded by a CIRCLE, creating the impression of a WHEEL and thereby becoming both a cosmic and a solar symbol. The letters A and W (see ALPHA AND OMEGA) were often added, as were the sun and the moon, which refer to the Crucifixion (at which the sun darkened and the moon appeared). See IHS; ANASTASIUS, CROSS OF.

Christmas Tree - The evergreen tree embellished with candles and decorated almost everywhere in the Christian world. It first became common in the 19th century, but can be traced back to the heathen custom of the so-called "raw nights" (December 25–January 6), when people feared the ramblings of evil spirits and, as protection, hung up green branches in their houses and lit candles. In Christianity, the Christmas tree is a symbol of Christ as the true tree of life (see TREE); the candles symbolize the "light of the world" that was born in Bethlehem; the apples often used as decorations set up a sym-

bolic relation to the paradisal APPLE of knowledge and thus to the original sin that Christ took away so that the return to Eden—symbolized by the Christmas tree—is again possible for humanity.

Chronos - The personified symbol of time, usually regarded as being identical with the god Cronus or Saturnus and portrayed together with its symbols of impermanence, namely, the SCYTHE and the HOURGLASS. See SATURN.

Chrysanthemum - In China and Japan, it is a symbol of happiness and long life. Because of the ray-shaped arrangement of its petals, it is also a symbol of the sun. It is the emblem of the Japanese imperial house.

Church - As a personification (see ECCLESIA) frequently contrasted with the blindfolded SYNAGOGUE (see BLINDFOLD), it is depicted with seeing eyes, a crown, and a triumphal flag. —The church itself, on the other hand, refers to the coming Holy Jerusalem, the kingdom of the chosen (see JERUSALEM, HOLY).

Church Construction - Determined by the needs of Christian services and genres of historical style. Materials: stone, wood,

CLUB: Heracles, with club in sun bowl, on night sea journey; base of an Attic vase, 5th century B.C.

COCK: Detail from a Corinthian crater (6th century B.C.)

brick; also concrete, steel and glass in modern times. Main types: since early Christian times, elongated structures, usually patterned on an "O" (common symbolism: altar = heaven = east, west portal = hell; by analogy: a person's head = east, feet = west, heart = intersection of the nave); a central structure, especially in Byzantine art (see BAPTISTERY); and the combination of both basic types in the cruciform church that has a cupola and in Baroque and modern churches that have oval, parabolic, or trapezoidal floor plans. During various epochs, the development and modification of characteristic component parts and special types corresponded to changing liturgical needs (for example, fortified and military churches; the changing of the elongated building plan to a broad and often centralizing building plan). Modern church construction is often influenced by secular architecture.

Cinnabar - Because of its color (see RED), it is a symbol of life or sometimes also of immortality.

Circle - One of the most common signs, often seen in relation and contrast to the SQUARE. The circle leads back into itself and is thus a symbol of unity, of the absolute and of perfection; it is thus also a sym-

bol of heaven in contrast to earth or of the spiritual in contrast to the material; there is a close association to the symbolic significance of the WHEEL. As an infinite line, it is a symbol of time and infinity, often symbolized by the figure of a SERPENT biting its own tail. —For practitioners of magic, the circle is an effective symbol of protection against evil spirits, demons, etc.; this is probably the reason for the protective function attributed to the BELT, the RING, the hoop, the circular amulet, etc. —In Zen Buddhism, concentric circles symbolize the highest level of enlightenment and the harmony of all spiritual powers; in other contexts, such as in Christianity, they symbolize various spiritual hierarchies or the various levels of creation. In Christianity, three intersecting circles symbolize the Trinity. —The circle inscribed in a square is a common Cabalist symbol for the spark of divine fire lying hidden within matter. —C.J. Jung sees the circle as a symbol of the psyche and of the self.

Circumambulation - The circumambulation of holy places, such as of the altar in Judaism, of the Kaaba in Islam, of the stupa in Buddhism, of the church in Christianity (processions), etc. is a widespread religious practice. As a simulation of the

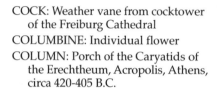

COCK: Weather vane from cocktower
of the Freiburg Cathedral
COLUMBINE: Individual flower
COLUMN: Porch of the Caryatids of
the Erechtheum, Acropolis, Athens,
circa 420-405 B.C.

movements of the sun and stars, it is possibly connected with cosmic symbolism as well as with the symbolic meaning of the circle (see above). The number of circumambulations is based primarily on holy symbolic numbers.

Circumcision - Generally: an ancient custom, still prevalent among many peoples, whereby a man's foreskin is cut off (Circumcisio) or incised (Incisio); less often, it involves cutting open the urethra (Subcision) and the circumcision of girls (for example, a clitorectomy, the removal of the clitoris), sometimes in conjunction with the removal of the small vulva. When infibulation is performed on girls, parts of the large vulva are also removed and the sexual organs are sewn shut. When infibulation is performed on boys, the foreskin is sewn shut. Circumcision is usually performed among primitive peoples at the time of puberty in conjunction with INITIATION; among pastoral peoples, it is performed during childhood (probably as a sacrifice of the first-born). Circumcision was known to most Semites (except the Babylonians) and the Egyptians, but not to the Indo-Germanic peoples. Among the Jews, circumcision is considered a symbol of the covenant with God and is traced back to Abraham (Genesis 17:9–14),

being performed on a boy eight days after his birth.

Citadel - A general symbol of protection and safety; often a symbol of retreat from the world and of an inner dialogue with God or one's self as well. See FORTRESS.

City - As a fortified, orderly arranged abode, the city is simultaneously a symbol of divine order. —Since the city protects its citizens like a mother her children, it was often personified as a maternal city goddess, often with a mural crown upon her head. —In Christian art of the Middle Ages, one encounters the city as Holy Jerusalem (see JERUSALEM, HOLY), for example, or in the juxtaposition of two cities, one of which, Jerusalem, represents the church of the Jews and the other, Bethlehem, the Christian church that grew out of the pagan church. In the late Middle Ages, the city, as an enclosed area, can also be a symbol of the Virgin Mary.

Clay - See VESSEL.

Cleansing - See BATH; WASHING OF HANDS AND FEET; BAPTISM.

Clothing - Or "garment." (According to the Bible, clothing has been worn ever since the Fall.) In contrast to NAKED-

COMPASS: The Creator measuring out the world with a compass; from a miniature in a Bible moralisée, France, 13th century

CORAL: Coral tree in the ocean; detail from an illustration in Dioscorides's *De materia medica*, 5th century

NESS, clothing is a consequence and manifestation of man's bashfulness; in widely varying forms and colors, clothing is a symbol of social conformity and social rank; it is often a sign of one's occupation; ethnic clothing is also a sign of being a member of a particular people. White, radiant garments are frequently a reference to the overcoming of earthly corporeality (as in the case of angels, persons having undergone transformation, deceased persons, etc.). Changing one's clothes is often a symbol of entry into a new stage of life, a new community; putting on of a monk's robes, as a sort of second baptism, symbolizes renunciation of the world, for example.

Clouds - Because of their mysterious cloaking character and because they are part of the SKY, clouds are often thought of as the abode of the gods and as an envelopment of high mountain peaks (such as Olympus). —Appearances by God in the Bible are also sometimes accompanied by clouds. —In Islam, clouds are regarded as a symbol of Allah's total inscrutability prior to creation. —In China, clouds that dissipate in the sky are a symbol of the necessary transformation to which the wise person must subject himself in order to extinguish his earthly personality

and to allow him to merge with the infinite. —As a bringer of rain, clouds can also sometimes be a fertility symbol.

Clover - Widely common papilionaceous flower; because of its vigorous growth, it is a symbol of vitality. —Among the Celts, it was a sacred magical plant. —During the Middle Ages, it was a symbol of the Trinity because it has three leaves. As a medicinal plant, it is sometimes associated with Maria. —Even today, the four-leaf clover (see FOUR) is thought to bring good luck; on the other hand, clovers having more than four leaves are usually thought to bring misfortune, and only the five-leaf clover is occasionally thought to be a reference to a happy marriage (see FIVE).

Club - A weapon for striking and throwing, made of metal or usually of wood. It is frequently a symbol of brutal force. — In antiquity, it was an attribute of Heracles. —In medieval and Renaissance depictions of virtue and vice, it is also an attribute of bravery, yet also, when in the hand of a half-clothed fool, of foolishness.

Club Moss - See PENTAGRAM.

Coal - A symbol of hidden, occult power: cold, black coal needs a spark of fire in

CORN: The Aztec corn goddess
Chicomecoatl
COW: The Egyptian goddess Hathor as
a cow; limestone, 18th Dynasty

order to be able to develop the dormant energy within itself. Burning coal thus symbolizes the alchemistic transformation of BLACK into RED. —Charcoal is also a symbol of purity, as it is wood that has been purified by fire.

Cock - As a morning herald of the SUN, it is a symbol of the sun and of fire among many peoples (such as the Syrians, Egyptians and Greeks) because of its brightly colored feathers and fiery-red comb. —In Japan, it was thought that the cock's crow brought the sun goddess out of her cave each morning. —Because of its close association with the breaking day, it is a symbol of light's victory over darkness as well as a symbol of vigilance. Folk belief often attributed the cock's first crow with apotropaic effect against the demons of the night. The cock, closely related to fire yet vigilant, was also supposed to protect against fire, which, as a red cock, is its antagonist. —Furthermore, its strong reproductive drive made the cock a fertility symbol; indeed, the sacrifice of cocks is sometimes a part of harvest rites. —Because of its belligerence, the cock is a symbol of battle, boldness and courage particularly in the Far East, but also, for instance, in the art of antiquity. —Among the ancient Germans and the Greeks, it also played a cer-

tain role as a guide of souls. —In Christianity, the cock, as the herald of day, is a resurrection symbol and a symbol for Christ's return on Judgment Day. Frequently mounted on top of church spires, the weathercock (weather vane)—which, due to its high position, is the first part of the church to be touched by the sun's rays—symbolizes the victory of the light of Christ over the power of darkness and is also a reminder that calls to early morning prayer. —In Europe today, the cock is usually regarded as a symbol of pride or "strutting," excessively masculine behavior.

Cocoon - In various cultures, the insect cocoon, and especially the butterfly cocoon, is a symbol of metamorphosis, a symbol of man's vulnerable, frequently withdrawn state before the advent of a new stage of maturity.

Coiffure - See HAIR.

Coin - See MONEY.

Cola Nut - Due to its bitter taste, it is a symbol among black African peoples of the difficulties of life and of the overcoming of those difficulties, and is thus also a symbol for virtues that lead to this overcoming, such as friendship and fidelity.

CRAB: Zodiacal sign Cancer (from a medieval woodcut)

Colors - Since time immemorial, colors have been laden with many symbolic meanings that, for their part, are frequently marked by the basic distinctions warm-cold and bright-dark. See BLACK; BLUE; BROWN; GREEN; GREY; RED; VIOLET; WHITE; YELLOW.

Colors, Symbolism of - 1) Colors as an expression and vehicle of psychological moods, human traits, hierarchical position, and the like; known already in antiquity, also common among primitive peoples; used in the Occident particularly during the Middle Ages. 2) In medieval art, use of red as a color of God, blue for the Son of God and therefore for Mary as well, green for the Holy Spirit and therefore for the apostles and bishops as well; as gold background in icons and paintings, a symbol of divine and heavenly glory. 3) Folklore: black is generally regarded as the color of night, death and mourning; red signifies blood, fire, passion; white, purity, light and joy; yellow, envy and arrogance; green, nature, confidence and hope. Blue is the color of fidelity and the sky and thus of infinity.

Colossal Statue - Or "colossus." A larger-than-life image (primarily of gods or rulers) that symbolizes supernatural powers (such as the sitting statues at Abu-Simbel or the Colossus of Rhodes, one of the Wonders of the World).

Colossus - See COLOSSAL STATUE.

Coltsfoot - A member of the Compositae family, found in temperate and northern zones, named because of the shape of its leaves. Because of its healing power and the blossom's radial configuration and light yellow color, coltsfoot is associated with Mary.

Columbine - A medicinal herb, containing prussic acid; member of a family of plants in the northern temperate zone. Originally sacred to the Germanic mother goddess Freya. In Christian art, it is a symbol of the Holy Spirit, its seven buds signifying the seven gifts of the Holy Spirit. Three buds are a symbol of the Trinity. Occasionally, it is exclusively a symbol of Christ or of Mary, often portrayed in manger scenes. See AGLA.

Column - A symbol of the connection between heaven (see SKY) and EARTH (see POLE); as a support of a building, the column is a general symbol of solidity and of tenability, yet, pars pro toto, also a symbol of the "edifice" of a strong commu-

CREMATION: During the process of cremation, spirit personified comes out of prima materia; illustration from *Tractatus qui dicitur Thomae Aquinatis de alchimia*, 1520

nity or institution. In its complete form, with a base and a capital, it is closely related to the symbolic meaning of the TREE OF LIFE (the base as the roots, the shaft as the trunk, and the capital as the leaves; compare, for example, Egyptian, Corinthian, Romanesque and Gothic columns). — Occasionally, it can also be thought of as an embodiment of the human figure, which is even suggested by the term capital (from "capitellum," meaning "little head") and by the atlantes and caryatids that are sometimes used instead of columns. —The Bible speaks of the columns upon which the world rests and that God will tear asunder on Judgment Day. —At the entrance to the atrium of Solomon's Temple stood two symbolically important columns called "Jachin" ("He lets one stand strong.") and "Boaz" ("In him is strength."); reproductions of these columns later played an important role in the Freemasons' temples. —In addition to and independent of these architectonically related columns, there are also individual, free-standing columns or pillars in many cultures, such as the Saxon Irmin column, which is probably a symbol of a world column (see WORLD AXIS) supporting the sky, or the numerous ancient triumphal columns symbolizing victory (such as Trajan's Column in Rome, which is decorated with scenic relief strips) or the ROLAND STATUES or Roland columns showing dominion and judicial power. In Christian usage, columns can serve as reminders at memorial sites as (among other things) prayer columns, atonement or votive memorials (such as wayside shrines, statues, or memorial tablets), as plague memorials, reminders of the Passion. — Columns can also have phallic significance, especially in fertility cults. —The column of fire and clouds, the form assumed by God when He led the people of Israel through the desert, appears many times as a mythical symbol in religious literature.

Column of Fire - See FIRE; COLUMN.

Comet - In many cultures (in antiquity, during the Middle Ages, as well as among American Indians and in Africa), the comet is interpreted as an evil omen (famine, war, pestilence, end of the world). — In the visual arts, though, the Star of Bethlehem is frequently represented as a comet.

Compasses - As a tool of planning, calculating intelligence, it is a symbol of active creative power and deliberate mental activity, of prudence, justice, moderation

CRESCENT: Maria in a crescent
moon; from Dürer

and truth; it is an attribute of various branches of knowledge and their personifications, such as geometry, astronomy, architecture and geography. The combination of the compasses with the T-SQUARE was regarded in esoteric symbolic languages (in China as well as in the West) as a symbol of the union of the CIRCLE or SKY (represented by the compasses) and the SQUARE or EARTH (represented by the T-square), i.e., as a symbol of perfection. —The symbolic tradition of the Freemasons correlates various degrees of the opened compasses with various stages of spiritual development: 90 degrees (correlation to the T-square), for example, signifies the balance of spiritual and material forces. Various combinations of the T-square and compasses can also symbolize the relationship of mind and matter; thus, a T-square atop a compasses signifies the domination of mind by matter, a crossed arrangement of the two tools symbolizes the balance of matter and mind, and a compasses atop a T-square symbolizes the domination of matter by mind.

Condor - In the mythology of the people of the Andes, the condor is the embodiment of solar powers and a symbol of the SUN. See VULTURE.

Cone - Shares in the symbolism of the CIRCLE and the TRIANGLE. As a symbol, it was presumably associated with fertility goddesses (Astarte, Ishtar and Aphrodite). —In another context, the conical shape, which comes to a point, sometimes appears as a paradigm of spiritual development; it symbolizes movement away from distracted wallowing in the diversity of matter to concentration, identity and self-discovery.

Coniferous Tree - See TREE.

Continents - See MAPPA MUNDI.

Copper - Among some African tribes, copper is a comprehensive symbol of light, life, and active agents, such as speech or sperm. —In alchemy, Venus, whose nature is described as warm, moist, feminine and conducive to beauty, idolness and voluptuousness, corresponds to copper. See METALS.

Coral - As an animal that lives in the sea and is frequently shaped like a branch or small tree, coral sometimes shares in the symbolism of WATER and the TREE. Its symbolic significance is also connected with the fact that these animal colonies, which look like plants and live in hard,

CROCODILE: The Egyptian earth god Geb in the form of a crocodile is prayed to by a deceased woman on the shore of the river of the world (detail); illustration in *The Book of the Dead of Heri-uben*, 21st Dynasty

often chalky skeletons, are apparently part of the three mineral, plant and animal kingdoms. Because of its red color, coral is sometimes a sign of BLOOD. It is sometimes used as an amulet or as material for amulets.

Corn - In some American Indian cultures, corn is a highly regarded edible plant that became associated with the cosmos, the SUN and the genesis of man. It was thought of as a symbol for prosperity and happiness.

Cornerstone - In practically all cultures, the "distinguished" stone with which the construction of a house of worship (such as a temple) was symbolically begun; the cornerstone of a Christian church is marked with a cross and consecrated; the KEYSTONE of a vault can be thought of in a similar manner.

Cornucopia - An attribute (symbol) of Fortuna or of the personification of autumn; a symbol for the superabundance of good fortune and for rich harvest. The cornucopia was originally regarded as the HORN of the GOAT Amalthea or of the river god Achelous, whose horn was broken off by Heracles during battle.

Correlative - According to the world view of MICROCOSM-MACROCOSM thought, a correlative is a relation, not existent "in itself," between (for example) external form and hidden potentials (the shape of a blossom, for example, "correlates" with an effect as a remedy). Ideas about correlatives can be found in many cultures; in the Occident, they can be found especially in the Renaissance as a legacy of Mesopotamian-Egyptian-Hellenic tradition, having been transmitted primarily from systems of astrology to the world views of alchemy and symbolism.

Cosmic Dances - In many cultures, cosmic dances are common ritual dances that represent the movements of the heavens. They are usually an expression of the conjuring up of cosmic forces. During the Middle Ages, they were occasionally performed in Christian churches, often in conjunction with LABYRINTHS. See TROJABURGS.

Courage - The cardinal virtue of FORTITUDO.

Cow - As a fertile domesticated animal that gives MILK, which is important for life, the cow is generally a symbol of the maternal earth, of abundance and of shel-

CROSS: Depiction of cross from 5th century: The Cross of Christ as a blooming Tree of Life; the two lights proclaim Christ as the light of the world, the 12 jewels symbolize the 12 Apostles (from Schmid's *Musterbuch*)

tering protection. —In Egypt, the cow was primarily venerated as Hathor, the goddess of the sky, who, as the mother and bride of the SUN, as mother of Horus and as wet-nurse of the Egyptian king, as goddess of joy, dance and music (in the form of a young woman), was regarded as a symbol of hope and the renewal of life, the living soul of trees, and the mistress over the mountains of the deceased; she could appear radiantly golden or in the shape of a lioness (see LION). —In India, the cow is revered as a sacred provider of nourishment; in addition, the white cow is associated with the sacred fire. Buddhism sees a close connection between the cow and man's step-by-step progress toward inner enlightenment; the white cow symbolizes the highest level of individual existence before its assumption in the Absolute. In the Vedic tradition, the cow is also known as a guide of souls. —For some peoples, such as the Sumerians, there was a symbolic relationship between the fertile cow and the MOON as well as between the cow's milk and moonlight. —In the mythology of the ancient Germans, the cow *Audhumla*, the primeval provider of nourishment and protector, played an important role; it was closely associated with WATER and RAIN.

Cowslip - See PRIMROSE.

Cowl - See MONK'S ROBE.

Cowrie - See SNAIL.

Coyote - A prairie wolf living in North America, it is considered in some American Indian cultures to be the root of all evil, particularly of winter and death.

Crab - As an aquatic animal, it is frequently associated with the symbolism of WATER or of the primeval ocean (see OCEAN). Because of its shell, which protects it from the external world, the crab is closely associated with the idea of the "embryo-uterus"; its relation to the complexes of "mother" and "sea" also connects it symbolically with the unconscious. —In Christianity, the crab is regarded as a symbol of the Resurrection, because it sheds its shell in the course of its development; in a more restricted sense, it is thus sometimes a symbol of Christ as well. —Since antiquity, the crab has also been regarded as a lunar symbol (perhaps because of the influence of the moon on the ocean and because of the crab's shape). —In Africa, the crab sometimes appears as a symbol of evil. —The crab, or Cancer, is the fourth sign of the zodiac, corresponding to the

CROSS: "Inhabited" cross, woodcut,
Florence, 1491

first month of summer; the Sun passes the sign between June 22 and July 22. Jupiter is exalted in Cancer; it is the house of the Moon. Since the time of Hellenic astrology, Venus, Mercury, and the Moon have been its decans; in Indian astrology, the Moon, Mars, and Jupiter are its decans. The triplicity of Cancer is water; Cancer is feminine, negative (passive), and a cardinal sign. The origin and name of Cancer as a constellation are still largely unexplained.

Cradle - A symbol of the maternal womb and of the security of early childhood.

Crane - In China and Japan, the crane is a symbol of long life and immortality (see STILTS) because people believed that it could live to be one thousand years old. The whiteness of its feathers was interpreted as being a symbol of purity; the red feathers of its head were thought to be a sign of vitality and connection with fire. —In India, the crane was regarded as a symbol of malice and betrayal. —Among some African peoples, a crowned crane appears as a symbol of language and thought, in part because of its apparently contemplative stance. —Because the crane, as a migratory bird, returns punctually in the spring, it was also regarded

as a symbol of spring. For that reason and because of its striking behavior during the mating season (crane's dance), it was also a symbol of love and joy of life, especially among the Greeks and the Romans. As a killer of snakes, the crane turns up as a Christ symbol.

Creation - The question of how the world came to be is as old as the consciousness by means of which man raises himself from his surroundings: So long as the child has not discovered itself, it is at one with its surroundings, yet the first time that it says "I," it has raised itself from its surroundings and discovers its surroundings and itself. The world comes to be when man discovers it; there are creation hymns in which consciousness does not proceed from existence, but rather existence from consciousness (according to H. Adler). Consciousness raises itself from fathomless unconsciousness, yet the unconscious existed at the beginning, and, in people's dreams about creation, it appears as chaos, as the sea, as night, as a black bird.... The illustration shows the so-called "creation portal" on the north side of the Freiburg Cathedral.

Cremation - A symbol of perfect cleansing, of transformation of matter into

CROSS

 Greek Cross: four arms of equal length

Latin Cross: Diagonal bar is shorter and higher; it is perhaps the form of the historical Cross of Christ; it is the usual cross form in depictions of the Crucifixion and of individual crucifixes

 St. Peter's Cross

 St. Anthony's Cross: "T"-shaped; trademark of the Order of St. Anthony that was founded in the 11th century and of the hermit St. Anthony, who often carries a crook with little bells. It is perhaps the form of the historical Cross of Christ; thieves are often depicted as being tied to "T"-shaped crosses (in contrast to Christ, who is on a Latin Cross).

Forked Cross: "Y"-shaped; used during the Middle Ages for thieves, but also for Christ Himself, in order to make His terrible suffering especially clear by showing His arms stretched up very high.

Cross of Andrew: "X"-shaped

 Crosslet: small crosses also appear on the four tips

 Moline Cross: Composed on four "T" crosses (crooks, see St. Anthony's Cross above)

 Jerusalem Cross: the five crosses refer to the five wounds of Christ. It is the insignia of the Order of the Riders of the Holy Sepulchre in Jerusalem

Maltese Cross or Cross of the Knights of St. John of Jerusalem: sign of the members of the Crusader orders

 Double Cross (Cardinal's and Patriarch's Cross): the upper, shorter crossbar is reminiscent of the inscription plate on the Cross of Christ

 Byzantine or Russian Cross: the third, lowest crossbar, diagonal or even, is reminiscent of the footboard of the Cross of Christ

 Papal Cross: has three different crossbars

Handle Cross: in Egyptian hieroglyphics, it is the sign for "life" and was thus appropriated by the Coptic Christians for the Cross of Christ as the true sign of life

 Coptic Cross

CROSSROADS: The choice of the
correct path of life; copperplate
engraving, circa 1620

ascending, spiritual substance (see HEIGHT; SMOKE); played a role in burial ceremonies (especially as bodily cremation), for example, and in alchemy.

Crescent Moon - Also called a "half moon." A common form in which the MOON is represented as a symbolic sign. —An attribute of female, and particularly virgin, deities (such as Artemis). Possibly with reference to its waxing phase, it is also closely related in meaning to "pregnancy" and "birthing." The relation that Christian art posits between the Moon and the Virgin Mary (who is frequently represented as Immaculata on the crescent moon), is probably connected in part with these two sets of meanings, even if the primary relation is to that of the woman of the apocalypse who is clothed in the SUN and has the Moon at her feet. —In Islam, the crescent moon is a sign that simultaneously symbolizes openness and concentration and refers to the victory of (eternal) life over death. A crescent moon surrounding one star has been a general emblem of the Islamic world since the Crusades (in the countries of the Near East, the Red Crescent corresponds to the Red Cross in the West).

Cricket - Among the Chinese, it is a sym-

bol of death and resurrection, since it lays its eggs in the earth and comes to the surface from the earth as a mature insect after a larval phase. —In China as in, for example, Mediterranean cultures, a cricket that likes to live in one's house and on the HEARTH is also thought to bring good luck.

Crocodile - Frequently associated with the symbolism of WATER; however, since it lives in the water and on land, its symbolic significance is often much more complex. —The crocodile enjoyed particular veneration in Egypt, where, like the Sun, it was thought to have been born from water; it was revered as a powerful, chthonic and sun-like deity (Sobek). The earth god could also become incarnate in the form of a crocodile. —Some American Indian cultures saw the crocodile, which lives in the primeval sea, as the creator of the world; for others, it was an animal that carried the entire world upon its back. —In the Bible, the name LEVIATHAN is also applied to the crocodile, which, in other places, symbolizes Egypt as well. —In Christian art, its symbolic significance is close to that of the DRAGON.

Crocus - A family of plants with more than sixty genera. In antiquity, the saffron spe-

CROWN: Maria with a crown; from H. Gerhard's Marian Columns, on the Marienplatz in Munich

cies was particularly highly regarded. Crocus wreaths were supposed to protect one from drunkenness. People prepared a yellow dye from the saffron flower's stigma, a symbol of light and majesty: the clothes of gods and kings were thus frequently colored saffron yellow. Because of its gold-colored pistil, the crocus in Christian literature is sometimes a symbol of GOLD and thus of the highest virtue, love.

Cromlech - From the Celtic. Circular arrangement of stone blocks in Neolithic and later pre-historic cultures; Stonehenge is an example.

Crooked Staff - See STAFF.

Cross - One of the most widely common and oldest symbols. Like the SQUARE, it shares in the symbolism of the number FOUR (if it is thought of in terms of its four tips); thus, for example, it became a symbol of the four cardinal directions. In China, on the other hand, it became associated with the number FIVE (see also TEN), as the midpoint was also taken into consideration. If one considers only the two arms of the cross, it can also be a symbol of the interpenetration of two opposing regions, especially of heaven (see SKY) and EARTH or of time and space.

—Especially in the architecture of sacred structures and entire city designs, the cross-shaped pattern plays a (not merely practical) role; the Greek cross, for example, determines the floor plan of many Byzantine and Syrian churches; the Latin cross determines the floor plan of Roman and Gothic churches. —The cross can also be thought of as a sign for the CROSSROADS (as a place where the paths of the dead and the living cross one another); among some African tribes, for example, it is frequently thought of in this sense (along with a meaning that encompasses the entire cosmos, i.e., people, spirits and gods). —In Asia, the vertical axis of the cross is frequently thought of as a symbol of active powers associated with the sky and thus as a symbol of the masculine principle, whereas the horizontal axis corresponds to the passive powers of water and thus to the feminine principle. In addition, both axes symbolize the equinoxes and the solstices. —A cross inscribed within a CIRCLE is thought of as a mediation between the square and the circle and thus symbolically emphasizes the connection of the sky and the earth. It is a symbol of the midpoint, of the balance of activity and passivity, and of the perfect human. If one thinks of the four arms

CROWN: Crowns as indication of position: 1) king's crown; 2) duke's crown; 3) count's crown; 4) noble's crown

of a cross inscribed within a circle as spokes, an image of a WHEEL arises, as does a sun symbol, which is found among Asiatic peoples as well as among the ancient Germans (even when not circumscripted, the cross can sometimes be a symbol of the sun, such as in Assyria). The SWASTIKA was another ceremonial and sun symbol common initially in Asia and then among the ancient Germans. —Because of the crucifixion of Christ, the cross acquired particular significance in Christianity as a symbol of the Passion of Christ as well as of His triumph and thus generally as a symbol of Christianity (which, however, was at first used quite hesitantly, as crucifixion was thought by the ancient world to be most offensive). —In Christian visual arts, it appears in many forms (the Greek and Latin crosses being most common); the ANCHOR is sometimes a concealed cross symbol. Aside from this, the shape of the cross also plays a role in the gesture of blessing and in crossing oneself. —The very old form of the forked cross, in particular, alludes to the symbolism of the TREE of life; in Christian art, the blooming and budding cross of Christ appears as a symbol of his resurrection and victory over death (see TREE CROSS). —See ANKH, the Egyptian looped cross.

Cross Flower - A cruciform, sculpted Gothic building ornament having stylized leafwork; the pinnacle of towers, gables, Gothic gables, and finials.

Crossing - See CROSSROADS.

Cross of Anthony - An Egyptian CROSS in the form of a Greek T (thus also called a "Tau cross").

Crossroads - In most cultures, the crossroads is an important place of encounter with transcendent powers (gods, spirits, the dead); often, it is closely related to the symbolic significance of the DOOR, as the crossroads can also symbolize a necessary transition to the new (from one stage of life to another, from life to death). In order to gain the favor of the gods or spirits of a crossroads, obelisks, altars or stones were set up at or inscriptions were affixed to crossroads. Almost everywhere in Europe, the crossroads is also thought to be a meeting place of witches and evil demons. This is perhaps not the least reason why Christianity is given to erecting crosses, statues of the Madonna and the saints, and chapels at crossroads. — Among many African tribes, the symbolism of the crossroads plays an important role in ceremonial rituals. —In Greek

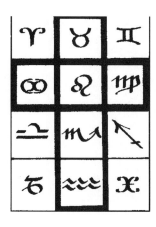

CUBE: General floor plan of a church; the 6 squares of the cube are in boldface, the entire figure is embedded in the system of zodiacal signs

mythology, Oedipus kills his father at a crossroads. The Greeks made sacrifices to a goddess of a triple crossroads who had three bodies or three heads: Hecate, goddess of ghosts and witchcraft, who was also closely related to the Underworld. The statue of the spirit guide Hermes also stood watch at crossroads and forked paths. A famous story by Prodikos tells of Heracles who, at a crossroads, opts for virtue over weakness. The Romans had a cult of deities of crossroads, by means of whom they wanted to gain the favor of fate. —In late Germanic law, legal actions were also conducted at crossroads.

Crow - For PHYSIOLOGUS, it is a symbol of monogamy. The interpretation reads: The synagogue of the Jews is earthly Jerusalem, Christ is no longer its consort; it will gain no new consorts, since it killed Christ. —Among the Celts, the crow is a sacred bird in whose shape the goddess Badb was given to appear at battles.

Crown - As an ornament adorning the noblest part of a person, the crown has a symbolic significance that ennobles the the person who wears it. Because of the ray-shaped points frequently used, the crown is closely related to several symbolic aspects of the HORN; because of its ring-like shape, it also shares in the symbolism of the CIRCLE. —The crown is always an expression of high position, power, consecration or of a solemn aloofness. In most cultures, it is worn by the sovereign. In Judaism, the golden diademlike crown is also an indication of the exalted position of a high priest. —The crowns of gods and kings were respected by the Egyptians as mighty, magical beings to which specific cults or ritual songs were dedicated. —In Buddhism and Hinduism, as well as in Islam, the crown (occasionally together with the lotus flower) is regarded as a sign of the elevation of the spirit over the body. —The Bible sometimes mentions crowns, such as the crown of life and the crown of immortality, which symbolize the state of eternal salvation. —In the Orient and the Occident, one encounters the marriage custom of the wearing of bridal crowns, which are regarded as a sign of virginity as well as of elevation to a special, new state. Deceased persons, especially unmarried ones, were sometimes given death crowns for the GRAVE as an indication of their impending unification with God. See illustrations.

Crown of Thorns - See THORN.

CUP: The Eucharistic chalice; detail from a painting by J.D. de Heem, circa 1650

Crux Gammata - See SWASTIKA.

Cry - The war cry was once common in most cultures as an expression and sign of the thrill of attack. The cry also embodies the force and joy of life, such as during certain ceremonies of antiquity (usually having to do with fertility rites).

Crystal - A symbol of purity and clarity, and therefore frequently a symbol of the mind. —The symbolic meaning of crystal is closely related to that of DIAMOND. —As a material body that, in contrast to other matter, is transparent, it is also a symbol of the unification of opposites, especially of spirit and matter. —Since crystal itself does not burn but can light a fire by means of the sun rays that pass through it, it is regarded in Christianity as a symbol of the Immaculate Conception and is therefore a symbol of Mary as well.

Cube - As a body bounded by six squares, the cube shares in the symbolic significance of the SQUARE; yet, more so than the square, it is a symbol of that which is solid, firm and immutable and also occasionally of eternity. —If the cube is unfolded in a certain way, a cross appears, which is interpreted esoterically as an astrological basis of the church floor plan.

St. John saw the "Holy City" in the shape of a cube (Revelation 21:1 ff.). See CHEST. Of the five PLATONIC SOLIDS, it represents the earth.

Cuckoo - According to Vedic tradition, the cuckoo is a symbol of the soul before and after incarnation; the body is thereby compared to a strange nest in which the cuckoo lays its eggs. —According to Occidental folk belief, the number of the cuckoo's calls is frequently thought to be a portent of life-span, marriage or expected money. —Because of the lasciviousness ascribed to the cuckoo, whores were sometimes called "cuckoos" during the Middle Ages. The devil was also euphemistically called a "cuckoo" ("The cuckoo take you!"). —Cuckoo eggs are thought to be a symbol of something that has been dishonestly substituted.

Cucumber Herb - See BORAGE.

Cup - Or "chalice." It is often a symbol of overflowing abundance. —In the Bible, the image of the cup appears in various contexts: the cup of the salvation or of the fate that man receives from the hand of God as though it were a cup or a cup's contents, God's cup of wrath. In the scene on the Mount of Olives, Christ speaks of

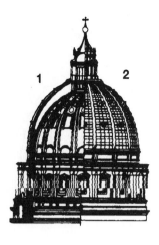

CUPOLA: 1) Cupola of St. Peter's in Rome (cross section of the left half); 2) constructions: a) hanging cupola (pillar cupola, Bohemian dome), the projected area of the cupola circumscribes the foundation of the lower structure; b) pendentive cupola, the projected area of the cupola is contained within the foundation of the lower structure

the cup of sufferings that awaits him. — As a vessel that provides nourishment, the cup sometimes appears as a symbol of the maternal, nourishing breast (in India, for example); as a sheltering and protecting vessel, it is also a symbol of the maternal womb. —Because of its shape, it became associated with the CRESCENT MOON (which, because of its milky white color, refers in turn to the maternal breast). — Cups in ritual use or in religious graphic arts frequently contain the potion of immortality. —In graphic representations, the cup that contains the blood of Christ also points beyond the celebration of the Eucharist, namely, to Christ and eternal salvation. —Drinking from a common cup or chalice within a community as a sign of solidarity or of belonging to a commonly recognized idea, religion, etc., is common in various cultures. Mutual exchange of drinking cups symbolizes fidelity (such as in Japan during wedding ceremonies). —In Islamic literature, the cup appears as a symbol of the heart; three cups, filled with MILK, WINE and WATER, symbolize Islam (milk as a symbol of the natural and right religion), Christianity (in which wine assumes sacred importance) and Judaism (in which water played a destructive role during the Flood and a helpful role during the crossing of the Red Sea). —The symbolic significance of the cup is sometimes also close to the cosmic symbolic significance of the SKULL. See GRAIL.

Cupola - Or "dome." In Buddhist, Islamic, Byzantine, Christian and other architecture, the cupola is frequently interpreted as being a symbol of the dome of the sky, which is indicated by paintings of stars, birds, angels, and sun chariots, etc.

Cyclamen - Based on the prophecy of Simeon in Luke 2:35, the cyclamen is the flower of Mary because of the blood-red color of the blossom's interior (symbolizing Mary's heart bleeding in pain).

Cypress - Among many peoples, the cypress tree is thought to be holy. As an evergreen, long-living plant, it, like all conifers, is revered as a symbol of long life and immortality. In contrast, it was regarded as a symbol of death in antiquity because it no longer grows after it has been cut down; it was therefore associated with Pluto and the realm of the underworld. —In China, the cypress seed was associated with the Yang principle (see YIN AND YANG); eating it was supposed to bring long life.

DANCE: Female acrobatic dancer; drawing on an ostrakon from the New Kingdom, Egypt

DANCE: Dancing bayadère; from an Indian Rajput miniature; 18th century

**Daisy -** A member of the Compositae family found in temperate zones. It was originally sacred to the ancient Germanic mother goddess Freia and frequently appears in medieval art as an attribute of Mary. It symbolizes eternal life and salvation, yet also, like the MARGUERITE, tears and drops of blood.

Dance - As rhythmically structured, yet simultaneously ecstatic movement, dance became associated in many cultures with creative as well as ordering powers. Thus, there are gods and heroes in many myths who bring forth and order the world by dancing (often with respect to cyclical changes of the planets, the seasons, and the periods of the day). In many cultures, ritual dances are regarded as means to establish a connection between heaven and earth, i.e., to entreat rain, fertility, or mercy, etc., or to gain insight into the future (especially in dances by shamans and medicine men). —Symbolic gestures during dances, especially with the hands (see HAND), are also common; their meaning is usually intelligible only to initiates. — In China, the art of dance, as an expression of cosmic harmony, was closely associated with the symbolism and rhythm of numbers. —Among black African peoples, dance was originally associated with nearly all activities of daily life and rites as a transcendent component. —The Egyptians had many different cult dances in which, as in many other cultures, personifications of the deities took part. — The Old Testament tells of dance scenes as an expression of spiritual joy (the celebration dance of the women after David's victory over Goliath, David's dance before the Ark of the Covenant), yet also tells of Salome's seductive, deadly dance.

Dandelion - A very common, milky member of the Compositae family; an ancient medicinal plant; probably for that reason and because of its flowers that radiate like the sun's rays, it was asssociated with Christ and Mary in Christian art of the Middle Ages. Like many lactating plants, it is also a symbol of the deaths of Christ and the martyrs.

Danse Macabre - Medieval representation of people of every age and social position who are doing a round dance with dead people, often with DEATH playing the music. Verse captions are common. The first picture shows a round dance in progress; in the next picture, people are

DANCE: Two dancers, Etruscan fresco, 520 B.C. (Tarquinia)

in pairs, the dance motif has disappeared, and death as a skeleton stands face-to-face with an individual. The motif probably has its origin in a legend from the Middle Ages and the popular notion that the dead left their graves for midnight dances in churchyards. The earliest depictions are on frescoes from the first half of the 15th century. In the graphic arts, the wood cut sequence "Danse macabre" (Paris, 1485) and that of Hans Holbein the Younger are especially well known. —In 1849, Alfred Rethel introduced an new iconographic version with the sequence *Auch ein Totentanz (Another Dance of Death)*.

Darkness - As pertaining to DUALISM, darkness is the complementary-contrary symbol of LIGHT.

Dawn - A general symbol of hope, youth, abundance of possibilities, and of new beginning. Among the Greeks, the dawn was personified as the goddess Eos, sister of Helios (see SUN) and of Selene (see MOON); as the "rose-fingered one," she rides preceding the chariot of the Sun; in Rome, she was identified with Aurora. — In Christian symbolism, Mary is sometimes called the dawn that brought us Christ the Sun.

Day - In contrast to NIGHT, day is a sym-

bol of clarity, reason, and candor ("to bring something to the light of day"). —The four periods of the day were often symbolically identified with the four seasons: spring with morning; summer with midday; autumn with afternoon or sunset; and winter with night. These identifications also play a role in astrology. See MIDDAY AND MIDNIGHT.

Dead-Nettle - A labiate flower; as a medicinal plant, it is sometimes an attribute of Mary in Christian art of the Middle Ages.

Death - In Greek art, death is portrayed as a lovely, naked youth (see THANATOS) or as an old, bearded man with wings, yet, as early as in late antiquity, it appears as a skeleton (in Pompeii); it was seldom portrayed during the Early Middle Ages and, when it was portrayed, it appears as an ugly old man or an ugly woman. From the 14th century on, depictions of skeletons predominate, most frequently in the DANSE MACABRE.

Deadly Sins - ACEDIA (sloth), AVARITIA (covetousness), GULA (gluttony), INVIDIA (envy), IRA (anger), LUXURIA (lust), and SUPERBIA (pride).

Death's Head - See SKULL.

DEATH

DEATH: Mors (death) and Vita (life) each have 4 letters, which are often put at the ends of a cross (from Schmid's "Musterbuch")

The Christian-Occidental symbolism of death did not develop until relatively late in the High Middle Ages; before then, resurrected, not dead, persons were usually portrayed. In the case of gravestones, one must also determine whether the monument is immortalizing "Death" or the deceased person.

As a personification or symbol, death appears in the juxtaposition of the words mors (death) and vita (life).

Not until the late Middle Ages did symbols commonly known to us appear in increasing numbers; among these are the portrayal of death as a skeleton (often bearing an hourglass and/or a scythe) or, even more forceful, the danse macabre cycles, which probably arose under the mark of the plague epidemics, which carried away poor and rich, young and old, woman and man.

DEATH: Death as a skeleton with a scythe and hour glass; detail from an engraving by Anders Trost

DEATH: A woman possessed by one of the seven deadly sins; English Bible illustration, 13th century

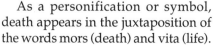

Small Basel (Klingental) Danse Macabre, 1440.
Danse macabre: Death and the shopkeeper by Hans Holbein the Younger
Danse macabre: woocut from *La danse macabre des femmes*, Paris, 1485

DIADEM: A headband made of cloth or metal, originally a sign of the priestly caste or a part of a ruler's tract, developed in Byzantium into the crown. The diadem, triumphal wreath and crown were originally symbols of magical protection. 1) Egyptian; 2) Greek; 3) late Roman; 4) Russian

Deciduous Tree - See TREE.

Deësis - A depiction of an enthroned Christ as judge of the world between Mary and John the Baptist, who are interceding on behalf of souls. It is often a symbolically truncated depiction of the Last Judgment.

Deformation - Bodily deformation frequently portends special and mysterious abilities (good or bad). See MONOCULARITY; ONE-LEGGEDNESS; LAMENESS.

Demon - From the Greek "daimon." The term was originally used to describe gods and later referred to mediary beings between gods and humans who could influence human destinies and cosmic events for good or evil. The Greek philosophers considered them to be the divine part or divine voice in man (Daimonion). Demons are characterized by their unpredictable, whimsical nature and often take possession of the mental powers of people. The Bible describes them solely as evil spirits, fallen angels who represent a power against God's dominion (see DEVIL; LILITH). —Demons are often central characters of later legends, appearing as superhuman beings such as GIANTS (in fairy tales they are no longer demonic, but rather often dumb and comical),

DWARFS (acquiring human characteristics, appearing as skillful smiths, and often representing higher ethical standards) and non-human beings.

Depth - As a symbolic image, it represents the region of darkness as well as the region of the essential, yet also of evil, of the impulsive and of the material in the negative sense.

Descent Into Hell - Christ's descent into Hell. The entrance of Christ's soul into the underworld (Matthew 12:40, The Acts of the Apostles 2:24–31), the dwelling place of the souls of the righteous from pre-Christian times. Represented in Byzantine art as an ANASTASIUS CROSS, represented less frequently in the Occident, but especially in the 10th–15th centuries.

Desert - An ambivalent symbol with negative and positive aspects. In Islam, it usually appears in a negative sense as a place of confusion. —In the Upanishads, the desert occasionally appears as a symbol of the undifferentiated primeval unity beyond the illusory world of all existence. —On the one hand, the Bible mentions the desert in connection with abandonment and distance from God and as a place where demons live; yet, on the other hand,

abracadabra
abracadabr
abracadab
abracada
abracad
abraca
abrac
abra
abr
ab
a

DISAPPEARING PATTERN:
Disappearing pattern by Agrippa
von Nettesheim
DODECAHEDRON: Above: from a
drawing by Leonardo da Vinci;
below: two-dimensional unfolding

it is also the place where God can show Himself with particular intensity (examples: the column of fire and clouds by which God led the people of Israel in the desert; John the Baptist proclaims the imminence of the Messiah in the desert). In connection with hermit legends, the desert also often appears in a double sense: on the one hand as a place of temptation by demons (as in the case of St. Anthony), on the other hand as a place of meditation and closeness to God.

Devil - From the Greek "diabolos," meaning "denier, divider"; called "Satan" in Hebrew. According to Christian teaching, devils are those ANGELS who rebelled against God, especially Lucifer, who tempted the first couple to sin and has since been "prince of the world." —In early Christian symbolic representations, the devil appears as a serpent, dragon, lion, basilisk, and asp; represented in the 9th century as a naked, dark angel; represented since the 11th century as a demon and fantastic, grotesque, satyr-like hybrid; greatly modified into the 16th century. The most powerful images are from the Age of Reformation (Dürer, J. Ammann, H. Bosch, P. Brueghel). Most common themes: the temptation of Christ or of saints (especially St. Anthony), expulsion of Luci-

fer from heaven, the Fall, the Last Judgment. During the Italian Renaissance and the Baroque period, the devil was portrayed predominately in human form; since the 19th century, the figure of the devil has increasingly undergone a process of psychological interpretation.

Dew - Also "dew drops." Dew is closely related to the symbolic significance of RAIN as an expression of the influence of the SKY upon the EARTH; however, since it falls inaudibly and at night, and glitters in the morning sun or looks like pearls (see PEARL), its symbolic significance is more mysterious and decidedly more strongly emotional-spiritual. Occasionally, such as in the Cabala, it appears as a symbol of salvation and of the renewal of life (being produced from a TREE OF LIFE); for the ancient Germans, dew was a supernatural element that drips from the world tree YGGDRASIL and is the food of the couple that survives after the end of the world. —In China, dew was thought to come from the MOON and to grant one immortality. —Buddhism, however, sees dew as a symbol of the impermanence and nothingness of our world. —The Greeks interpreted dew as being a symbol of fertilization and fertility.

DOLPHIN: Anchor and dolphin; catacombs, 2nd century
DOORS: Tabernacle doors

Diadem - See CROWN.

Diamond - The diamond is usually conceived of symbolically as a perfected CRYSTAL and is therefore a symbol of absolute purity, spirituality, and permanence. In India, it is sometimes a symbol of immortality; Buddha's throne is made of diamond. —Plato describes the world axis as diamond. —Popular belief in Europe attributes various magical qualities to the diamond: it is supposed to cure disease, render poisons impotent, drive off animals, witches and ghosts, make one invisible, and grant men good luck with women. — During the Renaissance, it was primarily considered to be a symbol of courage and strength of character. —PHYSIOLOGUS says that diamond is stronger than iron. Diamond is called "adamant" because it conquers all, which leads to the interpretation: "My Lord Jesus Christ also judges all, yet no one can judge Him."

Dice - See CUBE.

Dietary Taboo - A prohibition to touch or consume certain foods. Some groups within a society are subject to particularly rigid rules, such as shamans and chiefs. In the Old Testament and in Judaism, dietary taboos were emphasized especially strongly; for example, clean animals, i.e., those suitable and unsuitable for sacrifice, were strictly separated from animals that were unclean and not allowed to be eaten.

Disappearing Pattern - A procedure used in magic whereby a particular word (for example, ABRACADABRA) is repeatedly written underneath itself and the first or last letter is deleted until only the "A" remains. This procedure is supposed, for example, to dispel certain ailments, to make the ailment "disappear." Disappearing patterns were frequently written on AMULETS.

Disk - Like the CIRCLE, the disk is frequently a sun symbol (such as in India and Egypt); the depiction of a winged disk represents the course of the SUN and, by extension, the upswing into higher spheres in general. —In China, it is a symbol of heavenly perfection; a jade disk with a HOLE in the center (the *Pi*) symbolizes heaven.

Disk Cross - A cross or crucifix with a background disk that bears ornamental or figured decoration; especially common from the 11th century through the end of the 13th century.

Distaff - A forerunner of the spinning

DOVE: So-called Aphrodite with a
dove; gold plate, Mycenae
DOVE: Dove as the Holy Spirit; from
a miniature of the Holy Trinity;
from the so-called Landgrafen
Psalter

wheel, often identified with the SPINDLE
in symbolism.

Doctrine of Signs - The doctrine holds
that a (magical) relationship exists between parts of animate and inanimate
nature by virtue of the existence of a mark
or sign; in addition to CORRELATIVES,
it is an important basis of MICROCOSM-
MACROCOSM thought.

Dodecahedron - A solid body bounded
by twelve flat polygons. The pentagonal
dodecahedron, bounded by twelve equilateral pentagons, is particularly important symbolically, sharing in the symbolism of the numbers TWO and FIVE. It is
regarded as the most perfect of the five
PLATONIC SOLIDS and is therefore a
symbol of totality.

Doe - A symbol of the animalistic or maternal aspect of womanliness; women or
girls are frequently turned into does in
fairy tales. In Greek mythology, the doe
was sacred to Hera and Artemis; Artemis's chariot was drawn by four does or
stags (see STAG) with golden antlers. —
In the mythology of the Turks and Mon-
gols, the doe embodies the feminine, i.e.,
the earthly side of the mythic union of
heaven and earth.

Dog - Probably man's oldest domestic
animal. It has long given occasion for complex, often contradictory symbolic interpretations. In many cultures, it is associated with death; it guards the realm of the
dead, is a guide of souls or mediator between the world of the dead and the world
of the living (Anubis, CERBERUS); the
gods of ambiguous, nocturnal-dark regions sometimes appear in the form of
dogs, such as Hecate, the Greek goddess
of the CROSSROADS. —In some cultures
(such as in Africa), the dog's acknowl-
edged wisdom caused it to be thought of
as an ancestral father of civilization and
the bringer of fire to man; on the other
hand, the dog's strong sexual drive caused
it to become associated with the symbolism of the ancestors and progenitors of
man. —The dog's faithfulness, proverbial
to this day, made the dog a very common
symbol of fidelity and (in Japan, for example) a mythic helper and protector of
women and children in particular. —In a
negative sense, the dog appears as a symbol of impurity, vice and lowliness (such
as in the Old Testament and in Islam,
where, however, the dog is accorded good
characteristics as well); it is common in
nearly all cultures to invoke the dog as a
humiliating insult. During the Middle
Ages, a humiliating punishment involved

DRAGON: Dragon on a dragon vest; China, 17th century

DRAGON: The woman of the Apocalypse with the 7-headed dragon; from an illuminated manuscript by Konrad von Scheyern

requiring someone to carry a dog; hanging a dog along with a person was sometimes thought to make an execution worse. —In medieval art, the dog is an ambivalent figure: it can be a symbol of envy, wrath, and temptation by evil, but also a symbol of faith and fidelity. A white dog frequently signifies the goodness and piety of the person at whose feet the dog is portrayed as sitting; it can also be a symbol of a good marriage; in contrast, an ugly, usually dark-colored dog sometimes symbolizes disbelief or pagan belief. —The dog is the eleventh sign of the Chinese ZODIAC, corresponding to AQUARIUS.

Dolmen - From the Breton, meaning "stone table." A MEGALITHIC GRAVE constructed of vertically placed stones with a capstone. During the Neolithic Period, they were especially common in Brittany. See MEGALITHS.

Dolphin - As an astonishingly intelligent and agile animal friendly toward humans, the dolphin provided many peoples associated with the OCEAN occasion for mythic interpretations. It was regarded as god-like by the Cretan-Mycenaean civilization and the Greeks and Romans. In Greece, it was sacred primarily to the god of light, Apollo, but also to Dionysus (the protector of seafaring), Aphrodite (who was born from the ocean), and Poseidon (the god of the ocean). French successors to the throne had dolphins on their personal coats of arms and were therefore

DOLPHIN: Various depictions of dolphins on ancient coins

85

DRINKING HORN: Rhyton from the
Oxus [presently called Amu Darya]
trove

given the title "dauphins." The dolphin
was also thought to be a guide of souls
that safely brought the souls of the deceased to the realm of the dead on its back.
In this regard, it was appropriated by early
Christian art and applied to Christ, the
Savior.

Doors - Or "portal," "gate." Like the
BRIDGE, it is a symbol of transition from
one place to another, such as from this life
to the next, from the profane to the holy.
The idea of a gate of heaven or a sun gate
marking the transition to otherworldly,
divine regions, is common. According to
the ideas of many peoples, the underworld or the realm of the dead lies on the
other side of large gates. —A closed door
often signifies a hidden mystery, yet also
prohibition and futility; an open door represents a challenge to pass through it or
signifies an open secret. —Representations of Christ on medieval doors (in the
tympanum, for example) refer to the well-
known words of Christ, "I am the door."
Depictions of Mary, on the other hand,
often refer to the symbolic significance of
Mary as the portal to heaven through
which the Son of God entered the world.
—See JANUS.

Doorstep - See THRESHOLD.

Double Axe - See AXE.

Dough - A symbol of unformed matter or
of the union of WATER and EARTH. The
kneading and shaping of dough is also
occasionally compared with masculine
sexuality and creative power.

Dove - 1) In the Near East, the dove was
associated with the fertility goddess
Ishtar; in Phoenicia, it was associated with
the Astarte cult. In Greece, the dove was
sacred to Aphrodite. See PARTRIDGE. —
In India, and to some extent in ancient
Germany as well, a dark dove was regarded as a bird of the spirit, yet also of
death and misfortune. —Islam sees it as a
sacred bird because it supposedly protected Mohammed during his flight. —In
the Bible, Noah lets out three doves after
the Flood, one of which returns with an
olive branch; it is a sign of reconciliation
with God and has since then been a symbol of peace. The white dove is also a symbol of simplicity and purity and, especially in Christian art, a symbol of the Holy
Spirit; yet it can also occasionally be a
symbol of a baptized Christian, of a martyr (with a LAUREL or a martyr's crown
in its beak), or of the soul in a state of heavenly peace (for example, when it is
perched on the tree of life or on a vessel

bearing the water of life). —In conjunction with the four cardinal virtues, the dove symbolizes temperance. —A white dove pair is a popular love symbol. 2) "Eucharistic dove," a tabernacle in the form of a dove that hangs over the altar and has a tray for the consecrated host; first mentioned in the 7th century.

Dragon - The word is borrowed from the Latin; the Germanic name for it is "Wurm" (i.e., Lindwurm). A mythic image among many peoples, the dragon is a living, fantastic HYBRID CREATURE that frequently has many heads. In many religions, the dragon (often akin to the serpent) embodies primeval powers hostile to God that must be conquered. In conjunction with this, several myths telling of the killing of dragons have arisen (Indra, Zeus, Apollo, Siegfried, St. George —see DRAGON FIGHTS). —In the Old Testament, the dragon (akin to the LEVIATHAN) embodies the continued agency of the chaos that existed before the world, which threatens Creation and must be conquered. In the Book of Revelation, the dragon, as the principle of Satan (and symbol of the devil), pursues the sun-clothed woman who is giving birth to the child (baby Jesus); the dragon is felled by the archangel Michael. —In legends and fairy tales, the dragon frequently appears as the guard of a TREASURE or a kidnapped PRINCESS and thus embodies the difficulties that must be overcome before a lofty goal is reached. —C.G. Jung sees the dragon slayer myths as the manifestation of a fight between the ego and regressive forces of the unconscious. —In Hinduism and Taoism, the dragon is regarded as a powerful spiritual being that can produce the potion of immortality. In China and Japan, the dragon is revered as something that brings good luck and wards off demons. It grants fertility, since it is closely associated with the powers of water and thus with the Yin principle (see YIN AND YANG); yet, at the same time, it primarily represents the masculine active powers of the sky and thus the Yang principle; as a demiurge, it produces the waters of the primeval beginning or the world egg; its antagonist is the TIGER. Favorite decorative motifs include a dragon playing around a wish pearl (see PEARL) and a pair of dragons. As the powerful being that reconciles opposing principles, the dragon also became an imperial symbol. —The dragon is the fifth sign of the Chinese ZODIAC; it corresponds to Leo the LION.

Dragon Fights - Dragon fights are battles

with monsters, accounts of which have come down through history in various forms according to a set pattern: a horseman bearing either a spear or sword fights a serpent; or two beasts fight one another and the hero steps in; or a craftily waged fight against a monster ends with the hero tying up the monster.

Drawing Board - A master's symbol of the Freemasons; in some respects, it is identical to the WORK table.

Dream - A type of experience that has not yet been satisfactorily defined, dreaming is connected with sleep and perhaps related to fantasy. From the earliest literary sources up to the present and in all religions, dreams play an important role, whereby the question of whether dreams are directed from within or without has still not been convincingly answered. Independent of this is the role of the dream interpreter, an "occupation" that existed early in all civilizations. Joseph's role in interpreting the Pharaoh's dream (Genesis 41:25–27) and the meaning of Mordecai's dream in the Book of Esther are well known. Among Greek dream interpreters, such as Artemidoros Daldianus (2nd century A.D.), one finds the basis of today's widely common interpretation of dream symbols according to depth psychology. This offers *one* possibility of interpretation, whereby there is a division (which has grown since antiquity) between dreams that foretell the future and dreams that require interpretation because of the ambiguity that is always present in dream symbols. Dreams should be distinguished from visions, such as the vision of Jacob's Ladder, although overlappings are common; for their part, visions, like dreams that occur during sleep, are possibly connected with daydreams.

Drinking Glass - As a container for drinking that is given from hand to hand, it is a symbol of friendship and camaraderie. — It is an ambivalent symbol in the Bible: as a cup of wrath, it is a symbol of divine justice; as a cup of blessing and of joy, it is a symbol of God's closeness.

Drinking Horn - Or "rhyton." Adopted from the Orient, the drinking horn is an ancient Greek pitcher or drinking vessel in the shape of a HORN; there is a very small opening at the bottom from which a narrow jet streams.

Drum - A frequently used cult instrument; its rhythmically produced sound is sometimes equated with hidden sounds and

DUCK: Symbol of talkativeness; from Schmid's *Musterbuch*

DUCK: Detail from a mural in the grave of the Egyptian scribe Harmhab

forces of the cosmos (in Buddhism, for example). Often, such as among black African peoples, the drum served to call magically upon heavenly powers; the war drum, in particular, was usually closely related symbolically to LIGHTNING and THUNDER. —In China, the sound of the drum became associated with the path of the SUN and especially with the winter solstice, which is the point of the greatest influence of the Yin principle (see YIN AND YANG), yet also of the renewed rising of the sun and thus of the increasing influence of the Yang principle.

Drunkenness - See INTOXICATION.

Dualism - From the Latin "dualis," meaning "directed toward two opposing things." Dualism reduces the world to two original, ultimate principles; in a broad sense, dualism attains when two supreme beings face one another either as polar complements (heaven and earth; the feminine and masculine principle, such as Yin and Yang in Chinese religion) or as enemies (light and darkness; good and evil; life and death).

Duck - In Egypt, ducks were favored sacrificial animals. —In the Far East, duck pairs, which usually swim together, are regarded as a symbol of marital happiness (see KINGFISHER). The duck is not cited in PHYSIOLOGUS, but it can be found in early Christian representations, where it appears on church portals and, due to its chattering, symbolizes the babblers who should stay away.

Dung-Beetle - See SCARAB.

Durga - From the Sanskrit, meaning "that which is difficult to approach." In Indian mythology, Durga is the bride of Shiva. She appears in her horrible form as Kali, fights demons, and receives human sacrifices; she is also worshipped as a nourishing mother (being a type of Great Mother).

Dust - Occasionally a symbol of man's impermanence, such as in the Bible and in Christian literature; in the Book of Genesis, it is also a symbol of the huge number of Adam's progeny.

Dwarfs - Dwarfs are small, old, often duck-footed, goose-footed or bird-footed, sometimes visible, sometimes not, helpful or teasingly mischievous, human-like creatures of folk belief that can be interpreted as (among other things) symbolic embodiments of useful but ultimately uncontrollable natural forces as well as of experiences and actions of the subconsciousness that are only vaguely, or not at all, understandable. Aside from various skills that they possessed and the gift, attributed to them, of being able to tell the future, dwarfs were regarded as excellent smiths who practiced their trade under the ground. Many of the attributes that were characteristic of individual gods, give evidence of dwarfs' skill. They were also thought to be guards of treasure.

EAGLE: As a symbol of the spirit. From *The Hermaphroditic Child of the Sun and the Moon*, 1752.

EAGLE: Eagle and fish as symbol of baptism (from Schmid's *Musterbuch*); motive from the floor of the baptistery of Capua

Eagle - Very common symbolic animal, usually in conjunction with the SUN and the SKY, but occasionally with LIGHTNING and THUNDER as well. Its strength, stamina and skyward flight, in particular, gave it a symbolic character. In some American Indian cultures, the eagle, being related to the sun and the sky, is juxtaposed to the chthonic JAGUAR. Its feathers were used in cult jewelry as symbols of sun rays. —The eagle is considered the "king" of the birds and was already a symbol of kings and gods in antiquity. In Greco-Roman antiquity, the eagle was the companion and symbolic animal of Zeus (Jupiter). In Roman art, a soaring eagle embodies or carries the soul of the ruler that rises up to the gods after cremation of the body. The Roman legions had the eagle as a banner. —In the Bible, the eagle is a symbol of God's omnipotence or also of the strength of faith. —PHYSIOLOGUS ascribes the same legendary attributes to the eagle as to the PHOENIX; thus, it was also a symbol in the Middle Ages of rebirth and baptism (and thus occasionally appears as decoration on baptismal fonts) as well as an occasional symbol of Christ, especially with respect to Christ as conquerer of serpents, and as a symbol (also due to its flight) of Christ's Ascension. Mystics variously compared the soaring eagle with prayer. Since the eagle was alleged (by Aristotle) to look directly into the sun when it ascended, it was also regarded as a symbol of contemplation and spiritual knowledge. With respect to this and its high flight, it is also an attribute of John the Evangelist (see EVANGELISTS, SYMBOLS OF THE). —Among the seven deadly sins, the eagle symbolizes pride; among the four cardinal virtues, it symbolizes justice. —C.G. Jung sees a paternal symbol in the eagle. —In a continuation of Roman tradition, the eagle is present in many state insignia as a sign of sovereignty.

Eagle Pulpit - A reading lectern for religous services in the form of an eagle (usually made of brass, bronze or wood) with extended wings. Probably associated with the evangelistic symbol of John.

Ear - A symbol of hearing, of communication, and also of obeying; like the EYE, it is an organ of perception that, as the "eye of the spirit," can also be a symbol for inspiration; spiritual "hearing" is considered to be an older ability than spiritual "seeing."

EARTH: Earth as prima materia, suckling the son of the philosophers; from Mylius's *Philosophia reformata*, 1622

—In antiquity, the ear was seen as the seat of memory; pulling one's ear, a juridical practice common up into the Middle Ages, was regarded as an appeal to the memory of witnesses not to forget certain facts. —In China, for example, a long, broad ear was often thought to be a sign of judgment, wisdom and immortality. —In Africa, the ear frequently has sexual significance; the shape of the outer ear is often considered to be phallic, while the ear canal—as a receptive organ—is compared with the vagina.

Early Christian Art - Also called "ancient Christian art." Arose in the service of Christianity between the first half of the 2nd century and the 6th–7th centuries, particularly in North Africa, Egypt, Syria, Mesopotamia, Armenia, Asia Minor (Antioch), Italy (Rome, Milan, Ravenna), Greece (Salonica, Philippi) and Spain. At first entirely derived from ancient Hellenic forms, it changed over into Byzantine art during the 4th century, particularly in the Christian East. Frescos with Biblical scenes still exist, particularly in Dura-Europos; the earliest examples are in Rome in the catacombs and on sarcophagi with Judeo-Christian themes and Christian re-interpretations of ancient-pagan motifs (such as Orpheus and the Good Shepherd), representations of baptisms, heavenly banquet and Jonah scenes and, beginning in the 4th century, of the enthroned Christ with saints and martyrs. Moreover, there are icon paintings and figurative and decorative mosaics on floors, in cupolas and apses. Reliefs on sarcophagi were at first figured and had similar themes as those in paintings; beginning in the mid-5th century, they assumed a more schematic symbolic nature. —The interpretation of symbols of early Christian art is often very difficult and is the object of controversial discussions.

Earth - In contrast to the SKY, the earth is usually interpreted as being feminine, passive and dark; it often appears in mythology as a feminine deity. Myths about the creation of the world sometimes see the world's beginning as a reproductive act in which the earth was fertilized by the sky; it is sometimes thus compared with the WOMB as well. —Yet the earth is not only the womb from which all life issues, but it is also the grave into which it returns; its symbolic significance thus frequently corresponds to the ambivalent figure of the "Great Mother," who is experienced simultaneously as life-giving and threatening. INITIATION rites and, at times, customary ritual burial with

ECCLESIA: Ecclesia and Synagogue
(from Schmid's *Musterbuch*)

subsequent "resurrection" sometimes allude to a connection between the mortiferous and natal aspects of the earth. —In alchemy, the earth is often represented by the sign ⍒. —In astrology, it is associated with the zodiacal signs Taurus, Virgo and Capricorn (see ZODIAC).

Easter Egg - See EGG.

Easter Lily - The Yellow Narcissus; the symbolism of the NARCISSUS, in particular, applies to the Easter lily; specifically, it is a symbol of spring.

Eastern Orientation ["Ostung"] - Or "orientation." Looking toward the rising sun as a symbol of the presence of a divine power; customary in many countries and religions during prayer, sacrifice, and the construction of grave sites and temples. In Christianity, it is particularly common in church construction. The altar that faces east (and the entrance that faces west) is the most common form next to the portal that faces east (and the altar that faces west), of which there are many instances dating from early Occidental Christian times.

Easter Rabbit - See HARE.

Ebony - Because of its color, ebony shares in the symbolic meaning of BLACK. According to legend, the THRONE of Pluto, god of the underworld, is made of ebony.

Ecclesia - From the Greek "ekklesia," meaning "congregation." Ecclesia is a term for the community of those who believe in Christ, the Church. —Personified as a woman in early Christian art (in St. Sabina in Rome, for example), she has appeared since the 9th century particularly in dramatic juxtaposition to the SYNAGOGUE. She is usually depicted under a crucifixion, bearing a crown, chalice and victory banner, whereas synagogue is depicted with blindfolded eyes, a drooping crown and a shattered spear: in various symbolic contexts, they are symbols of the Church and of superceded Judaism. The Gothic portal sculptures at Strasbourg and Bamberg are famous.

Echidna - A HYBRID CREATURE of Greek mythology, consisting of a woman whose lower body is a SERPENT. She bore various other monsters, such as CERBERUS, the CHIMERA, Scylla and the SPHINX. She is variously interpreted as the dual psycho-physical/rational-impulsive nature of humans. C.G. Jung interprets her as a symbol of tabooed incestual desires: the mother as a beautiful young

EGG: The world egg, wound in a spiral by a snake that here represents time; illustration in J. Bryant's *Analysis of Ancient Mythology*, 1774.

EGG: Mercury in a philosophical egg; from *Mutus liber*, 1702

woman whose lower body evokes an association of horror.

Echo - In American Indian imagery, it is an attribute of the JAGUAR, which is interpreted as a chthonic deity, inasmuch as it is associated with mountains, wild animals and drum signals. —In Greek mythology, it is a nymph. —For many peoples, it is generally a symbol of repression and passivity; it is frequently also a symbol of ambiguity and shadow. It is sometimes associated with a golem.

Egg - As the seed of life, the egg is a common fertility symbol. —Encountered in the mythic notions of a great many cultures is the world egg, which—as a symbol of the totality of creative forces—is thought to have been present at the primeval beginning, when it floated on the primeval waters and issued from itself the entire world and the elements, or initially at least heaven and earth. —Mythic human figures, such as Chinese heroes, were sometimes depicted as breaking out of eggs. —Because of its simple shape, its frequently white color and the wealth of possibilities before it, the egg is often encountered as a symbol of perfection. —In alchemy, the philosophical egg played an important role as a symbol of PRIMA MATERIA, from which the philosophical fire hatched the PHILOSOPHERS' STONE. —Specifically, the yellow yoke was often interpreted as a symbol of GOLD and the egg white as a symbol of SILVER. —In Christianity, the egg is regarded as a symbol of resurrection, because Christ broke out of the grave like a fully developed chick breaks out of an egg; the Easter egg, which had already played a role as a fertility symbol in heathen rites of spring, thus acquired a specifically Christian meaning.

Egypt - According to the Old Testament, Egypt is the land of bondage of the people of Israel and the land of idolatry; it is therefore a symbolical negative counterpart of "the promised land." —Often regarded as a symbol of ancient mysteries, such as the building of the pyramids as a world mystery encoded in numbers, and the founding of astronomy, astrology and alchemy. Modern research has shown that much of this was "glorified" and mystified in the Hellenic world.

Egyptian Plagues - The ten afflictions that, according to Exodus 7–12, God visited upon Pharaoh so that Pharaoh would let the Israelites go free: frogs, lice, flies, murrain, boils, hail, locusts, darkness, death of all firstborn, and turning the Nile into blood.

ELEMENTS: The four elements of air, fire, water and earth that, as signs of the macrocosm, surround the microcosm man, made by God the Creator; Alsatian, 12th century

Elder - A bush or tree with white, fragrant blossoms and violet-black berries. It was a highly regarded medicinal plant even in antiquity; touching the plant was thought to be especially effective, as an illness supposedly was transferred to the plant in this manner. The elder was also used as a defense against sorcerers and witches. Cutting down and burning the wood of the elder was thought to bring

EIGHT

8 The first cubic number: $2^3 = 2 \times 2 \times 2 = 8$. According to Aristotle and Pythagoras, a number's perfection is attained in its third power, such as $3^3 = 3 \times 3 \times 3 = 27$. According to early Christian thought, this perfection is reflected in the octagon of the christening font and of the baptistery as a manifestation of the feminine and of the bosom of the church; it is a symbol of Christ's resurrection. 8, 2 $\times$ 2 $\times$ 2, is the number of the element earth, just as 27, 3 $\times$ 3 $\times$ 3, is the number of the element fire. Circumcision takes place on the eighth day after birth. —8 plays an important role in Hinduism and in Buddhism. It is frequently the number of spokes in the Buddhist symbol of the WHEEL; the symbolic LOTUS flower has 8 petals; 8 paths lead to spiritual perfection. The Hindu god Vishnu has 8 arms that must be seen in conjunction with the 8 keepers of space. —In Japan, 8 is also regarded as the number of greatness fundamentally immeasurable and innumerable.

18 As the product of 3 (fire) x 3 (fire) x 2 (earth), 18 is the symbolic number of the element air. 18 might also possibly be viewed as an astronomical symbolic number, since it represents the period (in years) in which solar and lunar eclipses recur in regular succession.

28 A perfect number, since the sum of its parts, 1 + 2 + 4 + 7 + 14, equals 28. 28 is also the lunar number, since all four phases are traversed in 28 days. 4 x 7 = 28 plays a role in the cult of Mithra and wherever 7 is already prominent. In Islamic tradition, there are said to have been 28 prophets before Mohammed.

ELEMENTS

The four elements play a crucial role in microcosm-macrocosm thought. Indeed, their combinations in antiquity's view of the world made possible the constitution of the microcosm of man and of the macrocosm of the world. Numerous speculations as well as analogies, correlatives, symbolic pictures, alchemist thought, and symbolic combinations of numbers are associated with the doctrine of the elements, having been handed down to us from Greek antiquity since the time of Thales of Milet and Empedocles.

Of particular interest is the diagram of the four elements that appears as a wall fresco in the crypt of the Cathedral of Anagni (located southeast of Rome) and depicts Hippocrates's conception of the interrelationships of the elements. Its particular significance derives primarily from the fact that it contains clearly represented symbolic speculations about numbers, whereby the third powers of the feminine number 2 ($2 \times 2 \times 2 = 8$) and the masculine number 3 ($3 \times 3 \times 3 = 27$) are correlated with the elements of earth and fire, respectively.

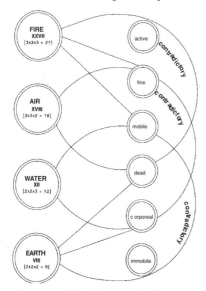

System of the elements in the
Cathedral of Anagni

The four elements according to Schmid's
Musterbuch

Man as the convergence of the four elements; from a woodcut by H. Weiditz in C. Plinius Secundus's *Historia Naturalis*, Frankfurt, 1582

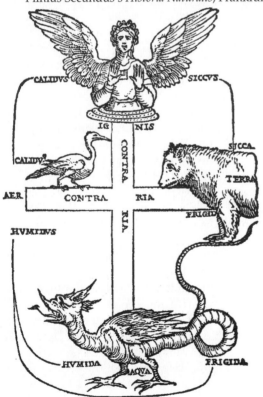

The four elements according to alchemy. Their similarity with the system of the elements of the Cathedral of Anagni is remarkable. The opposing pairs are represented in the form of a circle; the fact that the symbols themselves can be variously chosen (an elephant instead of a bear, for example) is also remarkable. The associations of the elements, which are abstractly depicted at left, can be clearly seen.

ELEPHANT: The elephant as a symbol of chastity (from Schmid's *Musterbuch*)

ELEPHANT: The Indian god Ganesha; sculpture, 12th century

misfortune and death. —On the other hand, because Judas is said to have hanged himself on an elder tree, the elder is sometimes associated with the devil. — Because its blossoms smell sweet yet its leaves taste bitter, the Christian Middle Ages saw the elder as a simile for Christians (blossoms) and Jews (leaves), who come from one root and one stem.

Eldorado - From the Spanish el dorado, meaning "the gilded man." A legendary land of gold in the Andes of northern South America. Figuratively, it is a symbolic place of greatest abundance, greatest wealth, and immeasurable surplus.

Elecampane - Compositae flowers. Helen of Troy is supposed to have been holding them in her hands when she was abducted by Paris (thus the Latin name Inula Helenium). The herb MOLY, given to Odysseus by Hermes so that he could free his journeymen from the magic of Circe, was occasionally thought to be elecampane (though it was usually thought to be the black hellebore root). —In Christianity, elecampane seldom appears as a symbolic plant; it signifies "salvation."

Elements - The fundamental principles that structure the world; various basic phenomena from other realms of being are frequently associated with them. — The Chinese doctrine of the elements arose as early as the second millenium B.C. and includes water, fire, wood, metal and earth. The number 1, depth, winter and the north corresponded to water. Similarly, the number 2, height, summer and the south corresponded to fire; the number 3, spring and the east corresponded to wood; the number 4, autumn and the west corresponded to metal; and the earth, which corresponded to the number 5, was the mediating element. — Like the Greeks (beginning with Empedocles), most other cultures distinguish four elements: FIRE, WATER, AIR and EARTH. Sometimes thought of as the "fifth element" since the time of Aristotle, ether, radiating brightly above the layer of air close to the earth, also corresponds to fire and air. —The doctrine of temperaments associated the four elements with the four temperaments: water with the phlegmatic, earth with the melancholic, fire with the choleric, and air with the sanguine. The four stages of a person's life, bodily fluids and organs, and the four times of the day and (as was already recognized in China) of the year were sometimes associated with the four elements. —C.G. Jung occasionally refers to the

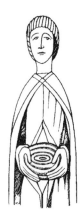

ENTRAILS: St. Mamas with entrails in his hands
EUCHARISTIC SYMBOLS: Cup and wine pitcher; from Schmid's *Musterbuch*

ancient distinction between masculine, active principles (fire and air) and feminine, passive principles (water and earth). —The Freemasons symbolically associated the four elements with the stages of spiritual development: man is born from the earth and is cleansed step by step by passing through air, water and fire. —The Renaissance was fond of personifying the elements as gods from antiquity: earth as Cybele, water as Neptune, air as Juno and fire as Vulcan. —The alchemists recognized not only the four elements of the Greek natural philosophers, but also the so-called "philosophical" elements of SALT, SULPHUR, and quicksilver (see MERCURY).

Elephant - In Asia, the elephant is the animal ridden by rulers, a symbol of power, wisdom, peace and happiness. It is ridden by the Indian god Indra; Ganesha, the beloved son of the god Shiva and remover of all obstacles, is depicted as having an elephant's head. In India and Tibet, the elephant is frequently encountered as the bearer of the entire universe; thus, it often appears in architecture as caryatids. —The white elephant combines the symbolic significance of the elephant with the symbolic significance of the color WHITE. According to Buddhist views, the Bodhisattva

entered the womb of his mother, Princess Maya, as a white elephant before his rebirth as a Buddha; thus, the white elephant became a popular symbol of Buddhism. —The elephant is revered as a symbol of strength, happiness and long life in Africa as well; for example, one sometimes encounters elephant cults that seek forgiveness from the elephants killed by hunters. —During the Middle Ages, the elephant was considered to be especially chaste, since, according to Aristotle, the male elephant abstained from sexual intercourse during the two-year gestation period of his mate; the elephant was thus also associated with the virtues of prudence and temperance (temperantia). PHYSIOLOGUS embellishes this view by maintaining that sexual drive could be extinguished by eating parts of the mandrake plant (see MANDRAKE). —The appearance of an elephant together with an OBELISK can be traced back to an elephant together with a tree of wisdom or life, as it first appeared in Indian mythology. —The elephant also appears as a symbol of the ELEMENT earth. —The elephant as a bearer of an OBELISK turned up as a symbol in Italy in the 14th century and is a mixture of ideas about the elephant that are found in Physiologus and bestiaries and the comparison with the tree of wisdom or life that was handed down from India to Persia and Byzan-tium: a combination of the wise, generous, pure and pious elephant and the tree of knowledge. See illustration on page 98.

Elixir - See POTION.

Elm - A long-lived tree with hard and tough wood; in ancient Greece, the elm was a symbol of death.

Emerald - The emerald shares generally in the symbolic significance of the color GREEN.—The Indians of Central America associated it with BLOOD (the colors green and RED are often regarded by American Indians as an expression of vitality), RAIN and the MOON. Due to its green color, the emerald is associated with fertility in Europe as well and thus with moistening, the moon and spring. — In Rome, the emerald was an attribute of Venus. —According to the Revelation of St. John, the emerald is one of the jewels of Holy Jerusalem. —During the Middle Ages, the symbolic meaning of the emerald was manifold; it was thought to be a highly effective talisman, as it (supposedly having come from hell) could be used especially well against the powers of hell. At the same time, though, people believed that, by having an emerald on one's tongue, one could conjure up evil spirits and hold a conversation with them. A consecrated emerald (that is, one deprived of its evil powers) was supposedly able to set prisoners free. In the symbolic thought of the Christian church, the emerald signifies purity, faith and immortality.

Embryo - Symbol of all possibilities still dormant and thus closely related to the symbolism of the EGG. —The Vedic golden embryo symbolizes the principle of life that is born by the primeval waters (clear parallel to the familiar notion of the world egg).

Encolpion - From the Greek, meaning "worn on the breast." In the Old Testament, it was a capsule worn as an AMULET; in Christian times, it was in the shape of a cross, an anchor, a fish, etc. and contained relics, Bible verses, the monogram of Christ, and the like. The medalion image of the Virgin Mary worn by dignitaries of the Eastern Orthodox Church is also called an encolpion.

Enhydris - An animal cited in PHYSIO-LOGUS and often identified (questionably) with the OTTER. It is interpreted as "the person of our Savior, who put on the cloak of the earth and went to Hell in order to vanquish death and devil."

Markus

Matthäus

Lukas

Johannes

EVANGELISTS, SYMBOLS OF: Detail from a miniature ; Pontificale of Chartres, beginning of the 13th century

Enlightenment - See LIGHT.

Entrails - According to popular belief in various cultures, entrails had significance relating particularly to the future. Augury from the entrails of sacrificial animals was especially common. See LIVER. Entrails were the symbol of St. Mamas in the vicinity of Venice and around Langres (eastern France).

Erinyes - In Greek mythology, the Erinyes (known in Rome as the Furies) are female avengers, primarily of murder. In art, they are depicted as being ugly, having wings, snakes in their hair and hands, torches and whips. —They are frequently interpreted as symbolic figures of an agonizing bad conscience. See EUMENIDES.

Ermine - A large, white weasel; because of its color, it is a symbol of purity, innocence and incorruptibility (in this sense, it frequently appears as fur trim on the robes of rulers). —In Christian art, it is a symbol of Christ the victor over the devil, since it hunts and kills SERPENTS.

Etimasie - A symbolic motif of the preparation of the throne for Christ's return; the empty throne is situated under the cross and appears with a lamb, a dove, the book of life or a scroll, the implements of the Passion, a crown, a purple robe, and so on; in the Orthodox Church, it is situated over the ALTAR.

Eucharistic Symbols - The Eucharist was originally celebrated as a form of a prayer of thanks; this occurred in the celebration of the Holy Mass of the Catholic Church and in the Communion of the Protestant church. BREAD, WINE, the chalice (see CUP), and a FISH are symbols of the Eucharist; the MYSTICAL WINEPRESS and the MYSTICAL MILL have a more allegorical character.

Eumenides - Forgiving goddesses in Greek mythology who were often interpreted as symbolic embodiments of divine mercy. They are identical with the Erinyes, yet it is a point of controversy whether this ascription of friendly characteristics to the avenging goddesses has to do with a euphemism or with the fact that the Erinyes, like other chthonic deities, were both terrible and beneficent.

Eutocius Stone - See VULTURE.

Evangelists, Symbols of the - Attributes that are associated with depictions of, or represent, the Evangelists in Christian art. The angel or MAN is associated with

EVANGELISTS, SYMBOLS OF THE

The four Evangelists, the authors of the four canonical Gospels, have been depicted since the time of Constantine either as human figures in the tradition of ancient images of philosophers and authors or by evangelistic symbols. These symbols have been represented since the 4th century usually as MONSTERS or as TETRAMORPHS, whereby the quadrumvirate is no doubt closely related to ancient astral-cosmological notions such as the "fixed cross" of the astrologers, which is composed of the four zodiacal signs Leo, Taurus, Scorpio and Aquarius, the four points of the compass, the four elements, the four winds, or the four rivers of Eden; the latter were already being interpreted as the four Evangelists themselves early on. Thus, the four symbols of the Evangelists, by virtue of their astral-cosmological background, became symbols of the foundations of heaven and the cosmic system, whereby old notions from microcosm-macrocosm thought no doubt played a role. Particularly in the Byzantine Church, one finds groupings on relic holders and books containing the Gospel; the groupings show the cross, as the true tree of life, and the four symbols of the Evangelists united with the four rivers of Eden, which are thought of as symbols of the four Gospels. The groupings thereby form the four bounds of the earth or the center of the earth, that is, Eden.

Depiction of the symbols of the Evangelists in Schmid's *Musterbuch*. A spring, fed by the cross of Christ, has its source in the beak of a dove (Holy Spirit), grows into a stream, collects in a basin, divides into four rivers (Gospels), and pours into the flowing river Jordan below (inscription). Stags and lambs (believers) quench their thirst with this holy water.

Mark with the lion; mosaic, Ravenna

Matthäus

Markus

Lukas

Johannes

Symbols of the Evangelists from Schmid's *Musterbuch*

The rivers of Eden, Pison, Gihon, Tigris and Euphrates, are interpreted as the cardinal virtues or the four Gospels.

Matthew, the LION with Mark, the BULL with Luke, and the EAGLE with John; this ascription derives from a vision (see TETRAMORPH) described in the Revelation of St. John. Originally, the symbols of the Evangelists were usually interpreted in conjunction with Christ: Christ became man by being born, died like a sacrificial bull, rose from the grave like a lion, and rose to heaven during the Ascension like an eagle. Later, another interpretation became common, whereby the (often winged) human near Matthew became associated with Jesus's lineage and birth (the account of which begins the Gospel of St.Matthew). The lion of Mark was thought to be a reference to the beginning of the Gospel of St. Mark, which recounts John's sermon in the desert. The bull (as a sacrificial animal) of Luke was considered to be a sign of the beginning of the Gospel of St.Luke, which begins with the offering of Zacharias. The eagle of John was thought to be a symbol for the spiritual heights of the Gospel of St.John.

Eve - Created by God from Adam's rib (see ADAM) on the sixth day of Creation, Eve, who is Adam's equal, is the ancestral mother of the human race in the three monotheistic world religions. According to Christian thought, she is the mother of all human life, whereby the aspect of giving birth is central and stands in contrast to the figure of Astarte-Ishtar-Venus in non-monotheistic religions. The problem of original sin is closely connected with the appearance of Eve (see ADAM AND EVE): as a counterpart to Mary, Eve is seen as one of the roots of original sin.

In Occidental civilization and in a metaphorical sense, Eve is the symbol of the life-giving primeval mother or Great Mother (Magna Mater) and an object of everlasting veneration (mother cult, matriarchy) in nearly all cultures; for instance, representations exist in statues from earliest prehistoric times (about 40,000 B.C. on) as so-called "Venus statues" (Venus of Willendorf, Venus of Malta, Venus of Macomar). Yet the name "Venus" is misleading, since the concept of the Magna Mater must be sharply distinguished from the Astarte-Ishtar-Venus goddess type that represents the erotic aspect not present in the Magna Mater. Today, the sexual emphasis on Eve as a seductress stands in the foreground ("Eve's daughter"), with the accentuation and goal-oriented utilization of feminine charms, especially in the case of the woman-child type ("Lolita"). The sexual and seductive aspects did indeed exist earlier as well; for the most part, though, the negative aspect connected with this is receding into the background in light of today's dissolution of taboos, as are the maternal and fertility aspects.

In this context, LILITH, for example, who appears in Talmudic literature, must also be mentioned. Lilith—who is probably of Babylonian origin—is often represented as a serpent and appears in the dual function as the seductress of the man, partially against his will (as in the case of ADAM), and as an element of endangerment for pregnant women and newborns.

It is significant that "Eve," who has been overshadowed in Christianity by the figure of Mary, has broken away from this context, found her own "niche" as a feminine principle, and, to an increasing extent, attained the equality of women (Eve) in the course of the struggle for emancipation.

Bibliography: W. Hofmannn (ed.), Eva und die Zukunft, München, 1986.

Eye - As the primary organ of sense perception, the eye is closely connected with LIGHT, the SUN, and the SPIRIT. It is a symbol of mental vision, but also—as the "mirror of the soul"—an instrument of soulful-intellectual expression. The right

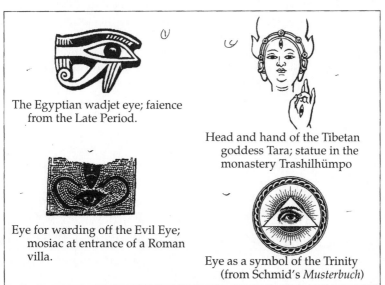

The Egyptian wadjet eye; faience from the Late Period.

Eye for warding off the Evil Eye; mosiac at entrance of a Roman villa.

Head and hand of the Tibetan goddess Tara; statue in the monastery Trashilhümpo

Eye as a symbol of the Trinity (from Schmid's *Musterbuch*)

eye was occasionally associated with activity, the future and the sun; the left eye was occasionally associated with passivity, the past and the Moon. —Buddhism recognizes a Third Eye as a symbol of inner vision. —In antiquity, the eye frequently appears as a symbol of the sun god.

A common AMULET in Egypt was the so-called "wadjet eye," the falcon eye of Horus, god of the sky, that rested on a crooked, rod-like scepter; the eye symbolizes broad vision and omniscience and the scepter symbolizes sovereign power. The entire amulet was supposed to provide invulnerability and fertility.

In the Bible, the eye appears as a symbol of God's omniscience, vigilance, and protective omnipresence. In Christian art, an eye surrounded by sun rays signifies God; an eye in God's hand signifies creative divine wisdom; and an eye in a triangle signifies God the Father in the Trinity (which first appeared during the Baroque period!). Eyes on the wings of seraphim and cherubim refer to the penetrating power of their knowledge. —Since antiquity, representations of the eye have been attributed with apotropaic effects. See MIRIBOTA.

Evening Star - Like MORNING STAR, evening star is a term for the bright planet Venus, yet, in contrast to the morning star, it refers to Venus's position in the evening. It is the herald of approaching night, and is thus occasionally a Christian symbol for the fallen angel Lucifer.

Evil Eye - A type of sorcery performed with the eye, based on a belief in the harmful effect of the eye of certain persons (especially of women and deformed persons). Defense against the evil eye is offered by amulets, veils, and protective signs.

Excrement - Particularly among primitive peoples, excrement was often regarded as a substance embued with various powers; it was sometimes associated symbolically with GOLD. —Among some African tribes, there was a prevalent notion that manure piles were inhabited by souls that entered the bodies of women. —Among some peoples, high regard for excrement led to the ritual eating of feces, which people believed would enable them to incorporate into themselves the powers of the departed person or animal; the role that excrement had often played earlier in the preparation of medicines, also had to do with these ideas. In addition, the imaginary world of the anal phase during early childhood, uncovered by Freudian psychoanalysis, has to do with the high regard for excrement.

Fabulous Creatures - HYBRID CREATURES that are depicted just as realistically as actually existing living creatures; they appeared in the earliest cultures. It is typical that many fabulous creatures were thought to live at the edges of the known world (today in strange galaxies!). In a more restricted sense, "fabulous creatures" (see MONSTER) refers to human-like beings with drastically mutated body parts. See page 108.

Faggot - In China, the faggot is a symbol of the coming and passing of humanity: just as a faggot is tied and untied, so does the entirety of the history of humanity consist of ever new formations that are repeatedly dissolved by death. —As a favored burning material, the faggot is sometimes associated symbolically with FIRE as well (as an attribute of witches, for example).

Falcon - The falcon is generally a sun-like, masculine, heavenly symbol. In Egypt, it was a divine symbolic animal because of its strength, beauty and high flight; it was, among other things, a sacred animal of the sun god Ra; the god Horus generally assumes the form of a falcon or of a human with a falcon's head, but other deities also appear in the form of a falcon. —The falcon was also a royal hunting animal and a symbol of the way of court life. As a stylization derived from the time of rule by the Vikings, the falcon appeared in Russia in 1918 on the coat of arms of Ukraine and was even used to stylize Russia's oldest coins (Oleg coins). —Especially during the Renaissance, a hooded falcon symbolized hope for a light to illuminate the darkness: Post tenebras spero lucem.

Fan - Used in Babylon, India, China, Persia, among the Greeks and Romans, and in other cultures. Made of palm leaves, ostrich or peacock feathers, the tail fan, in particular, was a symbol of a sovereign's high position. —In Hinduism, the fan is regarded, among other things, as a symbol of ritual sacrifice, since sacrificial fires are fanned with it. —Especially in China and Japan, the motions of a fan were associated with the warding off of evil spirits.

Fasces - From the Latin. In ancient Rome, the fasces were bundles of wooden rods carried by the lictors (lictor bundles) in front of high officials; outside of the city, they appeared with an axe.

FABULOUS CREATURES

Documented as having been first used in the 18th century, the term "fabulous creature" applies primarily to anthropomorphic beings that are often identified with monsters and less often with demons; a group of HYBRID CREATURES. Typical for fabulous creatures is, among other things, the assertion that they live in distant regions, on the edge of (known) and distant lands. Comparison with the modern fabulous creatures of science fiction films, who live on distant celestial bodies or galaxies, necessarily arises, as does comparison with the legendary Yeti snowman. According to antiquity, a monster, a Homo monstrosus, was a freak and thus a sign that pointed to coming events ("mon-strare" means "to show"). Fabulous creatures, or hybrid creatures, depicted particularly during the Middle Ages should not be called monsters, especially when they are in a symbolic-religious context, such as in ICONOGRAPHY.

Bibliography: H. Schrade, *Dämonen und Monstren*, Regensburg, 1962.

Left: Fabulous creatures from Schedel's *Weltchronik* (Chronicle of the World). Above: Table of "strange people" from Konrad von Megenberg's "Buch der Natur" (Book of Nature)

FASCES: Fasces
FALCON: Horis in the form of a falcon;
Egyptian mural in a grave

Fats - In various cultures, they were regarded as signs of prosperity (and thus also as a valuable sacrifice to the gods) or as being endowed with the particular powers of the specific animals from which they were taken. See OILS; BUTTER.

Feather Grass - A pleasant smelling plant symbolizing Mary; a type of grass that often appears painted at Mary's feet.

Feathers - Probably because of their leaf-like appearance, feathers are a symbol of vegetation for many primitive peoples; because of the their ray-like shape and close association with BIRDS, feathers are also closely related symbolically to the sky and the sun. The feather headdress of some American Indian tribes (usually made from the feathers of the prairie eagle) is a power symbol with close symbolic relation to the sun. —Among many peoples, feathers also serve as attributes of social position (for example, the decorative tuft of feathers on the helmets of medieval knights).

Feather Work - Among various primitive peoples of Oceania, America and Africa, feather works are clothes (such as royal feather robes on Hawaii), ornaments or cult objects (such as masks) made of feathers. The feathers were often fastened to fabric, leather, and other objects or woven into bast or cotton weavings.

Fennel - Because of its supposed ability to strengthen the eyes, it was sometimes used as a symbol for mental clarity. Because it supposedly caused skin shedding in snakes that ate it, it was also regarded as a symbol of periodic renewal and rejuvenation. In addition, the Middle Ages saw the fennel as an apotropaic plant. Because of its fragrance and valuable oil, it is also sometimes mentioned as a plant symbolizing Mary.

Fermentation - Among many peoples, such as Africans and American Indians, fermentation is a symbol of spirit permeating matter and of ebullient imaginative power. For that reason and because of their effect, fermented drinks were attributed with the ability to impart esoteric knowledge; they were thus frequently used in ceremonial rituals. —Because the process of fermentation is closely related to that of decomposition, fermented foods can also sometimes be associated with the symbolism of EXCREMENT. —In alchemy, fermentation symbolizes the "maturation" and transformation of organic substance and was thus also seen

FALCON: Since the time of the rulership by the Vikings, the visual representations of the falcon have played a special role in Russia, often stylized to the point of ornamentation. 1) Coat of arms of the state of Ukraine; 2, 3 & 4) Oleg coins with representation of falcon. Pendants from the early Middle Ages, found in Kiev, the capital of the Varangians, each show a falcon (illustrations 5 & 6).

---

thus also seen in connection with the transition from the state of death to that of life. —See YEAST.

Fertility Rites - Magical acts that are supposed to promote the growth and prosperity of cultivated plants, animals and people; they are common among most primitive peoples and are based on a belief in the power of spirits (ancestors, plant demons). They are manifest in fertility cults (sacrifices of humans, animals, or food, cult dances) and fertility spells (conjurations and defensive spells). Many folk customs, such as harvest and fasting rites, can be traced back to fertility rites.

Fetishes - Objects such as wooden or mud figures as well as parts of animals used primarily in West Africa and revered as magical, beneficial and protective sources of power. Occasionally, they were objects of ritual ceremonies; thus, for instance, they were driven with nails, which was symbolically supposed to transfer illnesses to the respective fetish.

Fica Gesture - The obscene gesture formed by closing one's hand and placing the thumb between the middle and index FINGERS.

Fides - Symbolic form of the theological virtue of faith. Its attributes are the CROSS and the chalice (see CUP).

Field - A plowed field (see PLOW) is a symbol of the womb; an unplowed field is occasionally a symbol of Mary's virginity.

Fig - Obscene gesture. See FINGER.

Fig Tree - Among many peoples, the fig tree is revered as a holy TREE; along with the OLIVE TREE and the GRAPEVINE, it is frequently a symbol of fertility and abundance (and thus a symbol of the tremendous multiplication of the people of Israel). In antiquity, it had erotic symbolic meaning and was sacred to Dionysus. — Especially in India, it is frequently encountered as a symbol in a religious context; a fig tree growing down from the sky is regarded as a symbol of the world, for example. The Bodhi tree is the fig tree under which Buddha attained Enlightenment (or "bodhi"); it is regarded as a symbol of knowledge. —The cursing of a fruitless fig tree by Jesus in the New Testament is interpreted as a condemnation of the Jewish people; a withered fig tree therefore symbolizes the synagogue in Christian art. PHYSIOLOGUS compares the fruit, which can be eaten only after it

FICA GESTURE: Fica gesture
FIG TREE: Symbolic depiction of
  Buddha's Enlightenment; relief
  from the stupa at Bharhut (Bodhi
  tree temple)

been cut open and the gall-fly has been removed, with Christ: "When the fig is cut open, it will become nourishment on the third day. So is our Lord, whose side was torn open, risen from the dead on the third day and become life and nourishment for all."

Finger - Among various African tribes, fingers play a very complex role with many symbolic associations relating to life and bodily sensations. —In astrology, the THUMB is correlated with Venus, the index finger with Jupiter, the middle finger with Saturn, the ring finger with the sun, and the small finger with Mercury. —In popular parlance, the ring finger used to be called the "heart finger" because people believed that it was directly connected to the heart by a special vein or nerve; the symbolism of love and fidelity of the ring finger, particularly of the left hand (the side of the heart), also has to do with this. —Finger and hand gestures have always been aids to emotional and intellectual expression. They have been particularly richly cultivated in Indian art and dance. —In antiquity, sticking out one's middle finger was considered to be an insult, while meshing one's fingers was considered to be a defensive gesture. In Mediterranean countries since time imme-

morial, the fig (formed by closing one's hand and placing the thumb between the middle and index fingers—see FICA GESTURE) has been regarded as a defense against the evil eye, a crude insult, and a sexual symbol as well. —In Occidental art, a finger laid on the mouth means silence. In contrast, the baby Jesus with a finger on his mouth or tongue refers to the Logos as the spoken word. See HAND.

Finger Glove - See GLOVE.

Fire - Fire is considered by many peoples to be holy, purifying and renewing. Its power of destruction is often interpreted as a means to rebirth on a higher level (see CREMATION; PHOENIX). Individual fire deities are sometimes worshipped, such as Agni in India or Hestia in Greece; the Chinese had several fire gods. —In the Bible, there are numerous images in which God or the divine is symbolized by fire: the Book of Revelation mentions, among other things, WHEELS OF FIRE (see WHEEL), fire-spewing animals, etc. In the Old Testament, God, for example, appears as a column of fire (see COLUMN) or in a burning THORN BUSH. Fire is frequently associated with the SUN, LIGHT, LIGHTNING, the color RED, BLOOD, and the HEART. In contrast to WATER, which is

FINIAL

FIRE: Marriage of water and fire, each of which has four hands as a sign of its power; from an Indian illustration

sometimes attributed with being the origin of the world, fire is often thought to come from HEAVEN. The myths of some peoples speak of a theft of fire, which is frequently interpreted as sacrilege. Greek natural philosophy saw fire either as the origin of all being or as a phenomenon that stood frequently in close connection with the symbolic complex of meanings of destruction, war, evil, the satanic, hell, or divine wrath. The fire of Sodom and Gomorrah was often thought of as a preview of hell-fire. —In many cultures, the production of fire by rubbing led to fire's association with sexuality; in numerous cases, the origin of fire itself is traced back to a sexual act of mythic beings or animals. —The apotropaic effect of fire plays a role among many peoples; thus, for instance, the hearth fire of the ancient Germans, which was thought to drive away evil spirits, was never allowed to go out. —In alchemy, fire is often symbolized by the sign Δ. —Astrology associates fire with the zodiacal signs (see ZODIAC) Aries, Leo and Sagittarius.

Firebug - With respect to its ability to shine in the dark by itself, the firebug is sometimes regarded as a symbol of souls that continue to live after death. —In China, the firebug is a traditional attribute

of poor students, since its light serves them as the only source of light when they read books at night.

Fireplace - In fairy tales and according to superstitious beliefs, communication with spirits and demons often takes place through fireplaces; witches, in particular, ride in and out of houses through them. The spirits of the deceased also leave houses through fireplaces. The reason for the association of the fireplace with the realm of spirits is probably the fireplace's cave-like shape (which is open at the bottom and the top (see CAVE)), the FIRE, the BLACK soot, and the rising SMOKE. —In another respect, fireplaces also share in the symbolic significance of the HEARTH.

Fire Water - See ALCOHOL.

Fireworks - A paradoxical pyrotechnical spectacle that combines the symbolism of water, light, fire, buildings and color. Since the 14th century (the first use of fireworks for enjoyment is dated at 1379 in Vicenza), fireworks have increasingly developed the potential for destruction and enjoyment provided by saltpeter, sulphur and coal (black powder), together with architecture, landscaping and music (Handel's

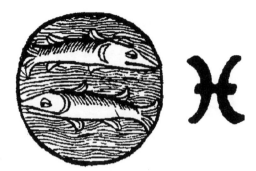

FISH/PISCES: Zodiacal image of
Pisces (from a medieval woodcut)
and the modern astrological symbol

Fireworks Music), into a representative "total art work." Baroque celebrations and, most recently, A. Heller's "productions" (quite rightly given the name "fire dramas") were high points of fireworks art combining allegory and symbol.

Fish - Closely related symbolically to WATER, its life element. As a symbol of life and fertility among many peoples, it is also a widely common TALISMAN. — In Egypt, most species of fish in a particular area or at a particular time were considered to be sacred, yet often threatening and uncanny as well. —The fish is one of the oldest secret symbols for Christ, at first probably due primarily to its relation to baptism by water. Later, the Greek term for fish (ichthys) was interpreted as being an acrostic of the words Jesous Christos Theou (H)Yios Soter (Jesus Christ, Son of God, Savior). Baptized Christians thought themselves to be fish newly born in the water of baptism. As an embodiment of Christ, the fish can also be a symbol of spiritual nourishment and, particularly when it appears with depictions of BREAD, a symbol of the Eucharist. —The fishes, or Pisces, are the twelfth and last sign of the zodiac, corresponding to the third month of winter. The sun passes the sign between February 18 and March 20.

Venus is ascending in Pisces; it is the house of Jupiter (Neptune). Since the time of Hellenic astrology, Saturn, Jupiter and Mars have been its decans; in Indian astrology, Jupiter, the Moon and Mars are its decans. The triplicity of Pisces is water; Pisces is feminine, negative (passive) and a movable sign. Its depiction and name can be traced back to Babylonian sources, in which a link between the two elements is particularly noted.

Fisher - See NET.

Five - See page 116

Flag - A symbol of rule as well as of national or group membership. In war, it is a symbol of military honor and fidelity that is to be defended by sacrificing one's own life if need be. In addition, a fluttering flag is often regarded as a symbolic expression of new beginnings and of resolve for future change. —In the symbolism of Christian art, Christ or a lamb carries a flag as a sign of the Resurrection and of the victory over the powers of darkness.

Flame - Symbolically identical with FIRE to a large extent, it frequently appears as a compact manifestation of fire, for example, as the fire of the Holy Spirit in de-

FISH: Two fishes with an anchor; grave of Licinia

pictions of the miracle at Pentecost or Christ's baptism. The "fieriness" of a speech or a look, in the sense of extraordinary power as well as destructive force, is sometimes illustrated by flames taking the place of a person's tongue or coming from a person's eyes. Vices such as greed, envy or lust are sometimes symbolized by flames, especially in literary contexts.

Flamingo - In the Upanishads, the flamingo is associated with the symbolism of LIGHT.

Flaming Sword - See SWORD.

Flammeum - See RED.

Flintstone - Among many primitive peoples, it is a symbol of LIGHTNING due to the spark that results when it is struck. According to PHYSIOLOGUS, "For they are of such nature, masculine and feminine…, that when they come very close to one another they ignite one another and everything in between…So you, too, flee the feminine form…so that all virtue burns within you…." —On Easter Eve, a flintstone is used to make the sparks that ignite the fire used to light the triple light of the Easter candles.

Floods - Floods are symbols of dangerous passions insofar as they symbolize the violent aspect of WATER, often engulfing or indifferently burying everything in their path. Jumping into a flood also often symbolizes a courageous venture into uncertainty. In the Bible, floods are a symbol of downfall and death. See WAVES.

Flower - Or "blossom." A symbol of crowning achievement, of what is essential. Most of all, it is a symbol of feminine beauty. The receptive relation to the SUN and to RAIN also makes the flower a symbol of passive acquiescence and of humility; on the other hand, it can also be a sign for the sun, due to the predominantly radial arrangement of its petals. Since it quickly whithers, it is often a symbol of instability and transiency. Flowers, like the BUTTERFLIES that call upon them, are sometimes associated symbolically with the souls of deceased persons. Differentiated according to color, yellow flowers are symbolically associated with the sun, white ones with death or innocence, red ones with BLOOD, and blue ones with dreams and mystery (see BLUE FLOWER). Gold flowers are occasionally encountered as symbols of highest spiritual life (such as in Taoism). —In Japan, the art of flower arranging (ikebana) developed into a form of symbolic expres-

FIVE

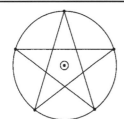

5

According to Pythagoras, the perfect number of man the microcosm; the secret sign is the pentagram. 5 as the sum of 2 (feminine element) and 3 (masculine element), i.e. 2 + 3 = 5, played and continues to play an important role in many cultures. As the unification of TWO and THREE, it was considered by the Pythagoreans to be a symbol of marriage and synthesis. It is the number of the hand's five fingers (and can also signify them), the number of the 5 senses, the 5 wounds of Christ, the 5 pillars of piety in Islam, etc. In China, 5 played a particular role as a symbol of the midpoint (see MIDDLE); moreover, the Chinese had 5 colors, 5 smells, 5 tones, 5 planets, 5 metals; 5 is also the number of the harmonic union of YIN AND YANG. —In Hinduism, 5 is (among other things) the number of the principle of life; the god Shiva was sometimes imagined as having 5 faces (the fifth one, directed upward, was identified with the WORLD AXIS and generally not represented); he was also occasionally worshipped in the form of 5 LINGAM representations. —In the QUINTESSENCE (the fifth essence, that is, the fifth element in addition to the four elements), the alchemists sought the life-generating and life-sustaining spirit; the number 5, occasionally encountered in the ornamentation of Christian churches of the Middle Ages (and elsewhere), possibly has to do with such considerations.

15

An arithmetic-mystical number, because, as the sum of $1 + 2 + 3 + 4 + 5 = 15$, it is also the product of the two sacred numbers 3 and 5, i.e. $3 \times 5 = 15$

25

As the second power of 5, i.e. $5^2 = 25$, indicating the perfection of the 5 senses, 25 is a number particularly rich in symbolism; it is interpreted as being significant also because it is the sum of the holy, odd numbers less than 10: $1 + 3 + 5 + 7 + 9 = 25$.

50

If one regards 50 as the product of 10 (Commandments) x 5 (senses) = 50, then it plays a role in connection with repentance and forgiveness and thus leads up to Psalm 50, which contains a lamentation of sin. In the decimal system, 50 is an indeterminate round number: 50 Nereïds (in Hesiod) is a number that cannot be overlooked; in the legend of the Holy Grail, 50 or 150 (i.e. 3 x 50) knights sit at the Round Table. In ancient Rome, a man at least 50 years old no longer had to serve in war.

55

A number playing a minor role, regarded as of the sum of all numbers from 1 to 10: $1 + 2 + 3 + 4 + 5 + 6 + 7 + 8 + 9 + 10 = 55$. Because it can be represented as the sum of $28 + 12 + 10 + 5 = 55$, it was used for many sorts of speculations about numbers.

FLAG: The Easter Lamb carrying the staff cross with a flag showing that Christ has prepared a new living way into the temple (from Schmid's *Musterbuch*)

sion having different manifestations in various schools; frequently occurring basic positions of flowers are sky (top), man (center), and earth (bottom).

Flower of John - See ARNICA.

Flute - As an attribute, the flute is frequently associated with the lives of shepherds. —The tone of a flute is sometimes interpreted as being the voice of angels or of mythological or enchanted beings. —The sound of the reed-pipe, which was played at dervishes' dances, symbolizes the call of the soul that is separated from God and wants to return to heavenly provinces.

Fly - In the Far East, the fly was regarded as a symbol of the immaterial, incessantly wandering soul. —Usually, though, it became associated with sickness, death, and the devil; it was a common notion that demons of sickness, in the form of flies, threatened humans. The chief devil mentioned in the Bible, Beelzebub (from the Hebrew Ba'al-Zebub, meaning "lord of the flies"), who is often depicted as a fly, is a perversion of the original Canaanite deity Balzebul; in popular belief, he plays a role especially in spells. —In Persian mythology, the principle of negation, Ahriman, sneaks into the world as a fly.

Flying Dutchman - Symbol of the eternally restless man at sea; associated with stories of an approaching ghostship boding ill fortune. See AHASVERUS [i.e., the Wandering Jew].

Fodder Bean - A plant useful as fodder and known even to antiquity. The black-spotted blossom was sometimes regarded as a death symbol. Its seeds became symbolically associated with fertility and regions beneath the earth and thus, in turn, with death as well. The dual symbolic association with death and life is apparent, for example, in the fact that beans became associated with the souls of the deceased and with embryonic, and especially male, children. —Accordingly, fodder bean sacrifices were made at planting and harvest times, at weddings and funerals. See BEANS.

Fog - A symbol of the indeterminate, of the transition from one state to another, as well as of the vague and the fantastic. According to the mythologies of some peoples, fog is the primeval matter of the universe. —Depictions of fog are frequently found in Japanese painting. See CLOUDS.

Foot - The animal and human body part that is most closely tied to the EARTH; as

FLOWER: Mexican Codex
    Magliabechiano
FLUTE: Flute player with a double
    flute; Estruscan, 5th century B.C.

the organ of locomotion, of "stepping out," it stands in symbolically relevant connection with the will. Thus, according to popular custom and law, for example, placing one's foot upon something was thought to be a sign of seizure. Especially during antiquity, it was common to place one's foot on the conquered enemy as a sign of the enemy's total submission. — As early as Roman times, getting up or entering a house with one's right foot was thought to bring good fortune, whereas doing this with one's left foot was thought to augur bad fortune. Bare beet are frequently a sign of humility (such as when entering a mosque or a temple); in monastic orders, they are a conscious expression of poverty. —Demonic beings are frequently depicted as having animal feet; thus, the devil has ram's or horse's feet and DWARFS or female demons have goose's or duck's feet. —Kissing of the feet (of persons of higher position) was—particularly with respect to the "lowliness" of the feet—a symbol of greatest submission. —Washing of the feet—an act of hospitality in the Orient—is a symbol of humility and love if it is done by a person of higher position; as a practice on Holy Thursday in the Catholic Church, it is usually a symbolic reenactment of Jesus's washing the feet of the disciples. —In psy-choanalysis, the foot is often attributed phallic significance, whereby shoes are a symbol of the vulva. In this regard, bare feet can also play an important role in rituals of fertility and maturity.

Footprints - The footprints of venerable persons are exhibited and revered in many cultures. Images of Christ's footprints were depicted especially in conjunction with the ASCENSION.

Footstool - An attribute of the highest deities as early as in Mesopotamian times; the footstool itself can also serve as a symbol of domination, such as in Psalms 110:1, "The Lord said unto my lord, Sit thou at my right hand, until I make thine enemies thy footstool," or in Matthew 5:35, "…by the earth, for it is his footstool…" The rainbow is also thought of as the "footstool of the Lord."

Foot Washing - Like hand washing, it is a symbol of ritual cleansing before holy observances. See WASHING OF HANDS AND FEET.

Forest - In the religious thought and folk superstitions of many peoples, forests play an important role as a sacred and mysterious place in which good and evil

FLY: Beelzebub; from Collin de Plancy's *Dictionnaire infernal*, 1845
FOUNTAIN: The Fountain of Life as fons mercurialis; from *Rosarium philosophorum*, 1550

gods, spirits and demons, wild men, wood pixies, moss pixies, tree pixies, fairies, etc. live. Sacred groves that offer protective asylum appear in many cultures. Depictions of a forest or forests as the scene of dramatic action often refer symbolically to things irrational, yet also to sanctuary. —As a place of isolation from the bustle of the world, the forest, like the DESERT, is a preferred dwelling place of ascetics and hermits and is thus also a symbol of mental concentration and inwardness. —Especially in German speaking lands, the mysterious, dark forest often appears in fairy tales, sagas, poems and song. —Psychoanalysis often sees the forest as a symbol of the unconscious, a symbolic relation that can be manifest in dream images as well as in real anxiety about dark forests; the forest (especially a forested hill) is also sometimes interpreted as a symbol of woman.

Forked Cross - Also called a "thief's cross." See CROSS.

Fortitudo - The personification of bravery, one of the four cardinal virtues; frequently represented with the attributes CLUB, SWORD, shield, victory flag, and LION.

Fortress - As a fortified residence often set up high or surrounded by a forest, it is a symbol of protection and of security. In the Bible and in Christian symbolic thought, it is a symbol of refuge in God or of faith that protects one from demons. Hell is also sometimes portrayed as a dark, occasionally subterranean fortress with numerous dungeons and chambers.

Fortuna - A Roman goddess of fate, eventually only of good luck. Identified with the Greek Tyche. Frequently encountered in the graphic arts of the Renaissance. As a personification of random or fickle good fortune, she is often depicted as standing on a WHEEL or a ball. A frequent attribute is also the cornucopia (see HORN).

Fountain - The fountain is symbolically associated with WATER, but also with the depth of mystery and access to hidden sources. Going down into a well (in fairy tales, for example) frequently symbolizes access to esoteric knowledge or to the region of the unconscious. Dipping into the water of a fountain often corresponds symbolically with drinking a special elixir (see POTION): it affords immortality, youth and health (such as the fountain of youth). —In the Bible, fountains are associated symbolically with cleansing, blessing, and the water of life. —Square,

FOX: Aesop listens to the words of the fox; from a bowl in the Vatican; circa 450 B.C.

walled fountains in Arabic countries are sometimes regarded as symbols of heaven. —The necessity of water for life and the religious/ritual importance led early on to the architectonic, artistic formation of fountains. The tradition of the Ancient Orient (the earliest evidence coming from Mohenjo-Daro in the 3rd century B.C.) was continued in the Greco-Roman city civilizations. Fountains for cleansing (including ritual cleansing) are located in the atrium of early Christian basilicas and in the vestibules of mosques (as well as magnificent fountain designs in Islamic art, such as in the Alhambra). A type of fountain in Romanesque times was the shell fountain, while Gothic art developed the pipe or tier fountain, which had a columnar structure and much sculptural ornamentation. In accordance with an instruction in the Regula of St. Benedict, fountain houses were built in the cloisters of medieval monasteries (such as Sluter's fountain in the Chartreuse at Champmol). The Italian Renaissance produced monumental fountains (such as the Fountain of Neptune in Bologna) and thereby had an effect on Germany (in Augsburg, for example). During the Baroque period, art on fountains was augmented by superstructures having many figurines; naturalistic fountains often had fantastic rock formations (some examples being Bernini's Fontana di Trevi in Rome and Donner's Flüsse Fountain in Vienna). Fountains, along with waterworks and canals, made their mark on Baroque landscaping (such as in Versailles and Schwetzingen).

Fountain of Life - Allegory of the saving power of Christ; as early as early Christian times, it was represented as a water container or a roofed fountain from which animals drank, later often in conjunction with the four rivers of Eden or a portrayal of saints.

Fountain of Youth - See FOUNTAIN.

Fox - In Japanese and Chinese myth, the fox played a significant role as a demonic, partially good, partially evil animal skilled in magic that could metamorphose into many forms, especially human ones. —In some American Indian cultures, the fox is a symbol of lasciviousness. —In Europe, it is frequently a symbol of slyness and cunning. In medieval art, it appears as a symbol of the devil, lying, injustice, intemperance, greed and lust. PHYSIOLOGUS thus compares Herod with a fox; the fox is comparable to all other fire-colored "satanic animals," such as squirrels and stag beetles.

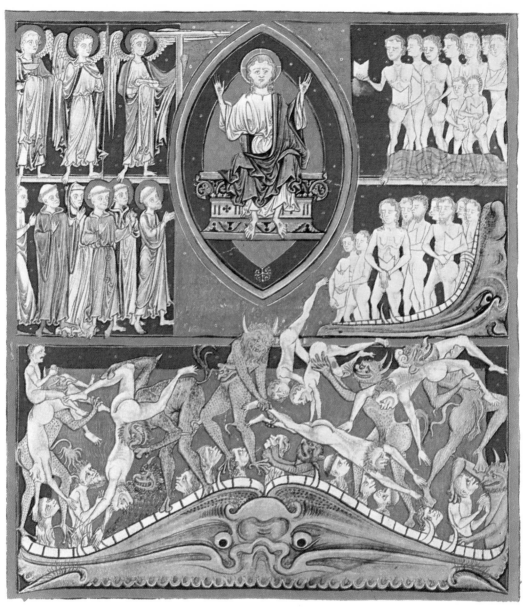

APOCALYPSE: This last and most symbolically rich book of the New Testament depicts in powerful visions the coming final events up to the Last Judgment and the coming of the kingdom of God.

The Last Judgment was especially frequently depicted. The basis was the vision, "And I saw the dead, small and great, stand before God; and the books were opened: and another book was opened, which is the book of life: and the dead were judged out of those things which were written in the books, according to their works And whosoever was not found written in the book of life was cast into the lake of fire."

The miniature *The Apocalypse of Queen Eleonore* shows the judge of the world in the mandorla, an angel with the implements of the Passions at left, and, below them, a queen and four important churchmen; at the right, the earth and the sea give up their dead with the "opened" books, and, below, the damned are thrown into the pit of fire (hell).

ASCENSION: In this picture by Hieronymus Bosch (*Ascension to the Light*), two human souls, leaving the world, rise up in order to look for, and finally to find, the way into heaven through a pipe-like path that is flooded with a cosmic light.

In art, people often sought to depict this ascension or ascent into the eternal light through symbolic representation. Its literary form in Dante's *Divine Comedy* is full of symbols; in it, as contemporary research shows, the author used number symbolism in the "construction" of the work.

BOOK OF HOURS: The zodiac man from the book of hours, *Les Très Riches Heures* of the Duke of Berry (made shortly before his death in 1416), turns up repeatedly in medieval manuscripts in conjunction with microcosm-macrocosm thought. The correlation of the zodiacal signs with the human body and its organs is conventional, only the meaning of the "double" figure framed by the astrological signs of the year is unclear: Is an androgyne supposed to refer to the ambivalence of some astrological statements and of the essence of man?

ISTI MIRANT STELLA

COMETS: Comets appear in the world picture of antiquity and of the Middle Ages as the visible manifestation of a crisis in the most literal sense of the word: a disturbance of the divine, regulated course of the stars and planets; comets on their paths in the sky, mocking all regularity, became heralds of extraordinary events, positive as well as negative. Our picture shows Halley's Comet during its appearance in 1066 as an episode on the Norman tapestry of Bayeux. Halley's Comet was already mentioned in cuneiform texts of late Babylonian times; it is the best known periodic comet.

CREATOR GOD: Biblical notions of a creator god became associated very early in the history of Christianity with ideas of ancient tradition: The creator god is compared with the Demiurge of Plato, the master builder, the overseer and "maker" of the cosmos. God the Father as master builder of the world became a topos, a frequently employed form of depiction; with the giant compass of the master builder in his hand, he circumscribes the round universe; the green represents the primeval sea that borders the world, the blue represents the atmosphere; the Sun, Moon, and stars have already been formed from chaos and hover above the center, which represents the as yet undifferentiated earth: the four elements, from which are made the world and everything that is in and on it, are also represented, namely, earth, fire (the Sun and the stars), air, and water. (From a miniature in a Bible moralisée from mid-thirteenth-century France)

DEATH MASK: The custom of putting masks on the faces of the dead was common throughout the world, as the skull (face) was often compared with the vault of the sky as a manifestation of the symbolic association of the significance of the human microcosm and the universal macrocosm: the face mask made of precious materials was supposed to hide the decay of death.

Our illustration shows an Aztec death mask; it is made of pieces of jade, whereby jade itself was either a symbol of the loss of life or the symbol of a divinized heart. In addition, jade was a symbol in Central America of vegetation, water, and rain due to its green, transparent color and was thought of as a symbol of blood due to the interchangeability of the symbolic meanings of red and green. (National Museum of Anthropology, Mexico)

ELEPHANT: In India, elephants were regarded as caryatids of the universe and as the riding
    animals of gods of high position; in our picture, the god of love, Kama, who is also
    regarded as the god of growth, is riding: when Shiva, the destroyer of the world, killed
    him, nature languished. Today, popular belief sees Kama more as a symbol of flippant
    frivolity.
The elephant's body is symbolically made up of nine women's bodies; it is not by chance
    that there are exactly nine, since nine plays an important role in Central Asian
    mythologies.
The practice of "constructing" fantastic human, plant, or animal objects is ancient; it was
    known even in Mesopotamia, where hybrid creatures were apparently "invented." Yet it
    was also known in classical antiquity and reached a grandiose high point in the fantastic
    and grotesque pictures of Arcimboldi (Second half of the sixteenth century).

EVANGELISTS: The symbols of the Evangelists are associated convincingly with the so-called fixed cross of the astrologers; the corner points of the cross are represented by Taurus and Scorpio (eagle), Leo and Aquarius (man); those are the constellations that are juxtaposed to one another in pairs in the zodiac.

These illustrations are probably ancient recollections from the time of the Jews' Babylonian captivity when the Jews became familiar with Babylonian cosmic hybrid creatures (Lamassu) and astrological views; these recollections have never fallen into oblivion, even if information concerning them has largely been lost.

FREEMASONRY: Sign for stability of
St. John's Lodge

Freemasonry - A secret fraternal order
that arose during the Enlightenment. It
espouses no religion per se, but it developed cult-like characteristics in its
striking symbolism, which pertains to
building, workmanship and light. It
strives toward a "world union of light"
for practicing the "Royal Craft," or "stone
masonry work" on one's own self and
construction work on the "temple of humanity." To a large extent, the greatly
varying symbolism was derived from the
customs of the old stonemasons' guilds
(see WORK). The meetings places are
called "lodges," as is the local congregation of Freemasons themselves who work
together. In recent years, some lodges
have been opened to women, that is,
women's lodges have been founded.

Frog - Usually interpreted in close conjunction with WATER, and particularly
with RAIN. It is frequently considered to
be a lunar animal and is tied to the Yin
principle (see YIN AND YANG) in China.
Analogous to the change from PHEAS-
ANT to SERPENT, there was a notion in
China of a seasonally changing predomi-
nance of the frog or the quail. —In Japan,
the frog was thought to be an augur of
good luck. —In India, people had the notion of a large frog that supported the
world; at the same time, one saw in the
frog a symbol of a dark life imprisoned
by matter or—in a positive sense—a symbol of fertile Mother Earth. In ancient
Mesopotamia, the frog was a symbol of
fertility. —According to the Bible, the frog
is an unclean animal. —In Egypt, there
was a goddess with a frog's head who
helped at births and granted long life and
immortality; the frog was primarily a symbol of resurrection, which probably has to
do with the change of its form during its
development and with the assumption
that the frog comes from the mud of the
Nile each year during the spring. —The
church fathers regarded the frog as a symbol of the devil or (due to its constant
noise) the heretic. —PHYSIOLOGUS distinguishes land frogs and water frogs; the
righteous members of the congregation
are like the land frog, since they resist the
fire of temptation; worldly persons are like
the water frog, since they plunge back into
incontinence and lechery if they are
touched by even the slightest heat of
temptation and desire. —Medieval folk
belief considered the frog to be a witch's
animal and used the tiny joints of frogs
for love spells.

Fruit - A symbol of maturity, of completed development. Several different

FOUR

4

The basic number of the feminine, also regarded as a cosmic number and a number of harmony; it is based on the second power of 2, i.e., 2^2 = 2 x 2 = 4; with the 4 seasons, it is a manifestation of Mother Earth = 4; the number 2, with its maternal principle, thus expands to include the cosmos, which is bounded by 4. As a symbolic number, 4 is closely related to the SQUARE and the CIRCLE. It is the number of the 4 cardinal directions and thus of the 4 winds, the 4 elements (see FIRE; WATER; AIR; EARTH), the 4 humors, the 4 rivers of Eden, the 4 Evangelists, and the 4 stages of life (childhood, youth, maturity, old age).

14

An important lunar number, because it is one half of the moon's 28-day cycle, i.e., 28:2 = 14; yet is can also be thought of as 7 x 2 = 14, i.e., as a doubling of the richly symbolic number 7. In Christian symbolic thought, it is the number of the good and of mercy, of rescue from trouble (14 Catholic saints) and of protection (14 guardian angels).

24

With respect to number symbolism, 24 is to be understood as the product of the richly symbolic numbers 3, 4, 6 and 8, i.e., 4 x 6 = 24 or 3 x 8 = 24; it can also be interpreted as 2 x 12 = 24 and as the number of hours in a day, and thus as a symbol of totality and of harmony between heaven and earth; it is also the number of letters in the Greek alphabet.

40

As far back as in ancient Mesopotamia, 40 was originally a number that had to do with the Pleiades rule: the new year was celebrated after the Pleiades had disappeared under the horizon for 40 days and reappeared. As the sum of 28 (stations of the moon) and 12 (signs of the zodiac), 40 possibily has a different origin. In the Bible, it is the number of expectation, or preparation, of penetance, of fasting or of punishment; the waters of the Flood fell upon the earth for 40 days and 40 nights; Moses waited on Mt. Sinai for 40 days and 40 nights before he received the Ten Commandments; the city of Nineveh did penance for 40 days in order to escape God's punishment; the wandering of the Israelites through the desert lasted 40 years; Jesus fasted in the desert for 40 days and appeared to His disciples for 40 days after His resurrection. In Islam, 40 is of great importance in conjunction with speculations pertaining to letters and numbers, as in the case of the 40-fold repetition of religious formulae.

64

64 is the second power of 8, i.e., 8^2 = 8 x 8 = 64; it is thought to be an especially lucky number; it is the number of possibilities (64 hexagrams) in the I-Ching and the number of squares of a chessboard.

84

84 is a number that appears especially often in areas in and around India, usually in thousands: 84,000 stupas for the Buddha's relics; the world mountain is 84,000 units high; some kings reign for 84,000 years.

FRUIT: Grave painting of fruits in the ancient Egyptian grave of Nakht (15th century B.C.)

fruits together frequently symbolize abundance, fertility and prosperity. — The forbidden fruit of Eden—which is not described specifically in the Bible— might be an apple, a grape, a cherry, a fig, according to the landscape in a given artistic representation; it symbolizes the temptation to sin.

Furies - See ERINYES.

Galium - A plant of Mary, also called "straw of Mary's bed"; a folk remedy (like many other plants of Mary) and a (red) dye.

Gaming - The free, pleasurable exercise of one's powers without an immediately useful goal. Play is characteristic of humans as an expression of life. Possible from the simplest to the most highly developed mental and physical form, it permeates language, cult, culture, and social and political life; it is often a symbol of a battle, be it against other people or against obstacles that must be overcome in accordance with rules. —Originally, games were usually associated with sacred ceremonies. —The outcome of games was sometimes thought to have magical or prophetic significance. —In association with events that are important for life, such as harvests, games can also be an expression of gratitude toward the gods (such as a symbolic representation of a battle of the elements or of the victory of plant life over the elements).

Garden - A symbol of earthly and heavenly paradise, a symbol of the cosmic or-der. —In contrast to the Holy City (see JERUSALEM, HOLY), which symbolizes the end of the world, the garden is an image in the Bible of man's original sinless state. Solomon's Song of Songs compares a garden with a lover. —In Greek mythology, the tree with the golden apples grew in the garden of the Hesperides, which is usually interpreted as a symbol of the tree of life. —In its isolation and as a refuge from the world, the garden is symbolically closely related to the oasis and the IS-LAND. —The walled garden that can be entered only through a narrow gate also symbolizes the difficulties and obstacles that must be overcome before one reaches a higher level of spiritual development. —In a similar sense, the enclosed garden also symbolizes, from a man's point of view, the intimate areas of a woman's body.

Gargoyle - A water spout projecting over a parapet or a drainage pipe on a roof extension used for draining rain water; since antiquity, gargoyles have often been sculpted, especially during the Gothic period. The Middle Ages often represented the devil as a gargoyle in the service of the church; they are also often regarded as symbols of vice; the basic symbolic idea behind the presence of gar-

GAMES

Senat, the Egyptian forerunner of race games like backgammon, has been a typical game of the Egyptians since the time of the Pharoahs; this type of game can be seen on murals in graves from the 3rd Dynasty (circa 2600 B.C.)

The game is an ancient phenomenon of life; board games in the widest sense, which exist in infinite variety, are the most important; they probably provide the oldest evidence of the desire of homo ludens to game.

Two basic types crystalized quite early on: those games determined by fortune—chance—and those based on practice, experience and tactical ability.

Clearly, one can assume that the first type of games was invented in societies in which control by supernatural forces, later articulated in microcosmic-macrocosmic thinking, played a role. What is essential for games of this sort is the use—to put it in modern parlance—of a "random generator," a die-like constituent of the game that makes the game's outcome dependent upon chance; the "king's game of Ur" and derivative games are probably among these.

The other type of board games is based solely on the tactical abilities of the players, none of whom has an advantage, yet any of whom can succeed in mastering the game through training and careful thinking. The classic example of this type of game is chess in all its regional and temporal variants.

Games in which chance and tactical ability are combined, seem to be relatively recent; the best known example is backgammon, in which a practiced player can use the result of a roll of the dice in such a way that a hopeless position can be turned into a promising one.

It is remarkable that there are apparently numerous cultural circles that have none of the above-mentioned sorts of games; such is the case, for example, among the Eskimos and the Australian aborigines.

Bibliography: R.C. Bell. Das grosse Buch der Brettspiele, Bochen, 1980; A. Borst. Das mittelalterliche Zahlenkampfspiel, Heidelberg, 1987 (each book has an extensive bibliography).

GARDEN: Fountains in a walled garden, symbol of stability and truth even under difficult circumstances; from Boschius's *Symbolographia*, 1702

goyles on medieval churches was that the draining water would also wash away the power of the devil from the church.

Garlic - Probably because of its strong odor, which was interpreted symbolically as a dispelling force, garlic was thought to offer defense against the evil eye and evil spirits; in Central Europe, it was thought to offer particular defense against vampires. In Greece, the mere mention of the word was supposed to offer protection.

Garment - See CLOTHING.

Garuda - The name of the animal ridden (see HYBRID CREATURES) by VISHNU and LAKSHMI.

Gate - See DOORS.

Gates of Heaven - See DOORS.

Gauntlet - See GLOVE.

Gazelle - A symbol of speed; became associated in India, for example, with air and wind. —In the Semitic world, it is a paradigm of beauty, particularly because of its eyes. —Because it supposedly had a particularly sharp eye, it was sometimes regarded in Christianity as a symbol of penetrating spiritual knowledge. —In the graphic arts, the gazelle is frequently encountered as a victim that is hunted down or killed by wild, rapacious animals: a symbol of the annihilation of the noble and defenseless by wild brutality; psychoanalytic interpretations also see these depictions as a symbol of self-destructive tendencies that stem from the subconscious.

Gemini - The constellation of the TWINS.

Genista - A shrub-like papilionaceous plant having yellow or white flowers. The thorned genista is a symbol for the sins of man, sins that force him to cultivate a field full of thorns and thistle; it is also a symbol for the suffering that Christ bore for humanity (it is sometimes depicted below instruments of torture), and is therefore a symbol of salvation as well (as is THISTLE).

Genius Cucullatus - A pictorial representation common in many areas that were settled by the Celts, showing a child in a robe with a hood. Aside from other possible interpretations pertaining to fertility and death, the idea of the Celts' belief in rebirth comes specifically to mind, accord-

GIANT: Detail from the Gundestrup cauldron; relief, silver, Celtic, 1st century B.C.

GOAT: Goat as witch's steed; detail from a woodcut in Praetorius's *Blockes-Berges Verrichtung*, Leipzig, 1669

ing to which the dead return to the world as children.

Gestures - See FINGER.

Giants - Giants are found in the mythic ideas and fairy tales of most peoples as larger-than-life, humanoid beings (titans, cyclopses, etc); originally, they were probably seen as the embodiments of tremendously powerful forces of nature; in most mythologies, they are the opponents of the gods, yet also the opponents and assistants of humans; now and then, individual giants possess great wisdom; in fairy tales, they usually eat humans; in popular funny stories, they are often clumsy blockheads. —Occasionally, though, one encounters positive portrayals of primeval giants who took part in the creation of the world or who support it. —Battle against giants often probably symbolizes man's self-assertion vis a vis nature.

Ginnungagap - In the Germanic history of creation, it is the gaping nothingness that stood at the beginning and out of which the world arose; comparable to the Greek CHAOS.

Ginseng - Due to the human-like shape of its root, ginseng, like MANDRAKE, is thought to possess special powers, particularly life-prolonging ones. Since it was also thought to increase virility, it became associated with the Yang principle (see YIN AND YANG).

Glass - Because of its transparence, glass, like CRYSTAL, is a symbol of LIGHT. In medieval images, glass, which allows all things to shine through it without sustaining damage to itself, is also a symbol of the Immaculate Conception. —Mica is a gypsum that looks like ice or glass and can be split into thin sheets; it was used during the Middle Ages to "doctor up" pictures of saints and had limited use as a glass substitute.

Glass Window - See WINDOW.

Glory - Aureola, see HALO.

Glove - Significant as a symbol of law and rule, especially in medieval chivalry. A glove thrown at another person was regarded as a sign of a duel ("throwing down the gauntlet"); it was a sign of striking someone with one's hand, since an actual blow was forbidden as unchivalrous. Knights, and later cavaliers, wore the gloves of the women they adored on their helmets or hats. Wearing thimbles was

GOAT-FISH: Illustration on a
Babylonian border marker
(Kudurru)

GOLDEN CALF: Dance around the
Golden Calf; woodcut from S.
Brant's *Narrenschiff* (Ship of Fools),
1494

long a privilege of nobles and thus a symbol of social position. —In Freemasonry, gloves are part of the ritual garb; they are usually WHITE and are a symbol of the work that is to be done as well as a symbol of purity. The use of gloves symbolizes purity and dignity in the Catholic Church as well.

Gnats - Like flies (and craneflies), they are thought to be animals symbolic of the devil. See FLY.

Goat - Employed in various ways as a useful domestic animal by fertility cults since ancient times, the goat was also associated with demonic powers. In ancient Jewish tradition, the roof of the tabernacle had to be made of goat's hair. In Greek mythology, Zeus was nurtured as a child by the she-goat Amaltheae (see HORN; AEGIS). —In India, the goat was a symbol of prima materia and of the embodiment of the primeval mother, probably (among other reasons) because the words for goat and "unborn" are homonymous.

Goatfish - The ancient name of a zodiacal sign that apparently came from Babylon to Greece and Egypt; its shape corresponds to the IBEX of medieval tradition; the Greek name is "Aigokeros,"

meaning "goat horn" or "Capricornus" in Latin. See HYBRID CREATURES.

Gog and Magog - Symbolic figures of the enemies of Israel (Ezekiel 38 f.); the war of Gog and Magog as war against God or His people is the decisive war at the end of the world that immediately precedes the coming of the Messiah (Revelation 20:8).

Gold - Since time immemorial, it has been regarded as the most precious of metals; it is malleable, can be polished, and is glittering, largely resistant to heat and acids and thus a symbol of immutability, eternity, and perfection. Because of its color (and other reasons), it became identified nearly everywhere with the SUN or FIRE. It is thus also frequently a symbol of (principally esoteric) knowledge. In Christian symbolism, moreover, gold is a symbol for the highest of virtues, love. —A gold background appearing in painted panels of the Middle Ages is always a symbol of heavenly light. It is a common notion that gold is the earth's most intimate and most sacred secret. —The alchemists' attempts to make gold, which had to do with the search for the PHILOSOPHERS' STONE, must be seen primarily in close connection with the attempt to purify the soul

GOOSE: The Egyptian primeval goose; illustration on a papyrus

(which is symbolized by gold). —From a moral point of view, gold is assigned a negative value as the epitome of all earthly goods (synonym for MONEY) and thus as a symbol for worldly attachment or ambition. See EXCREMENT.

Golden Age - See AGE.

Golden Calf - According to legend, a calf (or bull) idol made by Aaron at Mt. Sinai and around which the Israelites danced while Moses received the tablets with the Ten Commandments; a symbol for the constant temptation of the people of Israel to succumb to the cult of Baal. —The dance around the golden calf is today a symbol of excessive striving for material goods.

Golden Fleece - The golden pelt of a ram that was guarded by a DRAGON and stolen by Jason and the other Argonauts after they overcame numerous difficulties. C.G. Jung sees the golden fleece as a symbol for goals that—contrary to the judgment of mere thought—are nevertheless reached in the development of an individual.

Golden Oriole - In China, the golden oriole is a symbol of spring, weddings, and joy.

Golden Pheasant - See PHEASANT.

Golden Plover - The CHARADRIUS of PHYSIOLOGUS.

Golem - From the Hebrew. "That which is without form," inanimate matter. In Jewish (Cabalistic) mysticism, a mysterious, articifically created human being (homunculus); Golem legend of Rabbi Löw of Prague (1580).

Goldfinch - The goldfinch was said to have lived from THISTLE; because it sings so beautifully, it was a symbol in the Middle Ages of Christ (particularly of the baby Jesus) and of the devout soul that has been purified through suffering.

Gong - An ancient Chinese-Indian percussion instrument, usually a free-hanging bronze disk up to one meter in diameter, struck with a mallet; used as a cult and signal instrument as early as the 1st century B.C.

Good Luck Charms/Signs - The swastika and the wheeled cross were the most common good luck charms in Germanic lands; there is also the knot and the ring, ancient coins and their replicas (gold bracteates) worn as amulets, and various knotted

GORGONS: Gorgon as ornament on an
amphora (Attic, 7th century)

patterns reminiscent of the labyrinth symbol that Christianity appropriated from antiquity. The actual meaning and relevance of such good luck charms/signs is controversial; like the runes, they often have a rather ornamental character. Hammer-shaped amulets, for example, can be easily explained as good luck charms connected with the cult around Thor.

Good Shepherd - Symbolic representation of Christ as savior according to Luke 15:3 and John 10:1 ff.; can formally be traced back to ancient idyllic SHEPHERD scenes; did not appear as epic re-telling of the parable until later. It was common in early Christian art (except Byzantium), especially in sepulchral art; since the 12th century especially in illuminated manuscripts, on cyclic figured tapestries; in the late Middle Ages in many typological contexts; popular during the Baroque period.

Goose - In Egyptian mythology, the goose plays an important role as the primeval goose that either laid the world egg or—according to different versions—was born from it. In Egypt, as in China, wild geese were also regarded as mediaries between heaven (see SKY) and EARTH. —In Greece, the goose was sacred to Aphrodite and, in Rome, was sacred to Juno; it was

regarded as a symbol of love, fertility, and maritial fidelity, yet also of vigilance. Indeed, the vigilance of the geese at the Capitol supposedly saved it when Rome was destroyed in 387 B.C. —In Russia, Central Asia and Siberia, "goose" is a common term for one's beloved wife. —For the Celts, the goose was symbolically closely related to the SWAN and, like the swan, was thought to be a messenger from the spiritual world.

Goose Grass - It is supposed to impart likeability, eloquence, cleverness and intelligence to the person who carries the plant's root. It was thought to be a symbol of maternal love and thus of Mary's love, since its leaves fold up around the flower when it rains, thereby forming a protective cover.

Gordian Knot - See KNOT.

Gorgons - Hideous monsters of Greek mythology: three sisters (Euryale, Stheno and Medusa) at whose sight one turned to stone; represented as having SERPENTS in their hair or on their girdles and frequently as having wings. Often interpreted as the terrible aspects of the numinous. The singular form, Gorgon, generally refers to the one sister who was

GRAPE VINE: The return of the scouts from the Promised Land; from a children's Bible, presumably from the 19th century

mortal, Medusa, and whose head was chopped off by Perseus. In later times, she is often also portrayed as being youthful and beautiful. See GORGONEION.

Gorgoneion - Head of a Gorgon (see GORGONS) with a grotesque, horrible appearance, having a muzzle-like mouth with bared fangs; its tongue hangs out and it often has a beard. It was affixed to temples as a symbol of terrifying divine powers and an apotropaic sign (See APOTROPAIC FIGURES). The AEGIS had a GORGONEION at its center.

Gothamites - Symbolic figures of the narrow-minded bourgeoisie and of provincialness; originally referred to the inhabitants of Gotham.

Gourd - Because of the great number of its seeds, it, like the POMEGRANATE and the candied lemon (see CANDIED LEMON TREE), is a symbol of fertility. Among black African peoples and elsewhere, it is also a symbol of the world EGG and of the womb. —In Taoism, it is revered as a food that grants long life and corporeal immortality. —In China and elsewhere, drinking from two dried gourd halves symbolically signified the primeval unity that has been cleaved into two halves. —

In Christian art, the gourd, which grows quickly and withers quickly, is frequently a symbol of the brevity and frailty of life.

Graces - From the Latin, meaning "the graceful." Goddesses of grace in Roman mythology; figures symbolic of the youthful grace and beauty of woman; like many other mythological-symbolic figures, they were three in number.

Grafting (of Fruit Trees) - The fruits of grafted trees were regarded by the Jews as a product of an unnatural intervention in the divine order and thus could not be eaten. —In Christian art of the Middle Ages, a grafted shoot sometimes signifies a turn-around, refinement, or a new beginning brought about through grace.

Grail - A sacred object in medieval literature; in France, it is usually a vessel that contains the Host or a Communion cup or vessel in which Joseph of Arimathia caught the blood of Christ. In the German version of Parzifal by Wolfram von Eschenbach, the grail is a STONE with wondrous powers that provides nourishment and gives eternal youth. A symbol of highest heavenly and earthly happiness, as well as of Holy Jerusalem (see JERUSALEM, HOLY). It is attainable only

GRAVE: Various types of house urns

by the person who is pure and is thus a symbol of the highest level of spiritual development after passage through spiritual adventures.

Grain - See SEED.

Grain of Seed - A symbol of life, of a plethora of as yet undeveloped potentials. The grain of sand that dies in the ground so that a plant can sprout, is a symbol of the constant flux between death and new beginnings in nature, yet also a symbol of man's spiritual rebirth.

Grape - See GRAPEVINE.

Grapevine - A symbol of abundance and of life. In Greece, the grapevine was sacred to Dionysus; with respect to the Dionysus Mysteries, which celebrated the god of ecstasy as lord of death and of the renewal of all life, the grapevine was also a symbol of rebirth. —In Jewish and Christian symbolic thought, the grapevine is a sacred bush with much symbolic meaning; it was regarded as a symbol of the people of Israel (for whom God cares just as a person cares for his grapevine) and as the tree of the Messiah; the Messiah Himself is compared with a grapevine even in the Old Testament. Christ identi-

fied Himself with the true grapevine that, as a vital, strong stem, bears the faithful like branches, meaning that only the person who derives strength from Him can truly bear fruit. —An enclosed and guarded vinyard is a symbol of the chosen people; it was later allegorically related to the holy church. —The grape that the scouts brought back from the Promised Land is a symbol of God's promise; on early Christian sarcophagi, it is a symbol of the promised kingdom in the next life into which the deceased has entered. A single dove in the hand of Jesus is a symbol for His expiatory death and the Last Supper. See WINE.

Grass - See HAY.

Grasshopper - See CRICKET.

Grave - As a tumulus, it is perhaps a symbolic allusion to holy mountains (see MOUNTAIN); the form of many grave markers (including urns, such as so-called house urns) are related symbolically (or realistically, as in the case of the pyramids) to the idea of a place of residence (house, temple, etc.) for the dead. —In psychoanalysis, the grave as a place of death, yet also of quiet, of protection and anticipated rebirth, is sometimes associated with the

GRIFFIN: Depiction of a silk towel
(Cathedral of Sens)

loving and simultaneously horrible dual aspect of the Great Mother.

Graven Image - See IDOL.

Gravestone - See STONE.

Green - The color of the plant world and especially of spring in bloom; the color of water, life, freshness; the color of mediation between the RED of hell-fire and the BLUE of the sky. Green is frequently the antagonist of red, yet, as the color of life, sometimes also the substitute for red. As the color of annual renewal in nature, green is also the color of hope, longevity, and immortality. —In China, moreover, green is symbolically related to lightning and thunder and to WOOD and the Yin principle (see YIN AND YANG). —In Islam, green is the color of spiritual and material well-being, the color of wisdom and the prophets. —In the mythologies of many peoples, there are close connections and transformations between green and red. In Africa, for example, green, which represents the feminine, is sometimes thought to have arisen from red, which is masculine. The alchemists frequently saw transformation processes as interactions between regions that were symbolized by masculine red and feminine green. Green light plays a role among alchemists and occultists; it is encountered in nature during the burning of various chemical substances as well as during the rising and setting of the sun, where it appears as an extremely rarely observed manifestation of light known as the green ray, and is a symbol of illumination as well as a symbol of death and life. The alchemists also saw the so-called secret fire, the living spirit, in the image of a green, translucent and fusible CRYSTAL. In alchemy, green in compounds such as Green Lion and Green Dragon usually indicates solutions that are capable of dissolving even GOLD. —Christian artists of the Middle Ages sometimes painted the Cross of Christ in green as a sign of the renewal brought about by Christ and as an expression of hope for humanity's return to Eden. Yet green can also have a negative meaning in medieval art as the color of poison and a menacing luster.

Green Woodpecker - See WOODPECKER.

Grey - Grey consists of equal proportions of BLACK and WHITE and is therefore a color of mediation and compensatory justice. It is also a color of intermediary realms, such as in folklore, where it is the color of dead persons and spirits that wander about. In Christianity, it is the color of the resurrection of the dead and the color of the robe that Christ wears as judge of the world.

Greyhound - Or "whippet." In medieval pictures, the greyhound is a symbol of perception, since the greyhound, in particular, recognizes its master.

Griffin - A fabulous animal of antiquity having the head of an EAGLE, the body of a LION, and wings (see HYBRID CREATURES); an animal symbolic of the sun. Among the Greeks, it was sacred to Apollo and Artemis and symbolized strength and (due to its penetrating glance) vigilance. —Because it is at home in the sky as an eagle and at home on the earth as a lion, it was a symbol in the Middle Ages of the dual divine-human nature of Christ; as an animal related to the sun, it is also a symbol of resurrection.

Grimace - See BES; GORGONEION; APOTROPAIC FIGURES.

Ground Ivy - A creeping labiate flower usually having bluish-violet flowers. During the Middle Ages, it was a common medicinal plant and was thus sometimes a symbol of Mary as well. A wreath made of ground ivy that was picked during Walpurgis Night supposedly gave one the ability to recognize witches the following day.

Grove - See FOREST.

Gryllos - From the Greek grylloi, meaning "pig." Fantastic caricature that is part man and part animal; supposedly invented by Antiphilos, who lived in Alexandria and wanted to use it to mock a certain Gryllos ("pig").

Gula (Gluttony) - The female personification of one of the seven deadly sins; she rides on a pig or a fox with a goose in her mouth. Symbols (among others): wolf, bear, pig, raven.

Gynecocracy - From the Greek, meaning "rule by women." Political superiority of women that, in the form of genuine rule by women, exists only in legend (Amazons).

HAIR: Horus as a child with lock of hair on one side
HAIR: Pigtail-like "Suebic bun" from a Ice Age corpse found in a swamp

Hair - In many cultures, hair is seen as an actual bearer or symbol of strength (such as the hair of Samson in the Old Testament). This high regard for hair explains the significance of hair sacrifices (such as those among the Greeks when one was accepted as a citizen or at wedding and funeral ceremonies or those which took place in Christianity beginning in the Middle Ages vis a vis certain saints) as a sign of devotion and attachment or of repentance. The tonsure of monks and clerics must probably also be partially seen in this context. —Among the ancient Germans and during the Middle Ages, cutting off a person's hair had symbolic legal significance and was regarded as a way of dishonoring a criminal (indeed, at the end World War II, it still was a way to identify women collaborators). —In various cultures, particularly those oriented toward magic, a person's shorn hair can signify the person himself and is used as such in certain practices. —Coiffures can also have symbolic value: wild, disheveled hair, sometimes coursed with snakes, signifies terrible deities, furies, etc. (such as in Hinduism and Greek mythology). Different coiffures were also regarded as indications of profession, caste and class, age or sex. In ancient Egypt, for example, children wore a long, curled lock of hair on the right side. — Long, freely flowing hair, especially when worn by men, was sometimes regarded as a sign of freedom and noble parentage; when worn by women during the Middle Ages, it was regarded as a sign of virgins (yet also of whores). Long, uncut hair can also be a sign of a conscious animosity toward civilization, such as that of yogis, hermits or modern subcultures as well. People occasionally refrained from cutting their hair during a war or a journey or as an expression of mourning (in contrast, the Greeks of the Archaic Epoch cut off their hair as a sign of mourning). —Hair color also occasionally had symbolic importance: blond was frequently associated with light, whereas RED was considered from the High Middle Ages on to be a sign of evil. Among the ancient Germans and other peoples, hair buns played a role as well (see SUEBIC BUN); according to later medieval tradition, the hair bun and hooding are regarded as a sign of the married woman.

Hairstyle - See HAIR.

Halo - Patterned on the NIMBUS of an-

HALO: Different variants; radiant or disk-shaped halo with a cross for Jesus; square for living persons; triangle for God the Father
HAMMER: Thor's hammer, Mjöllnir, as an amulet; silver, 10th century

tiquity, it is a symbol in Christian painting (and sometimes sculpture) of divinity, majesty, or sovereign dignity and is in the form of a round, usually golden disk or rayed corona around the head of people (in contrast to the AUREOLE and MANDORLA); originally associated with Christ the Lamb, God the Father (where the halo is frequently triangular), and the dove of the Holy Ghost; often appears with an added monogram of Christ or CROSS as a cross nimbus; used since the 5th century for Mary, angels, apostles, prophets and saints as well; from the 4th–12th centuries, it was used for living persons (popes, bishops, donors, rulers), in which case it was usually square-shaped; in the art of the Middle Ages, it was also replaced by the gold background; during the Renaissance and the Baroque period, it was often down-played by perspectival-oval streaks of light, architectonic framing or radiant gleams of light, or avoided.

Hammer - A tool and originally a weapon and therefore a symbol of power and strength. It was frequently associated with thunder and is thus an attribute of Thor, the god of thunder, in ancient Germanic mythology. Among the Celts, it was a cult object, often depicted as having an especially long handle and a barrel-like head

(see SUCELLOS). In antiquity, it was the tool of Hephaistus, the god of fire and the art of metalworking. —Some cultures have ritually forged hammers that were attributed with the magical power to protect against evil. —In northern Europe, there are numerous depictions of hammers, such as those on gravestones; these possibly have to do with signs that are supposed to protect the peace of the dead from evil influences. Hammers are sometimes encountered as veiled cross symbols. —In Freemasonry, the hammer is a symbol of the strength of the will oriented toward reason. —In jurisprudence, the hammer is symbolically binding at auctions and other transactions. After the death of a pope, the pope's head and the walls of the death chamber are tapped three times with a golden hammer as a legal indication of death.

Hand - A symbol of activity and power; when used in gesticulating, it is also a symbol of apotropaic power. To be in the hands of a god or a ruler means to be at his mercy, yet also to be under his protection. —Reaching for or offering one's hand(s) is a sign of friendly openness, devotion, or pardon; thus, it has also long been an important symbol of a concluded marriage agreement and is laden with

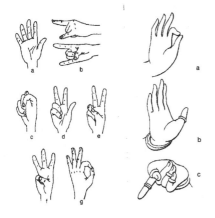

HAND: Apotropaic hand gestures: a) open "hand greeting"; b) cornuta; c) fica; d) oath; e) oath with "rabbit ears"; f) triple-sprout hand; g) hand forming "eye with eyelashes"

HAND: Examples of hand gestures in India: a) cinmudra or wakhyanamudra, meaning "meditation" or "teaching"; b) Aabhaya, meaning "granting of protection"; c) suci or tarjani, meaning "threat"

symbolic legal significance. —In Buddhism, a closed hand signifies silence about esoteric secrets; thus, the Buddha's open hand refers to the fact that he withheld no secret. Moreover, Buddhism and Hinduism have a great number of different hand gestures that have definite symbolic significance and play an important role in graphic art and in cult dance. For example, they can express threat, devotion, mediation, wonderment and prayer, argumentation and infertility. Hand and FINGER languages play a role in most cultures as a means of communication and expression; thus, placing one's left hand, fingers closed, in one's right hand is thought to be a sign of deference and respect in parts of Africa; hiding one's hand in one's sleeve had a similar meaning in ancient Rome. Covered or veiled hands were generally common in antiquity when one approached high dignitaries or received gifts from them. This gesture is also sometimes encountered later in Christian art as an expression of religious reverence; in liturgical ceremonies within the Christian church, it is common when holy objects are carried by persons who are not priests. —The symbolic significance between the right and left hands is very wide-spread (see RIGHT AND LEFT). It plays a role, for example, when

one lays one's hands upon someone as a sign of blessing, which is generally done with the right hand and is frequently thought to effect a genuine conveyance of powers. —In Christian art, God's intercession is often symbolized by a hand coming out of the clouds; God's hand was generally interpreted as being a symbol of the Logos incarnate. Since the Middle Ages, folding one's hands has been a gesture of prayer. —Lifting one's right hand while taking an oath is still thought to be legally binding today. See GLOVE.

Handle Cross - See ANKH.

Hanukkah Lamp - The candlestick with eight branches (a ninth branch serves solely to light the other candles) and eight candles used in the Festival of Hanukkah that commemorates Judas Maccabeus's reconsecration of the temple after its desecration by the Seleucids. It is a favorite object of skilled Jewish craftsmanship. See MENORAH.

Hare - Often identified with the rabbit; an animal symbolic of the Moon, because it sleeps during the day and is awake during the night and because it is very fertile (see MOON). In the fairy tales and legends of many peoples, the Moon is thus either itself a hare or the bright and dark surfaces on it are interpreted symbolically as being hares. Because of its fertility (and sometimes also because it likes to duck down into furrows in the ground), the hare is also closely related to the earth, insofar as the earth is conceived of as a mother, and is thus also a symbol for the constant renewal of life. —The playful notion of an egg-laying Easter bunny compounds this fertility symbolism by tying it to another fertility symbol (see EGG). Since the hare's plentiful progeny is traced back to its great sensuousness, it is occasionally encountered as an animal with a symbolic sexual reference. —Because of its timidity, it is sometimes regarded as a symbol of fear and cowardice; its alleged ability to sleep with its eyes open caused it to become a symbol of vigilance; because of its agility, it also appears as a symbol of rapidly fleeting life. —In the Bible, the hare is mentioned as an impure animal.

Harp - The most important stringed instrument of the ancient Orient, next to the LYRE, with which it is often symbolically identified (plucked strings!). The harp at first had seven strings, later nineteen or twenty, and the Greek harp had up to thirty-five strings. The harp is frequently mentioned in Old Nordic and Irish literary works.

Harvest - A symbol of fulfillment. In Christian art, it is frequently symbolic of the Last Judgment.

Hat - Sometimes symbolizes the head or thoughts; to change one's hat can also mean to change one's views. See JEW'S HAT, and PILGRIM'S HAT.

Hawk - As a very common bird of prey in the art of the Christian Middle Ages, it is a death symbol.

Hawthorn - Christ's crown of thorns is supposed to have been made of hawthorn. During the Middle Ages, it was a symbol of caution (which one needs in order to pluck the plant without hurting oneself) and of hope.

Hay - As a dried, that is, "dead" grass, it is a symbol in the Bible for the transitoriness of the world and of human life.

Hazel - In folklore and magic, it occasionally plays a role, possibly (among other reasons) because of its flexibility, because it is not hit by lightning, and because it blossoms early. It was thought to offer protection against evil spirits and serpents. The hazel sapling was a favorite tool among seekers of gold and water since it supposedly stuck out when it was over gold or water veins.

Head Coverings - As a WREATH and a CROWN, head coverings are symbols of high position, power and success; as a JEW'S HAT or PILGRIM'S HAT, they are a sign (symbol) of certain segments of a population. See HAT.

Heart - As a central organ vital to humans, it is associated with the symbolic significance of the MIDDLE. —In India, it is regarded as the place of contact with Brahma, the personification of the absolute. —In ancient Greece, it initially represented man's thinking, feeling, and wanting; later, the meaning shifted more in the direction of the spiritual. —In Judaism and Christianity, the heart is thought to be primarily the seat of the affective powers, especially of love, yet also of intuition and wisdom. —Islam sees the heart as the site of contemplation and spirituality; it is thought to be wrapped in various layers whose colors become visible when excited. —The heart played an essential role in Egyptian religion as the center of the powers of life, the will and the mind; it was allowed to remain in the dissected mummy together with a SCARAB because its weight at the judg-ment of the dead determined a person's fate in the next world. —Especially since the mysticism of the High Middle Ages, Christian art has developed an extensive heart symbolism modelled on the symbolism of love (the flaming, pierced heart of Christ, Mary, the saints). —Today, the heart is generally regarded as a symbol of love and friendship.

Hearth - Also called the "hearth fire." Symbol of the house, of human community, warmth and safety, of family, and of woman. The hearth played an important role in the religious ideas of many peoples; the deceased were thus buried next to the hearth even in prehistoric times; the hearth frequently served as a site of cult activity. Hearth cults exist in numerous religions, especially in Indo-Germanic lands. The hearth is often the ritual center of the house, the place of the cultic fire; among the Romans, it was the abode of household guardian spirits (called "lares") to whom sacrifices were made on the hearth; Hestia was the goddess of the hearth among the Greeks, Vesta among the Romans.

Hearth Fire - See HEARTH; FIRE.

Heaven - See SKY.

HARE: The hunter (the devil) chases the hare (man), the hare (the believer) can chase off the hunter (the devil); Schmid's "Musterbuch"

HARE: The crescent moon as a cup with the water of life in which a rabbit sits; Mexican illustration; Codex Borgia 55

Heaven's Door - See DOOR.

Hedgehog - In Japan and China, it is revered as a symbol of wealth; in Mesopotamia, Central Asia, and sometimes in Africa (possibly because of its spines), it was regarded as a sun-like animal that was associated with fire and thus with civilization. —On the one hand, it was thought to be a symbol of the devil during the Middle Ages (according to PHYSIOLOGUS); it is also encountered as a symbol of avarice, gluttony and—due to its quickly raised spines—wrath. On the other hand, it also appears in a positive vein as a hunter of SERPENTS and thus as a fighter of evil.

He-Goat - Also called a "billy goat." The he-goat is frequently thought of as a positive or negative embodiment of masculine sexual potency. —In India, the he-goat is a sun-like animal, sacred to the god of fire. —In ancient Greece, the he-goat was sacred to Dionysus and was the steed of Aphrodite, Dionysus, and Pan. —In the Bible, the he-goat is a sacrificial animal that takes the sins of the people onto itself, representing in this context the scapegoat that is cast out into the desert; as a stinking, dirty, demonic animal, it is also a symbol of the damned on Judgment Day.

—The Middle Ages attributed the devil with a he-goat's horns and feet. The he-goat was also thought to be the obscene steed of witches and of lust personified. —See LAMB, GOAT.

Height - As a symbolic-visual image, it represents the realm of spirit and of the divine; it is the goal of intellectual and moral development.

Hell - In contrast to the underworld (see (THE) HEREAFTER), the dead in hell lead an existence as shades; in many religions, hell is the place in the hereafter where punishment is exacted; it is the traditional counterpart of heaven, the realm of the merciless ruler of the underworld, i.e., of the DEVIL; usually portrayed as being a place of intolerable agonies of heat and fire, less frequently as a place of icy coldness.

Hell-Fire - See FIRE.

Helmet - A symbol of strength, invulnerability and occasionally also of invisibility.

Hem - Symbolically significant particularly in the Near East; kissing or touching a hem was regarded as a gesture of defer-

HARP: Detail from a grave painting
(Egyptian, 18th Dynasty)
HARP: Cycladian idol with harp, ca
2500 B.C.

ence or submission. —Among some peoples however, cutting off a hem was a humiliating punishment or at least the symbolic expression of the power held over a person (occasionally in conjunction with the symbolically related shearing of a person's HAIR).

Hen - Also called a "sitting hen." A symbol of caring, protective motherliness, occasionally also in the sense of an exaggerated caricature. See CHICKEN.

Henpecker - A symbol (more proverbial) of the dominance of the woman in marriage over the man ("henpecked husband").

Herbs - As plants that are frequently curative and unassuming, they are symbols of hidden power and modesty.

Hercules at the Crossroads - See CROSSROADS.

(The) Hereafter - In widely diverse cultures, the hereafter is a symbolic image of life after death; the realm of the living and the realm of the hereafter were frequently depicted as being separated by a river (see SKIFF; SHIP); yet the hereafter is usually not defined more specifically; it can be represented by the Island of the Blessed, Eden and heaven, as well as by hell or the underworld.

Herma - From the Greek. A pillar-shaped structure, crowned with a bearded head of Hermes, characterized by arm stubs at the sides and a phallus; originally sacred to the cult of Hermes; used as a road or border marker and erected at graves and house entrances; since classical times, the pillar shaft was in the shape of a body ("body herma"); in Roman art, there are portrait hermas (often with a name inscription on the shaft) and double hermas with two faces opposing one another; later it was used as an architectural sculpture.

Hermaphrodite - A hybrid creature. Symbol for the coexistence or the mediation of opposites as well as for the perfect human. In many religions, the divinity was imagined as being a bisexual creature. In his *Symposium*, Plato recounts the myth of humans who were originally bisexual. See ANDROGYNE. —The "materia prima" and the PHILOSOPHERS' STONE in alchemy, which was supposed to be produced by re-uniting the masculine and feminine principles (after previous separation), frequently appear in images as hermaphrodite. See MERCURY; REBIS.

HAT: Jew's hat, from an illustration in
Herrad von Landsberg's Hortus
Deliciarum
HEDGEHOG: Hedgehog symbol from
Schmid's "Musterbuch"

Hermes - In ancient mythology, Hermes was the god of trade and commerce; as a messenger of the gods, he held Caduceus in his hand. —Astronomically and astrologically, Hermes was known in antiquity as the planet (see MERCURY) that could be seen by all with the naked eye but that was the most difficult to observe (only in the morning and evening skies near the sun). —Hermes is quicksilver in alchemy and METAL and MERCURY in astrology.

Hermit - A symbolic figure of the ascetic living in total isolation who thereby strives toward union with God and perfection; aside from Christianity, they are also known in Hellenic Judaism and Buddhism.

Hero - According to the psychoanalytic interpretation of the symbolism of dreams and fairy tales, the hero is often an embodiment of victorious forces of the ego.

Heroic Age - See AGE.

Heron - In Egypt, the heron is occasionally a sacred bird; from time to time, the bird Benu (see PHOENIX) also appears in the form of a heron. —Because of its long beak, it is sometimes encountered as a symbol of the exploration of hidden wis-

dom (see IBIS), yet also of curiosity sticking its nose into everything. —During the Middle Ages, the heron, like other SERPENT-devouring animals, was a Christ symbol. —The grey heron was regarded as a symbol of penitence due to its ash-colored feathers. A heron with a white stone in its beak symbolizes taciturnity. —Since, according to Pliny, the heron sheds tears when it is in pain, it is also associated with Christ on the Mount of Olives.

Hesperus - See VESPER. The planet VENUS as the evening star.

Hexagram - Also called the "Seal of Solomon" and the "Star of David." A six-pointed star, formed by two triangles lying on or intertwined with one another; found particularly in Judaism, Christianity and Islam, yet is essentially the basis of the Indian YANTRA as well. In the broadest sense, the hexagram is often a symbol of the interpenetration of the visibile and invisible worlds; in Hinduism, it is a symbol of the joining of YONI and LINGA; in alchemy, it is also a symbol of the union of all opposites, since it is composed of the basic shapes of the signs of the elements FIRE Δ or AIR ⩘ and WATER ∇ or EARTH ⩒. One can also find numerous other speculations in alchemy that

HEIGHT: The union of height and depth; detail from a representation by Maria Prophetissa in Maier's Symbola aureae mensae, 1617

HELL: The devil Belial before the gate of Hell

assume a correspondence between the individual lines or points of the hexagram and planets, metals, and qualities. —The Star of David is a symbol of faith in Judaism and is the national emblem of the state of Israel. —C.G. Jung sees the hexagram as symbolizing the unification of the realms of the personal and the impersonal or also of the masculine and the feminine.

Highest Being - In religious studies, this is the term for the power standing over the world and over all supernatural forces (see GOD), especially as creator, originator and guardian of the moral order; manifold types of belief in a highest being existed in earliest times.

Hind - See DOE.

Hippopotamus - In Egypt, it was an animal feared because of its voracious appetite and was thus regarded as an embodiment of evil powers and a symbol of brutality and injustice; on the other hand, the female hippopotamus was revered as a symbol of fertility in the form of a hippopotamus goddess that was often depicted as being pregnant and standing upright; she was regarded as the protectoress of women. —In the Old Testament, the hippopotamus is a symbol of brutal force (behemoth) that can be tamed only by God Himself.

Hole - A symbol of opening, sometimes also of setting off into uncertainty, but also a symbol of nothingness and want. —Occasionally a symbol of the female genitals as well. —The Chinese jade disk made with a hole, called "Pi," is a symbol of heaven; in this case, the hole represents the shining of the spiritual world into the earthly world.

Hollyhock - See MALLOW.

Holy Jerusalem - See JERUSALEM, HOLY

Honey - Often associated with MILK, it is a symbol of sweetness, of tenderness or of the highest earthly or heavenly goods and thus of the state of perfect bliss, such as Nirvana; as a nutritious food, it is also a symbol of vitality and immortality. —In China, honey bore a close symbolic relation with the earth and the center, and was therefore always a part of the meals served to the emperor. —In the ancient world, honey was regarded as a "mystical" food, in part because it was gathered by an innocent animal (see BEE) from innocent blossoms in such a way that the blossoms

HELMET: Greek helmet
HERMAPHRODITE: Standing at the
center of the world; Frankfurt, 1550,
Rosarium Philosophorum

were only touched and not destroyed. It was thought to be a symbol of spiritual knowledge and initiation as well as of silence and peace. —An isolated practice encountered in initiation rites involves washing one's hands not only with WATER, but at first symbolically with honey, a practice that is derived from honey's importance as a medicine and an internally purifying substance. —Because of the way it is produced, which depends upon light and warmth, and because of its golden yellow color, honey was also sometimes associated with the SUN. — C.J. Jung's psychoanalytic interpretation of symbols sometimes sees honey as a symbol of the Self (the goal of maturation of the process of individuation). See BEE; MEAD.

Hood - An article of clothing of various gods, demons and sorcerors; part of monks' clothing. Aside from its practical aspect, it has symbolic significance as an expression of the concentration of spiritual energy or of self-concealment. Covering one's head with a VEIL or a hood symbolizes death in the initiation rites of the most varied cultures.

Hoopoe - In Arabic poetry, the hoopoe is a messenger of love. —During the Middle Ages, it was occasionally a symbol of the devil because of its crest, which is reminiscent of horns, and because of the foul-smelling fluid that it spews at enemies; thus, it also played a role among magicians and witches. In PHYSIO-LOGUS, it is a symbol of children caring for their frail parents; this trait is attributed to other birds as well (such as the KINGFISHER, STORK and crested lark).

Horn - Due to its importance in the animal kingdom, it is a symbol of strength and power, also in a mental sense. Dionysus and Alexander the Great were thus frequently portrayed as having horns, and representations of the horned Moses are part of this context (although they are probably based on a translation error, namely, the confusion of facies coronata and cornuta). —Horned animals were often regarded as fertility symbols. —Horns were used by many peoples as AMULETS against hostile forces. —The sacrificial altar of the Israelites had horns pointing in the four cardinal directions as a sign of God's omnipotence. The horn, whose shape is reminiscent of a crescent, is also associated with lunar symbolism. —Because of its shape (and also because of the aforementioned fertility symbolism), the horn is also a phallic symbol. —The horn's

HERON: The ibis-headed Egyptian god Thoth at the judgement of the dead; detail from a funerary papyrus, Ptolemaic age

HEXAGRAM: Symbol of the union of fire and water, air and earth; from Eleazar's *Uraltes chymisches Werk*, 1760

symbolic significance acquires a negative sense with the devil, who is frequently represented as having horns. —C.G. Jung pointed out the ambivalent symbolic meaning of horns: because of their shape and strength, they embody the masculine, active principle, yet, because of the lyre-like, open shape of their position, they can also symbolize the feminine, receptive principle and can thus be considered, all in all, as a symbol of psychological balance and maturity as well. —See CORNU-COPIA; HUNTING HORN; DRINKING HORN.

Horse - Representations of horses exist even in Paleolithic caves (see ROCK PAINTINGS); up into the Industrial Age, they played a large role in most cultures, which is why the symbolism associated with this animal is so rich. —Originally, the horse was usually thought of as a chthonic creature; it was associated with FIRE and WATER as life-giving, yet dangerous forces; thus, in many regions of Europe and in the Far East as well, it was said that the horse could produce wellsprings from the ground with a stomp of its hooves. It also frequently appears in a lunar context. It was close to the realm of the dead (such as in Central Asia and among many Indo-European peoples)

and thus also appeared as a guide of souls; it was therefore sometimes also buried together with the deceased or sacrificed in the event of death; horse sacrifices were often considered to be the most distinguished of all sacrifices; the cooking in cult CAULDRONS and the communal eating of sacrificial animals were social events—at least among the Celts and the ancient Germans. —The dark side of horse symbolism appears in a negative context in Zoroastrianism, for example, which often saw the diabolical spirit Ahriman embodied in the shape of a horse. Also associated with the dark side of horse symbolism are the horse-man hybrid creatures found in Greek mythology (CENTAURS; Sileni; SATYR), whose horse parts usually represent uncontrolled impulsiveness. PEGASUS, the winged horse of Greek mythology, is to be judged differently, being associated with the light symbolism of the horse, which was complementary to the chthonic and evolved later (such as in China, India, and antiquity). With respect to light, the horse, primarily as a white horse, became a sun-like and heavenly animal, a steed of the gods, a symbol of strength harnessed by reason (see the well-known comparison of the two horses in Plato's *Phaedrus*), or of joy and of victory (depiction on the graves of martyrs).

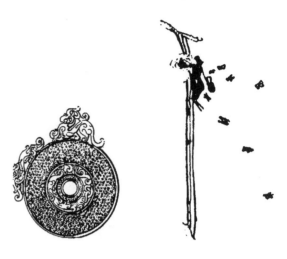

HOLE: Pi, the Chinese symbol of the sky, made of jade; fairly late Chou Dynasty

HONEY: Cave drawing of honey gatherers, painting in red; Valencia, Spain

In Christian symbolism, one encounters the horse, the white horse of "Christus triumphator," and the steeds of the "horsemen of the Apocalypse." —As a symbol for youth, strength, sexuality, and masculinity, the horse shares in the dark as well as the bright side of the above-mentioned symbolism. —The horse is the seventh sign of the Chinese ZODIAC; it corresponds to Libra (see SCALE). —See HORSEMAN; SLEIPNER.

Horseman - The horseman is a symbol of the mastery of wild strength (European statues of rulers as horsemen also share in this symbolism). —After the opening of the first four seals in the Book of Revelation, four horsemen appear one after another on a white, a fiery red, a black and a pale horse. The horseman on the white horse probably symbolizes Christ as victor; the others represent the angels of war, famine and death.

Horseshoe - Thought by many peoples to ward off misfortune and to bring good luck; it is possibly associated with the positive aspects of the symbolism of the HORSE.

Hortus Conclusus - The "enclosed garden" in which Mary is seated with a UNI-CORN in her lap; the hortus conclusus is a symbol of Mary's Immaculate Conception and derives from the enclosed garden in the Song of Solomon.

Hortus Deliciarum - The "Garden of Delights," a collection of excerpts from writings of the Bible, the church fathers, the church teachers and the Encyclopedists assembled around 1180 by Herrad von Landsberg, the abbess of the convent of Odilienberg in Alsace; the illustration of the convent textbook, preserved only in reproductions, is an inexhaustible source of symbolism of the High Middle Ages.

Hourglass - A symbol of fleeting time and of death (see CHRONOS). Because it must be turned over again after its sand has run down, the hourglass is also occasionally a symbol of the end and new beginning of cycles or epochs or of the changing influences of the sky upon the earth and vice versa. —Among the four cardinal virtues, the hourglass symbolizes temperance.

House - As an ordered, enclosed area like the CITY or the temple, it is a symbol of the cosmos or of the cosmic order. — Graves were sometimes fashioned like houses with respect to their significance as a person's final home (such as the pyra-

HOOD: Hermit; detail from a drawing by Urs Graf, 1512

HORN: The horned Moses; from the Fountain of Moses by C. Sluther, Carthusian monastery of Champmol, Dijon

mids of the Egyptians). —Like the temple, the house is sometimes a symbol of the human body and frequently (such as in Buddhism) associated with the idea that the body offers refuge to the soul only for a short time. Occasionally (such as in the psychoanalytic interpretation of dreams) the symbolic relation between body and house is sketched in even greater detail, such that the facade of the house corresponds to outward appearance, the roof to the head or spirit or consciousness, the basement to the instincts, impulses, and the unconscious, and the kitchen to psychic changes.

House Cricket - see CRICKET.

House Urn - See GRAVE.

Human - Man himself as well as parts and processes of the human body appear in many cultures as a symbol of phenomena not part of man. The interpretation of man as a microcosm in analogy to the universe (macrocosm) is common. —The coupling of human body parts, organs or basic substances to other phenomena is very common; thus, for example, the bones (as the supporting structure) correspond to the EARTH, the head (as the seat of the mind) to FIRE, the lungs (as the organs of breath-

ing) to AIR, and blood (as a fluid substance that binds everything together) to WATER. To a large extent, medicine of earlier times was based on the assumption of correspondences between phenomena of the human body and phenomena of the rest of the world (see ZODIAC). —Man (frequently winged) is the attribute of the Evangelist Matthew (see EVANGELISTS, SYMBOLS OF THE).

Humors - A notion developed during antiquity of the four humors that correlated with the four bodily fluids: blood–sanguine; gall–choleric; black gall–melancholic; phlegm–phlegmatic; these four humors are often components of pictographs and are often associated with other groups of fours (such as the elements, the stages of life, and the seasons).

Hundred - For thinking based on the decimal system, one hundred is the essence of a complete multiplicity within a larger whole, a high, large round number as the square of 10, the number of fulfillment, and, in the Hellenic world, the perfect good. In Christian literature, 100 sometimes appears as a symbol of heavenly bliss; the number one-thousand has a similar meaning. See TEN.

Hunt - As a goal-oriented pursuit of game,

HORN: Horned devil; detail from an illustration in *Le grant kalendrier et compost des Bergiers*, Troyes, 1496

HORSE: Winged horse, Sassanian, 10th century

the hunt is a symbol of the passionate search for spiritual goals, such as the soul's search for Christ in Christian mysticism. —As the conquering and annihilation of wild animals, it is also a symbol for victory over coarseness, disorder and ignorance (such as in the Near East and Egypt).

Hunting Horn - While hunting the UNICORN, the archangel Gabriel blows a hunting horn; the angels blow a horn at the Last Judgment. See HORN.

Hyacinth - This plant with blue-violet blossoms appears seldomly in Christian symbolism as a symbol of prudence and longing for heaven; since the 15th century, the Mother of God has been portrayed in art as wearing a hyacinth-colored (i.e., blue or purple) robe.

Hybrid Creatures - "Hybrid creatures" is the term for all types of living creatures that do not actually exist (nearly all are exclusively of animal or human origin, and, extremely rarely, some are solely of plant origin, as in the case of mandrake) and that are made up of a combination of artificial creatures or things and other various, actually existing creatures or things; they must be distinguished (in a narrower sense) from FABULOUS CREATURES, which in reality are basically only human figures, albeit ones usually having a grotesque distortion of particular body parts. Hybrid creatures of this sort were "invented" as far back as during the early ages of the great civilizations on the Euphrates, the Tigris, the Nile and the Indus; typical examples are hybrid creatures from the Akkad period (Mesopotamia, ca. 2200 B.C.) on cylinder seals, on which, for example, human parts and lion parts were combined, or in Ancient Egyptian images of gods that have an animal's head on a human's body. Over the course of time, there arose an immense variety of types, forms and variants of already existent types in the most varied cultures and for the most varied reasons, from sacred ICONOGRAPHY on Romanesque-Gothic church portals or Romanesque church ceilings up to our time (S. Dalí, P. Picasso and M. Chagall, for example); following H. Mode, one can set up a particular scheme for classification by forming four groups and classifying the types; the boundaries of the four groups are not rigid, of course, and can often be only arbitrarily established.

Bibliography: H. Mode. *Fabeltiere und Dämonen: Die phantastische Welt der Mischwesen.* Leipzig, 1977.

MYN GLAS LOOPT RAS

HORSEMAN: Statue of Charlemagne; statuette from 9th century, horse from 16th century

HORTUS CONCLUSUS: Hunt for the unicorn in Hortus conclusus (miniature from the Dominican breviary of the Library of the City of Colmar)

HOUR GLASS: Illustration in a work by Joost Hartgers, Amsterdam, 1651

Hydra - Also called the Lernaean Serpent. A serpent monster of Greek mythology that has many (at least nine) heads and lives in the swamps of Lerna; two new heads grew for each one cut off. Heracles conquered the Hydra by cauterizing the Hydra's necks with a log of firewood. The Hydra is a symbol of difficulties and obstacles that proliferate in the course of accomplishing a task.

Hyena - In Africa, the hyena is a symbolic animal with ambivalent significance: as a voracious, shy eater of carrion, it is a symbol of coarseness and cowardice; as an animal with powerful jowls and an excellent sense of smell, it is a symbol of strength, knowledge and cleverness. —In medieval art, it is a symbol of avarice, especially as the hyena head on the DRAG-ON in the Book of Revelation, which symbolizes the cardinal vices. According to PHYSIO-LOGUS, the hyena is gynandrous: one moment it is male, the next it is female. Physiologus's conclusion: Be not like the hyena, that you are amourous of males one moment and females the next, for, as it is written in Romans 1:27, men commit fornication with men.

Hyperboreans - A legendary people of antiquity that supposedly lived in the extreme north (beyond Boreas, the North Wind); it is unclear to what extent a historical people gave rise to these notions. The land of the Hyperboreans became more and more a symbol of light and bliss to whence Apollo occasionally retreated. Later, political utopias were situated there.

Hyssop - A small white or blue labiate flower having picant leaves; in Judaism and in Christian ritual, it served as a whisk for the sprinkling of the blood of sacrificial animals or holy water, which sometimes also contained hyssop. Since the simple plant grows in rocky grounds, it was also regarded as a symbol of humility; as a commonly used medicine, it was also an attribute of Mary in medieval art.

HYDRA OF LERNA: Heracles defeats the Lernaean Hydra

HYDRA OF LERNA: Heracles battling the Hydra; Greek vase picture

HYSSOP: The oldest Greek representation from the 6th century

149

HYBRID CREATURES

a.   b.   c.   d.   e.

f.   g.   h.

Animal-people: Hybrid creatures with human or animal bodies, clearly human stance, animal's head, sometimes only a few indications of an animal nature, such as a goat's foot in the case of the devil. a) cow-headed Hathor, Egyptian; b) Ganesha, Indian; c) elephant-headed spirit, French; d) Diva, Islamic; e) belly-face, Lycosthenes; f) Cernunnos, Celtic; g) Agrippiner, medieval; h) werewolf, medieval

---

a.   b.   c.   d.   e.

f.   g.   h.   i.

People-animals: Hybrid creatures with the body of an animal or in animal stance, having human's head, usually a human upper body or other purely human characteristics. a) man-bird, Akkadian; b) siren, Akkadian; c) sphinx, Mesopotamian; d) bird with soul, late Egyptian; e) lion-woman, Italian; f) winged centaur, Kassitic; g) lion-centaur, early Assyrian; h) fish-god, Assyrian; i) Mélusine, alchemistic, 16th century

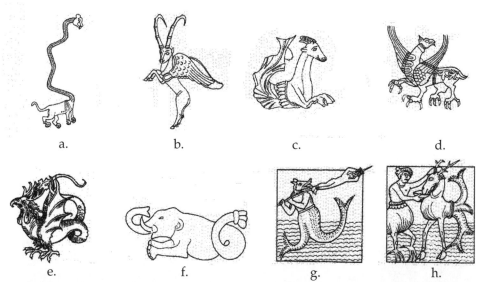

Hybrid animals: Hybrid creatures with animal bodies and animal heads of the most varying types with additional animal markings; their body parts are often greatly enlarged or multiplied. a) snake-necked lion, Egyptian; b) winged ibex, Persian; c) goat-fish, medieval; d) griffin, medieval; e) basilisk, medieval; f) elephant-fish, Indian; g) wolf-fish, medieval; h) sire and stag-fish, medieval

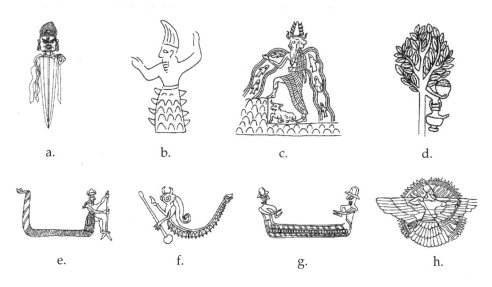

Hybrid creatures composed of all sorts of objects that have been anthropomorphized or put into animal form. a) dagger-man, Tibetan; b) mountain-god, Hettite; c) water-god, Akkadian; d) tree-man, Indian; e) boat-man, Mesopotamian; f) boat-god, Akkadian; g) double-body boat, Babylonian; h) Ashur in winged disk

Ibex (CAPRICORN) - A wild goat common in Eurasia and North Africa. The shape of its horns is remarkable, as they are bent backward or twisted; they sometimes appear as a symbol of the Moon, such as in rock drawings from the Stone Age. It was also known in Meso-potamia (in the Gilgamesh epic, for example). —The ibex or Capricorn is the tenth sign of the zodiac, corresponding to the first month of winter. The sun passes the sign between December 21 and January 19. Since the time of Hellenic astrology, Jupiter, Mars and the sun (Uranus) have been its decans; in Indian astrology, Saturn, Venus and Mercury have been its decans. The triplicity of Capricorn is earth; Capricorn is feminine, negative (passive), and a cardinal sign. The constellation Capricorn is clearly identical with the hybrid known as the GOAT-FISH, which is mentioned even in Babylonian sources.

Ibis - A sacred bird of the Egyptians, symbol of incarnation of the moon god Thoth, of the inventor of writing and of the god of wisdom (the bent shape of its beak was regarded as a reference to the crescent moon, and the beak's pointedness and length became associated, as in the case of the HERON, with the fathoming of wisdom). —PHYSIOLOGUS sees it as an impure animal according to the law, but also as a challenge: "Learn to dive spiritually, that you might enter the deep spiritual river, the depth of God's wealth, wisdom and knowledge."

Icarus - The son of Daedalus in Greek mythology. With wings made by his father and held together by wax, he went so close to the SUN that the wax melted and he fell into the sea, despite his father's warning. —A symbol for immoderate demands or unreasonable adventurism.

I-Ching - The "Book of Changes" used in ancient China (since about 1000 B.C.) for divinatory purposes and containing the practical application of the polarity of the masculine and feminine principles. Sixty-four hexagrams that can be formed from 8 x 8 trigrams, constitute the basis of the practice; solid lines represent the masculine element, broken lines the feminine. The sixty-four combinations constitute the system from which the future (and other oracles) can be read; according to tradition, the I-Ching was first done with yarrow stalks.

Ichneumon - An animal mentioned in

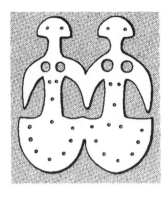

IDOL: Double idol from Alacahöyük

PHYSIOLOGUS that has nothing to do with the "modern" pine marten-like Viverridae family; often identified with the ENHYDRIS, although with a different interpretation; the ichneumon is an enemy of the dragon, which it kills: so, too, did Christ take the form of man and vanquish the devil.

Icon - From the Greek, meaning "image." A term for the religious pictures on panels in Eastern Orthodox churches and in private houses; according to Eastern Orthodox belief, the icon brings to mind the person portrayed and thereby becomes an object of ICONOLATRY.

Icon Dispute - Disagreement over the justification of ICONOLATRY, especially in 8th and 9th century Byzantium. Up until the Reformation, the dispute led to several instances of iconoclasm. In Byzantium, the problem of aniconic ornamentation played a special role.

Iconoclasm - The forceful removal and destruction of church images and SYMBOLS during the ICON DISPUTE, especially during the Age of the Reformation; this often led to the destruction of valuable artworks. Luther rejected iconoclasm, while Zwingli and Calvin were fanatical iconoclasts.

Iconography - A comprehensive term for the binding rules that determine the order in which symbols, figures, etc. must be portrayed in order to depict a certain event or a certain image. Iconography is determined by the educational level of an "elite" (usually literate scholars and clerics) who use iconography to educate the "uninitiated." Iconography is always dependent on the state of knowledge at a given time. Significant examples of iconography are the construction of some ROSE WINDOWS or the facade programs of medieval cathedrals or churches. See IMAGO MUNDI.

Iconolatry - The religious reverence of images or of SYMBOLS of a divinity, supernatural beings or people venerated as saints. Common in primitive religions and many civilized religions. In actual image worship (called "iconolatry" in Greek), the image is considered to be identical with the divine being or is supposed to make that being present, and the image itself is worshipped. The Old Testament (and thus Judaism) rejects all iconolatry as idolatry. —The Christian church initially allowed some iconolatry. During the ICON DISPUTE, the Second Council of Nicea (787) declared that reverence was due to the images of Christ and the Saints, since the

IHS: The abbreviation IHS with a cross and cross nails in two illustrations from Schmid's "Musterbuch"

person himself was revered in the image; however, only God was due worship. In 1564, the Council of Trent affirmed this teaching against religious reformers. Only icons are allowed in Eastern Orthodox churches.

Iconstasis - From the Greek word "ikonostas." In Eastern Orthodox chur-ches, the iconostasis is the wooden, triple-door partition that is decorated with icons and located between the altar and the central body of the church. The middle door, called the Holy Door or King's Door, symbolizes the Gates of Heaven and is passed through only by the bishop or the priest.

Icon Painting - In the art of the Eastern Orthodox church, icon painting is found on panels and is abstract, typified, usually frontal, two-dimensional and outlined; usually done by monks as an ecclesiastical office in strict accord with a canon.

Idol - From the Greek. A plastic, figured representation of supernatural beings who are thought of as living continuously or intermittently in the images. Idol cults are characteristic of ancient Oriental and American civilizations, West African cultures and the peoples of northern and central Asia. Idols were made in the shape of humans (particularly VENUS STATUES) in prehistoric times (especially during the Stone Age), usually of stone, clay, ivory and bones and probably of wood as well; from the Upper Paleolithic period up into the early Iron Age, they also existed as flat, abstractly stylized figures (pre-Mycenaean Greece, Troy, the Iberian Peninsula) as well as animal and mixed figures. The marble Cycladean idols ("island idols"), which date from the 3rd century B.C., are especially well known.

Idun - Also spelled "Ithunn." A goddess of the Aas race of man who possessed the golden APPLES that gave the gods eternal youth. A symbol of youth and immortality.

IHS - Also "JHS." The abbreviation of the name of Jesus (in Greek), interpreted during the Middle Ages as Jesus Hominum Salvator (Christ, Savior of Mankind); also as the inscription of the labarum as In Hoc Signo (In This Sign [be victorious]); it was later interpreted by the Jesuits as meaning Jesum Habemus Socium (We have Jesus as an ally); all three meanings are a symbol of Christ. See CHRIST MONOGRAM.

Ikebana - See FLOWER.

ICONOSTASIS

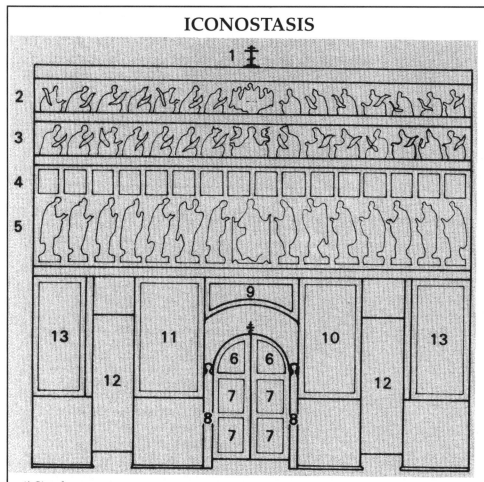

1) Simple cross
2) Forefathers with the image of the Trinity (rarely of the Crucifixion) in the center as the beginning of the convenant between God and man
3) Prophets with the Mother of God of the Sign; David is usually to the left, Solomon to the right
4) Old Testament preparation of the New Covenant: Feast days as primary stages of salvation, usually 6 feasts of the Lord, 4 feasts of Mary, Easter (Descent into Hell), Pentecost, Exaltation of the Cross during the progression of the year
5) Effect of God's having become man, the church of the New Testament; also the consummation during the coming age of the world, the sight of divine majesty and the church's intercession for the world through angels, apostles, holy father liturgists, primary martyrs, and occasionally local saints or founders of monasteries
6) Annunciation (on the Holy Door)
7) Evangelists (on the Holy Door)
8) (on the door columns) Holy father liturgists St. John Chrysostom and St. Basil with other important hierarchs (later, they sometimes appeared on the Holy Door; see #7)
9) Communion of the Apostles (institution of the Eucharist in both forms)
10) Icon of Christ, occasionally a "church icon" (patron or festival to whom or which the church is dedicated)
11) Icon of Mary with the Child

INCENSE: Scene of a sacrifice, offering of incense; relief on the temple of Osiris at Abydos, Egypt

Image, Ancestral - Pictorial or figurative portrayal of a deceased person. See TOTEM POLE.

Image Magic - A magic of analogy that believes in a close connection between an image (or symbol) and the person portrayed by that image, such that an action done to the image will affect the person himself, for example, that one can kill an enemy by putting a hole through his image.

Imperial Orb - One of the German imperial insignia; a sphere with a cross as a symbol of Christian world domination.

Incense - Incense is used in the cults of many peoples. The symbolic ideas connected with incense are based on its fragrance, SMOKE, and composition of imperishable resins; the rising smoke symbolizes prayers rising to heaven; the fragrance is supposed to drive away evil spirits; the RESIN symbolizes permanence. —In Christianity, incense was first used at burials, yet was later used generally in liturgical ceremonies.

Initiation - Among many peoples, initiation, with its attendant customs, marks the entry into a new stage of life (especially the transition into the role of a sexually mature adult); it is connected with tests and symbolic ceremonies (such as CIRCUMCISION). This usually involves a transformation process that is thought to be symbolic as well as actual and that generally embraces the phases of shedding one's old role, isolation, and finally the return and reintegration of the transformed person into the community. —In a more restricted sense, it is a term for rites that represent the condition for acceptance to secret societies or mystery cults. In such cases, the experience of a symbolic death (sometimes even in graves or coffins designed for that purpose) and a spiritual resurrection on a higher level, frequently play an important role. Practices that were thought of as a return to and reissue from the WOMB, were a part of various rites. Aside from this, the passing of various other tests symbolically related with the development of particular moral and spiritual abilities, was common (see LABYRINTH).

INRI - The (Latin) writing on the Cross of Christ, Jesus Nazarenus Rex Judaeorum (Jesus of Nazareth, King of the Jews); also appears in Hebrew and Greek.

Interpretatio Romana - The transference

IMAGO MUNDI

In contrast to the MAPPA MUNDI, the Imago Mundi is the picture of the world based on St. Augustine's idea of an ordered world, particularly in the medieval sense, which is of an order set by God and encompassing all creation (see MICRO-COSM-MACROCOSM; ELE-

MENTS). Thus, the idea of the Imago Mundi encompasses the earth and the cosmos. In contrast to the corresponding notion in antiquity, the Imago Mundi provides a theological relation to the act of creation and systematic use for all areas of life. The "picture of the world" is a mytho-graphic picture of the world, a picture of the world that is more exegesis than geography, more interpretation of the world than description of the earth. Thus, a comparison with that which we today mean by "world map" cannot be made. Rather, it bears an intellectual kinship with ICONOGRAPHY.

William Blake depicted the act of creation by the "great architect" of the universe very much in the sense of medieval painters of miniatures: a giant sun, still young, floods the act of creation with its light and is witness to the creation of the earth .

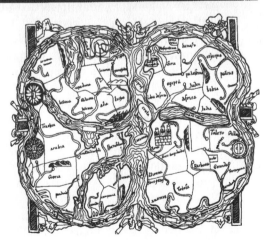

Half a millenium earlier, the draftsman of the map at the left joined the sun and the Moon (at the left edge of the map), Eden and the four rivers of Eden (top center), and the known world with Rome and Jerusalem near the center. The waters of a primeval ocean flow to the north, south, east and west through four arms of a river and divide the inhabited world into four symbolic parts that have hardly anything to do with geographic reality.

IVY

of the names and characteristic traits of Roman gods onto the deities of other peoples. —The Interpretatio Graeca has to do with a similar phenomenon, as does the Interpretatio Christiana.

Intoxication - Or "drunkenness." In some cultures, intoxication is closely related to rites of harvest and prayers for fertility. Because of its intensity, which transcends the bounds of everyday consciousness in various religions, intoxication induced by dancing, music, alcohol or drugs is regarded in some cultures as a manifestation of particular closeness to God.

Invidia (Covetousness) - A female personification of one of the seven deadly sins, riding on a dog with a bone in its mouth or on a dragon. Its symbols include the scorpion and the dog.

Ira (Anger) - A female personification of one of the seven deadly sins, riding on a bear or a wild boar. Its symbols include the dog and the hedgehog.

Iris - A plant found in northern temperate zones, having sword-shaped leaves; an ancient medicinal plant, and thus a symbol of Mary during the Middle Ages. The Greek name (in Greek mythology, Iris is the embodiment of the rainbow) also re-

fers to the RAINBOW as a symbol of a reconciliation between God and man.

Iron - A widespread symbol of strength, durability, and inflexibility. Occasionally (such as in China), it is contrasted with COPPER or bronze as the less precious metal. Iron and copper sometimes share in the opposition of the symbols WATER–FIRE; north–south; BLACK–RED; Yin–Yang (see YIN AND YANG). Yet iron is not seen as being inferior in all cultures and in every respect; thus, iron from meteorites that have fallen from the sky is frequently considered to be heavenly and divine. —Iron and iron tools are thought, on the one hand, to offer protection from evil spirits, yet, on the other hand, to be the instruments of evil spirits. —The fact that iron tools were forbidden in the construction of Solomon's temple in the Old Testament, has to do with similar notions: people were afraid that iron could drive away the numinous powers present in the altar stone. For similar reasons, the use of iron instruments for slaughtering sacrificial animals was avoided in various cultures. —In alchemy, iron corresponds to Mars, which, being masculine, the planet of war and strife, hot and dry, lightning and storm, is described as causing ferocity and cruelty. See METALS.

Iron Age - See AGE.

Island - As an isolated area that is hard to reach, it is often a symbol of that which is special or perfect; it sometimes appears—in dreams, for example—as a place of realized utopian wishes that cannot be reached until the future. —It is frequently conceived of as a carefree place in the hereafter, such as the Island of the Blessed of Greek myth, where the favorites of the gods continue to live after their physical death. —In a negative sense, it is also a symbol of a flight from the world that avoids contending with life.

Ivory - Because of its white color and uniform smoothness, it is a symbol of purity and stability. See IVORY TOWER.

Ivory Tower - Symbol of arrogant, aloof or aestheticized isolation from the world. —In Christianity, Mary—in an entirely different sense—is occasionally compared with an ivory tower; here, it symbolizes the Tower of David, that is, Mary is a pure VESSEL that bore the seed of the nation of David. See IVORY; TOWER.

Ivy - Like most evergreen plants, ivy is a symbol of immortality. In Etruscan art, it is something of a symbol of procreation and rebirth (often together with the PANTHER). The unchanging green color and climbing, yet "huggling" character of this plant also made it a symbol of friendship and fidelity, which is why, for example, it was presented to a bride and groom at their wedding in ancient Greece. —Because of its need to lean on something, ivy was sometimes regarded as a feminine symbol as well. —On the other hand, the richly verdant plant was a symbol of vegetative powers and sensuality in antiquity, which is why it played an important role in the cults of Dionysus and Bacchus; thus, maenads (or bacchants), satyrs and sileni were crowned with a garland of ivy and the thyrsus was decorated with ivy.

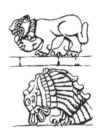

JACKAL: The Egyptian god Anubis; detail from a mural in the grave of Ramses I, Valley of the Kings, 19th Dynasty

JAGUAR: Jaguar and eagle; depiction on the pyramid of Quetzalcoatl in Tula

Jackal - The jackal was often thought to be an animal that roves about cemeteries and feeds on corpses; its appearance was thus often seen as a bad omen. It was sometimes also regarded as a symbol of greed and wrath. —The animal head of Anubis, the Egyptian god of the dead, is frequently interpreted as being a jackal's head, although it is probably that of a jackal-like greyhound.

Jacob's Ladder - A symbol of the providence with which God looks over mankind; angels often climb up and down ladders (see LADDER); visual representation of Genesis 28:10 ff.

Jade - Like gold, jade was thought in China to be closely associated with the Yang principle (see YIN AND YANG) and was thus a symbol of vitality and cosmic energies. It was seen as a symbol of perfection and of the unification of the five heavenly virtues (purity, immutability, clarity, harmony and goodness) and as a union of moral qualities with beauty. Jade was used as a general remedy and was thought to be the food of immaterial beings and an agent that granted immortal-

ity or long life and protected the bodies of the deceased from decomposition. — In Central America, jade was a symbol of the soul, the mind, and the heart.

Jaguar - Particularly among Central American Indians, the jaguar is a chthonic being associated with the powers of the Moon and the hidden secrets of the earth; for this reason, it is also a guide of souls. The coming of twilight is visually represented as the sun's being eaten by a giant jaguar. It is frequently juxtaposed symbolically to the heavenly, sun-like EAGLE.

Janus - One of the oldest Roman deities. As the god of doors, he was portrayed as having two faces: looking outward and inward, i.e., looking over those who come and those who go. In this sense, Janus is a general guardian of all beginnings and transitions (such as of the beginning of the year, the first month of which is named after him). —Later, the Janus head also became a symbol of ambiguity or of the evil and good sides of one and the same thing.

Jasper - A type of chalcedony that has impurities. When it is broken, many new stones seem to appear inside, which is why it is sometimes a symbol of preg-

JANUS: Janus on a Roman copper coin
JERUSALEM, HOLY: From an illuminated manuscipt in the Bamberg Apocalypse, circa 1020

nancy and birth (a notion passed down from the Babylonians to the Greeks and Romans and then to the Middle Ages). — During the Middle Ages, jasper was especially highly regarded because it was designated in the Book of Revelation as the first foundation of Holy Jerusalem (although the jaspoid opal which was on the crown of the emperor of the Holy Roman Empire and was called "the orphan," was meant). —The term "jasper" has undergone frequent changes in meaning, such that attributions made to it at a given time cannot always be explained unequivocally.

Jerusalem, Holy - Described in the Revelation of St. John as a city with twelve gates on a square plot of land; it is a symbol of the expected end of the world when God will dwell among His people. —The city is built upon twelve cornerstones bearing the names of the Apostles; the twelve gates are twelve PEARLS.

Jesse's Root - Having arisen during the 12th century, Jesse's Root is a representation of the family tree of Christ and Mary according to Isaiah 11:1; it features a stylized tree growing from a sleeping Isai and bearing images of Christ's ancestors (including David and Solomon) in its branches; Christ appears at the top, but, beginning in the 13th century, that position is usually held by Mary and the baby Jesus.

Jet - A very dense type of COAL that can be polished; as an AMULET, it is a commonly used agent against harmful influences, such as the evil eye, poisons, illnesses, and storms. —As far back as in Celtic times, as well as in the Middle Ages and during modern times, it was a symbol of mourning and thus frequently worn during mourning because of its deep BLACK color.

Jewelry - Jewelry is a symbol of distinction, power, and esoteric knowledge; yet it is also simply a symbol of material wealth; finally, in a negative sense, it is a symbol of nothingness, of the merely external appearance of all earthly things. — Among some peoples, the wearing of jewelry was attributed with having an apotropaic effect (see AMULET). Jewelry was often buried with the dead so that they would be bedecked for life after death.

Jewels - As hard, strong, sparkling, rare minerals that can be polished and cut, jewels are often symbols of "earthly stars,"

JESSE'S ROOT: From a depiction on
the bronze door of San Zeno,
Verona; circa 1000

of heavenly light on earth, or of truth (as well as numerous other specific meanings. See: AGATE; AMETHYST; CRYSTAL; DIAMOND; EMERALD; JADE; JASPER; SAPPHIRE; TURQUOISE). With respect to this symbolic content, kings' crowns, the breastplate of high priests of the Old Testament, and especially conceptions of utopian buildings and cities, as well as fairy tale castles and castles in the sky or Holy Jerusalem (see JERUSALEM, HOLY), were decorated with many jewels.

Jew's Hat - A pointed hat that Jews in Islamic and Christian lands had to wear during the Middle Ages. See HAT.

Job - Symbolic Biblical figure of the God-fearing, just man whose faith in God remains unshaken even by heavy blows of fate.

Journey - As the goal-oriented traversing of a path on which obstacles must also often be overcome, journeys are a symbol of the course of life or, in a more special sense, a symbol of the search for spiritual-psychological goals that often appear embodied as the Promised Land, as the Island of the Blessed, and as castles and temples (frequently upon mountains). — Initiation rites take place variously in the form of a series of tests that the adept had to go through like a journey (as in the case of Chinese secret societies, the Greek mysteries, and the Freemasons). —Many peoples have the idea of a journey that the deceased must undertake after death; the Egyptian and Tibetan books of the dead, for example, recount this in detail. This apparently has to do with a symbol of a cleansing and further development of the soul. —Buddhism compares the succession of a person's births, the sequence of incarnations of one's spiritual individuality up to the point of its release in Nirvana, with a journey. —According to psychoanalysis, journeys as a dream symbol can be understood in part as a wish for change.

Judas - Since the Middle Ages, he has been represented negatively in appearance, clothing and gestures as a Jew and an outsider (red hair, yellow robe, Jew's hat); he was the disciple who betrayed Jesus to the high priests (Matthew 26:14 ff., Mark 14:10 ff., Luke 22:3 ff. and John 13:2 ff.).

Jupiter - The Greek Zeus. In the mythology of antiquity, he is the lord of the sky, the omnipotent ruler who has a bundle of lightning bolts in his hand. —With respect to astronomy and astrology, Jupiter was

JUDAS: Kiss of Judas; detail from a miniature from Heinrich vom Blois's *Psalms*

already known to antiquity; it emits a yellowish white light and outshines all stars near it. —In alchemy, Jupiter is identified with PEWTER.

Justice - The cardinal virtue JUSTITIA.

Jusitia - Equivalent to the Greek Dike, Justitia is the personification of justice, one of the four cardinal virtues. She is frequently depicted with a SCALE, SWORD, BLINDFOLD, CORNUCOPIA, olive branch and law book as attributes. With reference to carrying out the law, she is also represented with a severed head in her lap.

KING: King as materia prima,
swallowing his son; detail from an
illustration in Lambsprinck's
Figurae et emblemata, 1678
KNOTS: Heracles knot, Isis knot

Kagami - A luxuriously decorated Japanese metal mirror for cult use that has no handle and reflects light in a special manner; it is usually round or calyx-shaped.

Kali - The bride of Shiva in Indian mythology. See DURGA.

Kauri Snail - See SNAIL.

Kendo - The Japanese competitive sport; a sword fight that has been imputed with symbolism since the age of the Samurai. See ARROW AND BOW; KYUDO.

Kerykeion - The Roman caduceus. A herald's staff, originally a magic wand. Two SERPENTS are intertwined around its top, their heads facing one another. An attribute of Hermes (Mercury) in particular. Variously interpreted, sometimes as a symbol of fertility: two serpents copulating over an erect phallus. Yet it must probably be understood primarily as a symbol of balance. In alchemy, it is a symbol of the union of opposing forces. See ASCLEPIUS, STAFF OF.

Key - The symbolic meaning of the key frequently has to do with the fact that it unlocks as well as locks. Janus, the Roman god of doors (later, of beginnings generally) was usually depicted with a doorkeeper's staff and a key. —In Japan, the key is regarded as a symbol of happiness because it opens up the rice pantry (and, in a broader, spiritual sense, hidden treasures as well). —In Christian art, the key— as well as the double-key—symbolizes the authority given to the Apostle Peter to dissolve and to bind (compare the two keys of the Papal coat of arms). —During the Middle Ages, handing over keys was regarded as a symbolic legal action that granted powers (compare to act of handing over the keys to a city). —In esoteric symbolic languages, the possession of a key often means "to be initiated." —The key appears in fairy tales and folk tales as well, often as a symbol of difficult entry to mysteries or (as in folk custom and folk song) as an erotic symbol.

Keys to Heaven - See PRIMROSE.

Keystone - A keystone is a wedge-shaped stone placed in the top of an arch or vault, often articulated by sculpted or ornamental reliefs or coats of arms; also especially well developed in the late Gothic period as a pendent capital.

KNOTS: A magician sells a seaman a rope; winds, either favorable (good magic) or unfavorable (defensive magic), are "buttoned" into the knots. Woodcut by O. Magnus, 1555

Kidney - Among some primitive peoples, but also in Judaism, the kidney is thought to be the seat of the feelings and of special power and passion; the use of the phrase "heart and reins" to refer to a person's inner powers was used as far back as in the Old Testament. —During the Middle Ages, the kidney was regarded as the seat of emotional excitement, especially of sexual drive.

King - Or "emperor." Frequently thought to be the embodiment of God, the sun or of heaven, or to be the center of the cosmos or the mediator between heaven, man, and the earth. —C.J. Jung sees the figure of the old king appearing in dreams as an archetypal figure that represents the wisdom of the collective unconscious. On the other hand, the fairy tale figure of the king (especially when someone "becomes king") must probably be usually thought of as a symbol of the goal toward which the development of the ego strives. —In alchemy, the king sometimes corresponds to the prima materia.

Kingfisher - Often flies in pairs; thus, it is a symbol of marital happiness, especially in China. —In Christian symbolism, the kingfisher is a symbol of resurrection, since, according to medieval belief, it annually moults all its feathers.

King's Daughter - Or "princess." In the fairy tale traditions of many peoples, the king's daughter is a symbol of a goal and highest good that the hero can reach only after overcoming various obstacles and dangers. —The king's daughter is also interpreted psychoanalytically as being the embodiment of the individual unconscious in contrast to the "old king," who is a representative of the collective unconscious. See KING'S SON.

King's Path - In contrast to crooked, winding paths, the king's path is the right and straight one that symbolizes the progress of the unwavering soul toward its inner goal; during the Middle Ages, for example, it was a common term for the way to God via monasticism and meditation.

King's Son - Or "prince." Encountered in numerous fairy tales as a shining hero, as the embodiment of youthful, active, moral action and change as well as of staunch endurance. Psychoanalytically, the king's son can be thought of as a representative of the victorious forces of the ego. See KING'S DAUGHTER.

Kiss - Originally probably thought of as a waft from the soul living in the BREATH; it was thus also thought to impart energy and to give life. —Usually an expression of emotional devotion and a sign of reverence. Aside from the actual erotic significance (which can also assume symbolic character in wedding customs), the kiss also has sacred relevance. In Egypt, for example, the feet of the god-ruler were kissed, a form of deference that was commonly shown toward rulers, priests and judges in many cultures. —In antiquity, people kissed the threshold of temples, altars, and images of gods. To this day in Islam, the Black Stone of the Kaaba is kissed as the goal and the high point of the pilgrimage to Mecca. —In the early Christian church, the kiss of peace or of brotherhood was a symbol of solidarity (compare the Easter kiss of the Eastern Orthodox church); the kiss of brotherhood is also common as a symbol of solidarity in secular contexts (such as among Communist comrades); the greeting kiss has a somewhat diminished symbolic significance among relatives and friends. —In Christianity, the kissing of the altar, the cross, the Bible, relics of the saints, etc. is thought of as a symbol, but also as spiritual union. —During the Middle Ages, kisses were also a symbol of reconciliation (reconciliation kiss). —Blowing a kiss can be a substitute for a kiss and is probably derived from ideas found in magic. —We are reminded of Judas's misuse of the kiss by the phrase "kiss of Judas."

Kite - In Japan, the kite (especially the golden kite) was thought to be a divine bird. —In Greece, it was sacred to Apollo and a symbol of prophecy because of its high flight and sharp eye.

Kneeling - A ritual symbol that is often legally binding. A sign of deference, humility and subordination.

Knife - Like the SCISSORS, the knife, as a sharp cutting instrument, is a symbol of the masculine, active principle that works feminine, passive matter. —In Hinduism, the knife is an attribute of terrible deities. —In many cultures, it is thought to ward off calamity, which possibly has to do with the symbolic significance of IRON. —A knife in the hand of Old Testament figures is a knife for circumcision and refers to membership in the Old Covenant.

Knot - Frequently a symbol of linkage, connection, or attachment to powers that grant protection, yet also a symbol of complication and adversity. —Among the Egyptians, the knot was a symbol of life and immortality; the Knot of Isis, a type of ANKH with arms folded down, was a common AMULET. —As a symbol of love and marriage, knots are sometimes found in wedding ceremonies. —The Islamic world sees the knot as a symbol that grants protection; Arab men, for example, tied knots in their beards as a defense against the evil eye. —The symbolic significance of untying a knot is widely common. Buddhism compares the wise person's untying himself from the world of mere appearance with untying a knot. —Death is also sometimes compared with the untying of a knot (see SUEBIC BUN). —In Marocco, for example, where a groom was not allowed to sleep with his wife until he had untied seven knots on his clothes, the untying of a knot was a symbol of opening oneself. —According to psychoanalytic dream interpretation, a knot can refer to complexes and psychological consolidations and, accordingly, the untying of a knot can refer to the overcoming of problems. —Alexander the Great's cutting through the Gordian Knot is proverbially used in a positive sense as a symbol of decisive action, yet sometimes also, in a negative sense, of crude impatience.

Knot of Isis - See KNOT.

Kyudo - See ARROW AND BOW.

LABARUM: Depiction on a Roman coin
LADDER: Ladder of Virtue, from a miniature from Zwettl

Labarum - From the Latin. A Roman standard that was introduced by Constantine the Great and became an imperial standard in 324 A.D.; a gold-plated cross staff with a purple cloth on the cross-bar and the CHRIST MONOGRAM at the top; derived from the Christian interpretation of an alleged vision of light (cross of light with the inscription *in hoc signo vinces*, see IHS) and subsequent dream epiphany that Constantine had before the decisive battle against Maxentius in 312 A.D.

Labyrinth - Originally a term for King Minos's palace on Crete that had a large number of tortuous corridors; it was later a term for the abode built by Daedalus for the MINOTAUR. From this, it finally became a term for all mazes in architecture and the visual arts. —Passage through a labyrinth was sometimes a part of INITIATION rites; it symbolized the discovery of a hidden, spiritual center as well as the ascent from darkness to light. See ASTRAL DANCES; GOOD LUCK SIGNS; TROJABURGS.

Ladder - Or "stepladder." In sundry variants, it is a symbol of a connection between heaven (see SKY) and EARTH (in this respect, it is sometimes closely related to the symbolic significance of the RAINBOW); a symbol of ascent; a symbol of a gradual heightening or of a development. The number of rungs often corresponds to a sacred number (frequently SEVEN) and the individual rungs sometimes have different colors (such as in Buddhism) or consist of different metals (such as in the Mithra mysteries); they thereby often correspond at the same time to various steps of a spiritual initiation. —The Bible mentions Jacob's dream of the Ladder of Heaven upon which angels climb up and down: a symbol of the living relationship betwen God and man. —In Christian art, one frequently encounters the Ladder of Virtue upon which virtuous people, threatened on all sides by demons, climb upward step by step. —As places of higher spiritual development, cloisters were also sometimes compared with ladders (Cistercian and Carthusian cloisters are also sometimes called *Scala Dei*). —See STAIRCASE.

Ladder of Heaven - See LADDER.

Lad's Weed - See ORCHIDS.

Lady Chandelier - Hanging chandeliers (candlestick holders) usually made of

LADDER: Jacob sees the ladder with the angels in a dream. Detail from Herrad von Landsberg's *Hortus Deliciarum*, 12th century

wood in the shape of a female trunk with a fish-tail, especially popular in the 16th century; a HYBRID CREATURE (see MÉLUSINE) probably related to the symbolism of the fish-tailed SIRENS; probably derivative of astrological symbolism (zodiacal opposition of Virgo and Pisces).

Lady's Ice - Ice of our Blessed Ladies, MICA.

Lady's Mantle - Frequently called "night mantle of our Blessed Lady" in popular parlance due to the shape of its leaves; associated with Mary.

Lady's Slipper - A type of orchid so called due to the shape of its flowers; it was occasionally also called "Kriemhild's helmet." In German-speaking lands it is associated with the Virgin Mary in many legends.

Lady World - An allegorical (symbolic) representation of evil in the world, whereby the "world" is regarded as a female deceiver and seductress (see PRINCE OF THE WORLD). The great majority of figurative depictions show a magnificent front; the disgusting back has been eaten away by vermin and other animals and is rotting.

Lake - Or "pond." Often visually interpreted as an open EYE of the earth. —It is sometimes thought of as the dwelling place of subterranean beings, fairies, nymphs, water men, etc. who attract people in order to draw them down into their domain. —In dream symbolism, it is often a symbol of the feminine or the unconscious.

Lakshmi - Or Shri (from the Sanskrit). Hindu goddess of beauty, wealth and happiness; bride of Vishnu, with whom she is often depicted as riding the GARUDA eagle. Symbol: the lotus.

Lamassu - Assyrian-Babylonian guardian spirit in the form of a steer with a human head; guardian of the gates of the city and of the palace; usually depicted as having five legs, such that one could see four legs from any vantage point.

Lamb - Or "sheep." Because of its simplicity and tolerance, and because of its whiteness, it is a symbol of meekness, innocence and purity. Next to the RAM, it was the most common sacrificial animal in antiquity and is thus also a symbol for Christ and His sacrificial death. In Christian art, a lamb amongst other sheep or

LABYRINTHS

Labyrinths were originally two-dimensional, more or less symmetrical patterns whose middles were connected to the exit by disproportionately long, yet clear-cut paths that neither crossed nor left open the possibility of a choice; they were thus distinguished from Meander patterns and angular spirals. Research on labyrinths was long made difficult by the fact that people did not clearly distinguish between the prison given its name by Minotaurus (Ovid, *Metamorphosis* 8, 158 ff.), which is a three-dimensional construction, and the older forms of labyrinths, which are flat (two-dimensional) constructions. Only the latter shall be considered here.

Precursors of labyrinths are already recognizable on the imprints of Mycenaean seals, but amulet fragments from ancient Egypt bearing labyrinth-like figures are also known, as are ones on painted Etruscan vases, which occasionally are interpreted as representations of a womb (the so-called Cretan type). The later so-called Roman labyrinths stand in contrast to these and include the many

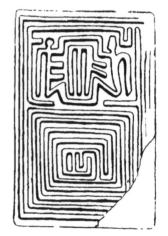

Left: Labyrinth graffiti in Pompeii; the writing reads: "LABYRINTHUS HIC HABITAT MINOTAURUS" ("Labyrinth, here resides Minitaur."); Right: Labyrinth-like amulet from ancient Egypt; it is probably a meander or angular spiral; Below: Etruscan vase painting with a labyrinth figure reminiscent of the much later Nordic form of the Trojan Games

medieval labyrinths as well, which are mostly symmetrical, leave an open space in the middle and are mostly constructed of concentric circles, while the Cretan type is distantly reminiscent of spirals and thereby gives rise to a possible astral interpretation as a symbol of the sun's path.

Labyrinths depicted on the floors of many old churches arose from the Roman labyrinths. The oldest Christian labyrinth is that from the year 324 in the Reparatus Basillica in Orleansville in Algeria. Through the skillful arrangement of letters in the middle, the words *Sancta Ecclesia* could be read more than 3,000 times. Another Algerian Labyrinth (ca. 440 A.D. at Tigziert-sur-Mer), with the christological lamb, forms an open wreath; the entirety of the labyrinth is construed as a symbol of human life with all its trials, tribulations and digressions, and, for this reason, the middle can symbolize the expectation of salvation in the form of Holy Jerusalem. In medieval tradition, religious dance is known as a type of symbolic pilgrimage on the labyrinth floors of Gothic cathedrals (Amiens and Chartres, for example). See ECCLESIA.

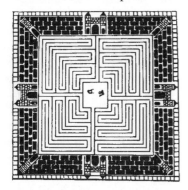 

Above left: Roman floor mosaic labyrinth from Orbe (Switzerland); the edge is 350 cm in length; it dates from circa 200 B.C.; Right: Labyrinth in the form of an octagon in the Cathedral of Amiens; the edge is 520 cm in length. The labyrinth is made of white and bluish-black stones.

Below left: The labyrinth made of white and black marble under the cupola of San Vitale in Ravenna; the diameter is 340 cm; the labyrinth was most probably not laid out until the 16th century. The directional movement, leading from the center toward the periphery, is remarkable. Below right: The preserved church labyrinth in the Cathedral of Chartres; the diameter is between 12.3 meters and 12.6 meters. Together, eleven concentric circles add up to a path that is 294 meters long.

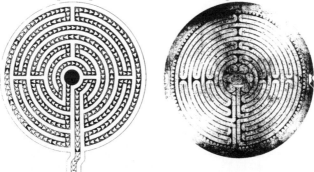

LADY'S SLIPPER
LAMB: The faithful as lambs with a
palm tree as the tree of life in
Schmid's Musterbuch

standing to the side, refers to the Lamb of God that bears the sins of the world. Groups of lambs or sheep also represent the faithful or the church of the martyrs (in which case Christ appears in the role of the Good SHEPHERD). The Last Judgment is sometimes represented as occurring under the image of Christ, who separates the sheep from the he-goats. —The sheep is the eighth sign of the Chinese ZODIAC, corresponding to Scorpio (see SCORPION).

Lameness - A manifestation of weakness or of injury; like BLINDNESS, lameness can also be a symbol of spiritual inadequacy, yet, like blindness, MONOCULARITY, or a hunched back, it can also indicate extraordinary abilities in certain areas (as is the case with witches, sorcerers, and fire gods, e.g. Hephaestus). In Greek mythology, lameness is also frequently a punishment given by the gods for disobedience (Hephaestus is lame because he protected his mother Hera from his father Zeus). —According to folk belief, the devil limps on one foot because he was thrown out of heaven.

Lamp - Frequently a visual representation of LIGHT, which cannot be represented, often with respect to individual spiritual light and the individual spiritual being; the lighting and extinguishing of a lamp can thus signify the birth and death of a person. The lamp was thus also thought of simply as a symbol of life and death, particularly in antiquity. —The clay oil lamp is a symbol of man in various respects: like man, it is made of "mud" and it harbors a sort of "life force" in the form of oil (see OILS); when lit, it appears as the bearer of the spirit, which is represented by the FLAME. —In the Biblical parable of the Wise and Foolish Virgins, the lamp carefully filled with oil is a symbol of spiritual vigilance and readiness. —The placing of burning lamps on graves is a custom common not only in Christianity but in other religions as well, as it refers to respective religious ideas about the divine light in the hereafter.

Lance - Like all weapons, it is a symbol of war and power; moreover, it is a symbol of the sunbeam and of the phallus, and is sometimes also closely related to the symbolic significance of the WORLD AXIS. See SPEAR. —In Christian art, animals that are pierced by lances often refer to vices that must be overcome; for this reason, the personifications of virtues are frequently represented with lances as attributes. In a more restricted sense, the

LANTERN: Lantern from the temple in Nikko, Japan
LAUREL: Laurel wreaths on ancient coins

lance is an attribute of the cardinal virtue of bravery. —The eucharistic use of a small lance in the Eastern Orthodox church refers symbolically to the lance of Longinus, who determined that Christ was dead by stabbing Him in the chest with a lance (the lance of Longinus played a large role during the Middle Ages, such as in the saga of the Holy Grail).

Lancet Window - In the symbolism of ROSE WINDOWS, the lancet window is thought to be masculine, whereas the simple rose (window) is thought to be feminine.

Language - Aside from numerous individual symbolic meanings that are connected with sounds and signs (see ALPHA; ALPHA AND OMEGA; LETTERS; OMEGA; TAU), language as a whole is a symbol of God's creativity; according to many religions, God's word or language was what existed at the beginning of the world; in addition, it is a manifestation of ordering reason that is the immanent basis of all things.

Lantern - To a large extent, the lantern corresponds symbolically to the LAMP. Lanterns are found particularly in Japanese temple and garden settings as symbols of light and mental clarity.

Lapis Lazuli - Because of its blueness and the many little golden speckles within it, it was thought of as a symbol of the starry heavens in antiquity. —In the Orient, it is regarded as a defense against the evil eye.

Lapis Philosophorum - See PHILOSOPHERS' STONE.

Lapwing - Erroneously considered to be an evil bird because it was confused with the HOOPOE.

Larch - A pine-like, deciduous tree found in northern temperate zones. —In Siberia, the world TREE was envisaged as being a larch on which the sun and the Moon, in the form of a gold and silver bird, climbed up and down.

Lark - A bird that ascends vertically into the sky and builds its nest on the ground; it is thus a symbol of the connection of heaven (see SKY) and EARTH.

Larkspur - A ranunculus plant; during the Middle Ages, it became associated with the knightly nobility due to its spur-like flowers and was thus thought of as a symbol of chivalrous virtues; in pictures of Mary, it is also a symbol of the loftiness of Mary as Mother of God.

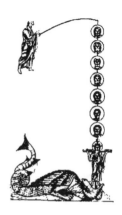

LEOPARD: Maenad with leopard from a bowl, circa 490 B.C.

LEVIATHAN: Catching the leviathan with the seven-part fishing hook of the family tree of Jesse and the Crucified as bait; from Herrad von Landsberg's *Hortus Deliciarum*, 1180

Laurel - Like all evergreen plants, the laurel is a symbol of immortality. —During antiquity, it was thought to be physically and morally purifying; it was attributed with the ability to give poetic inspiration and the power to tell the future; it was also thought to ward off lightning. It was especially sacred to Apollo. —In conjunction with victory parades, the laurel initially appeared due to the powers of purification attributed to it: people wanted to cleanse themselves of the blood that had been spilled in battle; later, it was thought of simply as a symbol for victory and triumph and—with respect to its significance for immortality—as a symbol of the immortality thereby attained; in this respect, it was also used (usually as a laurel wreath) as an award for particular achievements in science and art (especially literature).

Lavender - A simple blossoming labiate flower of the Mediterranean region having a very picant fragrance; since antiquity, it has been used for bathing, and washing and as a remedy. During the Middle Ages, it was sometimes related symbolically to the virtues of Mary.

Lazarus - According to Luke 16:19 ff., Lazarus is a symbolic figure of man who suffers from disease and poverty on earth and who is compensated for this in the HEREAFTER. The account of "poor Lazarus" is a common component of medieval iconography.

Lead - Because of its high specific gravity, lead is a symbol of heaviness as well as of oppressive burden. In antiquity, lead was also thought to have magical powers. In alchemy, lead is identical with Saturn, which is often portrayed as a hunched old man with a SCYTHE or occasionally as a grey drawf. It was thought to make one cold, damp, sick and melancholy; positively, however, it was thought to be close to philosophy and to systematic thought and asceticism generally. —In Christian symbolism, lead occasionally signifies a person burdened with sin. See METAL.

Leaf - The leaf is a general symbol of the plant kingdom, common in the ornamentation of peasant cultures. —In eastern Asia, it is a symbol of happiness and prosperity; a branch with leaves symbolizes the cooperation of individuals in a collective effort. —In Christianity, a three-petaled leaf (see CLOVER) symbolizes the Trinity; a four-petaled leaf symbolizes the CROSS, the four Evangelists or the cardinal virtues; a seven-petaled leaf symbol-

LIGHT: Personification of light; detail from an Alsatian miniature from the 12th century

LIGHTNING: Detail from an illustration of the Revelation of St. John; woodcut by M. Greyff, 1492

izes the gifts of the Holy Spirit. —The fig leaf (see FIG TREE), being the first clothes of Adam and Eve after the Fall, symbolizes bashfulness.

Left - See RIGHT AND LEFT.

Legenda Aurea - An important collection of medieval legends about saints (Legenda sanctorum); its enormous circulation made it the most important source for Christian symbolism and themes for pictures; it served mainly as edification and catered to the religiously tinged thirst for miracles and adventures in continuation of the encyclopedias of the church fathers; over the course of time, its contents were constantly expanded: the oldest handwritten manuscript of 1288 has 182 chapters, whereas the first printing of 1470 has 488. The author was the Dominican Jacobus a Voragine (1228/30–1293), who eventually became Bishop of Genua.

Legume - Symbol of corporeality as the covering of the soul and the mind.

Lemon - In Judaism, the lemon is a symbol of the human heart. During the Middle Ages, it was regarded as a symbol of life and was thought to offer protection against powers hostile to life, such as bewitchment, poison and plague; it was placed in graves and played a customary role in baptisms, weddings, confirmations, communions, etc. During the late Middle Ages, it was regarded as a symbol of purity and was an attribute of Mary.

Lenten Altar Cloth - A large cloth used since the year 1000 to cover the altar during Lent; very common during the 14th and 15th centuries; it was painted or embroidered with small scenes from the Passion or implements of the Passion; originally a white linen cloth, it later appeared in liturgical colors (black, violet, brown) as well.

Leo - The constellation of the LION.

Leopard - Frequently a symbol of wildness, aggression, battle, or pride. —In China, the leopard, in contrast to the sunlike LION, was thought of as a moon-like animal. —On the other hand, it became associated with the light of the morning sun in African myths. —In antiquity, the leopard was an attribute of Artemis and Dionysus; it was regarded as a symbol of strength and fertility and, in this respect, also played a role in the cults of Dionysus and Bacchus; because of its wild leaps, it was also compared with the maenads. See PANTHER.

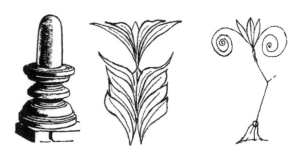

LINGA: Phallic symbol of the Indian god Shiva

LILY: Two lily-like flowers on containers for the bones of a dead person (late Biblical and Mishna age)

Lernaean Serpent - See HYDRA.

Letters - Letters are laden with symbolic meanings in most cultures. Islam, for example, distinguishes between airy, fiery, earthy, and watery letters, each of which, as materializations of the divine word, is a specific bearer of a particular meaning, referring (among other things) to past, present and future. —According to the Cabala, there is a complete system of mystical speculation having to do primarily with the shape of individual letters as well as with their numerical values. —In antiquity, the seven Greek vowels (the vowels "e" and "o" each being represented by two letters) were thought to be symbols of the seven spheres of heaven and of the seven sets of stars moving within them; they were also thought to be symbols of the spirit. In contrast, the consonants symbolized matter. The alphabet—as a combination of vowels and consonants and thus of "spirit" and "matter," and as the entirety of linguistic signs—was felt to be a symbol of wholeness and completion; thus it was also used apotropaically. Its occasional use in early Christianity up until the Middle Ages should probably be understood in this vein as well, since it was sometimes drawn on graves, for example. See AL-PHA; ALPHA AND OMEGA; OMEGA; and TAU.

Leviathan - In Ugaritic myth, Lotan is a many-headed monster of chaos that was conquered at the time of the creation; compare Psalms 74:13 f. According to Job, sorcerers can re-awaken the leviathan and God will not finally destroy him until the end of the world. The monster of chaos is also called *Rahab* or "dragon." —In Psalms 104:26 and Job 40/41, the leviathan is only a huge aquatic animal and creature. Later, though, in the Book of Revelation, the notion of this mythic being serves in the portrayal of Satan (Revelation 12:3 ff.) and of his earthly image, the seven-headed animal that represents world power.

Liber Mundi - See BOOK.

Libra - The constellation of the SCALE.

Lictors' Bundles - See FASCES.

Life, Stages of - Since antiquity, the stages of life have usually been subdivided into different periodic intervals and compared to external periodic intervals, whereby number mysticism plays a role: four stages of life correspond to the four seasons, the four Evangelists or the four

LILY: Kaiser Friedrich I ("Barbarossa") with a lily septer; from a miniature from the *Weltchronik* (Chronicle of the World), Altdorf (today named Weingarten), last quarter of the 12th century

LION: Youthful deity in the rising sun, carried by two lions who symbolize the eastern and western horizons; from an illustration in the funerary papyrus of Heri-uben 21st Dynasty

continents, seven stages correspond to the seven planets or the seven rungs of the ladder or of the wheel of fortune; intervals of three, six and (frequently) ten also occur. See TEN.

Light - Omnipresent phenomenon that is well known to us in its effects but whose essence is largely unintelligible. It is thus a favored symbol of immateriality, spirit, and God as well as of life or happiness. One occasionally encounters a finer distinction between the light of the SUN, which symbolizes inspiration and spiritual vision, and the light of the MOON, which, as reflected light, symbolizes mediate forms of knowledge through rational, discursive thought. —Light is frequently encountered as a border of darkness, which then usually appears as a symbol of ignorance and spiritual dullness, of morally underdeveloped or inferior areas and conditions, of death, misfortune or also of "mystery." —In symbolic thought, the spatial notion of "up" and "down" (see HEIGHT; DEPTH) corresponds to the relation between light and darkness. — Nearly all fundamental principles based on a division of the world into a duality, refer to this distinction of light and darkness, such as Ormuzd and Ahriman, YIN AND YANG, angels and demons, spirit

and matter, masculine and feminine. The idea of an ascent from darkness to light plays an important role for many peoples with respect to the development of humanity as well as to that of the individual; numerous initiation rites are thus based on this duality. —The separation of light and darkness as a postulate of the initial order at the beginning of the world is encountered in the cosmogonies of many peoples. —Mystics sometimes speak of a darkness that lies "beyond" (rather than "beneath") the light of knowledge and that symbolizes the essential incomprehensibility of God. —In the visual arts, the spiritual enlightenment of a person is frequently shown by an AUREOLE, a NIMBUS, or a HALO. See FIRE; SOLAR ECLIPSE.

Lighthouse - In early Christian art, the lighthouse is a symbol of the heavenly harbor into which the soul sails after a dangerous life journey; during the Baroque period, it was a symbol of the exemplary (guiding) Christian life.

Lightning - In many cultures, lightning is regarded as a symbol or expression of divine power that manifests itself as terrible or creative. In the mythological conceptions of many peoples, lightning and THUNDER are originally traced back to

LION: Lion from a Phrygian pitcher
from Gordion (circa 700 B.C. in
Ankara)
LION: Zodiacal image of Leo (from a
medieval woodcut) and the modern
astrological symbol

the highest god (for example, Jupiter/ Zeus, and Indra). —In the Bible, lightning frequently appears in conjunction with the wrath of judgment: the punishing god of fire, of lightning and thunder. —Zeus of antiquity, hurling lightning bolts, can appear as a fructifying, enlightening divinity as well as a punishing one. —Particularly in the Orient, the association of lightning with thunderstorms and rain— and thus lightning's symbolic association with fertility—is emphasized; it can thus clearly have phallic significance as well. —Until modern times in some regions of Asia and Europe, milk offerings were made to lightning to calm it.

Ligure - One of the stones in the breastplate of the high priest (Exodus 28:19 and 39:12); it is usually thought to be jacinth, but it is probably amber or a particular transparent type of amber.

Lilith - Corresponds to the Assyrian Lilitu, a female demon. In Hebrew, she became associated with Laila ("night"). Lilith became a nocturnal ghost.

Lily - The white lily is an old and very common light symbol; aside from this, it is also regarded as a symbol of purity, innocence and virginity, especially in Chris-

tian art (particularly common in depictions of Mary, where, for example, it appears very often in conjunction with the Annunciation by the archangel Gabriel); perhaps this has to do with the sublimation of an originally phallic significance that had been attributed to the lily due to the striking shape of its pistil. A lily protruding from the mouth of Christ in representations of Him as judge of the world is a symbol of mercy. —The Bible speaks of the "lilies of the field" as a symbol of trusting devotion to God. —The lily is also a very old regal symbol and also plays an important role of varying significance in heraldry; for example, it can refer to the patronage of Mary, Mother of God, or, if the three leaves of its blossoms are emphasized, to the Trinity.

Lily of the Valley - A medicinal plant used for numerous ailments; a common attribute of Christ and Mary (sometimes appearing instead of the LILY in depictions of the Annunciation); symbolizes the "salvation of the world."

Lime Tree - The lime tree was venerated as a holy tree by the ancient Germans and the Slavs. It was thought to ward off lightning and to attract diseases to itself when touched. It frequently embodied the cen-

LOCUST: The apocalyptic vision of locusts (detail); from an illustration in the Apocalypse of Saint-Sever, *Satan et les sauterelles*, 11th century

LOTUS: Smelling a life-giving lotus flower; detail from a mural in the Grave of the Night near Thebes, 18th Dynasty

ter of communities or buildings, such as in courts, cemeteries, fountains and villages. —In contrast to the OAK TREE, the lime tree is frequently thought to be feminine.

Lindwurm - (The "radiant dragon") Another term for DRAGON.

Linga - The plural form is lingam. A common sculpted phallus depiction in India that exists as a cult image; it is a symbol of the god Shiva; exists as a naturalistic image and as a truncated column, often on a square base with an eight-sided shaft and a cylindrical capital (sometimes with one or more heads); symbolizes the divine and masculine power of creation and probably also the WORLD AXIS. The feminine counterpart of the linga is the YONI. A linga wound by a kundalini SERPENT symbolizes the power of knowledge; when it appears in conjunction with the yoni, it is (among other things) a symbol of awakening knowledge and of the union of form and matter.

Lion - Regarded as the "king" of the beasts of the earth (along with the EAGLE as "king" of the birds); a very common symbolic animal, usually having significance associated with the sun or a close associa-

tion with light, probably due in part to its strength, its goldish-yellow color and the ray-like mane that surrounds its head. The lion's relation to light is also expressed in the characteristic attributed to it of never shutting its eyes. It is primarily the lion's characteristics of courage, wildness and supposed wisdom that give it its symbolic significance. —As a symbol of power and justice, its likeness is often found on the thrones and palaces of rulers. —In China and Japan, the lion, like the DRAGON, was thought to ward off demons, which is why, for example, it was frequently depicted as a temple guardian. Egyptian, Assyrian and Babylonian temples were also often guarded by lion statues. —In Egypt, one finds depictions of two lions with their backs facing one another, which symbolizes the rising and setting of the sun, east and west, and yesterday and today. —The Indian god Krishna as well as Buddha are compared with lions. —Especially in antiquity, the lion, due to its tremendous strength, was also closely related to gods of fertility and love, such as Cybele, Dionysus (Bacchus) and Aphrodite (Venus). —The Bible frequently mentions lions; they are encountered in a positive and a negative symbolic sense: God is like the lion in His power and justice; the tribe of Judah is compared with a lion;

Christ Himself is called "the lion of Judah"; on the other hand, though, the devil is also associated with a rapacious lion. —The Middle Ages—PHYSIOLOGUS, for example—saw the lion as a symbol of the resurrection of Christ, partially because of the view, recounted by numerous authors, that the lion is born dead and is awakened to life after three days by the breath of its father. Depictions of roaring lions can also refer to the resurrection of the dead on Judgment Day. — Medieval depictions of the mighty lion that show the lion eating people or other animals, are also related to its negative, threatening aspect: they are usually symbols of pernicious, menacing or punitive powers. The lion's strength is similarly negative in depictions or mythological stories of lion battles or hunts, in which the lion, as a representative of untamed wildness, is conquered by heroes (Heracles, Samson). —The winged lion is an attribute and symbol of Mark the Evangelist (see EVANGELISTS, SYMBOLS OF). —Usually with respect to its strength, the lion frequently appears in heraldry on coats of arms and holders of coats of arms. —The lion or LEO is the fifth sign of the zodiac and corresponds to the second month of summer; the sun passes the sign between July 23 and August 22; Leo is the house of the sun; since the time of Hellenistic astrology, Saturn, Jupiter and Mars (Pluto) have been its decans; the sun, Jupiter and Mars have been its decans in Indian astrology. The triplicity of Leo is fire; Leo is masculine, positive (active) and a fixed sign. The name "lion" as a constellation can be found even in Babylonian sources.

Lion Dogs - Similar to the Assyrian-Babylonian LAMASSU, lion dogs are guardian animals on Japanese temples; they are symbols of stamina and vitality.

Lion's Throne of Solomon - Representation of the throne of Solomon usually having twelve lions on the side; during the Middle Ages, it was thought of as the Sedes Sapientiae, the seat of wisdom embodied in Ecclesia and Mary.

Little Gallows Man - See MANDRAKE.

Little Rose of Mary - The LYCHNIS plant, a symbol of Mary.

Liver - Among various peoples, the liver was regarded as the seat of vitality, of desires, of rage, yet also of love. People believed that they could use animal livers to predict the future (liver reading), which gave rise to an elaborate system of interpretation primarily in Babylon, but, for example, among the Etruscans as well. — Eating liver was supposed to enable one to counteract spells.

Liverwort - As a curative plant, it is a symbol of Mary in the symbolism of the Christian Middle Ages; because it has three leaves, it is also a symbol of the Trinity.

Living Creature - See TETRAMORPH.

Lizard - Because of its fondness for the SUN, the lizard is closely related to the symbolism of light and the sun. It often appears as a symbol of the soul that seeks LIGHT (of knowledge, of God, of the hereafter) and is often encountered in this context on Greek graves and urns as well as in Christian art. Representations of Apollo as a lizard killer (sauroktonos) also derive from this meaning: it symbolizes the longing to die by the hand of the god of light and to pass through death into the light of the hereafter. —The Middle Ages drew a connection between the longing for Christ and the subsequent alleged ability of the lizard (as reported in PHYSIO-LOGUS, for example) to regain its sight in its old age by slipping into a crack in a wall that faces eastward and looking un-

flinchingly into the rising sun: so should man, whose inner eye threatens to grow dark, look toward Christ as the sun of justice. —The lizard's annual shedding of its skin also made it a symbol of renewal and resurrection. —The lizard sometimes has negative symbolic significance in hot countries, where its frequent appearance coincides with periods of heat and drought.

Locust - Especially the migratory locust, which in great swarms destroys whole tracts of land by eating them barren, is a symbol of voracity and destruction. In the Old Testament, the plague of locusts that befalls Egypt is a scourge sent by God (see EGYPTIAN PLAGUES). The vision of locusts in the Book of Revelation is interpreted either as a symbol of heretics or as a vision of demonic powers. —In China, the occasional rapid increase in the number of locusts was sometimes seen as a manifestation of a disturbance of the cosmic order, yet, in earlier times, as a symbol of bountiful progeny and thus of happiness and prosperity, perhaps because the locust's quadruple moulting was seen as a symbol of the soul.

Locust Tree - See ACACIA.

Loin Cloth - As a protection from feelings

of shame, the loin cloth is often a symbol of masculine or feminine dignity among some primitive peoples. See NAKEDNESS.

Lord's Supper - Depicted in Christian art since the 5th century. Pre-forms: ancient banquet scenes (see BANQUET) with respect to Eucharistic symbolism. The basic types of the Lord's Supper are that of a ceremonial liturgical administration of bread and wine and that of the historical event according to the Biblical account.

Lorelei - See SIRENS.

Lotus - An Egyptian and Asiatic variety of water lily; plays an important role as a symbol in Egypt, India and eastern Asia. Since it closes its flower in the evening, draws back into the water, and does not re-surface and open up again until sunrise, it is an old light symbol; as a white, blue or red flower rising from slimy waters, the lotus flower is a symbol of purity's overcoming of impurity. —In Egypt, the lotus, which carries the sun within itself, was thought to have arisen from the primeval waters and was thus also a symbol of the genesis of the world from wetness; thus, it was especially associated with the sacred, life-giving Nile.

It was an attribute of various deities, was used in burial and sacrificial rites, and played an important role in the architecture and ornamentation of temples. The fragrance of the blue, aromatic lotus was thought to be rejuvenating. —The lotus is rich in symbolism in Buddhism and Hinduism as well (see LAKSHMI). Like the world EGG, the bud of the lily flower floating upon the primeval waters is thought of as a symbol of the entirety of all as yet unrealized possibilities before the creation of the world (in isolated instances, it is also a symbol of the human heart); the opened blossom is a symbol of the creation. The eight-petaled lotus flower is a symbol of all cardinal directions and thus also a symbol of the cosmic harmony; in this respect, it is frequently encountered as a meditation sign. Brahma is usually depicted as sitting on a lotus leaf; Buddha is usually depicted as sitting on or coming out of a lotus flower. The "jewel in the lotus" (*mani padme*) is Nirvana that is already latently present in the world. The thousand-petaled lotus flower is regarded as a symbol of the entirety of all spiritual revelation. In India, one also frequently distinguishes between the reddish lotus flower as a symbol of the sun and the bluish one as a symbol of the Moon. —The association of the lotus

LYRE: Orpheus with a lyre; from a crater from Gela, circa 450 B.C.

or water lily with ideas of purity extends into the European Middle Ages in a somewhat alienated form: because its seeds and roots were thought to be agents for quieting sensual urges, they were recommended to monks and nuns as a medicament.

Love Slaves - Famous men from the Bible, antiquity or German medieval epic poems who let themselves be fooled by women's wiles; the symbol of Christian love and chastity, namely, the virgin with the UNICORN (see HORTUS CONCLUSUS), is often contrasted with the consequences of earthly love.

Lucifer - 1) Or "Luciferus," the highest angel who opposed God (see DEVIL). —According to ancient German notions, it is he who brings the fire of the devil. 2) Phosphorus (luciferous), the planet VENUS as the morning star.

Lunar Eclipse - See SOLAR ECLIPSE.

Lure - A northern European form of a wind instruments, depicted even in cave drawings; see TRUMPET.

Luxuria (Lust) - Feminine personification of one of the seven deadly sins, riding on a swine or a ram; symbols include mirrors and the Sirens.

Lychnis - A common meadow flower in Europe and northern Asia that has rosy red bright blossoms; in Christian art of the Middle Ages, it is a symbol of Mary.

Lynx - Probably because of its rusty red coat, it was usually a symbol of the devil in medieval symbolism. Because it was attributed with being able to look through the walls of buildings and rooms, it is encountered in depictions of the five senses as a personification of sense of sight.

Lyra - Strictly speaking, it is the Greek LYRE; next to the kitara, it is the most important stringed instrument of Greek antiquity; it is strung with seven strings. See HARP.

Lyre - A symbol of divine harmony and of the harmonic connection between heaven (see SKY) and EARTH. —The lyre is an attribute of the Greek god Apollo as well as a common symbol of music and poetry in general. —The sounds of the lyre were sometimes thought to have magic effects (as in the myth of Orpheus), especially ones that calmed wild animals. —In the Bible, harp-playing often appears as an expression of thanks to and praise of God.

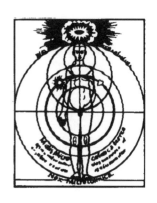

MAGNET: A magnet draws nails from
a ship; woodcut, 1509

MAN: Man as microcosm with regions
of light and shadow; from an
illustration in Roberto Fludd's
Utriusque Cosmi Historia, 1619

Macrocosm - The universe with its stars, planets and signs of the zodiac; the world in its entirety. Its opposite is the MICRO-COSM, which is the world in its particulars, particularly man. See MICROCOSM-MACROCOSM.

Magic - Among those who lived at the dawn of history, among primitive peoples, and in folk belief, magic is comprised of those practices commonly used to achieve beneficent results (white magic) or to cause harm (black magic) by means of secret powers and the entreaty of spirits and higher powers. Magicians (witches, medicine men, shamans) derive their abilities from animals, natural objects and spirits; their sometimes extraordinary strength is also based on special subconscious psychological forces in the sense of depth psychology and parapsychology. One must distinguish among magic used for defense, fertility, healing, injuring, weather, etc., where concentrated thought, magic formulas and spells, gestures, songs, dances, trance, ecstasy, mimetic actions (see ANALOGY, MAGIC OF), efficacious material objects (see IMAGE MAGIC), certain accoutrements (noise-

makers, wands, figurines, masks), etc., are employed; in black magic, a person's hair, fingernails and toenails, etc., are used *pars pro toto*.

Magic Squares - Quadratic arrangements of whole numbers in such a way that the sums of files, ranks, and diagonals are equal to one another; they played an important role as early as in ancient mathematics—also in the Far East. —In astrology, a particular magic square was associated with each planet, which is why one speaks of "planet seals." Magic squares having 3 (9 total numerals), 4 (16 total numerals), 5 (25 total numerals), 6 (36 total numerals), 7 (49 total numerals), 8 (64 total numerals), and 9 (81 total numerals) numerals on each outer edge, were of particular importance; as planet seals, they corresponded to Saturn (*Sigilla Saturnis*), Jupiter (*Sigilla Jovis*), Mars (*Sigilla Martis*), the sun (*Sigilla Solis*), Venus (*Sigilla Veneris*), Mercury (*Sigilla Mercuris*) and the Moon (*Sigilla Lunae*). The Jupiter square became especially well known because it was used by Albrecht Dürer in his famous etching *Melencolia I* (see MELENCOLIA). In conjunction with the symbolism of numbers and letters (see NUMBER SYMBOLISM), number squares could also be written in letters. Yet genuine letter squares

MANDALA: Two basic types, schematized

in the sense of the SATOR-AREPO FORMULA must be distinguished from these. Magic squares were once viewed as an expression of the harmony between the astral world and that of the "magician" and were reflected in ideas about the MICROCOSM-MACROCOSM.

Magnetite - Magnetite was called *lapis amoris* during antiquity because it, like love, signifies God's attraction to His creations; it was thus also called lapis gratiae (stone of mercy), such as in PHYSIOLOGUS. —A fable handed down from antiquity and very common during the Middle Ages, tells of a magnetic mountain in the sea that drew all passing ships toward it due to their iron parts and caused them to wreck upon it; it was thought of as a symbol of the sin upon which the SHIP of life must wreck if it is not oriented toward Mary, the STARFISH.

Magpie - In medieval art, the magpie frequently signifies evil, persecution or early death, especially when it appears with an OWL in depictions of the Nativity.

Maiestas Domini - In Christian art, it is a symbolic depiction of the eternal glory of the exalted Christ: frontal representation of an enthroned Christ who is surrounded by a MANDORLA, has a raised right hand, and holds the BOOK OF LIFE in His left hand; frequently surrounded by the symbols of the Evangelists (see EVANGELISTS, SYMBOLS OF) or the twenty-four elders of the Apocalypse.

Mallow - Or "hollyhock." A plant found in northern temperate zones and used as a remedy. Even in ancient times, the leaves of the mallow were thought to be a sign of a plea for forgiveness; in Christian art, the mallow is sometimes found to have the same significance.

Mana - In Melanesian and Polynesian belief, mana is a mysterious, supernatural force that people strive to harness and to use to control animals, plants and things.

Mandala - An ancient Indian term for "CIRCLE"; later, the word primarily signified circular or polygonal Indian religious meditation signs that were abstract or interspersed with sculptured elements; the mandala symbolically represents religious experiences and is supposed to assist one in achieving union with the divine through meditation. —C.G. Jung interpreted mandalas as individuation symbols and also found mandalas in the

MAGIC SQUARES

Of the infinitely large number of magic squares, those of the form n^2 (n = 3-9) play a special role.

The two-part magic square cannot be constructed due to mathematical reasons and is thus assigned to unordered chaos. In contrast, the other squares from 3 to 9 are assigned to the plants, the sun and the Moon in the Chaldean order (Saturn, Jupiter, Mars, sun, Venus, Mercury, Moon).

The origin of magic squares should possibly be sought in India; they probably came to Europe via Arabia.

Saturn square (left) and sun square (below) in ancient Chinese depictions (the "modern" number notations are below each of the Chinese squares)

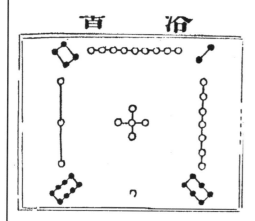

4	9	2
3	5	7
8	1	6

Saturn square in Hebrew letters

27	29	2	4	13	36
9	11	20	22	31	18
32	25	7	3	21	23
14	16	34	30	12	5
28	6	15	17	26	19
1	24	33	35	8	10

1 (Venus square)

22	47	16	41	10	35	4
5	23	48	17	42	11	29
30	6	24	49	18	36	12
13	31	7	25	43	19	37
38	14	32	1	26	44	20
21	39	8	33	2	27	45
46	15	40	9	34	3	28

2 (sun square)

6	32	3	34	35	1
7	11	27	28	8	30
19	14	16	15	23	14
18	20	22	21	17	13
25	29	10	9	26	12
36	5	33	4	2	31

3 (Jupiter square)

16	3	2	13
5	10	11	8
9	6	7	12
4	15	14	1

4 (Mars square)

17	24	1	8	15
23	5	7	14	16
4	6	13	20	22
10	12	19	21	3
11	18	25	2	9

5

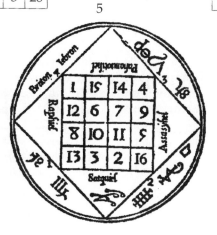

6 (Saturn square)

2	9	4
7	5	3
6	1	8

7 (Moon square)

37	78	29	70	21	62	13	54	5
6	38	79	30	71	22	63	14	46
47	7	39	80	31	72	23	55	15
16	48	8	40	81	32	64	24	56
57	17	49	9	41	73	33	65	25
26	58	18	50	1	42	74	34	66
67	27	59	10	51	2	43	75	35
36	68	19	60	11	52	3	44	76
77	28	69	20	61	12	53	4	45

8 (Mercury square)

1	63	62	4	5	59	58	8
56	10	11	53	52	14	15	49
48	18	19	45	44	22	23	41
25	39	38	28	29	35	34	32
33	31	30	36	37	27	26	40
24	42	43	21	20	46	47	17
16	50	51	13	12	54	55	9
57	7	6	60	61	3	2	64

1) Venus square; 2) sun square; 3) Jupiter square; 4) Mars square; 5) Jupiter square by A. Kirchner (1652); 6) Saturn square; 7) Moon square; 8) Mercury square

MANDORLA: Christ in a mandorla;
from a miniature, pontifical of
Chartres, beginning of the 13th
century
MANDRAKE: Mandrake from *Hortus
sanitatis*, German, 1485.

dream symbolism of modern man that correspond to Asiatic ones.

Mandorla - An almond-shaped AURE-OLE, having the symbolic meaning of the ALMOND. Since early Christian times, it has been used primarily for representations of the glorified Christ and Mary.

Mandragon - The root of the MANDRAKE plant.

Mandragora - The root of the MANDRAKE plant.

Mandrake - Term for the root of the mandragon or mandragora plant, a nightshade plant that, according to popular belief, grew underneath a gallows from the sperm of hanged men (the root was therefore frequently called "little gallows man"). The rootstock has a turnip-like, frequently forked shape often reminiscent of the shape of a person. Since antiquity, the mandrake has had many uses as a medicinal agent and a charm, and as an aphrodisiac and a narcotic before operations. In Egypt and among the Hebrews, for example, it was thus regarded as a magical, efficacious symbol of love and fertility due to its effects as an aphrodisiac and narcotic. In the Song of Solomon

7:13 and Genesis 30:14, "love potion" or "love plant" refers to the mandrake, as the Hebrew name *duda* means love plant.— According to popular belief during the Middle Ages, the mandrake was attributed with the power to bring happiness, fertility and wealth. Since then, the word is often used in this sense, especially in proverbial sayings. See ELECAMPANE; GINSENG; MOLY.

Manito - Among the Algonquin Indians, manito is the mysterious force and magical power living in things, sometimes personified as the Great Spirit.

Manna - The miraculous food that fell from heaven for the children of Israel during their trek through the desert; according to Talmudic tradition, manna was created during the evening of the sixth day of creation. It is a symbolic designation for any supernatural food. It has also been interpreted by Jewish and Christian authors as a symbol of the Logos.

Mantled Bamboon - See APE.

Marabou - See STORK.

Marguerite - Or "meadow daisy." A member of the Compositae family having radiant white blossoms; as the name mar-

MARIONETTE: Miniature from Herrad
von Landsberg's *Hortus Deliciarum*
MASK: From New Guinea

---

guerite indicates (Latin *margarita* means "pearl"), the plant was compared with the PEARL and thus also with tears, yet also with spilled drops of blood. On Christian panel paintings of the Middle Ages, it thus frequently refers to the deaths and sufferings of Christ and the martyrs.

Marian Plants - Plants that, because of their shapes, characteristics or fragrance (or combinations thereof), are supposed to symbolize Mary, such as AGAVE, ARNICA or LYCHNIS, COLUMBINE, LARKSPUR or ROSE, LILY or TANSY, and MARIGOLD

Marian Wheat Dress - In symbolism pertaining to Mary, this is the Biblical depiction of Mary wearing a dress that is decorated with patterns shaped like heads of wheat (a variant shows Mary standing in a wheat field); based on the Song of Solomon 7:2, they made their appearance in German nunneries in the 14th century.

Marigold - A member of the Compositae family having yellowish-gold to orange colored flowers in a radial arrangement. In popular parlance, it is also called "sun bride"; it is an ancient medicinal plant; it is found on Christian panel paintings of the Middle Ages as an attribute of Mary and a symbol of salvation.

Marriage - See WEDDING.

Mars - From the Greek "Ares." In ancient mythology, Mars is the god of war and keeper of fields. —In terms of astronomy and astrology, Mars is the reddish shimmering planet that was already known in antiquity and that dominates the night sky at times of optimal visibility. —Mars is IRON in alchemy and METAL in astrology.

Masculine-Feminine - See YIN AND YANG; LIGHT.

Mask - From the Arabic. Facial coverings made of various materials that make the wearer unrecognizable and transform him into the embodiment of that which is represented. Cultic, magical ideas are the basis of everything having to do with masks. Wearers of masks embody the gods and demons that appear at ceremonial masked dances when conjurations, hunting spells and initiation rites are performed. Masks are also often signs of a secret society. The function of nearly all masks is to frighten, which is why they usually have grotesque, terrible features, often mixed with human, animal characterisitics. —Theater masks on the sarcophagi of late antiquity allude

MAPPA MUNDI

In a more restricted sense, *mappa mundi* refers to the graphic representation of the inhabited (habitable) world, whereby close connections exist with the notion of the IMAGO MUNDI; the world is experienced not only as a geographical space, but also as a well-ordered cosmos.

The world is T-shaped, divided according to the sacred number 3 into Asia, Europe and Africa. Jerusalem, specifically Holy Jerusalem (see JERUSALEM, HOLY), was placed at the intersection; Eden, as the second important and distinguished location, lies in the east or, as in some variants of the mappa mundi, at the top. In mappa mundi representations, the shape of the world can be spherical (like the IMPERIAL ORB, for example), yet it can also be disk-shaped or rectangular and flat. Many maps typically show the primary winds, which usually number twelve, a reference to the fact that the original naming of the directions in antiquity was based on the winds. Many people believe that this eight- or twelve-fold subdivision of the circumference (of the horizon!), such as the one also found in the signs of the zodiac, derives from the naming of the primary directions of the wind.

The demise of ancient and medieval world maps came when Jerusalem no longer lay at the center and Eden no longer lay at (or "behind") the edge or in the north; unknown and unexplored regions became populated with HYBRID CREATURES or FABULOUS CREATURES of all types.

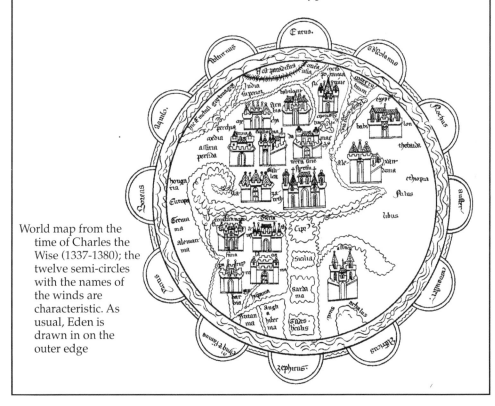

World map from the time of Charles the Wise (1337-1380); the twelve semi-circles with the names of the winds are characteristic. As usual, Eden is drawn in on the outer edge

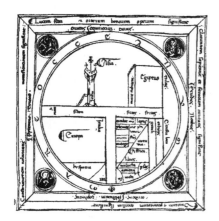 

Two types of T-maps: left, a map from a Sallust manuscript from the 14th century; right, the first printed world map (1472), a T-map in the tradition of the church father Isidor von Sevilla from the end of the 6th century

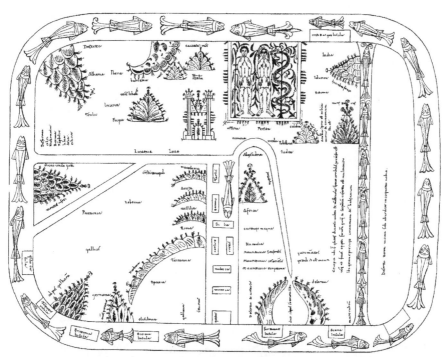

The world map of the Benedictine monk Beatus ("Beatus map") from the year 787. The rectangular world is surrounded by the world sea; this special type of world map, which is also basically a T-map, was made up into the High Middle Ages

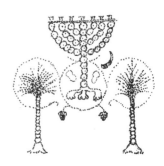

MÉLUSINE: A winged, fish-tailed mermaid, leaving her husband's castle after a breach of confidence

MENORAH: Variation of the prophetic motive in synagogue mosaic in Máon: candlestick with two date trees

---

to the "drama of life." —Today, masks are often thought of as symbols of the ego hiding behind an artificial face.

Materia Prima - See HERMAPHRODITE; MERCURY; PHILOSOPHERS' STONE; WATER.

Maya - See VEIL.

Mead - A fermented (see FERMENTATION) drink made of HONEY and WATER; in ancient Germanic mythology, it is the drink of gods and heroes. The intoxicating effect was sometimes interpreted as being a sign of the conveyance of divine powers onto men.

Megalith Civilizations - From the Greek and Latin. Cultural groups of the Neolithic period in Western and Northern Europe, named after MEGALITHIC GRAVES. The megalithic style of building also existed in the Mediterranean region and exists (or existed until recently) in large areas of Africa, Asia, America and Oceania.

Megalithic Chambers - Rectangular megalithic graves of various sizes that have been sunk into the ground and capped with stone slabs. In the Neolithic

Age and northwestern European Bronze Age, they were at first used for mass burials, yet, later, for individual burials as well.

Megalithic Graves - Pre-historic graves made of large unhewn or roughly cut slabs (see DOLMEN) or blocks of stone; often covered with a mound; usually mass graves or graves containing kin.

Melencolia - Or "Melancholia." The name of the famous etching by Albrecht Dürer; iconographically, it is regarded as the visual culmination of a humanistic apology of human freedom of the will and of virtuous striving for knowledge that establishes an elaborate relation between mathematics, astronomy, and astrology (such as PLATONIC SOLIDS, MAGIC SQUARES) a relation that ultimately leads to a divine unity.

Melon - Like most fruits that have many seeds, it is a fertility symbol.

Melothesia - An attribution system in MICROCOSM-MACROCOSM thought, according to which the members and organs of the human organism (microcosm) are correlated with the members of the universal organism (macrocosm). See CORRELATIVE; DOCTRINE OF SIGNS.

MEGALITHS

"Megaliths" is a general term for circular, elliptical or linear constructions erected by members of MEGALITH CIVILIZATIONS from large stones (see DOLMEN; MENHIR) that were often transported long distances. To this day, they give rise to the most widely varying speculations that run from their being centers and symbols of the Druid cult, to pre-historic sites for observing the sun, Moon and stars by means of ingenious systems in order to forecast eclipses and to construct calendars. Of all possibilities so far suggested, these conclusions of archeo-astronomy are the most likely, even if some questions are still open, such as the question of how current knowledge is interpreted *into* theories concerning these sites (see STONEHENGE). PASSAGE GRAVES of the same time, which are oriented according to the heavens, are also included among the megaliths; they are especially common in northern Europe, yet also—like all other megaliths—in most peripheral areas of the Mediterranean (such as on Malta).

Bibliography: S. von Reden. *Die Megalith-Kulturen*. Köln, 1978.

R. Müller. *Der Himmel über dem Menschen der Steinzeit*. Berlin, Heidelberg, New York, 1970.

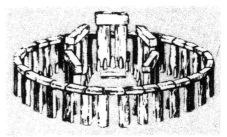

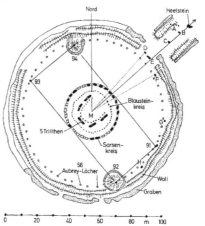

MEGALITHS: Above: The circle of stones at Stonehenge. Reconstructive drawing of the entire site, with a schematic outline below

MEGALITHS: Left: Tumulus near Rhives (Hebrides). The placement is related to the calendrical date of Lammas or Samhain.

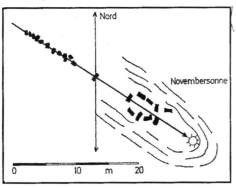

MERCURY/HERMES: Mercury/
Hermes as Sun-Moon
hermaphrodite, standing on Chaos,
which appears as a sphere; from
Mylius's *Philosophia reformata*, 1622

METALS: The seven wandering stars of
antiquity (Mercury as the seventh in
the center), which were associated
by the alchemists with certain
metals

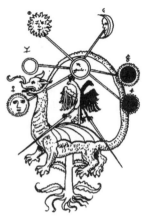

Mélusine - A mermaid who was the wife of a human; leaves her husband (who originally, according to French legend, was probably a nephew of the Count of Poitiers) and returns to the sea; one of the numerous HYBRID CREATURES of the Middle Ages; was regarded as a herald of calamity.

Menhir - From the Celtic, meaning "long stone." An upright stone that often probably has cultic significance, usually from the late Neolithic period; it is possibly a common phallus symbol in the broadest sense and thus also a symbol of power and protection; perhaps also associated with the symbolism of the WORLD AXIS. See MEGALITHS.

Menorah - From the Hebrew. The seven-branched CANDLESTICK in the temple; one of the most frequently portrayed Jewish motifs and the oldest symbol of the Jewish people. See HANUKKAH LAMP.

Mercury - Ancient Roman God of trade (later identified with Hermes). Name of the planet closest to the sun; in alchemy, Mercury is the sign for quicksilver (the earthly counterpart of the planet) and for *materia prima* (primeval matter) as well as

for the PHILOSOPHERS' STONE. Next to SALT and SULPHUR, mercury is considered in alchemy to be one of the "philosophical" elements and world principles; it represents the ephemeral (spiritus). In contrast to the "masculine" planets sun, Mars, Jupiter and Uranus and the "feminine" planets Venus, Saturn and Neptune, Mercury was interpreted as HERMAPHRODITE; it thus played an important role as a symbol of all practices of alchemy that mediate opposites. See HERMES.

Metals - Their symbolic significance is ambivalent; the working of metals (see SMITH) was frequently seen in conjunction with hellfire. On the other hand, the extraction of metals from ores and their refinement were a symbol of purification and spiritualization. —In certain metals, the alchemists saw earthly correspondences to the individual planets, which were thought of as the seven wandering planets of antiquity. —Because of metal's "subterranean" character, C.G. Jung saw metal as a symbol of sexuality in need of purification. —The common custom at initiation rites (including those of Freemasonry) of disposing of all metal that one is wearing as a sign of cleansing or of renunciation of all earthly possessions, refers to the negative symbolic signifiance of metal.

MILK: The Egyptian king is suckled
by Isis, who appears in the form of
a sacred tree; grave of Tuthmosis III

METALS: Metals: Scheme of alchemistic
correlations between metals and planets:

Sun = gold

Moon = silver

Mercury = quicksilver (in antiquity, steel
and pewter)

Venus = copper

Mars = iron

Jupiter = pewter (in antiquity, brass or
electrum)

Saturn = lead

Meteorite - See STONE.

Mica - Or "selenite." See GLASS.

Microcosm - The world in its particulars.
Its opposite is the MACROCOSM. Since
Boethius, the microcosm has been a term
for man as a "mirror of the world." According to Hildegard von Bingen, Gior-
dano Bruno, Leibniz, and many others
(particularly during the Renaissance, such
as Agrippa von Nettesheim), the microcosm is also a term for the human soul.
See MICROCOSM-MACROCOSM.

Microcosm-Macrocosm - The parallel between MICROCOSM and MACROCOSM;
probably very old, having existed in the
ancient Near East: "that, which is below,
is equal to that, which is above, is equal
to and corresponds to that, which is

above." (See CORRELATIVE; MELO-
THESIA; DOCTRINE OF SIGNS; ANAL-
OGY, PRINCIPLE OF) Microcosm-
macrocosm thinking probably originated
in ancient myths, according to which "everything" was supposedly formed out of
a single pre-temporal being. The alleged
parallel is one of the most important basic ideas in astrology and in many areas
of alchemy, having persisted from antiquity ("Tabula smaragdina"), through the
mystical-symbolic thinking of the Middle
Ages (as with Hildegard von Bingen and
Agrippa von Nettesheim), into modernity
(as with Boehme, Goethe and Novalis),
and up to present forms of esoterica. Microcosm-macrocosm thinking had a decisive influence on symbolism in antiquity and in the Middle Ages.

Midday and Midnight - Like the summer
and winter solstices, midday and midnight are temporal turning points that
have been attributed with special significance since antiquity; in China, they are
thought to be the highpoints of the YIN
AND YANG influences. —In esoteric
thinking, midnight is often the time of the
highest position of the spiritual (in contrast to the physical) SUN and is thus connected with contemplation, spiritual
knowledge and initiation. In folk belief,

MICROCOSM-MACROCOSM

The church father Gregory the Great (540-604) said, "Homo quodammodo omnia," "in a certain way, man is everything." Man, the microcosm, is also a macrocosm, a complete, yet small universe carrying within himself the inanimate order of minerals, the animate order of plants and animals, and the mental, the spiritual order that is common to men, the angels and God. Petrus Damiani (1007–1072), a church father, states even more emphatically: Man is named "microcosm," or "world in miniature," after a Greek word because he is composed in his material being of the same four elements as the universe.

Up into modernity, man, the microcosm, always stands in the foreground; only the surroundings or the zodiac in its variously depicted forms constitute the macrocosm, as was the case even with Robert Fludd (1574–1637).

1

3

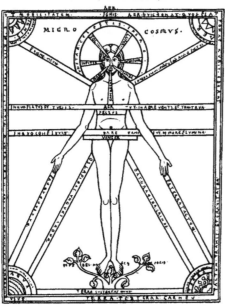

2

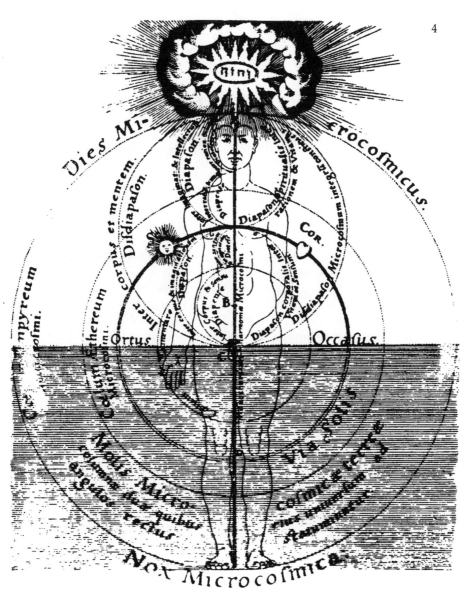

1 The man who stretches out his arms feels that he is the center of the world (fresco from Pedret, Catalonia)

2 Man as microcosm is subject to the influences of the four elements and the planets; the seven planets have their effect through the four openings of a person's head (from a pen and ink drawing from the *Glossarium Salomonis*, Prüfening, circa 1160)

3 Man is subject to the influences of the signs of the zodiac (zodiac man according to a French woodcut). Melothesia, or the correlation of the zodiacal figures to individual organs and body parts, has remained nearly unchanged since earliest antiquity.

4 Man as microcosm from R. Fludd's *Utriusque Cosmi Historia* (1617); all aspects of microcosm-macrocosm thought are included here.

MILKY WAY: The genesis of the Milky Way and of lilies from Hera's milk; V. Cartari, 1647

midnight is commonly thought of as the "bewitching hour" during which it is easiest to establish contact with spirits and lost souls. The hour of midnight and that of bright midday, when no shadows fall, are often the hours of mysterious decision in fairy tales. In antiquity, the summer midday heat was thought of as the hour of Pan.

Middle - As the center from which everything proceeds, it is a symbol of God or of the divine (sometimes also as the midpoint in the structure of pictures). —The middle of the world (see WORLD AXIS) was often thought of as a holy MOUNTAIN, a TREE, or a NAVEL.

Midgard Serpent - See SERPENT.

Milk - As the first and most nutritious food, milk is a symbol in many cultures of fertility, mental and spiritual nourishment and immortality. Because of its color and its mild taste, it is often associated with the MOON, which, in contrast to the sun, radiates a soft, white light. —In some areas of Asia and Europe, there was a prevalent notion that LIGHTNING or fires started by lightning could be extinguished only with milk. —According to Indian cosmogonical ideas, the world in the very beginning was a sea of milk that

was turned into BUTTER, the first food of living creatures, by a giant whisk or whiplashes (see WHIP). —Christian art, which is fond of portraying the Mother of God as nursing (*Maria lactans*), distinguishes between the good mother, who gives the milk of truth, and the evil one, who suckles SERPENTS at her bosom. — Milk in conjunction with HONEY appears in antiquity as well as in the Old Testament as the essence of the most precious divine gifts and of the blessed life (compare, for example, the Promised Land, in which milk and honey flow). Milk and honey thus played an important role in various ancient mysteries; in customs of the early Christian church, milk and honey also appear as a liturgical symbol and were given to neophytes at their first receiving of the Eucharist as a sign of the promise of salvation.

Milky Way - In the religious ideas of many peoples, the Milky Way is a link between our world and a transcendental one; it was compared with a white SERPENT (such as in American Indian cultures), a RIVER, FOOTPRINTS, poured MILK, a TREE, an embroidered garment, etc. Sometimes (such as in the Orient and among the ancient Germans), it was thought to be a path upon which the souls of the deceased

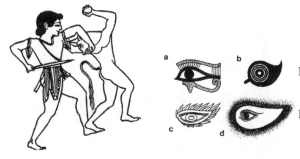

MINOTAUR: Theseus killing Minotaur; from a depiction on a Greek plate
MIRIBOTA: a) Ancient Egyptian eye; b) eye in Greek vase painting; c) eye from Burma; d) white eye make-up of a Tembu girl (South Africa)

had to wander after their death; some primitive peoples thought of it as a dwelling place of the dead. In Japan, India and Egypt, the Milky Way was seen as the river of a fertile land on whose banks gods lived. —Among some peoples, it was closely associated with the symbolic significance of the RAINBOW. —It was also sometimes thought of as a tear in the celestial vault through which heavenly fire shone into our world.

Millet - Originally a very common type of folk food; in China, it was regarded as a symbol of the fertile earth and the natural order.

Mill, Mystical - A medieval allegory that illustrates the relation of the Old Testament to the New Testament: the wheat of the Old Testament is ground by the mystical mill to flour, from which the bread of life of the faithful is made.

Mimosa - A weed, bush or tree with double-pinnated leaves. The leaves of the *Noli me tangere* (touch-me-not) variety fold together at the slightest touch; the mimosa is thus a symbol of sensitivity and bashfulness. —The yellow-flowered mimosa (often identified with the genuine ACACIA) is a symbol of light and of the certainty of salvation.

Minotaur - A HYBRID CREATURE of Greek mythology having the body of a human and the head of a steer; held captive by Minos in a LABYRINTH, the Minotaur was there fed Athenian boys and virgins annually or every nine years and was finally conquered by Theseus with the help of the THREAD of Ariadne. A symbol of dark, destructive powers working in secret. Sometimes also identified with the symbolic significance of the CENTAUR.

Mint - See PEPPERMINT.

Miribota - A term suggested by O. Koenig for a type of decoration that can be thought of as a "ritualization of the eye" (the EYE considered as a primeval symbol); known throughout the world by the most various names and for the most varied uses, from rug patterns to tie patterns.

Mirror - With respect to the replicative and "reflecting" function of thought, the mirror is a symbol of knowledge, self-knowledge and consciousness as well as of truth and clarity. It is also a symbol of creation, which "mirrors" the divine intelligence; it is a symbol of the pure human heart that, for example, God (in Christian mysticism) or Buddha-nature

MIRROR: Depiction of vanity in
 Sebastian Brant's *Narrenschiff* (*Ship
 of Fools*), Basel, 1494
MOLOCH: Illustration from
 Athanasius Kircher's *Oedipus
 Aegyptiacus*, Rome, 1652

assimilates. One also encounters the proverbial comparison of the eye or face as
the mirror of the soul. —Because of its clarity, the mirror, as an indirect source of
light, is a symbol of the sun, yet also of
the Moon; because of its passivity, it is a
symbol of the feminine; in China, it is also
a symbol of the contemplative, inactive
wise man. —In Japan, where the mirror is
a symbol of the perfect purity of the soul
as well as of the sun goddess, there are
holy mirrors in many Shinto temples. —
Because it appears similar to the surface
of water, it is used in rain magic as a symbol of water among some black African
peoples. —In the graphic arts of the
Middle Ages and the Renaissance, the
mirror appears as a symbol of vanity and
lust as well as of prudence and truth. In
medieval art, it also occurs as a symbol of
the virginity of Mary, in whom God "mir-
rored" His image in the form of His son.
—In the folk beliefs of various peoples,
the mirror was attributed with an apotropaic effect.

Mistletoe - Was often thought of as a defense against disease, lightning and sorcery, as a bringer of good luck and, since
it is an evergreen, as an immortality symbol; plays a significant role primarily in
Celtic customs, such as at the new year.

Mithra - From the Greek. Indo-Iranian god
of light, originally the keeper of the cosmic
and legal order; beginning in the 5th century B.C., Mithra existed as a synthesis of
Iranian and Greek religious elements that
became the "mysteries of Mithra"; initially
encountered in the East, Mithra was found
in the Roman Empire beginning in the 2nd
century A.D. With the Christianization of
the Empire came the decline (complete by
the 5th century) of the cult, which was open
only to men. The places of worship were
usually caves (*Mithraeum*). Fundamental
tenets of astrological systems were disseminated by the Mithra cult.

Moderation - The cardinal virtue of
TEMPERANTIA.

Moirai - Greek goddesses of fate who,
through their actions, symbolize the ca-
price of fate; according to Hesiod, they are
the daughters of Zeus: Clotho, the spin-
ner of the THREAD of life; Lachesis, the
appor-tioner of lots; and Atropos, the cut-
ter of the thread of fate (see SCISSORS).
They were identified by the Romans with
the Parcae.

Moloch - Originally a Canaanite god to
whom human sarcifices were offered.
Later, he was a general symbol of authori-

MONEY: Money-shitter of Goslar
MONOCULARITY: The blinding of
  one-eyed Polyphemus; ancient
  Greek vase picture, 6th century B.C.

ties that corrupt or destroy humans, especially inhuman political systems.

Moly - An herb that protected Odysseus from being enchanted by Circe. Probably should not be thought of as a botanically identifiable plant, but rather as a symbolic one. See ELECAMPANE and MANDRAKE.

Money - Money as such is a symbol for economic goods in the broadest sense. — Like GOLD, money (as the abstract form of all earthly goods, as it were) is also interpreted as a symbol of worldly attachment or ambition. —As a minted coin (like the SEAL), it is sometimes a symbol in Christianity of the devout soul that bears within itself the image of God (just as coins bore the emperor's image). —In the view of psychoanalysis, money is closely related to EXCREMENT.

Monk's Robe - Or "cowl." In monastic tradition, it is usually a symbol for poverty, detachment from the world, membership in a religious community; in Christianity, it is interpreted symbolically with reference to the baptismal gown.

Monocularity - Like BLINDNESS, LAMENESS, or a humpback, monocularity is usually a sign of a certain limitation, but it is also an indication of capabilities of a specific kind, frequently for extraordinary, primitive strength (as in the cases of Polyphemus and the Cyclopes) as well as for divine knowledge (as in the case of Odin).

Monolith - From the Greek. A large block of stone, upright (see MENHIR), cut as a monument (pillars, COLUMNS, OBELISKS, stelae) or part of a structure.

Monster - Monsters are often probably the personification of anxieties (see, for example, CERBERUS) relating to the external world as well as to threatening aspects of one's own mind. —In the Bible (see LEVIATHAN), monsters are embodiments of the order opposed to God. — They are often encountered in sagas and fairy tales as a keeper of treasure or a robber and guard of a maiden who must be fought and conquered; from a psychoanalytical point of view, this can be interpreted as a symbol of the trials and tribulations on the path of the development of one's personality. See FABULOUS CREATURES; HYBRID CREATURES.

Monstrance - From the Latin *monstrare*, meaning "to show." Also called an

MOON: Luna with a torch and horn, walking on clouds, with two wheels and the zodiacal sign Cancer; woodcut, 15th century

MOON: The Moon as the feminine principle (Luna); Vatican, 15th century

"osten-sorium." A container, usually finely crafted, consisting of a foot, a shaft with a carrying knob (*nodus*), and a showcase in which the host, born by the lunula (a crescent-shaped holder), is displayed on the altar. The shape of the monstrance varies from suggestions of sun, Moon and tree symbolism to wreath symbolism. As a symbol of the church, the monstrance has taken a partial position alongside the CHALICE since the 16th century.

Moon - In the geocentric system of ancient astrology and astronomy, the Moon is thought of as a normal planet; in the heliocentric system of modern astronomy, the Moon is the celestial body closest to the earth. The path of the Moon around the earth and the rhythmically changing phases of the Moon have been important bases of the calendar since the beginnings of astronomical observation, insofar as the month is in harmony with the sun and the year. —In astrology, the Moon, like the sun, is simply called "light." —The Moon plays an important role in the magical and graphic symbolic thought of most peoples. In this regard, it is especially important that the Moon appears to "live" due to its constantly changing shape, that it is apparently associated with various life

rhythms on the earth, and that it became an important fixed point in the measurement of time. In the ancient Orient, it thus often played a more significant role than the SUN. Among many peoples, it was revered as a god or (usually) goddess (such as among the Greeks, who knew it as Selene, and among the Romans, who knew it as Luna). —Because of its "waning" and "waxing" and its influence upon the earth (especially upon the female body), it has been associated with female fertility, rain, moistening, and with all becoming and passing in general since time immemorial. —Among some peoples, there were certain rites that were supposed to strengthen or rescue the Moon during the phase of the new moon or lunar eclipses, which were thought of as weaknesses of and threats to the nocturnal heavenly body. —In contrast to the self-luminescent sun, which is usually interpreted as being masculine and is closely related to the Yang principle (see YIN AND YANG), the Moon usually appears as a symbol of that which is gentle, in need of support, and feminine, and is usually associated with the Yin principle. In contrast to this, one sometimes encounters the notion of the Moon as a(n) (old) man (in German-speaking lands, for example). In many myths, the Moon appears

MOTHER CULT: One of the "mother goddess statues" of the El-Obeid civilization (Iraq, circa 4000 B.C.)

as a sister, woman or lover of the sun. In astrology and in depth psychology, the Moon is thought of (among other things) as a symbol of the unconscious, of fertile passivity, and of receptivity. See CRESCENT MOON; HARE; MILK.

Morning Star - The morning star, like the EVENING STAR (see HESPERUS), is a term for the bright planet Venus, yet, in contrast to the evening star, it refers to Venus's position in the morning (see PHOSPHORUS). As the herald of the new day, it is a symbol of constant renewal or of eternal recurrence, of light triumphing over night. In Christianity, it is thus a symbol of Christ or Mary.

Mother Cult - The cultic-religious worship of mother deities (such as Demeter, Isis, Cybele, Ma), usually in connection with fertility cults; mother cults were particular common in the Near East and influenced Greco-Roman and ancient Germanic cults.

Mourning Veil - See VEIL.

Mouse - In contrast to the other mouses, the shrew was revered as a sacred animal among the Egyptians. —White mice were regarded by the Romans as a sign of good luck. —Folk belief of the Middle Ages saw mice as embodiments of either witches or of the souls of the deceased; white mice, in contrast, were sometimes thought to be embodiments of the souls of unborn children. Infestations of mice, on the other hand, were frequently thought of as a punishment by God.

Mouth - As the organ of speech and breath, the mouth symbolically embodies the power of the spirit and of the creator, especially the "inspiration" of the soul and of life; as the organ of eating and swallowing, it is also a symbol of destruction, especially the mouths of monsters (the "bottomless pit"). —The mouth-opening ceremony performed on mummies in Egypt was supposed to enable the deceased to speak the truth before the gods and to enable the deceased to eat and to drink again. —In paintings of the Middle Ages, small, black demons coming from a person's mouth signify evil words and lies. Christ as judge of the world frequently appears with a SWORD or a sword and a LILY coming from His mouth.

Mouth Opening - See MOUTH.

Moth - As a BUTTERFLY that is irresistably drawn to LIGHT and carelessly burns

MOUNTAIN

Three basic viewpoints and symbolic meanings are joined together in the idea of a mountain; they constantly overlap with one another, each viewpoint being more or less clearly contained in the other two.

In nearly all cultures, mountains represent a connection between earth and sky, between microcosm and macrocosm; this is also (especially) true of artificially created "mountains" such as the Babylonian ziggurats, the Indian stupas, the Egyptian or ancient American pyramids, and the Christian churches and cathedrals that so often crown mountains or lend them their characteristic appearance.

As in the case of the LADDER, the connection between heaven and earth is thought of symbolically as the possibility of spiritual ascent and of the higher level of development thereby arduously acquired. Regarded in this manner, the mountain is the path of ascent for earthly beings, the path to closeness to God; for non-earthly beings, it is the path to earthly beings, if they want to intervene in earthly events. Everywhere in the world—often hidden by clouds or covered forever with ice—there are holy mountains that were regarded as the homes of the gods and the place where spiritually important events originated: the Chinese emperors made sacrifices on mountain tops; Moses, the "man of the moun-

The woodcut by Agricola shows the search for metals within the mountain; notable for the depiction of people using divining-rods

tain," received the tablets with the Ten Commandments on Mt. Horeb; Mesopotamian and Aztec priests made sacrifices on the highest platforms of their "simulated mountains," the ziggurats or pyramids. Yet Western legends of emperors also have the symbolic desire of not thinking of the hero or ruler as dead, but rather as only waiting within the mountain ("retreat into the mountain") and always ready to help. This is the case with King Arthur or Frederick Barbarossa, for example, to name just a couple. A long beard growing through a table is regarded as a symbol of magic sleep....

In the cosmologies of many peoples, the Holy Mountain constitutes the center of this world, the center that symbolizes absolute reality, the image of the world, the place of crossing. This center of the world (see NAVEL of the world, *omphalos*) is often illustrated in the IMAGO MUNDI as a pyramid-shaped mountain or a post: the vertically aligned mountain can be symbolically thought of as the axis of the world, an image strengthened by the apparent observed rotation of the starry heavens around a fixed point in the celestial vault. According to this view, a tree, the world tree, can take the place of the mountain.

Finally, the Holy Mountain can be placed on a par with the temple. Indeed, in a roundabout manner, the WORLD AXIS can also be associated with the temple, whereby the altar can be thought of as a Holy Stone. And, finally, caves can also be associated with mountain symbolism. The fear, prevalent among many people up into modern times, of setting foot on the untouched summit of the highest mountains, is associated with the fear of setting foot on the numinous. If one considers the multifarious symbolism of mountains, then it is self-explanatory why the alchemists construed the inner mountain as the site of the PHILOSO-PHERS' STONE in their system.

Bibliography: P. Huber. *Heilige Berge*, 1982, Zürich–Einsiedeln–Köln.

Moses receiving the harvest laws on the mountain top; woodcut by Holbein the Younger

Moses receiving the Ten Commandments on Mt. Horeb; the "neighboring" Mt. Sinai is the resting place of St. Catherine. Woodcut by W. Waltersweyl illustrating caravan of pilgrims to the Cloisters of Catherine

MOUTH: The Egyptian king Ay conducts the mouth opening ceremony on his deceased predecessor Tutankhamen (represented as Osiris); detail from a mural in Tutankhamen's grave

MRA: The written name of Mary in an illustration from Schmid's *Musterbuch*

up in it, the moth is a symbol of the soul's mysterious, self-sacrificial, selfless love for the divine light.

MRA - Like the name of Jesus (see CHRIST, MONOGRAM OF; IHS), the name of the Mother of God, Mary, is also rewritten in abbreviated form and, like the name of Jesus, was the object of particular devotion during the Baroque period. The form MRA is the most common one, often surrounded by rays and having a crown over it. In Byzantine art, the abbreviation MP ΘY was common (Greek MHTH ΘEOY, Méter Theoú, meaning "mother of God").

Mugwort - A member of the Compositae family of plants. Various types of mugwort were thought of as bridal flowers and were thus associated with Mary, the heavenly bride. See WORMWOOD.

Mulberry Fig - See SYCAMORE.

Mulberry Tree - In China, the mulberry tree was associated with the rising SUN. Arrows that were shot from a bow made of mulberry wood in all four cardinal directions were supposed to drive off evil influences.

Mullein - A plant commonly found in Europe, Africa and Asia; it was already being used as a medicinal plant in ancient times; supposedly protects one from fear and harm. —During the Middle Ages, it became associated with Mary.

Mundus - In ancient Roman symbolism, the mundus was the center of the ordered world or of a city. See NAVEL.

Muses - In Greek mythology, the Muses are deities of the arts and sciences, daughters of Zeus and Mnemosyne or of Uranos and Gaia. They dwelt in Pieria east of Mount Olympus (Pierian Muses), on Mount Helicon in Boeotia (Boeotian Muses) and on Mount Parnassus near Delphi (Delphic Muses), which often lay near springs and streams. Originally, they numbered three, but they appear as a group of nine sisters as early as in Homer, whereby each one was accorded a particular function of artistic endeavor, usually attached to a symbol, albeit one that could change. The invocation of the Muses when beginning an artistic work was a practice cultivated by poets in Homeric times and was later practiced in places of intellectual life, such as in schools, philosophers' circles, and the like. —The Romans identified the Muses with the Camenae.

MULLEIN

MUSSEL: Birth of Venus from a
mussel; from Botticelli

MUSES: The Nine Muses
 Erato (erotic poetry)
 Euterpe (lyric song)
 Calliope (epic song)
 Clio (history)
 Melpomene (tragedy)
 Polyhymnia (sacred songs)
 Terpsichore (dance)
 Thalia (comedy)
 Urania (astronomy)

Mushroom - Especially in China, mushrooms are a symbol of long life (possibly because they can be kept in dry storage for a long time). Mushrooms supposedly grow only in peaceful and orderly times, and are thus also a symbol of prudent statecraft. —In some areas of Africa and Siberia, mushrooms were also interpreted as being a symbol of the (newly born) human soul.

Musical Instruments - Of the great number of string, wind, and percussion instruments, the BELL, GONG, HARP, LYRE, ORGAN, SHOFAR and TRUMPET are especially laden with symbolic meaning.

Mussel - As an animal that lives in the sea, the mussel is frequently an attribute of sea deities. The mussel was sometimes symbolically associated with the MOON (and thus with the Yin principle), such as in China. —As "she who rose up from the foam of the sea" (anadyomene), Aphrodite is sometimes portrayed as standing on a mussel. It might have become associated with Aphrodite (and in India with Lakshmi, the goddess of happiness and beauty) because of the fact that the mussel is shaped like the female sex organ, because it shares in the symbolism of the fertile WATER of the SEA, and because the beautiful PEARL grows within it. —In Christianity, the mussel, as an object placed in a grave, symbolizes the grave from which man will rise from the dead on Judgment Day. The mussel became a symbol of Mary because Mary carried Jesus, the "precious pearl," in her womb and because it was believed during the Middle Ages that the mussel was fertilized "virginally" by dew drops. The mussel shell became a symbol of the Holy Sepulchre and the Resurrection and thus a sign of all pilgrims; the mussel shell was usually worn on the pilgrim's hat. The Jacob Mussel became a sign particular to pilgrims on the pilgrimage to Santiago de Compostela.

Myrrh - A resin of various types of balsam trees and bushes. Because of its fragrance and its beneficent and curative effect, myrrh played an important role in Indian, Oriental, Jewish and Christian cults; it was, among other things, an ingredient of the holy anointing oil of the Israelites; in the Bible, it is mentioned as one of the gifts of the Three Kings. Because of its bitterness, its medicinal efficacy and its use in the mummification of corpses, it is frequently associated symbolically with the Passion and death of Christ as well as with the penance and asceticism of faithful Christians.

Myrtle - An evergreen tree or bush with white flowers found in warmer regions; for the Jews, myrtle was a symbol of divine grace, peace, and joy. —In antiquity, myrtle was sacred to Aphrodite and was thus a love symbol; as an evergreen plant, it was also a symbol of immortality. In contrast to the LAUREL that adorns the victor after bloody battle, the myrtle wreath was a symbol of victory gained in a bloodless manner. —The myrtle wreath for brides was already a common sign of joy among the Jews; in antiquity, brides decorated themselves with wreaths made of roses and myrtle, which referred to Aphrodite, the goddess of love and marriage. Today, the myrtle bridal wreath is frequently a symbol of virginity.

Mystical Mill - See MILL, MYSTICAL.

Mystical Winepress - See WINEPRESS, MYSTICAL.

Myth - From the Latin *mythus*. A history or story about the deeds of gods and spirits and about the effect of these powers in heaven, on the earth and in the underworld. These mythic events, recounted as actual occurrences outside of real time, are supposed to reaffirm temporal events by their own recurrence and to trace those events back to divine actions. There are various types of myth based on their content: theogonic myths (pertaining to the origin of the gods); cosmogonic myths (pertaining to the origin of the cosmos and its conditions for existence), which are often connected with anthropogonic myths; primeval myths, which treat the conditions of human life with respect to established extra-temporal orders; soterio-logical myths, which tell of salvationary divine assistance; and eschatological myths, which treat the end of the world. — Myths are often handed down in the form of images and live on—often in transmuted form—as symbols.

NAVEL: The Omphalos of Delphi

Nails - In medieval Christian art, nails are part of the symbols of the implements of the Passion; during the High Middle Ages, four nails were usually depicted; beginning in the 13th and 14th centuries, only three nails were usually depicted. —Nails can also be part of the WORLD AXIS around which the universe rotates.

Nakedness - Since time immemorial, nakedness has been symbolically equivocal; with respect to the clearly apparent sexual appeal of the body, nakedness (thought of negatively especially in the Biblical, as opposed to the Greek, tradition) is a symbol of seduction and lust; it is often a component of love-spell practices and is also an element in the questioning of oracles and in sooth-saying. —As openness and honesty, it is a symbol of purity and truth (compare the proverbial phrase "the naked truth"). —The nakedness of Adam and Eve in Eden is a symbol of their innocence before the Fall. —As the renunciation of CLOTHING (which, for its part, can be a symbol of worldly attachment), nakedness is also a symbol of asceticism; as a reminder that we were all born na-

ked, it is a symbol of unconditional subjugation to the will of God. —On the other hand, condemned criminals were sometimes stripped of their clothing as a sign of the loss of their social position. See VEIL.

Narcissus - A widely common amaryllis plant; in Greece, it became symbolically associated with sleep (presumably because it draws back into a bulb after it blooms and sprouts again early the next year as one of the most striking flowering plants). It was planted on graves as a sign of the kinship between death and sleep. It was sometimes also thought of as a symbol of spring and fertility. —Because of its straight stem, it is sometimes a symbol among the Arabs of the upstanding person who acts in accordance with God's commandments. —In medieval art, it is sometimes a symbol of Mary (probably because of its lily-like appearance).

Nard Oil - See VALERIAN.

Nativity Scene - Scenic depiction of the story of the birth of Christ, often having movable and luxuriously clothed figurines on a set that is constructed like a stage. Nativity scenes were probably inspired by the spiritual plays of the Middle

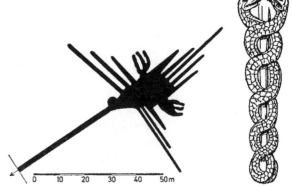

NAZCA LINES: A fabulous animal flying toward the point where the sun rises at the summer solstice (in the direction of the arrow)

NEHUSHTAN: Serpent staff from the cult vase of the Sumerian prince Gudea

0	10	20	30	40	50m

Ages and gradually broadened to include other Biblical scenes (adoration of the Magi, for instance). The earliest nativity scene in a church was at Naples (1478); they were introduced to Germany by the Jesuits in the 16th century. Popular nativity scenes in houses have existed since the 17th century, especially in southern Germany, the Tyrol and the Erzgebirge; isolated depictions of the Passion of Jesus also exist as so-called Lenten mangers.

Navel - In the myths of various peoples, the navel is a symbol of the center of the world from which creation is supposed to have originated. The omphalos of Delphi is famous; it is a cylindrical stone with a rounded top that was also a symbol of the connection between the realms of the gods, of man, and of the dead. —The pole star is sometimes thought of as the navel of the sky around which the heavens seem to rotate. —Contemplation of one's navel as a meditation on cosmic and human basic principles is found in Indian yoga and occasionally in the Eastern Orthodox church as well.

Navel Contemplation - See NAVEL.

Nazca Lines - A series of lines, often in the shape of geometric figures or giant animals and humans, that were found around 1939 in the high desert approximately 400 kilometers south of Lima; the lined constructions were made by "tilling" the upper layers of soil by up to thirty centimeters in depth and thereby exposing the lighter colored topsoil. The meaning of the Nazca Lines is debated; perhaps they are astronomical sighting lines of up to six miles in length that served to point out the rising and setting of stars (calendrical construction); perhaps they could also be cosmological-mythological figures (extending up to 300 meters) or replicas of constellations. They are thought to have been made in the time between the 5th century B.C. and the 13th century A.D. (perhaps by members of the Paracas/Nazca civilization).

Nehushtan - The name of a cult object (composed from the Hebrew words *nahash*, meaning serpent, and *nehoshet*, meaning "brazen") that was worshipped in Jerusalem and was traced back to Moses, but that was nevertheless deemed a heathen idol and destroyed by Hezekiah (II Kings 18:4).

Ner Tamid - From the Hebrew. The lamp that constantly burns in front of the ark in synagogues; prescribed in Exodus 27:20 f.

NER TAMID
NET: Apostles as fishers; ceiling panel in Zillis

Nest - A symbol of security and quiet; in medieval art, birds in nests often symbolize the peace of heaven.

Net - A symbol of extensive interconnectedness; yet it is primarily a symbol of catching and gathering. Oriental deities were sometimes portrayed with nets that they used to bring people down or draw them in. —In Iran, on the other hand, man (primarily mystics) appears as equipped with a net that he uses to seek God. —In the New Testament, the net appears as a symbol of the workings of God; in addition, it is associated with the apostles, the "fishers of men," as an allusion to the occupation of fisher. In this respect, a net with FISH can also be a symbol of the church. —According to depth psychology, fishing with a net can also be a manifestation of an active discourse with the subconscious.

Night - In contrast to DAY, night is a symbol of mysterious darkness, of the irrational, of the unconscious, of death, yet also of the protective and fertile maternal womb. The OX can symbolize the night on the capitals of Roman columns. See MIDDAY AND MIDNIGHT.

Nightingale - Because of its sweet, yet la-menting song, the nightingale is a symbol of love (especially in Persia), yet also of longing and pain. —In antiquity, its song was regarded as a good omen. —Folk belief frequently sees it as a damned soul, but also as the herald of a gentle death. —In Christian symbolism, it is a symbol of the longing for heaven.

Nimbus - In ancient and Oriental art (especially painting), the nimbus is a circular or oval disk or corona around the head of a god, hero, or saint; it possibly represents the SUN or a CROWN; it is a symbol of divinity, sublimity, enlightenment or sovereignty. See HALO; MANDORLA.

Nimrod - According to the legend mentioned in Genesis 10:8 and Micha 5:6 (the particulars of which are unknown), Nimrod was the hero, hunter, and founder of the Assyrian-Babylonian empire. Perhaps the Babylonian war god Ninurta was the basis of the legend of Nimrod.

Noli Me Tangere - See MIMOSA.

Norns - In Germanic mythology, the Norns are the three goddesses of fate, Urth, Verthandi and Skuld, interpreted as past, present and future. They are thought to be sisters who, in contrast to the gods,

NINE

9	The number 9 is the second power of 3: $3^2 = 3 \times 3 = 9$, the amplification of the sacred 3; this is the reason why the Kyrie eleison in the Roman Catholic liturgy is repeated nine times and why there are 9 choirs of blessed spirits; 9 plays an important role in Indo-Germanic and Central Asian mythology as well, as in the case of the 9-storied pagoda, which is a symbol of heaven.
19	During the Christian Middle Ages, 19 was thought of as the sum of 12 (signs of the zodiac) and 7 (planets), or $12 + 7 = 19$; the symbolic meaning is probably derived from the so-called Metonic cycle, which ties 19 solar years with 6140 (almost exactly 235 synodical lunar months) and is the basis of the ancient Greek lunar calendar that was known even in Babylon.
39	A symbolic number that probably arose by "underestimation" of the Jewish "taboo number" 40: by doing something (such as tasks on the Sabbath) only as many as 39 times, people did not come into conflict with the upper limit of 40.
49	As the square of the sacred number 7, it is seen as being especially efficacious, or $7^2 = 7 \times 7 = 49$; in the New Testament, it is the number that follows the coming of the Holy Ghost to the disciples; in Jewish thought, 50, when thought of as $(7 \times 7) + 1 = 50$, refers to the stillness of God.
99	The total of the digits of the number 99 yields $9 + 9 = 18$, which, in turn, yields $1 + 8 = 9$, whereby a striking characteristic of 9 is revealed. According to the symbolism of letters and numbers, AMEN (in Greek letters) corresponds to the sum 99, because $A = 1$, $M = 40$, $E = 8$ and $N = 50$, or $1 + 40 + 8 + 50 = 99$. In Islam, the rosary has 99 pearls, which is either a reference to the 99 Most Beautiful Names of Allah or a reference to the 99 names of the prophet Mohammed.

Above right: The nine steps to the holy city in Raymundus Lullus's mystical world view. Below left: According to Islamic world view, the universe is made up of nine spheres. Right: Corresponding to the nine spheres of the world, which proceed out of the sky from the symbol of the three-headed serpent and come together in the earth, are the nine Muses. Athanasius Kircher, 1650

NIGHT: Detail from: Day and Night as a Winged Spirit; mosaic depicting Genesis, San Marco, Venice, beginning of 13th century

NILE HORSE: The Egyptian goddess Thoueris, in the form of a Nile horse, propped up on the hieroglyph "protection"; statuette made of green schist, 26th Dynasty

know fate not only in part, but in toto. The Norns live on the banks of the spring Urdarborn next to the world ash tree and bring humans fortune and misfortune, whereby Skuld also determines the end of life, or death; the Greek MOIRAI and the Roman Parcae are similar.

Nose - In literature, the nose is sometimes encountered as a veiled symbol of the penis.

Numbers - In most cultures and religions, numbers are the bearers of symbols having rich, often complicated meaning that is today by no means apparent. Numbers were often regarded as the manifestation of cosmic and human orders or of the harmony of the spheres (Pythagoreans). Even numbers were often thought of as being masculine, bright or good, the odd ones as feminine, dark or evil. The interchangeability of numbers and LETTERS occasionally played a role (such as in the Cabala). Certain numerical relationships were often heeded in architecture, sculp-

ture, painting, music, literature and in sacred and profane customs, as in the case of the Golden Section. —In the process of assigning symbolic meanings and specific numbers, considerations of number theory also often played a role, considerations that, for their part, were associated with the counting system in question.

Nut - Or "walnut." Symbolically, the nut corresponds to the ALMOND to a large extent. —In Christian literature (mostly according to St. Augustine), the nut is sometimes mentioned as a symbol of man: the green covering as a symbol of the flesh, the hard shell as a symbol of the bones, and the sweet kernel as a symbol of the soul. As a symbol of Christ, the bitter tasting covering represents the flesh of Christ that suffered the bitter Passion, the shell represents the wood of the cross, and the kernel, which nourishes and whose oil gives light, represents the divine nature of Christ. —In pictures of the Madonna, the nut often plays the role of a fertility symbol.

NUMBER SYMBOLISM

The idea that numbers have symbolic (magical) significance is very old; it probably existed even in Mesopotamia, and is closely related to the development and modification of MICRO-COSM-MACROCOSM thought. Periodic cosmic events (the changing of day and night, the phases of the moon, the cycles of the year and the planets) as well as the Babylonian sexagesimal system, with its great number of divisors of the number 60, possibly played a role; it is also striking that many symbolic numbers were yielded by multiplication, yet hardly any by division; this, too, is possible evidence of a Babylonian origin, because the Babylonians did not divide, but rather multiplied with reciprocal numbers.

Number symbolism enjoyed its first flowering among the Pythagoreans and their successors; other flowerings of note were those at the time of Cabalism and in medieval speculations on magic.

Odd numbers are thought of in number symbolism as being active, masculine, "high striving" and as representing things limited; in modern notation, they are expressed as $2n + 1$ (where n is any number equal to or greater than 0).

Even numbers are thought of in number symbolism as being passive, feminine (because they can be divided into 2 equal parts), "receptive" and as representing things unlimited; in modern notation, they are expressed as $2n$ (where n is any number greater than 0).

Prime numbers are numbers that cannot be divided by even or odd numbers without leaving a remainder; they are divisible only by 1 or by themselves;

Where is the symbolism of a number explained?

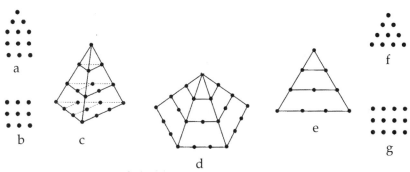

Examples of figured numbers:
a - Pentagonal number; b- quadratic number; c- pyramid numbers; d- pentagon
numbers; e - triangle numbers; f - triangle number; g- rectangular number

they play a somewhat important role only up to 19 (such as 2, 3, 5, or 7), and higher ones play only a minor role; it is generally the case that their symbolism is more complex if they are larger. 1 is not regarded as a prime number. It is striking that 2, 3 and 5 should be the primary factors upon which the numbers of the sexagesimal system are based.

Zero plays a subordinate role in number symbolism, which suggests that zero, as a number, was integrated into the numerical order relatively late (with the place system of counting).

Multiplication increases the "effect" of a number if that number is multiplied by another symbolically important number; in this regard, 2, 3, and 5 and their exponents are especially important: $2^2 = 2 \times 2 = 4, 2^3 = 2 \times 2 \times 2 = 8,$ $3^2 = 3 \times 3 = 9, 3^3 = 3 \times 3 \times 3 = 27, 5^2 = 5 \times 5 = 25.$

Diagonal addition, or mystical addition, is also important in number symbolism. 374, for example, is thought of as the sum of $3 + 7 + 4 = 14$, 14 yielding the diagonal sum $1 + 4 = 5$, 5 being a symbolic number.

Number-letter symbolism is an im-

An example of number/letter symbolism: The Greek word for dove, "peristerá", and alpha and omega have the same numerical value, 801; thus, they can be represented alternately by that numerical value.

portant operation that is based on the fact that Hebrew and Greek letters also have numerical value; in Greco-Roman antiquity, Cabalism, and medieval magic (gematria), the alternating interchanges of letters and numbers, often together with diagonal addition, yield an almost unfathomable number of numerically symbolic interpretations.

The linking of (arithmetic) numbers with (geometric) figures has played a role ever since the beginning of number symbolism, as in the case of figured or polygonal numbers. MAGIC SQUARES must also be seen in this regard.

Especially in esoterica, number symbolism has endured into modern times in the form of numerology, usually offering completely wild speculations.

Bibliography: F.C. Endres, A. Schimmel. *Das Mysterium der Zahl*. Köln, 1984.

NUMBER SYMBOLISM IN ISLAMIC MYSTICISM

Number	Geometrical Correspondence Static	Dynamic	Macrocosm	Microcosm
1	•		**Creator** The One, The Eternal	**Creator** The One, The Eternal
2	•——•		**Intellect** inherited, acquired	**2-Part Bodies** left, right
3	△		**Soul** plant, animal reasonable	**Structure of Living Creatures** 2 extremities, 1 truck
4	□	⊗	**Matter** Primeval Form Physical Form Artificial Form	**Four Humors** Phlegm, Blood Yellow gall Black gall
5	⬠	⛤	**Elements** Ether, fire, air, water earth	**Five Senses** Sight, hearing, touch, taste, smell
6	⬡	✡	**Bodies** over, under, before, behind right, left	**Six Movements** up, down, forward, backward, toward the right, toward the left
7	⬡	⛤	**Universe** 7 visible planets 7 days of the week	**Activities** attraction, repulsion nourishment, digestion, growth, preservation of life, formation
8	⬡	⛤	**Qualities** cold, dry, cold, wet warm, wet warm, dry	**Qualities** cold, dry cold, wet warm, wet warm, dry
9	⬡	⛤	**Constituents of the World** minerals, plants animals, three main divisions of each	**Nine Elements of the Body** bones, brain, nerves, veins, blood, flesh, skin, nails, hair

HEART: *Lao-tzu's Disciples Pray to Buddha*—this painting from the eighteenth century on a heart-shaped mulberry leaf contains many symbols that relate to one another: in ancient China, the mulberry tree was associated with the rising sun and the heart; the heart and Buddha, as "true suchness, the timeless," stood in the center of learned discussions (our picture), with statements like "the heart is the 'truth,'" or "when nature unites with knowledge (consciousness), there is the concept of 'heart,'" or "if one makes one's heart big, then it can embody the things in the world ... But the Holy One exhausts nature ... Whosoever exhausts his heart, knows nature." In Chinese thought, the heart, because of its central location in the body, becomes the vehicle of functions that "comprehend the entire universe ..."

MICROCOSM-MACROCOSM: *Man in the Microcosm* (Vision II of Hildegard von Bingen, described by H. Schipperges):

The microcosm as a naked man stands in a circle of air that surrounds the earth and extends with its limbs to the system of the spheres, which, for their part, are surrounded by the macrocosm with outstretched arms (the double-headedness is remarkable: God the Father or Christ?): "With widely open arms, He who first lived surrounds the entire cosmos in His love and goodness and thus carries in His heart the large and the small world with all its elements. In the middle of the world, man stands on his earth."

MONSTER: In Mathis Nithart Gothart's (aka Grünewald) *Temptation of Saint Anthony*—our
picture shows a detail from the so-called Isenheim altar in Colmar—the large
congregation of horrifying hybrid creatures represents the personification of anxieties,
symbols of the trials and tribulations that the father of Christian monasticism had to
endure and overcome.

Yet the demons also symbolize the hell-fire that threatens to consume the sick who were
afflicted with "Anthony fire" when they ate contaminated grain and suffered a terrible
death.

ROCK PAINTING: Magic hunting sorcery is presumably the mythological background of
these cave pictures from the Mtoko cave in south Rhodesia, which were done, some of
them several thousand years ago, by bushmen. Important European discovery sites are in
France and Spain.

Rock pictures — their existence from the most various epochs of history and from nearly all
regions of the inhabited world has been shown in our time — almost always operate on
the level of the magical, thereby usually constituting a preliminary stage of the complex
language of myth or symbol. For that reason, rock pictures and etchings have also been
called the language of the absent; they are means of communication, thoughts and words
made visible.

ROSE: One of the most magnificent depictions of the rose in the Christian Occident are the
rose windows, which can also be interpreted as symbols of the sun, especially when they
are part of Gothic churches.

Our illustration shows the rose — which is also called an "alchemist's rose" — on the north
side of Notre Dame in Paris; its construction is based on the symbolic meaning of the
number 16 (it is regarded as a symbol of Christian perfection); in the innermost circle, the
prophets of the Old Testament are depicted, the kings and judges in the next circle and the
kings and high priests in the outermost circle. They all surround the Virgin Mary with the
baby Jesus in the center.

In Dante's *Divine Comedy*, the rose is often a symbol of love and of the creation—of the
creation as a sign of divine love: the circles of heaven as roses, corona, ghirlanda, la
gloriosa ruota, la santa lola, sempiterne rose.

SAND PAINTING: The sand paintings of the Navajo Indians depict a particular type of creation myth in an especially impressive manner: father and mother, who pass on life in their children, find their counterpart in the cosmic dimension as sky and earth. Father Sky is represented with symbols of the Sun, Moon, and Milky Way; Mother Earth is represented with symbols of the four plants sacred to the Navajo that yield food and tobacco and that grow in the important freshwater lake, which is at the same time a symbol of development and growth. Sand paintings are often made in entire series and tell the entire creation myth. (Private collection)

WHEEL OF FORTUNE: (From a manuscript by John Ludgate, *Troy Book and Story of Thebes*, England, circa 1455-1462)

As goddess of the moment, Fortuna is the goddess of fortune and misfortune; her attribute is the wheel; the wheel is a symbol of the cyclical recurrence of time. The whims of fate, which bring happiness and success to some people, yet ruin and misery to others, are often associated with the changing appearances of the planets: the wheel and the planets are kept in motion by an angel who turns the world axis. Fortuna is often portrayed as being blind or having a blindfold over her eyes, because her choice is morally blind.

ZODIAC: The zodiac of Bet Alpha is a centerpiece of a floor mosaic in a synagogue in present-day Israel (southwest of Haifa) that was made under the rulership of Emperor Justinian I (518-527); the synagogue was probably destroyed by an earthquake in the sixth century. In the center is Helios (*Sol invictus*) with the sun chariot; representations of the four seasons are in the four corners; the form of the twelve zodiacal signs is in accordance with the canon of its day.

Zodiacs in synagogues were more common in the time between 350 and 600 A.D.; their occurrence is understandable, as the place of worship—not only in the synagogue—is a depiction of the cosmos. The floor with these zodiac mosaics is only a reflection of the ceiling, i.e., of heaven. Mosaic floors with zodiacs in churches still exist in Romanesque churches—such as in the Cathedral of Aosta—and are intended to symbolize the basis of belief; indeed, in the widest sense, they can be interpreted as ascension scenes.

NUMBER SYMBOLISM IN ISLAMIC MYSTICISM

Number	Geometrical Correspondence		Macrocosm	Microcosm
	Static	Dynamic		
10			**The Holy Tetraktys** The first four universal characteristics	**Primary Body Parts** Head, neck, chest, abdomen, trunk, thoracic cavity, pelvis, 2 upper legs, 2 lower legs, 2 feet
12			**Zodiac** Fire, warmth, dryness, east/ earth, coldness, dryness, south/ air, warmth, wetness, west/ water, coldness, wetness, north	**Twelve Body Openings** 2 eyes, 2 ears, 2 nostrils, 2 nipples, 1 mouth, 1 navel, 2 excretion openings

Number/Letter Symbolism

A	alpha	1	Ξ	xi	60	א	aleph	1	ל	lamed	30
B	beta	2	O	omikron	70	ב	beth	2	מ	mem	40
Γ	gamma	3	Π	pi	80	ג	gimel	3	נ	nun	50
Δ	delta	4	ϙ	koppa	90	ד	daleth	4	ס	samekh	60
E	epsilon	5	P	rho	100	ה	he	5	ע	ajin	70
F	digamma	6	Σ	sigma	200						
Z	zeta	7	T	tau	300	ו	waw	6	פ	pe	80
H	eta	8	Y	ypsilon	400	ז	zajin	7	צ	zade	90
Θ	theta	9	Φ	phi	500	ח	cheth	8	ק	qoph	100
I	jota	10	X	chi	600	ט	teth	9	ר	resch	200
K	kappa	20	Ψ	psi	700	י	jod	10	ש	schin	300
Λ	Lambda	30	Ω	omega	800	כ	kaph	20	ת	taw	400
M	my	40	ⲁ	san	900						
N	ny	50									

OAK: Oak

OCTAGON: Floor plan of a Gothic tower constructed with the help of an octagon. 1: The width of the middle aisle (a) is the foundation for the square socle level. 2: Sketch of an octagon (b) within the inner square

Oak - The oak is sacred among many Indo-Germanic peoples. Primarily because of its majestic form and its habit of attracting LIGHTNING, it was sacred to Zeus in Greece (especially Dodona), to Jupiter among the Romans, and to Donar in ancient Germany. Druids seem to have ingested acorns before telling fortunes. Because of its hard, durable wood, it has been a symbol of strength, masculinity and tenacity since antiquity; because its wood was thought during antiquity and the Middle Ages to be incorruptible, it was also a symbol of immortality. Oak groves are centers of cult activity. —In the 18th century, the oak became a symbol of heroism in Germany; since the beginning of the 19th century, oak leaves have been victory laurels.

Ocean - The ocean is a symbol of inexhaustible vitality as well as of an all-consuming abyss. According to psychoanalysis, then, it is related to the two-faced character of the Great Mother who gives and takes, permits and punishes. As a reservoir of countless untapped treasures and forms shrouded in darkness, it is also a symbol of the unconscious. —As an im-measurably large surface, it is a symbol of infinity; among mystics, for example, it is a symbol of union with God. See WATER.

Octagon - In Gothic architecture, the octagon is a scheme of proportions frequently used in the construction of foundations for towers and pillars; it is also a symbolic reference to universality and perfection.

Octopus - Even in earliest times, it became a symbol of the spirit of the devil and of hell in general because of its eight tentacles.

Oil Lamp - See LAMP.

Oils - In many cultures, oils are thought to bear special powers; as a product of the OLIVE TREE that bears fruit in arid ground, olive oil, in particular, is a symbol of spiritual power, yet, since it is burned in oil lamps, it is also a symbol of light. —In Shinto mythology, oils were thought of as symbols of the undifferentiated primeval state of the world: the "primeval waters" were made of oil. —In the Eleusinian mysteries, olive oil was employed as a symbol of purity. —In Mediterranean countries, people made

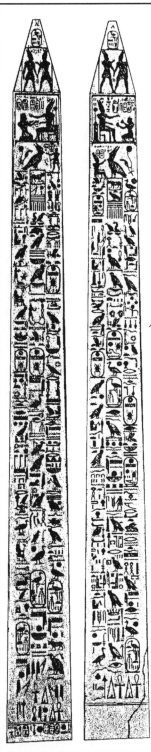

OBELISK

A tall stone pillar tapering toward the top and having a square foundation and pyramidal tip. In Egypt, especially in the Eighteenth and Nineteenth Dynasties, it was a cult symbol of the sun god: in the morning, its tip was struck by the first rays of the SUN. In addition, its strongly emphatic, directional shape represents the connection between the EARTH and the SKY or sun. —In ancient Egypt, obelisks usually stood in pairs in front of temple entrances. Today, thirty obelisks are still ′standing or have been re-erected, about fourteen of which are in Rome (they were first consecrated by exorcism and crowned with a cross); only five obelisks are still standing in Egypt. —Since the Renaissance, they have been a decorative architectural component and are used today as a type of monument as well. See ELEPHANT.

The installation of the Lateran obelisk in Rome, ordered by Pope Sixtus V and technically rendered by Domenico Fontana in 1588, was a remarkable event for the world at that time.

The erection of the obelisk itself was ordered by Tuthmosis III and completed by his successor Tuthmosis IV at the southern portal of the temple at Karnak.

The four drawings at left and right, made by Athanasius Kircher, are depictions of the Lateran obelisk.

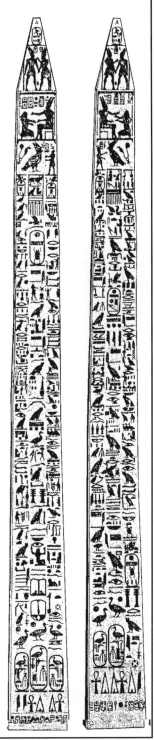

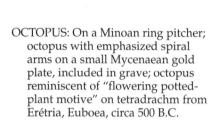

OCTOPUS: On a Minoan ring pitcher; octopus with emphasized spiral arms on a small Mycenaean gold plate, included in grave; octopus reminiscent of "flowering potted-plant motive" on tetradrachm from Erétria, Euboea, circa 500 B.C.

sacrifices of oil—pouring it onto stone altars, for example—as a sign of a prayer for fertility. —Anointment with oil played an important sacred role in various religions; in Judaism, for example, things (such as the Stone of Bethel) and people (priests, prophets and kings) were anointed with oil as a sign of divine blessing and of the authority given to them by God. The word *Christus* (*Messias* in Hebrew) means "the anointed"; it thus designates the royal, prophetic, and priestly authority of Jesus. —Oil—also mixed with balsam and spices (see CHRISM)—is sometimes used for consecration (for baptisms, ordinations, and extreme unction, for example) in Christian ritual.

Olive Tree - The olive tree is an ancient cultivated plant rich in symbolic meaning; in Greece, it was sacred to Athena and was regarded as a symbol of intellectual force and knowledge (because it supplied oil for oil lamps, it was thus akin to LIGHT), of purification (because of the cleansing power of its oil), of fertility and vitality (it is very resilient and can live to be many hundreds of years old), of victory, as well as of peace and reconciliation (because of the calming effect of its oil). —With respect to the olive branch brought back by the DOVE that Noah sent from the ark, the olive tree and its branches are primarily a sign in Christianity of reconciliation with God and of peace. See OILS.

Om - A sacred meditation syllable of Hinduism, Buddhism and Jainism (where it is pronounced "aum") laden with an abundance of esoteric meanings; it is thought to be everlasting and inexhaustible, and is interpreted in part as a symbolic expression of the creative spirit, the word, or (with respect to its three sounds) the three states of man (waking, dreaming, deep sleep), the three times of day (morning, afternoon, evening), the three capacities (acting, knowing, desiring).

Omega - The last letter of the Greek alphabet. Particularly in Christianity, it is a symbol of the end and of the completion of the world. See ALPHA; ALPHA AND OMEGA; and TAU.

Omphalos - See NAVEL.

Onager - A wild ass. A sub-species of donkey that is difficult to tame; in the Bible, it is a symbol of the person who does not want to accept reason, especially for disobedient Israel that does not want to yield to God's commandments. —It is sometimes also a symbol for hermits living in

OLIVE TREE: Olive harvest; detail from a painting on an amphora, 6th century

OM: The sacred syllable in written form

the wilderness. —Since it is often portrayed with a horn on its forehead, it can also be thought of as a variant of the UNICORN with a phallic emphasis.

One-Leggedness - One-leggedness is associated in the mythologies of many peoples with beings (deities, witches, sorcerers, animals) that are responsible for RAIN and THUNDER. In China, for example, the appearance of a one-legged bird was regarded as an augur of impending rain; dances done on one leg are supposed to bring rain.

Orange - Like most fruits that have many seeds, it is a fertility symbol.

Orant - From the Latin. *Orans* is the masculine or feminine form, *orante* the feminine, meaning "the prayer." A common motif of early Christian art: man or (more frequently) female figure (often in long robes) in a position of prayer ("orans position"), usually standing, with raised and extended arms; it was a heathen, ancient motif that apparently existed even in cave drawings (such as at Val Camonica).

Orchids - An orchis plant found mostly in moist, warm areas; many terrestrial orchids, such as the orchis indigenous to

Europe and neighboring regions, have testicle-shaped bulb roots (*orchis* in Greek means "testicles"); in antiquity, they were thus considered to be an aphrodisiac and a fertility symbol; they were seen as a favorite food of the satyrs; they were sometimes used for love-spells and were supposed to protect one from sickness and the evil eye, to give one good luck in gambling, and to make one rich. —The Chinese used orchids in spring festivals to drive away evil spirits. —The spotted orchis was originally sacred to the ancient Germanic goddess Freya and was later a plant of Mary.

Organ - A widely common symbol of Christian church music; because it is sounded by air, it quickly became a symbol of the Holy Spirit.

Orpheus - A Greek symbolic figure of the musician, often identified with the Biblical harp king David; in early Christianity, it was a symbol of Christ.

Ostrich - Ostrich feathers were regarded by the Egyptians as symbols of justice and truth (and a personification of the goddess of world order, Ma'at). —According to medieval ideas about nature (see PHYSIOLOGUS), the ostrich does not hatch its

ORANT: Maria in orans position;
 "Gold glass" in the Vatican
 Museum, 4th century (from
 Schmid's *Musterbuch*)
ORPHEUS

ONE

ONE: The numerical sign of one   ONE: St. Ursula as a protective patron
saint

1	Symbol of the still undifferentiated primeval beginning as well as of the totality to which all things and beings strive to return; as a unity, it is also a symbol of God; moreover, though, it is also a symbol of individuality. In number mysticism, 1, like 2 and 0, is not regarded as an actual number as the numbers beginning with 3 are.
11	Sometimes the number of sin and repentance, since it exceeds 10 (the number of commandments, for example) yet does not reach the equally holy and important number 12 (the number of the 12 Apostles, for example); it is the first "silent" number in the series of "silent" prime numbers after 10 (such as 17, 19, 23, etc.). It is perhaps a number of the zodiac as well, since, of the 12 signs, one is always invisible "behind" the sun. As the sum of $(2 + 3) + (2 \times 3) = 11$, it is also a connecting number between heaven and earth. In Christian symbolism, St. Ursula protects 11 (thousand) virgins with her robe.
21	The product of the sacred number 7 and 3, i.e. $7 \times 3 = 21$; in the Old Testament (The Wisdom of Solomon, 7:22–23), 21 characteristics are listed in praise of wisdom.

OSTRICH: The sun hatching ostrich eggs; detail from a Marian panel in Ottobeuren, circa 1450/60

OSTRICH: From an Egyptian illustration; 20th Dynasty

own eggs, but rather incessantly stares at them until the chicks hatch. The ostrich egg was thus regarded as a meditation symbol. According to other ideas, the ostrich hatches its eggs by the SUN; it is thus also a symbol of Christ, who was awakened by God. The ostrich egg is also regarded as a symbol of Mary's virginal motherhood. In a negative sense, the ostrich, which leaves its eggs, is a symbol of the person forgotten by God. In addition, synagogues occasionally appear under an image of an ostrich, which supposedly sticks its head into the sand (occasionally also a symbol of the deadly sin of sloth). This symbolic meaning has persisted up to today with respect to people who close their eyes to unpleasant facts.

Otter - A animal symbolic of the Moon. In some American Indian cultures and in Africa, its coat plays a role in initiation rites. —In Europe, it is occasionally encountered as a guide of souls.

Ouroboros - See UROBOROS.

Oven - The oven is symbolically related to FIRE; especially in ALCHEMY, it is important for transformation processes of metals, WATER, AIR, EARTH, etc. and the mystical and moral processes connected with them. —The baking oven, in particular, is a symbol of the maternal womb; "being shoved into the oven" can thus also be interpreted as a return to an embryonic state; "burning in the oven" can be interpreted as a symbol of dead and re-birth.

Owl - As a night bird that cannot bear the light of the sun, the owl as a symbol is frequently contrasted with the EAGLE. —In Egypt and India, the owl was a bird of death; from antiquity up until today, the owl itself and its call have been thought to be eerie and an omen bringing misfortune and death. —In China, it played an important role as a terrifying animal associated with lightning (which brightens the night), the drum (which pierces the silence of the night) and generally with the preponderance of the Yang principle (see YIN AND YANG) to the point of destruction. —Yet because it can see in the dark and is thought to be serious and thoughtful, it is also a symbol of wisdom penetrating the darkness of ignorance and was thus an attribute of the Greek goddess of learning, Athena. —The Bible counts it among the unclean animals. — In Christian symbolism—such as in PHYSIOLOGUS, which actually mentions only the screech owl—it appears negatively as a symbol of spiritual darkness,

OWL: Owl on an ancient Athenian coin

yet also positively as a symbol of religious knowledge or also of Christ, or of the light that illuminates the darkness; yet it is also a reference to His early death.

Ox - Or "buffalo." In contrast to the wild STEER, the ox is a symbol of contentedness and good-natured strength. In eastern Asia and Greece, oxen and buffalo are sacred and are popular sacrificial animals. In eastern Asia, the buffalo is thought to be the steed of the wise; Lao-tzu, for example, rides a buffalo westward. —Like the ASS, the ox is almost never absent in representations of the Nativity of Jesus. On the capitals of Roman columns, the ox can symbolize the night. —The ox is the second sign of the Chinese ZODIAC; it corresponds to Taurus.

Ox-Eye Daisy - See DAISY.

OX: Ox and ass at the crib of Jesus; relief
    from baptismal font of the Stiftskirche in
    Freckenhorst; first half of 12th century
OX: Talc seal with depiction of a humped ox;
    from Mohenjo-Daro

PALM: Darius hunting in the grove of palms, rock crystal, Mesopotamian

Palm Ass - A wooden replica of an ass that was carried along in Palm Sunday processions, usually with a figure of Christ.

Palm Tree - This refers primarily to the date-palm, a tree more than twenty meters high that has a supple trunk that the wind cannot break; it can live to be more than 300 years old. Among the Babylonians, it was regarded as a divine tree. —In Egypt, it was probably associated with the symbolic significance of the TREE of life and was frequently a model for the fashioning of columns (see COLUMN). —In antiquity, branches of the palm tree were victory symbols at public games. As the tree of light, it was sacred to Helios and Apollo among the Greeks. Its Greek name, PHOENIX, points to a close symbolic connection with this legendary people. — Palm branches are a widespread symbol of victory, joy and peace. The evergreen leaves of the palm tree are also a symbol of eternal life and resurrection. In Christian art, palm branches are thus often encountered as an attribute of martyrs. — C.G. Jung sees the shape of the palm tree as a symbol of the mind.

Pandora - From the Greek, meaning "she who was given everything." In Greek mythology, Pandora was the first woman, created by Hephaistos at Zeus's command and distinguished by her great beauty and given many alluring gifts by the gods. She was brought to the world by Hermes along with a box that contained hope and all the evils of the world. Pandora was supposed to punish humanity for Prometheus's theft of fire from the gods. Although Prometheus warned his brother Epimetheus, the latter married Pandora, who immediately opened the box, whereupon great ill came upon humanity. Only hope remained in the container; Pandora is thus the symbolic figure for the origin of all evil from the feminine sex.

Pansy - A variety of violet; the botanical name Viola tricolor refers to the fact that the pansy often has three colors, which is why it is repeatedly encountered as a symbol of the Trinity. —In addition, widely varying symbolic meanings were ascribed to the pansy; it is regarded as a symbol of the coyness of young girls, the fidelity of lovers, as well as envy, a trait that was attributed especially to stepmothers.

Panther - A common term for the black

PARADISE: The four rivers of Eden, from Herrad von Landsberg's *Hortus Deliciarum*, 12th century
PARASOL: Royal parasol; Sassanian relief; 5th century

LEOPARD; in contrast to the spotted leopard, though, it is less a symbol of wild animals. The panther was regarded as an attribute of Dionysus and was a symbol of procreation and re-birth; this holds similarly for IVY; both were also Etruscan symbols. PHYSIOLOGUS reports that the panther sleeps for three days after it eats and then gives off a wonderful fragrance that irresistibly attracts people. It was therefore thought of as a symbol of lust and sensuality, on the one hand, but also as a symbol of death and Christ's resurrection, on the other hand (due to its awakening after three days).

Pantokrator - A Byzantine-Christian symbol; the most important type of Christ icon, glorifying Christ as the Almighty.

Pantry - In the symbolism of the Middle Ages, the pantry is a symbol for Mary, the Mother of God, who carried within her the bread of life.

Paradise - In most cultures and religions, paradise is an expression of ideas about a happy, blissful state at the beginning or end of the world. —In the Old Testament (Genesis 2:8–15), paradise is described as a "garden in Eden" in the east, with "trees of all sorts," among them the tree of life and the tree of knowledge of good and evil. Four rivers flow through Eden. Earthly paradise was lost to man due to the Fall; the man who pleases God hopes to regain it in heaven. —The Islamic view of paradise is distinguished from the Christian view in large measure by the inclusion of sexual pleasures for men who are received into paradise. —During the Middle Ages, paradise was posited at the edge of the inhabited world (see MAPPA MUNDI).

Parasol - Occasionally a symbol of the vault of the heavens; in antiquity, it was held over rulers by servants; it is a symbol of power and high position. In China and India, parasols often had several levels as a symbol of the hierarchies of heaven.

Parcae - See MOIRAI.

Park - A landscape constructed according to the rules of horticulture (see GARDEN), whereby the contour of the ground as well as trees and bushes determine the form.

Parrot - The parrot is a Christian symbol of Mary's virginity, because its feathers supposedly do not get wet, but rather stay dry when it rains; a German association is with "Eva, who has her absolution through Mary," since the parrot can say "Eva," or the reverse of the "Ave Maria"—a play on the German word for Eve, "Eva."

Partridge - Because of its dance-like mating ritual, it is sacred to Aphrodite, as is the DOVE; it frequently appears in Etruscan grave paintings. —PHYSIO-LOGUS says that the partridge hatches eggs that are not its own and raises the young, who later return to their parents and leave the partridge standing "high and dry." The partridge is compared with the devil, who wishes to catch people although they follow the call of Christ.

Paschal Lamb - A symbol of Christ, His sacrificial death and resurrection. See LAMB.

Passage Grave - A megalithic grave from the Neolithic period that had a narrow entrance and was covered with stones; apparently, many passage graves were consciously positioned according to the heavens and occasionally sealed with a stone ("spirit hole").

Passion Columns - Or "martyr columns," "whip columns." During the 15th and 16th centuries, Passion columns were columns with sculpted depictions of the implements of the Passion (see PASSION, IMPLEMENTS OF THE) and the cock of Peter at the top.

Passion, Implements of the - Or "weapons of Christ." The objects involved in the Passion and martyrdom of Christ. —In art, up to thirty such implements are represented; particularly common are the cross, lance, whip, sponge, crown of thorns, and nails, as well as a ladder, hammer, ropes and sudarium.

Path - A many-layered symbol in the most various cultures and religions; the problems of searching, of flight, of imitation of exemplary persons, and of inward and outward journeys always play a role. See KING'S PATH; LABYRINTH; JOURNEY; CROSSROADS.

Path - The path is an ancient symbol of human life: man is a wanderer, his path is characterized by aimlessness and timelessness, and, what is altogether essential, the path leads back to the beginning. It is in this manner that religions regard themselves in a certain sense as paths, such as the path to purification and the path to enlightenment in Christian mystic piety and its prayers.

PAUPER'S BIBLE: Page from a Dutch
Pauper's Bible
PEACOCK: Peacock's tail as a symbol
of entirety; from Boschius's
Symbolographia, 1702

The motif of the two paths is of particular symbolic significance, known to everyone from the first Psalm, which speaks of the "way of the righteous" and the "way of the ungodly," or Psalm 139, which juxtaposes the "everlasting path" to the "wicked path." —The Pythagoreans regarded the letter Y as a symbol of the forked path; in the Occident, this meaning was forgotten at the end of the 18th century.

Pauper's Bible - From the Latin *Biblio pauperum*. A Christian instructional and devotional book with pictures from the New Testament. In accordance with early Christian TYPOLOGY, the pictures are contrasted with paradigms from the Old Testament and the Prophets. The book served poor clerics in particular. The book was probably widely distributed from Bavaria between 1300 and 1500 A.D. in the form of handwritten manuscripts, block-printed books, and early movable-type printed books.

Peace Pipe - Also called a *calumet*. A smoking pipe used by North American Indians that was smoked in turns when pacts and peace treaties were made and as a sign of friendship. It is usually thought to be a sort of primeval image of a human being whose strength and immortality it represents. Particularly with respect to its SMOKE, it was regarded as a symbol of the connection of man with nature as well as with heaven.

Peach Tree - Because it blossoms early, it is a symbol of spring and of fertility in China (and elsewhere). In Japan, the peach blossom is a symbol of virginity. In China, the wood of the peach tree (and of the MULBERRY TREE) was regarded as an effective agent against evil influences; similar powers were also attributed to the fruit. The tree, the blossom, and the fruit were also regarded as symbols of immortality.

Peacock - In India and elsewhere, it was thought of as a sun-like bird, probably because of its tail (see WHEEL); it is ridden by various deities; in Buddhism, for example, it is ridden by Buddha; with a SERPENT in its beak, it is a symbol of LIGHT victorious over darkness; the beauty of its feathers was sometimes thought to be the result of a transformation caused by poison that it absorbed during a battle with a serpent. —In antiquity, the peacock was associated with Hera and Juno, probably because of its beauty. —Islam sees the peacock that is spreading its tail as a symbol of the universe and sometimes of the full Moon or of the midday sun. —Likewise, there are representations of peacocks in early Christianity as sun symbols as well as symbols of immortality (Aristotle maintained that the flesh of the peacock was incorruptible; St. Augustine writes that he himself verified this), and of the joys in the next life. —In esoteric tradition, the tail of the peacock, which brings together all colors, was thought of as a symbol of completeness. —In the symbolic thought of the Middle Ages, the peacock also embodies the deadly sin of pride (superbia). —In modern times, the peacock is often thought of as a symbol of self-satisfied vanity because of its pompous, ostentatious behavior at mating time.

Pearl - A generally common symbol of the Moon and of women, such as in China, where it is closely associated with the MOON, WATER, and women and thus with the Yin (see YIN AND YANG) principle. Because of its spherical shape and its inimitable luster, the pearl is also sometimes thought of as a symbol of perfection. —Because of its hardness and immutability, it is also a symbol of immortality in China, India, and elsewhere. In China, the "flaming pearl" was regarded as a sun symbol and a symbol of things most precious. —Among the Greeks, it was a symbol of love, probably due primarily to its beauty. —In Persia, the undamaged pearl was regarded as a symbol of virgins. Persian myth also saw the pearl in conjunction with the original shaping of matter by spirit. —However, the pearl owes its profound (and simultaneously extensive) symbolic significance to the fact that it grows in a MUSSEL (i.e., in darkness) at the bottom of the sea. It is thus a symbol of the child growing in its mother's womb, yet it is primarily a symbol of light shining into darkness; among some peoples, there is the notion that it arose from specks of light or dew drops that came from heaven or the Moon. Gnosticism and Christianity, in particular, emphasize this set of meanings and frequently associate it with Christ as the Logos that was born from flesh (Mary). PHYSIOLOGUS associates the pearl with the AGATE. —Folk belief often associates pearls with tears as well. —The string of pearls is a symbol of a unity joined together from multiplicity.

Pear Tree - Pitted fruit wood having completely white blossoms that are a symbol of mourning in China due to their softness and rapid ephemerality. —During the Middle Ages, the pear tree was re-

PEGASUS: Bellorophon on Pegasus

PELICAN: A pelican ripping open its own breast; relief in the paradise of the Cathedral of Münster, Westfalia, 1235

---

garded as a symbol of Mary (probably because of the pure whiteness of its blossoms). —Due to its shape, which is vaguely reminiscent of female forms, the pear is frequently interpreted sexually in the psychoanalytical interpretation of dreams. —According to popular belief, many pears mean that one will be blessed with many children.

Pectorale - The BREAST CROSS.

Pegasus - In Greek mythology, Pegasus is the winged horse that sprang from the neck of Medusa (see GORGON). He is supposed to have created the spring Hippocrene, which was dedicated to the Muses, with a stamp of his hoof; thus, he was later a symbol of intellectual, and especially poetic, creativity.

Pelican - According to PHYSIOLOGUS, the pelican is a bird that kills its ugly offspring (in other representations, they are killed by a SERPENT), but reawakens them to life after three days with blood from self-inflicted wounds. It is a symbol of sacrificial paternal and maternal love. In medieval art and literature, its killing of its offspring retreated into the background in favor of the legend that the pelican feeds its progeny with its own blood

until the pelican itself dies; it therefore became a common symbol of Christ's sacrificial death. —In the symbolic language of the alchemists, the pelican was an image for the Philosophers' Stone that dissolves (i.e., dies) in order to allow GOLD to arise from LEAD.

Pentagonal Dodecahedron - See DODECAHEDRON.

Pentagram - Or "club moss." A five-pointed star drawn in one set of movements; an ancient magical sign. —Among the Pythagoreans, it was a symbol of health and knowledge. —It was frequently depicted by the Gnostics on ABRAXAS gems. —During the Middle Ages, it was a commonly used sign to ward off demonic powers, among them nocturnal witches. —As a self-contained shape, it is sometimes a symbol of Christ as ALPHA AND OMEGA; as a five-pointed shape, it is also a symbol of the five sacred wounds of Christ.

Peony - In China, it is a symbol of wealth and honor. In antiquity, it was thought to offer protection against the tricks of satyrs and fauns. —During the Middle Ages, it was often used as a medicinal and magical plant; peony seeds served as amulets.

PENTAGRAM: Gothic, 13th century
PHALLUS: Rock drawing from Val
Camonica, combination of phallus
and sun symbol

—As a "rose without a thorn," it is a common symbol of Mary in medieval panel paintings.

Peppermint - Or "mint." A labiate flower with a strongly aromatic, essential oil; known even to antiquity as a medicinal agent; in Christian art, it is a plant of Mary due to its curative properties.

Peridexion - A tree cited in PHYSIO-LOGUS that is supposed to grow in India; it is interpreted as being a symbol of the Trinity: whoever lives from the fruits of the Holy Spirit is protected from the devil's snares.

Periwinkle - A creeping shrub indigenous to southern and central Europe, having leathery, evergreen leaves and blue blossoms. Like all evergreen plants, it is a symbol of eternal life and fidelity; it was also regarded as a defense against witches and sorcerers.

Pewter - In alchemy of the Middle Ages, pewter was identified with Jupiter, which is described as a benevolent planet, a mediator between hot and cold, Mars (see IRON) and Saturn (see LEAD), bringing prudence and vivacity. See METALS.

Phallus - From the Greek *phallos*, a term for "penis." As a powerful presence of a deity or a sign of magical power, it is a symbol of fertility and of special powers (including cosmic ones) and is revered as a source of life, especially in agrarian cults (where it is thus often worn as an AMU-LET and sometimes exists as a magical trophy). Phallus cults existed or exist in antiquity (Dionysus, Demeter, Osiris), in Hinduism, in Shinto and among primitive peoples. See HERMA; LINGA.

Pheasant - Particularly in Chinese mythology, the pheasant is a symbol of cosmic harmony due to its song and dance; its call and the sound of its flapping wings became associated with THUNDER and thus with storms, RAIN, and the spring. The pheasant was thought to be associated with the Yang principle (see YIN AND YANG). In the course of the seasons, the pheasant changed into a SERPENT, which was associated with the YIN principle, and vice versa. —During antiquity and the Middle Ages, the golden pheasant was closely associated with the PHOE-NIX.

Philosophers' Stone - Or "lapis philosophorum." In alchemy, it is a substance that can supposedly be produced from materia prima by complex processes, that is sup-

PHOENIX: Illustration of the Phoenix
in Schmid's *Musterbuch*

---

posed to transform unprecious metals into precious ones, and that is supposed to rejuvenate and heal. In these processes, the separation and rejoining of opposing principles, especially the feminine and the masculine, played an important role, which is why the Philosophers' Stone was also frequently depicted as a HERMAPH-RODITE. All initial attempts to find the Philosophers' Stone must probably also be interpreted as symbolic actions that were basically visible accompaniments of psychologically and religiously motivated efforts: by a sort of death, the originally formless *materia prima* decomposes into its constitutent elements and achieves a resurrection on a higher level in the Philosophers' Stone. —C.G. Jung interprets these actions as an individuation process.

Phoenix - A sacred bird (Benu or Boine) among the Egyptians; it was originally represented as a water-wagtail and later as a heron or as a golden falcon with a heron's head; it was regarded as the embodiment of the sun god (who is supposed to have settled down on a primeval hill while the world was created), of the daily course of the sun and of the annual flooding of the Nile. This relation to ever-recurring renewal was reinterpreted by the Greeks, Romans and finally by the Christian church fathers

(especially in PHYSI-OLOGUS) as the widely common symbol of the bird that is periodically consumed by fire (every 500, 1,000 or 1,461 years) and rises anew from the ashes. In this regard, it is a symbol of Christ and of resurrection overcoming death and of immortality in general.

Phosphorus - LUCIFER. The planet VE-NUS as the morning star.

Physiologus - A text written in Greek (probably in Alexandria) between 150 and 200 B.C.; it existed in many variants and originally contained forty-eight chapters with statements or short accounts of the characteristics of animals, plants and stones; they are usually introduced with the sentence, "Physiologus says," and conclude with the sentence, "Physiologus says well of the . . ." At that point, a Christian exegesis follows, usually supported by Bible quotes. Typically, the "scientific" selection of the characteristics is made with the Christian-allegorical exegesis in mind. The (Greek) New Testament and the Greek translation of the Old Testament (the Septuagint) were the basis of the text. In addition to Ethiopian, Syrian, Arabic and other translations, Latin translations have existed since the 5th century; Spanish, English and French versions, the so-called Bestiaires, are based on

PIG: Sacrifice of a pig to the fertility goddess Demeter; from an illustration on an Attic vessel

these. Many ideas in Christian animal and picture symbolism are derived from Physiologus. See BESTIARUM.

Pi - See HOLE; DISK.

Pictish Stones - Symbolic stones in Celtic-Germanic areas; the meaning of the symbols is still largely puzzling, despite the clear depictions (usually in pairs) of animals or objects of daily life. They came into being between approximately the 7th and 9th centuries A.D.

Pig - The pig is a symbolic animal with various meanings; because of its numerous offspring, the sow or mother pig, in particular, is a fertility symbol among the Egyptians, Greeks and Celts; it was therefore used in illustrations as an AMULET that brought happiness and fertility (however, the expression "to have a pig," which means "to have undeserved good fortune," was at first probably meant derisively and is derived from medieval games in which the last prize, i.e. the undeserved one, was frequently a pig). —In Greco-Roman antiquity, the pig is among the favored sacrificial animals. —On the other hand, however, the pig was despised among many peoples; among Jews, Moslems and others, it was thought to be

a unclean animal. Because of its voracity and its rooting about in the dirt, it is also a common symbol of lowliness and crudity; in medieval art, it is primarily a symbol of intemperance—especially gluttony and unchastity—or of ignorance. —The wild boar sometimes played a special role; the boar was especially revered as a symbol of strength and pugnacity, as among the Greeks or in Japan. Among the Celts, the wild boar was a symbolic animal of the warrior and priestly classes and was eaten at sacred feasts. —In medieval art, it was a symbol of the demonic. —The erroneous belief that the name "boar" (*eber* in German) is derived from the Hebrew word *ibri* (meaning "progenitor of the Hebrews"), comes from the strange fact that the boar occasionally appears as a Christ symbol in Christian art of the Middle Ages.—The pig is the twelfth and last sign of the Chinese ZODIAC and corresponds to Pisces (see FISH).

Pilgrim - In numerous religions, the pilgrim is a symbol for the life of man on this earth, a life that is not final, but rather is only a transitional stage to another life.

Pilgrim's Hat - A broad-brimmed slouch hat bearing a MUSSEL, the sign of the pilgrims.

PILLOW: Seating pillows and foot pillows for God the Father; detail from Herrad von Landsberg's *Hortus Deliciarum*

PINE: Ancient bronze pine cone from a fountain in the Vatican

Pillow - A symbol for a person of high rank who uses a pillow; the pillow itself raises the seat (or the couch) to the throne.

Pine - In antiquity, pine was a term for all cone-bearing coniferous trees (pinus). In a narrower sense, the stone-pine was a fertility symbol (probably due primarily to the constant production of new cones). As an ornamental motif, the pine cone appears even in Assyrian art as a symbol of fertility, on ancient gravestones and as a gargoyle (the same is true of the cone of the Aleph Scots pine, whose resin was used to preserve wine); it topped the THYRSUS STAFF of Dionysus and his entourage. In Christian symbolism, it was closely related symbolically to the TREE OF LIFE, whose crown it often forms in depictions.

Pine Cone - See PINE.

Pisces - The constellation of the FISH.

Pitcher - In Indian art, it is sometimes encountered as a symbol of overflowing fertility and abundance; it is also a symbol for the potion of immortality. —In China, it is a symbol of the sky and particularly of thunder (because of the sound that one can make by tapping on an empty pitcher). —In early Christian art, one frequently finds representations of a pitcher; leaves and creeping plants or drinking birds refer to the water of life that the pitcher contains. Pitchers often symbolize the four rivers of Eden; they less frequently symbolize the River Jordan.

Planet Seals - See MAGIC SQUARES.

Plantain - In China, it is a symbol of fertility because of the great number of its blossoms and seeds.

Plants - As the lowest and thus basic level of the organic world, plants are a symbol of the unity of all living things; in mythic stories of peoples, one finds many examples of total or partial transformations of plants into humans or animals or vice versa. —The constant change of a plant from growth, blossoming, maturity and death, between sowing and harvesting, makes the plant kingdom as a whole a symbol of cyclical renewal. —Plants in fertile abundance are often the quintessence of "Mother Earth."

Plant Symbolism - Symbolic association of individual plants with spiritually significant meanings in language, art, national custom and religion, often tied to shape, season, healing power or name of the plant; see CORRELATIVE; DOCTRINE OF SIGNS.

Platonic Solids - The five regular polyhedra: tetrahedron, cube, octahedron, dodecahedron, and icosahedron. The Platonic solids are convex and bounded by regular polygons of the same type; they were already playing a large role in Greek natural philosophy; Kepler imagined the world to be constructed in such a way that the orbital paths of the planets were intersected by Platonic solids that were contained within one another. See illustration on page 239.

Plow - The work of the plow in the earth is compared in many cultures with a man's impregnation of a woman. The plow is thus a phallic symbol and a symbol of fertility.

Plowing - Widely thought of as fertilization of the earth or, in the same vein, as a joining of the SKY and EARTH by man. See PLOW.

Plum Tree - Due to the early blossoms that appear on the tree even before the leaves, the plum tree is a symbol of spring, of youth, and of purity in the Far East. —In

psychoanalytic dream interpretation, the plum is sometimes regarded as a symbol of female sexuality.

Plummet - Or SOUNDING-LEAD. A symbol of verticality, sometimes of the WORLD AXIS as well. Especially in Freemasonry, it is a symbol of mental and spiritual balance and of an upstanding mind and spirit, teaching one to search for truth and to procure justice for truth. In the graphic arts, it is sometimes a symbol of architecture and geometry as well as of moderation and justice.

Point - Especially in meditation, the point can be a symbol of the center (see MIDDLE), the merging of all realities or all potentialities, or both. It is usually depicted as the mid-point of a CIRCLE.

Pole - Or "pillars." As a symbol, it is a sign for the connection between heaven and earth or for the world axis itself; to some extent, MENHIRS and OBELISKS should be considered in this sense. Poles also appear in conjunction with serpents: see BRAZEN SERPENT. See COLUMNS.

Pole Star - A pole star is a star on which the heavens appear to rotate; it was thus often thought of as the center of the

PLANETS

The symbolism of the planets is closely tied to astrology (planetary astrology in contrast to zodiacal astrology) and alchemy within microcosm-macrocosm thinking and plays a disproportionately larger role than the symbolism of stars. Astrologically, the positions of the planets (including the sun and the Moon, which were regarded as planets) at the moment of one's birth were regarded as fundamental quantities. Furthermore, the position of the planets within the system of the zodiac, the interrelation of the planets among one another (aspects), and the position of the planets in the system of "houses" (a system concurring with the zodiac), are all held to be important in astrological interpretation.

The planets, like the signs of the zodiac, are correlated with all sorts of "sub-lunar" objects, as, for example, the planets are correlated with the prophets in Islamic astrology.

The tree of the planets; from an alchemical writing

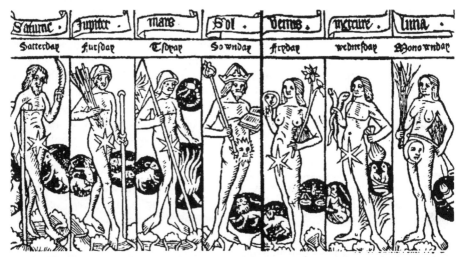

PLANETS: The seven planets as the regents of the seven days of the week; the symbols of the associated houses are given next to the symbols of the planets (from Shephard's Calendar, 1579)

The "ancient" planets (Mercury, Venus, Mars, Jupiter, Saturn and, in the old geocentric system, the sun and Moon as well) and the "modern" planets (Uranus, Neptune and Pluto) bear the names of gods from Greco-Roman mythology and are supposed to represent the characteristics of these gods. By means of this theomorphism, astrologers acquired a basis of inexhaustible possibilities: all characteristics and capabilities of the Babylonian-Greco-Roman gods and of the myths handed down by them, were transferred to the planets and played a role in the interpretation of each constellation; on this basis, the hypothesis of the "children of the planets" arose, as did speculations regarding number symbolism, magic squares, and planet seals.

The planetary system in its astrological form. The system correlating the planets and the days of the week, with the aspects and zodiacal signs, is in the center, surrounded by the seven planets with their houses and simplified depictions of the children of the planets and notes for iatromathematics. Woodcut from the end of the 15th century

The woodcut series, "The Children of the Planets" by Hans Sebald Behaim, shows how ancient thinking — the names of the planet gods determine the lot of those born under them — has continued to have an effect even up to most recent times.

The sun on a one-wheeled wagon; the wagon's wheel is the sole domicile of Leo; children of the sun love power and dominion.

The Moon on a one-wheeled wagon; the wagon's wheel is the sole domicile of Cancer; children of the Moon love places where water and fertility are associated with one another.

Mercury on a wagon; the wagon's wheels are the domiciles of Virgo and Gemini; children of Mercury are characterized by mental abilities, skill, and finger dexterity. Their home is the city.

Venus on a wagon; the wagon's wheels are the domiciles of Taurus and Libra; children of Venus love pleasure, love and unconventional occupations. Their home is the open country, gardens, and parks.

Mars on a wagon; the wagon's wheels represent the domiciles of Aries and Scorpio; children of Mars are among the warriors, the butchers, but also among the inventors and investigators.

Jupiter on a wagon; the wagon's wheels are the domiciles of Pisces and Sagittarius; children of Jupiter are characteristized by religiosity and dignity.

Saturn on a wagon; the wagon's wheels are the domiciles of Aquarius and Capricorn; children of Saturn can be found in architecture and farming; they are leaders in business, law, and politics.

PLATONIC SOLIDS: The Platonic Solids

	Solid	Element	Defined by	According to Kepler, intersects paths of
	Hexahedron	earth	6 squares	Saturn - Jupiter
	Tetrahedron	fire	4 triangles	Jupiter - Mars
	Octahedron	air	8 triangles	Mars - Earth
	Dodecahedron	——	12 pentagons	Earth - Venus
	Icosahedron	water	20 triangles	Venus - Mercury

The 5 possible isohedra — according to mathematicians, *only* these five solids exist — and their speculative correlates

cosmos, the NAVEL of the world, the gate of heaven, a cosmic hub, or the highest peak of the world mountain range.

Pomegranate - Like other fruits that have many seeds (see CANDIED LEMON TREE; GOURD; LEMON; ORANGE; TOMATO), it is a fertility symbol, which is why, for example, it was sacred in Greece to Demeter, Aphrodite and Hera. With reference to this symbolic meaning, recently married women in ancient Rome wore garlands made from branches of the pomegranate tree. In India, the sap of the pomegranate tree was thought to be a remedy for infertility. —Opening a pomegranate is occasionally also seen in symbolic relation to deflowering. —Because of the bright red color of the fruit's flesh, the pomegranate was also a symbol of love, blood and thus also of life and death. —Among the Phoenicians, the pomegranate was closely related to the SUN and signified life, power and renewal. —In Judaism, the pomegranate was a symbol of adherence to the laws of the Torah. — During the Middle Ages, the pomegranate's aroma and the large number of its seeds were interpreted as a symbol of Mary's beauty and many virtues. Yet its round shape, large number of seeds and pleasant smell were also regarded as a symbol of the perfection, infinite number of qualities, and goodness of God. Its large number of seeds, brought together in a core, could also be thought of as a symbol of the church. The red juice of the pomegranate became associated with the blood

239

of the martyrs. Finally, the pomegranate, which has a hard and inedible skin yet contains sweet juice within, was sometimes interpreted as a symbol of the perfect Christian, especially the priest.

Pond - See LAKE.

Poplar - Or "aspen" (Populus tremula). Because of its leaves, which tremble at the slightest blowing of the wind, it is a symbol of pain and lamentation; among the Greeks, it was thought to be a tree that grew in the underworld, and thus bore particular association as a symbol of wakes.

Poppy - In the Eleusinian mysteries of Demeter, it was offered as a symbol of the earth, yet also of sleep and forgetfulness.

Portal - See DOORS.

Pot - Common symbol of the WOMB and thus often of women as well. See VESSEL.

Potion - Also called "elixir." As the potion of immortality, it is a symbol of a heightening of consciousness, which is associated with knowledge of eternal existence. The negative counterpart is the potion of forgetting.

Prayer String - The prayer string, common in many religions, is a string or chain with beads or knots; its individual parts symbolize various spiritual facts, attributes, prayer forms or names of saints, enlightened beings and gods, etc. —The prayer string common in Buddhism has 108 beads and corresponds to the various stages of development of the world. —The prayer string in Islam has ninety-nine beads, which symbolize the ninety-nine names of Allah. —The rosary of the Catholic Church is the visual portrayal of a series of prayers. See ROSARY.

Primrose - Also called "keys of heaven," "cowslip." A spring flower found primarily in northern temperate zones; it usually has yellow umbels on sturdy stems, which gives the plant a certain key-like appearance; among the ancient Germans, it was sacred to the mother goddess Freya. During the Middle Ages, it was a medicinal and magical plant and was thought to be effective in "opening" hidden treasures in particular. It is a symbol of spring since it "unlocks" spring and the sight of it drives off gloomy thoughts of winter. It is a symbol of Mary because, through her son Jesus, Mary opens the gate of heaven for men.

Prince - See KING'S SON.

Prince of the World - Allegorical (symbolic) representation of evil in the world, whereby the "world" is regarded as a female deceiver and seductress (analogous to LADY WORLD).

Princess - See KING'S DAUGHTER.

Privy Purse - In medieval pictures (of Mary), it is a symbol of virginity.

Prostitution - See SACRED PROSTITUTION.

Prudence - The cardinal virtue of PRUDENTIA.

Prudentia - The personification of prudence, one of the four cardinal virtues; frequently represented with the SERPENT, MIRROR, SIEVE, and TORCH as attributes.

Puppet - A figurine that is held up and moved by threads, wires or sticks; a symbol of man's dependence on superior powers; in a more restricted sense, it is also a symbol of a personality that has no will and is directed from without.

Purple - Shares to a large extent in the symbolism of the colors RED or VIOLET. In earlier times, genuine purple, which was yielded from the dye of the *purpura* mollusk, was reserved for the clothes of rulers and priests due to its costliness and thus became a symbol of power and high rank; later, it was thought of as a general sign of luxury and affluence, especially among the Romans.

Pyramids - Like the OBELISK, the Egyptian pyramid, that monumental grave structure of Egyptian kings during the Old and Middle Kingdoms, is a symbol (sign) of Egypt and Africa. In conjunction with the story of Joseph of Egypt, pyramids can be thought of as granaries (a symbol of wealth). —In esoterica, pyramids are symbols of the comprehensive, secret, but lost, knowledge of the ancient Egyptians, a knowledge that cannot be confirmed.

Pythagoras - A Greek philosopher; a symbolic figure of science in conjunction with the Seven Liberal ARTS; as head of the Gnostic school of the Pythagoreans, he is also a symbolic figure of representatives of esoterica in the broadest sense (such as NUMBER SYMBOLISM).

 **Quadrivium** - The four final paths of learning (arithmetic, geometry, music and astronomy) that, together with the TRIVIUM, constitute the Seven Liberal ARTS.

Quail - In China, the quail is a symbol of spring because it is a migratory bird that returns in the spring. It is closely associated with fire, light and thus with the Yang principle. Its annual coming and going also made the quail a symbol of the alternating influence of the opposing forces YIN AND YANG. See FROG.

Quicksilver - See MERCURY.

Quince - In antiquity, the quince was a symbol of happiness, love and fertility and was sacred to Aphrodite (Venus); the "apple" in antiquity was probably a quince, as were probably the apples of the Hesperides. In Greece, women brought a quince into the house of their husbands at their wedding as a symbol of an anticipated happy marriage.

Quintessence - The fifth ELEMENT that, along with fire, water, earth and air, was suggested in some speculations in alchemy in order to posit a purely spiritual element (world spirit) over the other individual elements. The PENTAGRAM is its graphic representation. See FIVE.

RAHAB: Battle with the chaos serpent (from an Assyrian cylinder seal)

RAM: Zodiacal sign Aries (from a medieval woodcut) and the modern astrological sign

Rabbit - See HARE.

Radish - During the Middle Ages, the radish had a predominantly negative symbolic meaning as a symbol of quarrel and strife. Because the radish, like the turnip, was said to be related to evil spirits, radishes and turnips were sometimes consecrated, that is, rendered harmless.

Rags - A symbol of material poverty; especially in fairy tales, inner wealth can be hiding behind them: a symbol of the superiority of the essential *vis a vis* mere appearance.

Rahab - The name means "turbulent." It is a monster of chaos, an embodiment of the primeval waters, vanquished by the creator; at the same time, it is a symbolic name of Egypt.

Rain - Rain is thought of all over the world as a symbol of heavenly workings on the earth, as a symbol of fertility, and frequently as a fertilization of the earth by heaven (rain drops as the sperm of the gods); in this sense, it is also a visual symbol of the spiritual-mental influence of the gods upon the earth. See ONE-LEG-GEDNESS.

Rainbow - The rainbow is frequently a symbol of the union of heaven (see SKY) and EARTH. According to Talmudic tradition, the rainbow was created on the evening of the sixth day of Creation. In Greek mythology, the rainbow is the embodiment of the messenger of the goddess Iris; in Germanic mythology, it is the bridge Bifröst joining Asgard and Mid-gard. — After the Flood, God placed a rainbow in the sky as a sign of His covenant with humans; in medieval depictions of Christ as ruler of the world, for example, Christ reigns on a rainbow, which is to be understood in this sense. Thus, the rainbow also became a symbol of Mary, the intermediary of reconciliation. —The symbolic interpretation of the colors of the rainbow depends on how many colors one distinguishes; in China, for example, FIVE colors of the rainbow are recognized, their synthesis symbolizing the union of YIN AND YANG. —In accordance with the Aristotelean tradition of a three-fold division, only the three primary colors (a symbol of the Trinity) are distinguished in Christianity; yet the colors blue (the water of the Flood or the heavenly origin of Christ), red (the coming destruction of the

RAINBOW

The rainbow, a striking and central symbol and sign, articulates man's hope for a better world. Is it any wonder that the rainbow, one of the greatest symbols, became the one that was most misused, robbed of its meaning, and commercialized? - If one pursues the history of the rainbow symbol back to the beginnings of literary tradition, then we find the rainbow in Babylonian literature as a sign of wrath, of terror, and of ill, and as an attribute of the goddess Tir-an-na, bringer of misfortune. This aspect also appears in ancient Jewish writings. Specifically, an apocryphal writing claims that God removed the layer of wrath from the bow in the clouds, meaning that He detached the band of fury from the devastat-

Christ on a rainbow; from a depiction of the Last Judgement, 1543

ing waters of the Flood, which came from the high windows of heaven, and then spread out the bow in the clouds: instead of the flood waters, the rainbow, created on the eve of the first sabbath, now shines as the arch of peace. Thus, the rainbow underwent a complete change in meaning: the bow went from being a symbol of wrath and terror of the goddess Tir-an-na to the symbol of peace, the sign of the covenant between Yahweh and man.

In this context, Alfons Rosenberg has an interesting idea. In particular, he suspects that the bow mentioned in Genesis 9:8–17 does not at all refer to a rainbow, but rather to the arc of the zodiac. This would indeed be a much deeper embedment of the mundane event of the Flood in a larger, more comprehensive cosmic context than would be possible with the rainbow image.

Top: Rainbow with zodiacal symbols from Schedel's *Weltchronik* (Chronicle of the World);
Above: Dürer's Melencholia I refers to ancient astrological-esoteric ideas that associate the rainbow with prophesy and divination. The meaning of the rainbow here is still puzzling.

world by fire or the Passion of Christ), and green (the new world or Christ's workings on earth) are also distinguished. See BRIDGE.

Rainbow Coins - Celtic coins that were supposedly found at the ends of a rainbow; in reality, they were revealed by heavy storm rains. The coins bear no writing, but have images that are typical of Celtic symbolic thought.

Ram (Aries) - A symbol of strength. In antiquity, the ram was one of the most favored sacrifical animals. —The Egyptian god of creation, Chnum, was depicted with a ram's head. —Greeks and Romans worshipped the (originally Egyptian) wind god Amun as the incarnation of the highest god in the form of the ram-headed Jupiter-(Zeus-)Ammon. —The ram is an attribute of Indra and Hermes. —In Christianity, representations of the ram occasionally allude to Isaac's "sacrifice" as a symbolic auger of Christ's martyr death. —The ram, or Aries, is the first sign of the zodiac; it corresponds to the first month of spring; the sun passes the sign between March 21 and April 20; the sun is exalted in Aries; Aries is the house of Mars; since the times of Hellenic astrology, Mars (Pluto), the sun and Venus have been its decans; in Indian astrology, Mars, the sun and Jupiter have been its decans. The triplicity of Aries is fire; Aries is masculine, positive (active) and a cardinal sign. Nothing specific is known of the origin of the name of the constellation.

Ranunculus - Very common family of plants having many species; some species with particularly powerful medicinal properties are encountered in medieval images as attributes of Mary. Often confused with pink root.

Rat - In Asia, the rat is often a symbolic animal that brings good luck; in Japan, it is an attendant of the god of wealth; in China as well as in Siberia, the absence of rats in one's home and yard is regarded as an unsettling sign. —In Indian mythology, the rat is ridden by the elephant-headed god Ganesha (see ELEPHANT). —In Europe, on the other hand, the rat is considered by folk belief to be the sign of sickness, witches, demons and goblins. When rats leave one's house or ship, this is, however, also regarded as a sign of misfortune (it is usually an entirely rational indicator of waning provisions or of impending inconveniences). —The rat is the first sign of the Chinese ZODIAC; it corresponds to Aries (see RAM).

Raven - Because of its colors, its croaking call and its obtrusiveness, it is regarded by many peoples (of the Orient and the Occident) as an evil omen that portends sickness, war and death. The Bible counts it among the unclean animals. In the symbolic thought of the Middle Ages, it sometimes symbolizes the deadly sin of gluttony. —On the other hand, though, it was thought to be divine and sun-like in many cultures (possibly due in part to its intelligence). —In Japan, the raven (especially the red raven) was a divine messenger and symbol of the sun. In Chinese thought, a three-footed raven lives in the sun. —In Persia, ravens were sacred to the god of light and to the sun and thus played a role in the MITHRA cult (images exist on numerous Mithra stones). —Greeks and Romans saw white ravens in connection with the sun god Helios and with Apollo. —In Nordic mythology, two ravens, called Hugin (thought) and Munin (memory), were associated with Odin, the highest of the Aases. —An intelligent raven also plays a role in various flood legends: Noah sent one out to look for land; similar events are recounted in Babylonian legends. —Ravens were sometimes regarded as terrible parents who neglect their young, which is why we today still have the expressions "raven father" and "raven mother." —Because the raven likes to live alone, it is also a symbol of self-imposed solitude; this is perhaps why it symbolizes the rebellious and the faithless in Christianity. —The Romans thought of the call of the raven as a symbol of hope: *cras, cras* ("tomorrow, tomorrow").

Rebis - From *res bina*, meaning "the twofold." A term in alchemy for the HERMAPHRODITE.

Red - Red is the color of FIRE and BLOOD and, like these, it is symbolically equivocal. Positive: color of life, of love, or warmth, of enthusiatic passion, of fertility. Negative: color of war, of the destructive power of fire, of the spilling of blood, of hate. —In antiquity, there was a widely held belief that red protected one from dangers. Thus, people occasionally red-washed things such as animals, trees and possessions in order to protect them from evil influences or to make them fertile. In Egypt, red, the color of the red-hot desert, was regarded as a symbol of that which was "evil" and "destructive"; that is why scribes, for example, used a red ink made specifically for writing disparaging words on papyrus; as the color of the crown of Lower Egypt, though, red has a positive meaning. —Among the Romans, brides

REINDEER: 2 fighting reindeer, cave painting (grotto Font-de-Gaume, Dordogne)

wore a fiery red veil, called a "flammeum," a symbolic reference to love and fertility. As a symbol of power, red was also the color of emperors, the nobility, and generals among the Romans. —Highly placed officers of the law were also inclined to make use of the color red; during the Middle Ages, for example, executioners, as lords over life and death, wore red robes (even today in many countries, red is the color of judges, especially of senior ones). —Cardinals wear red as a reference to the blood of the martyrs. —Yet Satan, the lord of hell, and the Whore of Babylon are also clothed in red: an expression of the consuming power of hell-fire or of unchecked desires and passions. — In alchemy, red was often thought to be the color of the PHILOSOPHERS' STONE, which was thought of as a stone that bore the sign of sunlight. —As a bold color promising new beginning, new life and warmth, red is also the banner color of revolution.

Reed - Because it easily quivers in the wind, it is a symbol of vacillation and weakness; because of its pliability, though, it is also occasionally a symbol of flexibility. —According to Shinto mythology, the creation of the world began with reeds spouting up everywhere from the prime-

val waters. —Because the Roman soldiers mocked Jesus by putting a septer of reeds in His hand, it is also occasionally an attribute in *ecce homo* representations.

Reindeer - Reindeer are found even in CAVE PAINTINGS from pre-historical times, where they probably served cult purposes. —In the northern areas of Eurasia, the reindeer plays an important role as an animal that is symbolic of the Moon and that, as a guide of souls, is closely related to night and the realm of the dead.

Resin - Because of its non-perishability and because it is usually extracted from evergreen trees, it is a symbol of immortality. See MYRRH; INCENSE.

Revelation, Book of - The final canonical and only prophetic book of the New Testament, written by St. John the Divine on the island of Patmos. It contains seven epistles to Christian communities in Asia Minor and presages the imminent end of the world. These visions, some of which are difficult to explain, depict impending horrors, the dominion of the Antichrist, and his overthrow.

Rhombus - Because of its shape, which is

reminiscent of the female genitalia, the rhombus is a female sexual symbol; it is thus occasionally a general symbol of earthly and chthonic powers.

Ribbon - Frequently a symbol of sovereign or judicial power. The ribbon designates the power to bind and to set free. In other contexts, it can also be a symbol of obligations freely entered into.

Rice - Rice in Asiatic countries corresponds to WHEAT in Europe as an important food and thus has essential symbolic meanings in common with the latter. —In Japan, rice, and especially the stocked rice pantry, is also a symbol of abundance and of spiritual wealth as well. —In China, red rice, in particular, was regarded as a symbol of immortality. —The laborious task of rice cultivation was often thought to be a consequence of the rift between heaven (see SKY) and EARTH.

Right and Left - In folk belief and in many religions, the right side is regarded as the better side that brings good luck (see MELOTHESIA). —Frequently (such as in antiquity), the right arm (which carries weapons), and thus the right side in general, was a symbol of strength and success. —The seat at the right-hand side of God, a ruler or a host is regarded as a preferred place of honor. —At the Last Judgment, the chosen stand at the right side of God, the damned at the left. —In knowingly switching the valuation of right and left, black magic assumes that ceremonial actions are performed with the left hand, the left side, etc. —In China, the left side—which is thought of in the Christian-Occidental tradition as being passive—is associated with heaven, the active, masculine principle, and thus with Yang (see YIN AND YANG), whereas the right side is associated with the earth, fertility, harvest, the feminine principle, and thus with Yin. Accordingly, one gives with the left hand and receives with the right in China, for example. —In Cabalistic tradition, the right hand of God symbolizes mercy, the left hand justice; the right hand is thus used for giving blessings, and is the hand of the priestly caste, whereas the left hand is that of kings.

Ring - Because of its shape, which has neither beginning nor end, the ring is a symbol of eternity; furthermore, it is a symbol of union, of fidelity, of belonging to a community and is thus also a distinction and a sign of office and high position as well (official rings of Roman senators, civil servants, knights, university doctors).

RIVER: The four rivers of Eden; from an Alsatian miniature, 12th century
ROCK: Sisyphus with the rock; picture from a Greek vase

The idea pertaining to the magical power of the CIRCLE is also a part of the symbolism of the ring; thus, the ring is often attributed with having an apotropaic effect (against the evil eye, for example) along with the characteristic of being a magical agent; for that reason, it is also worn as an AMULET; according to folk superstition, the loss or breaking of a ring signifies ill.

River - Because of their importance for agrarian fertility, rivers were often worshipped as deities, such as among the Greeks and Romans, who worshipped them as local, masculine gods. —Rivers generally bear close symbolic relationship to WATER. Because of their fluidity, rivers are a symbol of time and impermanence, yet also of constant renewal. —The confluence of all rivers into the ocean is regarded as a symbol of the unification of individuality and the absolute, such as in Buddhism and Hinduism, where it is a symbol of merging with Nirvana. —In Judaism, for example, a river rolling down from the mountains is interpreted as being a symbol of heavenly mercy. The notion of four rivers of Eden is encountered in Judaism and Christianity as well as in India; in Christian art, they often spring from a hill on which Christ or the Lamb

of God is standing and symbolize the four Evangelists.

Rivers of Eden - See RIVER.

Robe - A symbol of protection (such as the protective robe of the Madonna in Christian art of the Middle Ages) or of high position (such as the king's robe). It is sometimes also a symbol of the wearer. A veil can also have the function of a robe.

Robed Madonna - See ROBE.

Rock - A symbol of solidity and immutability. In the Bible, rock is a symbol of the strength and fidelity of God the protector. The water-giving rock in the desert is thought to be a symbolic herald of Christ as the giver of the water of life. As the cornerstone of the church, Peter (the surname of Simon, from the Greek *petros* meaning "rock") is compared with a rock. —In Chinese landscape painting, rock appears as firm, corresponding to the Yang principle (see YIN AND YANG) and frequently the opposite of the unstable, continuously moving waterfall, which embodies the Yin principle. —The rock that, according to the Greek myth, Sisyphus must constantly roll up a mountain and that rolls backs down again and again

ROCK PICTURE: Cave picture with hunting scenes from the cave at Los Caballos (Castellón, Spain)

at the last moment, is a symbol of futile effort, but also generally of the wishes of human life that are never ultimately satisfied.

Rock Paintings - Also called "cave drawings." A term for permanent paintings, drawings, and reliefs (see BAS-RELIEFS) made on rock walls; in a more restricted sense, the terms refers to the rock paintings, drawings, scratchings, and engravings on cave walls and roofs dating from the Paleolithic and Neolithic periods. Rock paintings are found all over the world and some even date from historic times; they are still to be found among isolated hunting cultures. The earliest rock paintings can be dated at about 30,000 B.C. Rock paintings—now generally appreciated as convincing evidence of primitive artistic skill—are characterized by a great wealth of expression and, in part, by stark naturalism, yet also by a limitation of motifs (usually animals, more seldomly humans, as well as symbolic signs). Their significance should not be sought in the context of picture magic (hunting magic), but rather in a cultural-religious context. The rock paintings of the limestone caves in southern France (such as at Lascaux, Les Combarelles, and Font-de-Gaume), on the northern slope of the Pyrenees (such

as at Trois-Frères) and in northwestern Spain (such as at Altamira and El Castillo) are from the Upper Paleolithic period. Mammoths, bison, stag, bear and wild horses are represented in mostly black, red, or brown drawing. In the Neolithic period, starkly abstract depictions of humans appear (still existent in eastern Spain and in the Sahara). The rock paintings in central and southern Africa (art of the bushmen) and in Australia occupy a special position.

Rods - The bundle of rods, the lictors' bundle, the FASCES.

Roland Statues - A term for large statues of a horseman with a shield and sword; located on squares and markets, they are symbols of freedom and the rule of law; they are probably named after the hero Roland of the Song of Roland, whereby Roland is a symbol of the Christian-Occidental empire under Charlemagne; the sword of these statues typically has a relic in its pommel and the horseman typically is wearing a rose on his clothing as a symbol of martyrdom. Seventeen known Roland statues no longer exist, three exist as fragments, and twenty are entirely preserved, such as those in in Brandenburg, Bremen and Halberstadt. Roughly speak-

ROCK PICTURE: Scene from Swedish landscape at Bohuslän

ing, Roland statues were located in a wide swath along the Elbe and the Saale.

Room - Or "chamber." Many initiation rites involved the locking of the initiate in a secret room, a chamber, an underground space (see CAVE), etc.—a symbol of the maternal womb or of the grave—where he frequently spent the night and where he became privy to spiritual experiences and knowledge. — The secret room that hides forbidden knowledge and that can be entered only under pain of punishment, is also a common fairy tale motif; it appears, for example, as a thirteenth (see THREE) room that, in contrast to the other twelve, is taboo.

Rosary - Rosaries are prayer chains (see PRAYER STRING) whose individual beads represent assistance in meditation and prayer. During the Middle Ages, chains called a "rosary" or *rosarium* became common in the worship of Mary due to the symbolism of the ROSE, which is related to Mary. Fifty (or 150) small beads represent so many "Hail Mary" prayers (Gabriel's words to Mary when telling her of the Gospel), in five (or fifteen) sections, each of which is separated by a larger bead (an "Our Father" prayer). Reflection on an event from the life of Jesus or Mary is associated with each section.

Most hand rosaries usually have a trailer of 1 + 3 + 1 beads and a cross.

A large rosary in which the joys and sorrows of Mary are integrated, surrounds the figure of the Mother of God at rosary altars.

Rose - Because of its fragrance, its beauty and its charm (despite its THORNS), it is one of the most frequently encountered symbolic plants. In the Occident, it plays a role similar to that of the LOTUS in Asia. —In antiquity, the rose was sacred to Aphrodite (Venus). The red rose is supposed to have come from the blood of Adonis; it was a symbol of love and affection, of fertility and also of reverence toward the dead. Roses were used to garland Dionysus (Bacchus) and festival participants at drinking bouts, in part because they, like the VIOLET, were attributed with having a cooling effect on the brain. In addition, they were supposed to remind the drinkers not to divulge anything while they were intoxicated. The rose, often in conjunction with the cross, was still a symbol of secrecy in early Christianity as well. In addition, it was attributed with numerous other meanings in Christian symbolism: the red rose refers to the spilled blood and the wounds of Christ; it also symbolizes

ROSARY: Symbolic representation of the joyful (left), painful (center), and glorious (right) rosary (from Schmid's *Musterbuch*)

the chalice that caught the holy blood; because of its symbolic association with the blood of Christ, it is also a symbol of mystical rebirth. Since the rose was a symbol of virgins during the Middle Ages, it is also a symbol of Mary; the red rose is also a symbol of divine love generally. —The rose windows of medieval churches are symbolically closely related to the CIRCLE and the WHEEL and thus probably with the SUN as a symbol of Christ as well. —In alchemy, the rose, usually seven-petaled, played a role as a symbol of complex relationships, be they, for example, of the seven planets with their corresponding metals or of the various steps within alchemistic operations.

Rosemary - A small, fragrant bush found in Mediterranean countries; it was frequently burned in sacrifices by the Romans because of its pleasant smell. In folk custom, the rosemary was thought to be an agent against diseases and evil spirits and was used as such especially at births, weddings, and deaths. As a hardy, evergreen plant, the rosemary is also an ancient symbol of love, fidelity, fertility, and—as a funerary flower—a symbol of immortality as well; in earlier times when they were not yet being braided of myrtle, bridal wreaths were often woven of rosemary.

Rosette - See ROSE; ROSE WINDOW; TRACERY.

Ruby - Because of the ruby's intense color, the symbolic significance of the ruby frequently corresponds to that of RED; since the Middle Ages, it has been attributed with therapeutic effects.

Rue - A strongly fragrant, pleasant smelling plant; it is a symbolic and magical plant that is supposed to protect a bride from black magic because it is protected by Mary; it is also called a "death herb" because people lay wreaths of wound rue onto the chest or neck of corpses.

Rune - Gothic "runa"; Middle High German "rûne" (meaning "secret"); borrowed early on by Finnish as "runo" (meaning "song"); it possibly originated from the Celtic, but its etymology is debated. Runes are the oldest scripted signs of the ancient Germans; with the coming of Christian civilization into Germanic regions, runes were gradually supplanted by Latin

f u þ a r k

g w h n l j

e p R s t b

e m l ng o d

ROSE: Rose as a rose cross; from Robert Fludd's *Summum Bonum*
RUNE: Runic alphabet

script. Each rune designates both a letter and a word; aside from their use as a script, runes also had cultic-magical significance (rune magic). —In Germanic mythology, some gods were attributed with a particularly high level of mastery of runic doctrine and runic magic, especially Odin, who was often thought of as the creator of runes.

Rush Plant - A grass-like, long-lived plant. In Christianity, it is a symbol of God's indefatigable love. In conjunction with the BEE, it is a part of Egyptian royal titulary.

RUNE: Rune engravers with their implements that are covered with rune-like markings; from Olaus Magnus

ROSE WINDOW

Some rose windows of the High Middle Ages embody a particular form of medieval ICONOGRAPHY, such as the rose of the cathedral of Lausanne, where the number 4 (which, as the squared number 2 x 2, manifests the perfection of the maternal number 2) is the determining factor in the arrangement of squares and circles to which day and night, sun and Moon, seasons and months, rivers of Eden and hybrid creatures, elements and signs of the zodiac, fortune-telling techniques and winds are subordinate. The knowledge and world image of an era, written down in many encyclopedias dating from the conclusion of antiquity and the beginning of the Middle Ages, have been made accessible in a form comprehensible to the eye, thereby imparting early Christian doctrinal teaching by means of the geometric conceptional schemes of illustrated manuscripts and encyclopedias and of the figured wheel of the High Middle Ages in particular (according to H.R. Hahnloser). A depiction of the unusual construction of this rose (albeit variant in some important details) was made by Villard de Honnecourt (1225?–1250), the great French illustrator of the 13th century. Most large rose windows are of the wheel construction, such as those at Chartres or Strasbourg, but the rose window of Lausanne is marked by the alternate penetration of squares and circles, whereby it becomes apparent that an attempt was made to combine the finite with the infinite by means of the interpenetration of the square and the circle.

Bibliography: Ellen J. Beer, *Die Rose der Kathedrale von Lausanne*, Bern 1952; Painton Cowen, *Die Rosenfenster der gotischen Kathedralen*, Freiburg–Basel–Wien 1972.

ROSE WINDOW: Left: Design of Villard de Honnecourt's rose; above: rose window: idealized gothic rose window

The Creation (inner square)
I Annus = God of the Year
II Sol = Sun
III Dies = Day
IV Luna = Moon
V Nox = Night
Time: Seasons and Months
(semi-circles on inner square)
A Autumpnus = autumn
A_1 September
A_2 October
A_3 November
B Hyems = winter
B_1 December
B_2 January
B_3 February
C Ver = spring
C_1 March
C_2 April
C_3 May
D Estas = summer
D_1 June
D_2 July
D_3 August

The 4 Primary and Secondary Winds
(outer circle)
a Euroauster = southeast wind
b Subsolanus = east wind
c Volturnus = northeast wind
d Septentrio = north wind
e Corus = northwest wind
f Zephirus = west wind
g Austrozephir = southwest wind
h Auster = south wind
Eden and the Bounds of the World
(outer square)
I Tigris = River of Eden in the south
Ia Oculos
Ib Cynomology
II Pison = River of Eden in the north
IIa Pingmei
IIb Satyri
III Euphrates = River of Eden in the
west
IIIa Sciapodes
IIIb Ceffi
IV Gihon = River of Eden in the east
IVa Aethiopes
IVb Gangrida

The Elements, the Signs of the
Zodiac and the Arts of
Divination (semi-circles on
outer square)
1 Ignis = fire (element)
1_1 Cancer
1_2 Leo
1_3 Virgo
1_4 Pyromancia = divination by
fire
2 Terra = earth (element
2_1 Libra
2_2 Scorpio
2_3 Sagittarius
2_4 Geomancia = divination by
earth
3 Aqua = water (element)
3_1 Capricorn
3_2 Aquarius
3_3 Pisces
3_4 Hydromancia = divination
by water
4 Aer = air (element)
4_1 Aries
4_2 Taurus
4_3 Gemini
4_4 Aerimancia = divination by
air

SALAMANDER: Salamander in fire;
from an illustration by Charles
Pesnot, Lyon, 1555

SCALE: Zodiacal sign Libra (from a
medieval woodcut) and the modern
astrological sign

Sacred Prostitution - Usually conducted in temples; common in the Ancient Orient, Greece, India and elsewhere; it was thought to be a symbol of union with the gods and a fertility ritual.

Sacrifice - As a ritual act, it is (among other things) a symbol of a renunciation of earthly goods for the benefit of a union with God, gods or ancestors (although it is frequently a magical act that simultaneously has a purpose). Sacramental offerings of food are also common, whereby only a portion of the gifts (usually consisting of sacrificial animals) is burned and the rest is eaten communally by the sacrificers as a sign of a sacramental community or also of a union with God, gods, etc. —C.G. Jung interpreted certain sacrificial animals, such as the sacrificial steer of the MITHRA cult, as a symbol of victory of man's spirituality over his bestiality.

Sacrificial Animals - See SACRIFICE.

Saffron - See CROCUS.

Sage - A labiate flower having fragrant leaves; it is a multipurpose medicinal plant and is thus also an attribute of Mary in Christian art of the Middle Ages.

Säge - An unknown sea creature mentioned in PHYSIOLOGUS; it is probably a DOLPHIN.

Sagittarius/Archer - The archer, or Sagittarius, is the ninth sign of the zodiac; it corresponds to the last month of fall; the sun passes it between November 22 and December 20; it is the house of Jupiter; in Hellenic astrology, Mercury, the Moon, and Saturn are its decans; in Indian astrology, Mars and the sun are its decans. The triplicity of Sagittarius is fire; Sagittarius is masculine, positive (active) and a moveable sign. Sagittarius's name and image as a constellation are clearly derived from Babylonian representations of a centaur (with wings) and bow, as could originally be found on Babylonian border markers (Kudurrus).

Sal - See SALT.

Salamander - According to folk belief of the Middle Ages, the salamander is an elementary spirit that can live in fire unharmed and that is thus a symbol of flames *in toto*; it was regarded, among

SCALE: Creation scene; the scale as a symbol of divine justice; from an illustration in the *Cotton Psalter*, 11th century

SCALE: The archangel Michael weighing souls; 13th century, Meister von Soriguerola

other things, as a symbol of the righteous person who maintains peace of mind despite attacks. PHYSIOLOGUS associates the fire-quenching characteristic of the salamander with the statement that, like the three men in the furnace (Daniel 3), the righteous man sustains no harm.

Salt - Because of its importance for life and because of its rarity in earlier times, it was of high value. It was often thought to be a symbol of vitality and was thought to ward off ill. Since it is often yielded from WATER through evaporation, it was sometimes also seen as a symbol of a combination of water and FIRE. On the other hand, the grain of salt that dissolves in the ocean is a symbol of the assumption of individuality in the absolute. Because of its necessity for life, its ability to season foods and to cleanse, its incorruptibility and ability to preserve foods as well as because of its clear, transparent appearance, it is also a common symbol of moral and spiritual powers. In the Sermon on the Mount, Christ compares the disciples with the salt of the earth. In another passage in the Bible, there is talk of the salt of sorrow through which the apostles and Christ must pass in order to attain eternal life. —In Japan, salt was frequently used ritually as a symbol of inner cleansing and protection; accordingly, salt was strewn, for example, on thresholds, the edges of water wells, floors after funeral services, etc. To this day, some Japanese strew salt in their houses after an unpleasant person has left. —With particular respect to its agency as a food seasoning, salt is also a symbol of intellectually stimulating talk and of wit. —Among the Semitic peoples and the Greeks, salt, often in conjunction with BREAD, is a symbol of friendship and hospitality. Bread and salt are also frequently paradigmatic of basic, necessary nourishment. —In the Bible or among mystics, for example, salt appears in a negative sense as a symbol of destructive power and, especially in the case of the salt desert, as a symbol of barrenness and damnation. —In alchemy (where it is usually called by its Latin name *sal*), salt is one of the philosophical elements and world principles, next to SULPHUR and quicksilver (see MERCURY); it represents that which is solid and corporeal (corpus).

Samaritan - A symbolic figure of the selfless helper of the injured (Luke 10:29 ff.); the Samaritan is interpreted by the church fathers as being Christ.

Sand - Because of the innumerability of its grains, it is a symbol of infinity.

SATOR-AREPO FORMULA

A square, closely related to the MAGIC SQUARES, that contains letters and whose oldest authenticated specimens (in Roman Pompeii and in Syrian Dura Europos) are comprised of the series Rotas - Arepo - Tenet - Arepo - Sator. The form Sator - Arepo - Tenet - Opera - Rotas, preserved in Greek, Coptic and Ethiopian letters, did not become prevalent until the 6th century. The five words can be read vertically in both directions as well as from left to right or from right to left.

The translation of the Sator-Arepo formula is usually given as "The sower Arepo holds the wheels with difficulty," but "The sower holds the plough, the worker the wheels," or satanic conjurings and many other more or less reasonable translations (combinations) have been suggested. The Sator-Arepo formula also became tied to symbols of the Evangelists and, in alchemy, to the signs of the zodiac. Many so-called palindromes are known, such as Satan - Adama -

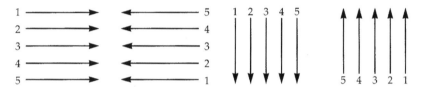

The four possible ways of reading the SATOR-AREPO formula

The magical letter square from a mosaic floor of the parish church of Pieve Terzagni near Cremona, circa 11th century (from J.B. Bauer)

Alchemistic seal with symbols of the zodaical signs Taurus, Leo, Scorpio and Aquarius

Tabat - Amada - Nadas, an equivalent to the Sator-Arepo formula that became associated with the order of the Knights Templars, which was destroyed in 1314. Interpretation is not easy; one cannot decide, for example, whether a meaning is to be "read into" or "read from" the square. Recent research has plausibly suggested that the Sator-Arepo formula is of neither Jewish nor Christian origin, but that its roots rather are probably in Stoic thought; the basis of this view is the meaning of the "central" word TENET around which the other words have probably been "sought" by the required palindrome form: TENET is supposed to mean that God the Creator "ties together" all His works, which thus leads to the phenomenon of SYMPATHY in MICROCOSM-MACROCOSM thought.

Bibliography: F. Focke. *Sator arepo* from *Würzburger Jahrbücher für die Altertumswissenschaft* 3, 1948, pp. 366–401.

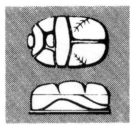

SCARAB: Egyptian (obverse view and side view)
SCORPION: Zodiacal sign Scorpio (from a medieval woodcut) and the modern astrological symbol

Sand Pictures - Representations made from multi-colored sand specifically by the Navajo Indians (even in the 20th century); they deal primarily with myths of the creation; they emphasize the duality of man and water, Father Sky and Mother Earth, together with the four holy plants, etc.

Sapphire - During antiquity and the Middle Ages, the sapphire was thought to be curative (although it was frequently identified with the LAPIS LAZULI); because of its blue color, it is a symbol of the sky, or heavenly protection or—among the alchemists—of air. In the Book of Revelation, sapphire is among the foundations of Holy Jerusalem. —In the Orient, the sapphire, like all blue stones, is regarded as a particularly effective defense against the evil eye.

Satan - The Hebrew word for the DEVIL. Other frequently used names are Beelzebub or Belial.

Saturn - The Greek Chronos. In ancient mythology, Saturn is the father of Jupiter (see CHRONOS). —Astronomically and astrologically, Saturn is the white-pale blue shimmering planet that was known even in antiquity and is not particularly

striking. In alchemy, Saturn is LEAD; see METALS.

Satyr - Hybrid creatures in human form having an animal's ears, horns, tails and hooves; they are in the entourage of Dionysus.

Saxifrage - A short shrub that usually grows on stones and also works its way into cracks and crevices, which is why people once said that it could break apart rocks. With respect to this, it appears as a symbol of the resurrected Christ, before whom "rocks split apart."

Scale (Libra) - A symbol of moderate balance and of justice and thus of judging and of the public pronouncement of verdicts. It is also a symbol of the judgment of the dead; in Egyptian books of the dead, Horus and Anubis weigh the hearts of the dead against a feather (see OSTRICH) before Osiris, a representation that one often encounters in Egyptian art. —In antiquity, the scale appears in Homer in the form of Zeus's golden scale as a symbol of authority and justice, for example. — In Christian art, depiction of the archangel Michael as a weigher of souls, especially in depictions of the Last Judgment, is very common. —The scale or "Libra" is

SCYTHE: Death as a skeleton with scythe and hour-glass; detail from an engraving by Anders Trost

SEA-HORSE: Copy from a French bestiarium

the seventh sign of the zodiac; it corresponds to the first month of autumn; the sun passes the sign between September 23 and October 22; Saturn is exalted in Libra. It is the house of Venus; since the time of Hellenic astrology, the Moon, Saturn and Jupiter have been its decans; in Indian astrology, Venus, Saturn and Mercury are its decans. The triplicity of Libra is air; Libra is masculine, positive (active) and a cardinal sign. The origin of the constellation Libra is still largely unclear.

Scalloped Stones - Basin-like indentations in MENHIRS or protruding cliffs, usually found in conjunction with Bronze Age MEGALITHS or rock drawings of megalith civilizations; their meaning is controversial; it is conjectured that they are (for the most part) sights used to determine the fixed points of calendars or images of constellations.

Scarab - Also called "dung-beetle," "sacred scarabaeus." The scarab makes "pills" out of dung that are then sunk into the ground and into which the female lays eggs. In Egypt, the apparent origin of the scarab from these balls made it a sacred, sun-like animal (its name corresponds with the word for "rising sun") and a symbol of resurrection, widely common in the form of seal stones or amulets. Larger versions were laid upon mummies' hearts; they carry a passage from the book of the dead in which the heart is called upon not to speak badly of the deceased person at the judgment of the dead.

Scissors - As tools for cutting, scissors are a symbol of the active, masculine principle. In Greek mythology, they are a symbol of the Moira (see MOIRAI) Atropos who used them to cut the THREAD OF LIFE: a symbol of man's dependence on the powers that control fate and a symbol of sudden death.

Scorpion (Scorpio) - In Egypt, it was thought of as a dangerous and feared, yet sacred animal that was accorded divine reverence; an Egyptian fertility goddess and protectoress of the deceased was portrayed with a scorpion on her head; one also sometimes encounters representations of scorpions having the head of Isis. —In Africa, the scorpion was often so much feared as an embodiment of dangerous powers that people did not dare say its name. —In the Bible, scorpions appear as punishments from God, as a symbol of the apostate Israelites or as a symbol of the devil. —In medieval art, the scorpion symbolizes Satan, the heretic,

SEAL: Opening the book with the 7
   seals; from a miniature from the 2nd
   half of the 13th century
SERAPH: Seraph from the Cathedral of
   Reims; 1st half of the 13th century

death or envy. —The scorpion or Scorpio is the eighth sign of the zodiac and corresponds to the second month of fall; the sun passes it between October 23 and November 21; it is the house of Mars (Pluto); since the times of Hellenistic astrology, Mars, the sun (Uranus) and Venus have been its decans; in Indian astrology, Mars, Jupiter and the Moon have been its decans. The triplicity of Scorpio is water; Scorpio is feminine, negative (passive) and a rigid sign. The constellation name "Scorpio" can be found even in Babylonian sources.

Scots Pine - A species of coniferous trees found in northern temperate zones. Because it is an evergreen tree and because of its non-perishable resin, it is a symbol of immortality in China and Japan; in Japan, moreover, it is a symbol of life force and of the personality that overcomes the difficulties of life unharmed, since it is a tree that holds up to wind and weather. Two Scots pines are a symbol of love and marital fidelity. See STONE-PINE.

Screech Owl - See OWL.

Scythe - Like the SICKLE, the scythe is a symbol of all-destroying time (see CHRONOS) and of death. Since the Renaissance, it has

especially been an attribute of the personifications of time and death, portrayed as a SKELETON.

Sea Horse - A bringer of good luck for fishermen on the Mediterranean as well as an AMULET against fevers; as animals that draw the chariots of Mediterranean deities, they are associated with cosmic power and the "swelling of the foaming sea"; for the Chinese, sea horses were bastard sons of the dragon. In antiquity, they were escorts of souls to the next life.

Seal - Very common as a representative of individual property law, authority, etc., especially in the ancient Orient. In the Bible and in Christian literature, the seal, like the coin (see MONEY), is sometimes mentioned as a symbol of belonging to God. Divine mysteries are also sealed, such as in the Book of Revelation, in which the LAMB opens the book with the seven seals.

Seal of Solomon - See HEXAGRAM.

Seasons - In art, the seasons are frequently represented by personifications, especially by feminine figures or genies with attributes, such as flowers, lambs or kids for the spring, sheaves of grain, a sickle

SERPENT: Serpent staff on a Sumerian vase

SERPENT: The uraeus serpent with sun disk; bronze

or fire-spewing dragon for the summer, a hare, cornucopia or fruit for the autumn, and venison, salamander, wild duck or a hearth fire for winter. In Christian art, the seasons sometimes appear as symbols of the stages of life; since they return each year, they are symbols of the hope of resurrection.

Sea Urchin - Echinodermata that live primarily in the coastal areas of the world's oceans. Petrified sea urchins played a role among the Celts as symbols of the world EGG.

Sempervivum - A yellow-flowered perennial having fleshy leaves. Popular belief thought that it offered protection against lightning and storms ("thunder plant"). As an extremely long-lived plant, it was also a symbol for eternal life (compare the Latin name), especially in nativity scenes.

Scepter - A symbol of highest power and authority; was often regarded as a vehicle of divine power; often also an attribute of the gods; developed from the STAFF.

Seraph - The plural form is *seraphim*; from the Hebrew. The seraph is a being (similar to the cherubim) of rather high position that has four or six wings, is men-

tioned in the Bible, and whose name means "the burning one"; it is also encountered as the "fire serpent"; it is the embodiment of spiritual power closely related to the symbolic meaning of LIGHT, FIRE and the bird (see BIRDS).

Serpent - Among most peoples, the serpent plays an extraordinarily important and extremely diverse role as a symbolic animal. The primary characteristics that gave the serpent its symbolic significance were the special place it occupies in the animal kingdom (movement over the ground without legs, living in holes in the ground, yet slipping out of eggs like a bird), its cold, slick and shiny exterior, its poisonous bite and its venom that can be used for medicinal purposes, as well as its periodic shedding of its skin. —It is frequently encountered as a chthonic being, as an adversary of man (but also as an apotropaic animal), as a protector of sacred precincts or of the underworld, as an animal having the soul of a human, as a sexual symbol (masculine because of its phallic shape, feminine because of its engulfing belly), and (because of its shedding) as a symbol of constant power of renewal. —In Africa, the serpent was occasionally revered in cults as a spirit or deity. —In ancient Central American civi-

SERPENT: The kundalini snake with the primary canals of the Nadi system as a serpent staff

lizations, the feathered serpent, in particular, played a large role; it was originally a symbol of rain and vegetation and later became a "night sky serpent covered with green quetzal feathers" that stood opposite the "turquoise serpent or day sky serpent" and, united with the latter, represented a symbol of the cosmos. —In China, the serpent was thought to be connected with the earth and water and was thus a Yin symbol (see YIN AND YANG). —In Indian mythology, there are *nagas*, serpents that function as beneficent or maleficent mediators between gods and humans and were sometimes (like other serpents in other civilizations) associated with the RAINBOW. The kundalini serpent, imagined as being rolled up at the bottom end of the spine, is regarded as the seat of cosmic energy and is a symbol of life and (psychologically formulated) libido. —The oldest evidence for a staff of Aesclepius (see AESCLEPIUS, STAFF OF) comes from Mesopotamia (end of the 3rd millenium B.C.). —In the symbolism of the Egyptians, the serpent played an essential and greatly varying role; there were, for example, several serpent goddesses, such as a cobra goddess who presided over the growth of plants. Fate (good or bad) was also sometimes worshipped in the form of a serpent, that is,

as a "house spirit." In addition, there are numerous mythological serpents (winged, with feet, many-headed). The *uraeus* serpent was regarded as a representative of a goddess who had many names; in it, one saw the embodiment of the eye of the sun god; according to mythology, it rises up on its tail end on the sun or on the forehead of the sun god and destroys its enemies with a breath of fire; its likeness appears on the forehead of Egyptian kings as a symbol of protection and rulership. Apophis, the arch-foe of the sun god and of world order, is also in the form of a serpent. In addition, the symbol of the UROBOROS, the serpent biting its own tail, first appeared in Egypt. —The Jews considered the serpent primarily as a threatening creature; the Old Testament counts it among the unclean animals; it appears as the idealized image of sin and of Satan and is the seductress of the first couple in Eden; on the other hand, though, it also appears as a symbol of prudence. When God punished the disobedience of the Israelites with a plague of poisonous, winged serpents, He commanded Moses, who asked for help, to make a BRAZEN SERPENT; whoever was bitten by poisonous serpents and looked upon the brazen one, was to remain alive. Thus, a Brazen Serpent of this type was long a ritual ob-

SERPENT: The Brazen Serpent of
Moses on a cross; alchemistically
interpreted as "serpens
mercurialis"; from Eleazar's *Uraltes
chymisches Werk*, 1760

SERPENT: Serpent swallowing a
person (Mexican codex)

ject of the Jews and was considered by
Christianity to be a symbolic portent of
Christ due to its salutary character; the
serpent figures on bishops' crooks refer
in part to that Brazen Serpent as well as
to the serpent as a symbol of prudence.
—There were numerous mythological and
symbolic serpent figures in antiquity as
well, frequently in the form of monstrous
hybrid creatures (see CHIMERA; ECHID-
NA; HYDRA). In the cult of the god of
healing, Asclepius (Aesculapius), the serpent (with respect to its shedding of its
skin) played an important role as a symbol of the constant self-renewal of life (see
ASCLEPIUS, STAFF OF). Serpents were
often kept in Roman houses as symbols
of house and family spirits. —The Midgard Serpent of Old Norse mythology is
a giant, destructive serpent that closely
surrounds the earth (*Midgard*), which is
thought of as a disk; it is a symbol of constant threat to the world order; in early
Christianity, it was identified with LEVIA-
THAN. —Christian art of the Middle Ages
often emphasizes the seductive aspect of
the serpent of Eden by a close association
with woman (such as depictions of serpents having a woman's head and breasts),
whereby an inner relation to the tempted
Eve is suggested. —In PHYSIOLOGUS,
the serpent is discussed with respect to the

text of Matthew 10:16, "Be ye therefore
wise as serpents, and harmless as doves."
—The serpent is the sixth sign of the Chinese ZODIAC and corresponds to Virgo
(see VIRGIN). —See ASP.

Sesame - An ancient, common cultivated
plant having thimble-like blossoms and
capsular fruits that contain oleiferous
seeds. In China and in the ancient Orient,
the seeds were thought to be a food that
extended one's life and strengthened
one's mind. —The phrase from *1001 Ara-
bian Nights*, "Open, sesame," which was
supposed to cause the treasure cave to
open and reveal its riches, is possibly associated with the sesame plant as well; the
connection would be that one could get
to the treasured seeds only after breaking
open the seed capsule.

Shadow - On the one hand, the shadow
is the opposite of LIGHT; in this respect,
for example, it is an aspect of the Yin principle (see YIN AND YANG); on the other
hand, it is a sort of copy of every physical
phenomenon and, in that respect, it is often interpreted as a particular form of
earthly creatures; in Africa, for example,
the shadow is frequently thought of as the
second, death-related nature of all things.
—In many American Indian languages,

SEVEN

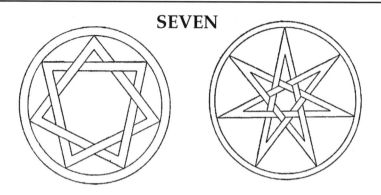

7

A holy number yielded by adding the basic number of the masculine, 3, and the basic number of the feminine, 4, i.e. 3 + 4 = 7. It is the number of the planets (in antiquity) and the number of the days of the week that the planet names bear, as well as the number of days of an individual phase of the Moon. —In Buddhism, there are 7 different heavens. —The Chinese saw the 7 stars of Ursa Major in connection with 7 openings of the body and 7 openings of the human heart. —Among the Babylonians, one also encounters the "evil seven," a group of demons that usually appear together. —In Greece, 7, which was sacred to Apollo and others, played an important role; there are the 7 (or 3) Hesperides, the 7 Gates of Thebes, the 7 sons of Helios, the 7 sons and daughters of Niobe, the Seven Wise Men, the Seven against Thebes, etc. The "Seven Wonders of the World," a collection of the most magnificent buildings and artworks of antiquity, are famous. — 7 is a particularly important number in Judaism. In the Bible, 7 often appears, in positive as well as negative portents, yet also as an expression of a totality: 7 churches, the book with 7 seals, 7 heavens in which the angelic hierarchies dwell, 7 years in which Salomon built the temple, etc., as well as 7 heads of the beast of the Apocalypse, 7 vials of divine wrath, etc. —7 plays an important role as a number of totality in fairy tales and folklore as well: 7 brothers, 7 ravens, 7 kids,

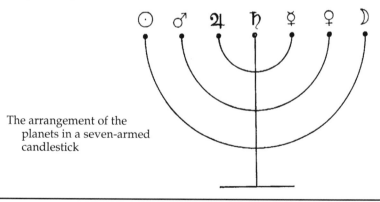

The arrangement of the planets in a seven-armed candlestick

7 different foods on special days, etc. In the Mithra cult, all Mithraea were oriented toward 7: 7 gods, 7 planets, 7 arches, 7 stages of wisdom, 7 colors (correlated to the planets), etc. In ancient Judaism, the SEVEN RACES play an important role, as does the seven-armed CANDLESTICK; in antiquity and during the Middle Ages, the 7 liberal ARTS were the basis of education.

17

As the sum of $1 + 3 + 5 + 8 = 17$, 17 is thought of in alchemy as the fundament of all other numbers. In medieval theological interpretation, it is the sum of 10 (commandments) and the 7 gifts of the Holy Spirit, i.e., $10 + 7 = 17$. It is closely related to the number 153, since 153 is the polygonal number (triangular number) of 17 (see NUMBER SYMBOLISM); 153 is the number of the fish in John 21:11, for example. —In antiquity and in the ancient Orient, it was a widely common symbolic number; for example, the Flood began on the 17th day of the second month and ended on the 17th day of the seventh month, and Odysseus wandered around for 17 days on his raft; the Greek alphabet has 17 consonants, which also gave rise to many sorts of speculations.

27

As the third power of 3, i.e., $3^3 = 27$, it is the amplification and perfection of 3; it is the number of the element fire (see EIGHT). Under favorable conditions, the Moon is visible for $3 \times 9 = 3 \times 3 \times 3$ nights.

70

As the product of $7 \times 10 = 70$, it is an amplification of the holy number 7; according to the writer of Psalms, it is the number of a fulfilled life; it is the number of years the Jews spent in Babylonian captivity. 70 is occasionally identified with the symbolic significance of 72; there were 70 or 72 languages after the confusion of the languages at Babel; it is the number of scholars who are supposed to have translated the Old Testament into Greek (Septuagint). According to Islamic belief, $70 \times 1,000 = 70,000$ veils separate God from His creatures.

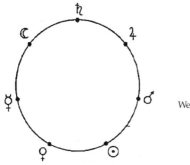 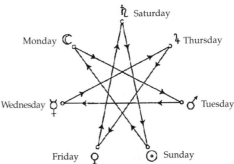

The regents of the days are produced from the Chaldaean series when the planets are placed on a circle equidistant from one another and connected with one another by a heptagram that is drawn in one motion.

SERPENT: Serpent as female temptress on the tree in paradise; woodcut by Steffen Arndes, from *Hortus sanitatis*, Lübeck, 1492

SERPENT: Serpent in paradise on the Tree of Knowledge; detail from a woodcut by H. Baldung (a.k.a. "Grien"), 1505

one word means shadow, image and soul. —In various ideas pertaining to the hereafter, the dead are thought of as shadows. —Yet the soul and vitality themselves were sometimes thought of as shadows; accordingly, spirits in human form or humans who have sold their soul to the devil, have no shadow. —In philosophy, the shadow, as a "bloodless" and only seemingly animate figure, also appears as a symbol of the illusory character of the earthly world, such as in Buddhism, or as a symbol of knowledge that is trapped in mere opinion and not oriented toward the world of the Ideas, such as in Plato's CAVE analogy. —C.G. Jung conceives of the shadow as the entirety of subconscious layers of personality that are consciously assimilated and transformed step-by-step by the process of individuation.

Sheaf - A symbol of harvest and plenty. During rites of harvest, the first or last bound sheaf was frequently attributed with special powers that would have negative effects if certain rules were not adhered to, such as giving the sheaf away or throwing it onto a neighbor's land. — As a conglomeration of many individual elements, the sheaf corresponds symbolically to the BOUQUET.

Sheep - See LAMB.

Shepherd - In many cultures, the shepherd has religious symbolic significance in the sense of a circumspect, caring father figure. God and ruler were occasionally thought to be shepherds. —The insignia of ancient Egyptian rulers were derived from the world of shepherds. — God is the shepherd of the people of Israel; Jesus Christ is the Good Shepherd, which is the most frequently depicted type of Christ of early Christianity that is traced back to the depiction, common in Mesopotamia and Greece, of a shepherd who carries a LAMB (or calf) on his shoulders or in his arm.

Ship - A symbol of journey and passage and thus also of life and its course; early examples of this existed even in Mesopotamia. —In Christianity, the ship, often with concomitant respect to Noah's ARK, is a symbol of the church (see CHEST) steering a safe course through the waves of worldly dangers. The architectonic shape of churches was compared with a ship, often in great detail (as is suggested by the terms middle aisle, aisle, and transept). Occasionally, one also encounters altars in the shape of a ship. See SKIFF.

SHIP: The ship symbolizes the church as the place of peace (from Schmid's *Musterbuch*)

SICKLE: Illustration in Herrad von Landsberg's *Hortus Deliciarum*

Ship Burial - Burial of the dead in ships (among the Vikings as well as in Oceania), ship-shaped megaliths (during the Bronze Age in northern Europe), or ship-shaped buildings (such as on the Balearics; based on the idea of a journey into the hereafter.

Shiva - High god of Hinduism, next to Vishnu and Brahma; an ancient, probably non-Aryan god; originator of cosmic illusion and destroyer of the world. Often represented as a dance king, many-armed, having serpents, a necklace, and a face of the Moon as head dressing; worshipped in the form of a LINGA. See DURGA.

Shoe - In antiquity, the wearing of shoes was the privilege and symbol of a free man and of power; slaves went barefoot. In addition, the shoe (which has a female form, as it were) is related to the symbolic phallic significance of the FOOT and was a fertility symbol in various harvest and wedding customs.

Shofar - In ancient Jewish rituals, the shofar is the ram's horn that was blown only on specific occasions (such as on Rosh Hashanah or Yom Kippur); the TRUMPET probably developed from the monotonal shofar.

Sickle - Because of its shape, the sickle is often associated with the CRESCENT moon. It is a symbol of the harvest that is renewed each year, and is thus also a symbol of time and of death (which appears as the reaper), as well as of hope for renewal and rebirth. See SCYTHE.

Sieve - A symbol of selecting, of critical dividing and distinguishing, particularly a symbol of separation of the good from the bad or evil; in this sense, it is frequently mentioned in symbolic context with divine justice or the Last Judgment, especially in connection with metaphors that relate to the sifting of wheat. —In connection with the four cardinal virtues, the sieve represents prudence.

Silver - As a shining white metal, it is a symbol of purity; among the Sumerians, in antiquity and up to late medieval alchemy, it was associated with the MOON and thus with the feminine principle as well (in contrast to masculine, sun-like GOLD). —According to Egyptian mythology, the bones of the gods were made of silver, their flesh of gold. —In Christian symbolic language, silver obtained through refinement symbolizes the purification of the soul. In Psalms, the word of God is

SICKLE: The Lord with a sickle; from a
  miniature in the Bamburg
  Apocalypse

SIRENS: Odysseus and the Sirens; the
  scene shows Odysseus, who has
  plugged the ears of his shipmates
  with wax, tied to the shipmast so
  that he can be drawn into the spell
  of the sweet song of the Sirens;
  Stamnus, painter of the Sirens, circa
  475 B.C.

compared to silver. As a pure virgin, Mary is also associated with silver.

Silver Age - See AGE.

Silver Tree - See ARBOR PHILOSO-PHICA.

Sirens - In Greek mythology, the Sirens are demons having the bodies of birds, the heads of women, and often breasts as well; they dwell on sea cliffs and are endowed with supernatural knowledge and a song that confuses one's senses; they use this song to lure sailors, whom they then kill and eat. They are often interpreted as being a symbol of the dangers of seafaring or of seductive, deadly dangers in general. Psychoanalytically, they can also be thought of as a symbol of impulsive self-destructive tendencies. —Later interpretations in antiquity saw the Sirens more positively as minstrels of Elysium who were associated with the harmony of the spheres. Because of this connection to the hereafter, they were often depicted on sarcophagi. —The Middle Ages, which often portrayed them as having fishtails, saw them as a symbol of worldly and devilish enticement, such as in PHYSIOLOGUS, where they are explained together with CENTAURS. —The Lorelei, who dwells on the Rhine, can be thought of as a German river Siren.

Sirona - A Gaulish goddess normally portrayed as the companion of Apollo Grannus and whose attributes (symbols), fruits and ears of corn, refer to a fertility deity; she is sometimes shown with a crescent on her head.

Sisyphus - See ROCK; TANTALUS.

Sitting Hen - See HEN.

Skeleton - A personification of death, often depicted as being in a contemplative position or having a SCYTHE and HOUR-GLASS; such representations existed even in late antiquity (the Greeks personified death as the still adolescent brother of sleep or as a spirit with a lowered torch). —The late medieval DANSE MACABRE motif shows people of all ages, genders and position doing a round dance with skeletons by whom they are being whisked away; in later representations, the skeleton also approaches people as an unexpected menace in the middle of life.

Skiff (Boat) - Frequently a symbol of transition from the realm of the living to the realm of the dead, or vice versa.

SIX

 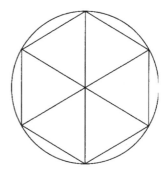

6

In antiquity and during the Middle Ages, the number 6 was regarded as the most perfect number because it can be represented as the sum of its parts and as their product, i.e., $1 + 2 + 3 = 6$ and $1 \times 2 \times 3 = 6$. It can also be thought of as the product of the first masculine number and the first feminine one, i.e., $3 \times 2 = 6$. —In China, 6 was associated with the influences of the sky. —In Christian symbolic thought, 6 is ambivalent: as the number of the days of creation, it is holy; it is also significant as the number of works of charity; in the Book of Revelation, however, 6 appears as the number of evil; 666 is the number of the beast of the apocalypse. See HEXAGRAM.

16

The number 16 is a number symbolic of completeness and perfection and is probably associated with the four elements in their squared form, i.e., $4^2 = 4 \times 4 = 16$.

36

36 is the product of the squares of the first 3 numbers: $1^2 \times 2^2 \times 3^2 = 1 \times 4 \times 9 = 36$, yet also the sum of the cubes of the first 3 numbers: $1^3 + 2^3 + 3^3 = 1 + 8 + 27 = 36$; since 36 is simultaneously the second power of 6 as well, it emphasizes the significance of the latter: $6^2 = 6 \times 6 = 36$. On the other hand, 36 is associated with astrological speculations, as it is the product of the cosmic numbers 12 (signs of the zodiac) and 3 (number of aspects per zodiac sign in the ancient Egyptian zodiac), or $12 \times 3 = 36$.

46

In letter/number symbolism, ADAM (in Greek) yields $1 + 4 + 1 + 40 = 46$; this number is also the number of years taken to build the temple (John 2:20).

60

is the base number of the sexagesimal system in Mesopotamia (see NUMBER SYMBOLISM) and thus one of the fundaments of all number speculations in the ancient Orient. It is also thought of as the product of the important numbers $3 \times 4 \times 5 = 60$.

66

is an important symbolic number in the Islamic tradition and represents the name of Allah in letter/number symbolism.

SKELETON: "Meditating skeleton" from Vesalius's *Anatomia*

SKY: The Egyptian goddess of the sky, Nut, on whose body the sun rises and sets, bends over the earth, which is represented as a disk; relief from a sarcophagus, 30th Dynasty

Encountered in the myths of many peoples. In Greek mythology, for example, the ferry-man Charon ferries the dead over the border river Styx or Acheron to the underworld in a skiff. —According to Egyptian lore, the sun god Ra sailed across the sky in a sun skiff during the day and through the underworld in a night skiff during the night. —The comparison of the CRESCENT moon with a skiff is very common. —Because of its shape, which allows nagivation in both directions, the skiff is also a symbolic embodiment of the ancient Roman two-faced god JANUS.

Skull - Or "death's head." It is frequently compared symbolically with the celestial skies (a manifestation of the symbolic union of the significance of the human microcosm and the universal macrocosm). —Especially in art of the Occident, it is a symbol of impermanence. —As the material "vessel" of the spirit, the skull was favored by alchemists as a container for use in transformation processes. Skull cults, documented in various cultures, are also probably based on the idea of the skull as the "seat" of the spirit. —The skull frequently portrayed under the Cross of Christ is Adam's skull (see ADAM).

Sky - The sky, earlier often seen as a semisphere arched over the surface of the earth, plays a large role in the mythological and religious notions of nearly all peoples as a place from which gods and divine beings are thought to act and to which the soul ascends after death. Crucial to this interpretation, which was initially thought of quite literally and not symbolically, were probably the fact that the sky is "above" (see HEIGHT), the lawfully ordered movements of the stars, the fertilizing rain that comes from the sky and is necessary for life, and fear- and awe-inspiring natural occurrences such as storms, LIGHTNING, comets, meteorites, and RAINBOWS. —One frequently encounters the idea that the sky and the earth were originally united. According to this point of view, then, the sky represents only one half of the entire world; the parallelization of the sky as masculine and active and of the earth as feminine and passive, is connected with this idea; not until the sky fertilizes the earth can all earthly beings come to exist (in Egypt, though, the opposite idea prevailed: the maternal goddess of the sky, Nut, was the bride of the god of the earth, Geb). —Also common are notions of several heavens or heavenly spheres atop one another, which corresponded to the various hier-

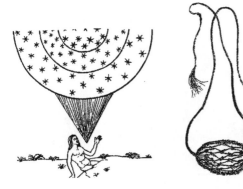

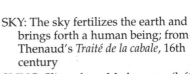

SKY: The sky fertilizes the earth and brings forth a human being; from Thenaud's *Traité de la cabale*, 16th century

SLING: Slings from Madagascar (left) and Kenya

archies of spiritual beings or to the various degrees of the purification of the soul.

Sleipner - Sleipner is the gray, EIGHT-legged horse of Odin for whom no obstacle was too high; among the ancient Germans, it was regarded as the fastest of all horses. See HORSE.

Sling - Along with the ARROW AND BOW, the sling is one of the oldest "distance weapons" that is today still used, with great accuracy, by shepherds; through his fight against the giant Goliath as the best known "slinger," David—the keeper of sheep—has become a symbolic figure of the (physically) inferior fighter who can defeat a (physically) superior giant. —In some American Indian cultures, the sling is an attribute of the storm god, probably because of the sound that it makes when it shoots.

Smith - As a forger of METALS (especially of IRON) and as a powerful, creative agent of change, the smith is a cosmogonic symbolic figure; in the religious thought of many peoples, a smith attends the principle god as an assistant (as in the case of Zeus and Hephaestus). —As a human, the smith often appears as a ruler over fire, as a healer of diseases and as a rainmaker;

the negative counterweight to this is the equally widely common notion of the smith who is allied with the powers of subterranean fire, with black magic, and with hell. —Smiths appear as artisans, especially as armorers in Germanic and Celtic mythology, where they play an important role. In many cases, dwarfs are also famed as skillful smiths. —In the minds of African peoples, the smith—who is, among other things, a producer of images of ancestors and other cult images—plays an important, and occasionally feared role and therefore often occupies a high social position; among some tribes, however, he is also despised.

Smoke - Smoke is a symbol of the union of heaven and earth, spirit and matter. Smoke columns are sometimes associated symbolically with the WORLD AXIS. See PEACE PIPE; INCENSE.

Snail - In numerous cultures, the snail is a lunar symbol since it alternately shows and withdraws its antennae and itself and is, in that regard, an image of the constantly waxing and waning moon; in this respect, it is also a general symbol of constant renewal. —American Indian wind gods were often depicted in the form of snails as an sign of their ability to reach

SMITH: Illustration from *Hortus sanitatis*, 1509

every nook and cranny of a person's house (just as the snail retreats into its house). —Like the MUSSEL, the snail was sometimes compared with the female genitalia; for that reason and because of its protective house, it was a common symbol of conception, pregnancy and birth in some American Indian cultures. —In Christianity, it is thought of as a resurrection symbol since it bursts the top of its shell in the spring. —Because of the shape of its shell, the snail is also symbolically related to the SPIRAL. —Cowries or porcelain snails were prized by various primitive peoples not only as jewelry and money, but also as amulets and fertility symbols.

Sneezing - Sneezing was thought by some primitive peoples to be influenced by demons who thereby sought to drive the soul from a person's body.

Snow - Because of its color (see WHITE), its purity and its coldness, it is a symbol of chastity and virginal innocence and is therefore a symbol of Mary in Christian symbolic thought.

Snowdrop - One of the first spring flowers and therefore a symbol of hope; in Christian panel paintings of the Middle Ages, it is an attribute of Mary, since Christians thank Mary for the "birth of hope"; in these representations, the snowdrops are usually on the left side of Mary and the Christ child.

Sodom and Gomorrah - Biblical cities that were destroyed by Yahweh because of their godlessness and moral decadence; they were a proverbial symbol of vice and decadence even in the Old Testament and are still such today. See FIRE.

Solar Eclipse - As a rarely occuring event that brings all life to a halt, a total eclipse of the sun, in particular, has terrified humans in all ages and often given rise to evil omens and prophecies of catastrophes. —In Islam and Buddhism, yet in other cultural circles as well, the solar eclipse (and the lunar eclipse) is frequently associated with the death of the heavenly body, which people imagined to be eaten by a monster; Chinese uses the same word for the eclipse of a heavenly body and for "to eat." In China, a solar or lunar eclipse was interpreted as being a disturbance of the macrocosmic order that was based on a disturbance of the microcosmic order, specifically, by rulers or their wives. —The reappearance of a heavenly body after an eclipse was often thought of as the beginning of a new cycle, of a new era.

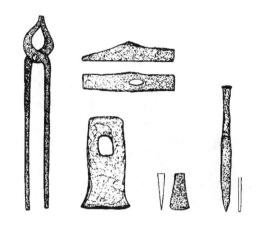

SMITH: Celtic smithing tools from various excavation sites; 1st and 2nd centuries B.C.

Sol Invictus - See SUN.

Solstice - In Christian symbolic thought, the solstice is sometimes associated with John the Baptist and Christ: the summer solstice (decreasing amount of daylight) as a symbol of John the Baptist ("He must grow, yet I must diminish."), the winter solstice (increasing amount of daylight) as a symbol of Christ or the birth of Christ.

Soma - An intoxicating drink from a like-named plant from which people in India prepared a ritual libation; it was often identified symbolically with the MOON.

Song of Songs - The Song of Solomon in the Old Testament, part of the so-called Books of Wisdom; the theological explication and the images from the text are the basis for many symbols of the virgin Mother of God; the LILY and the HORTUS CONCLUSUS are especially well known.

Soul - Among peoples of all levels of civilization, there is the idea of a spiritual, life-giving principle in humans. Several (at least two) souls are often assumed to exist. Typology: the vital soul, which is identical with breath and localized in the heart, blood, liver and bones; the ego soul, which

is the center of thinking, desiring, feeling, continues to live after death in the hereafter; the free soul, which can separate from the body, roam around in dreams, substantiate itself in animals (animals with human souls), etc.; and the androgynous soul, meaning that every person has a male and a female soul. Humanoid souls can also be attributed to animals and things.

Sounding-Lead - A symbol of the Freemasons; it is one of the "moveable treasures" used together with a square and a level to determine the "correct vertical" (a notion pertaining to the world axis). See PLUMMET.

Sow - See PIG.

Sparks - Particles of light that, according to ancient and medieval notions, are symbols of matter that hover high above, in the sense of down/up, and change from matter into spirit. Sparks are produced by striking a FLINTSTONE and are used to light Easter candles (Light of Easter).

Sparrowhawk - In Egypt, it was the bird of Horus and is thus a sun symbol; among the Greeks and the Romans as well, it was associated with the SUN. —The fact that the female is larger and stronger than the

275

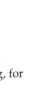

SNAIL: The snail is a symbol of resurrection and thus bears the grave of St. Sebald in Nürnberg, for example (from Schmid's *Musterbuch*)

SNAIL: Mayan wind god rising up from a snail

male, sometimes made the sparrowhawk a symbol of the dominance of the woman in marriage.

Spear - One of the oldest weapons used for jabbing and throwing; originally, it was a wooden stick that came to a crude point; later, its head was made of stone, bamboo, bone or metal, sometimes with a barb (especially spears for hunting fish and birds). The harpoon was an early modification (having a separate head attached to the shaft). See LANCE.

Spear Catapult - A staff-shaped device or long, flat board with a recessed section at the end, occasionally with a grooved guide and a loop made of bast or leather, used for shooting spears and harpoons. There is also a rope that sets the projectile into rotatory motion when it is thrown. The spear catapult was once very common (in pre-historic Europe and elsewhere); today, it can still be found in Australia, Oceania, and Eskimo kayak hunts.

Speedwell - Also called "Veronica." Most species are blue-flowering figworts. The Latin name can perhaps be traced back to the Greek word *berenike* (meaning "she who brings victory"); from this, the word play *vera unica medicina* was derived and the plant was related symbolically with Christ as the "true, sole medicine." —Because speedwell was said to attract lightning, people avoided taking it into their houses.

Spes - A symbolic figure of the theological virtue of hope; its attributes are the ANCHOR, CROWN, and FLAG.

Sphere - To a large extent, the sphere corresponds symbolically to the CIRCLE; it is a symbol of the universe, the globe, the starry sky, the entirety of all opposites that cancel one another, and thus also sometimes of the HERMAPHRODITE, for example. —In architecture (especially Islamic and Christian), the sphere or semi-sphere, like the circle or the arch, usually represents the SKY, whereas the CUBE or the SQUARE represents the EARTH.

Sphinx - (The plural forms are "sphinxes," "sphinges.") An animal-human HYBRID CREATURE with the body of a lion and the head of a king or (seldom) queen; it is an ancient symbol of rulers. Among the Egyptians, it is usually a representation of the pharaoh or sometimes of the sun god as an unshakable, powerful protective power. Among the Phoenicians, Hittites and Assyrians, it is represented as a winged lion or steer with a human head.

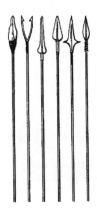

SPEER: Types of speers among various primitive peoples

—Among the Greeks, the sphinx, which is usually female and winged, was originally a puzzling, often terrible being to which our current proverbial use of the word still refers. —In modern times, such as in *fin de siecle* symbolistic art, the sphinx was often seen as a symbol of the incomprehensibility of women.

Spider - A symbolic animal with contrasting meanings. Because of its artful, radially constructed web and its central position within that net, it is thought of in India as a symbol of the cosmic order and as the "weaver" of the world of the senses. Because it produces the fibers of its web from itself, just as the sun produces its rays, it is also a sun symbol; in this respect, the web can also symbolize the emanation of the divine spirit. Because it runs up on the fiber that it itself spun, it appears in the Upanishads as a symbol of spiritual self-liberation as well. —In Islam, white spiders are thought to be good, black ones bad. —In the Bible, the spider appears as a symbol of futility, of vane hope and of "evil desire." — Folkish ideas sometimes juxtaposed the lethal spider with the BEE; according to superstition, its appearance prophesied good or bad luck, depending upon the hour of the day.

Spindle - Because of its constant turning motion, it is a symbol of unchangeable regularity, of merciless fate as well as of eternal recurrence; it is sometimes also a sexual symbol.

Spine - See WORLD AXIS.

Spiral - Even in pre-historical times, the spiral was a favorite ornamental motif of controversial symbolic meaning that nevertheless is probably associated with cyclic development, the phases of the moon and their influence on water, fertility, etc., the movement of involution and evolution in the entire cosmos generally (especially the double-spiral), with recurrence and renewal, and perhaps with the LABYRINTH as well.

Spirit Hole - A stone slab used in some PASSAGE GRAVES and stone cists (see MEGALITHS), having a round opening; it is interpreted as being a symbolic opening through which the soul can exit and enter.

Spittle - Among black African peoples, it is often seen in close symbolic conjunction with speech and sperm, and thus with creative powers. —In Germanic mythology, Odin's spittle is used to brew beer. In

SPINDLE & DISTAFF: A woman holding a spindle in her hand (left, Hittite bas-relief); at right, a woman holding a spindle (forerunner of the spinning wheel) in her hand and pulling a thread from the full distaff, turning a freely hanging spindle with her other hand (Attic vase painting, 6th century)

fact, spittle is still used today among primitive peoples to activate the fermentation process.

Spleen - In Europe and the Arab world, the spleen was thought to be the seat of humor and laughter; proverbs occasionally refer to this.

Spring - In general, springs are revered as the origin of life-giving powers, as a symbol of purity and fertile abundance; among many peoples (such as the Greeks), the spring is personified as a female deity. —In the Bible, it is sometimes a symbol of eternal life and rebirth, but is also a symbol of Mary. —C.G. Jung sees springs as a symbol of inexhaustible spiritual-emotional energy.

Square - One of the most common symbolic signs; it is a static, non-dynamic symbol, often seen in relation and in contrast to the CIRCLE, a symbol of the EARTH in contrast to heaven (see SKY) or of the limited in contrast to the unlimited. It is also a symbol of the four cardinal directions. —It is frequently used as a foundation of temples, altars, cities or as an architectonic unit, such as in the Romanesque style. —In China, the cosmos and the earth were thought to be quadratic. —The Pythagoreans saw the square as a symbol of the united workings of the four ELEMENTS and thus of the powers of Aphrodite, Demeter, Hestia and Hera, the synthesis of whom was thought to be Rhea, mother of the gods. According to Plato, the square, next to the circle, embodies absolute beauty. —In Islam, the square plays a role in various contexts; the hearts of normal people, for example, were thought to be square, because they were open to four possible sources of inspiration: the divine, the angelic, the human, and the devilish (the hearts of the prophets, on the other hand, are triangular, because they are no longer subject to the devil's attacks). —In Christian art, the square is sometimes a symbol of the earth in contrast to heaven. Square HALOS of people (then) still living thus indicate that the figure is still of this earth. —C.G. Jung sees the square as a symbol of matter, of the flesh, and of earthly reality. See CUBE; MAGIC SQUARES; FOUR.

Squaring the Circle - The unsolvable task of converting a given CIRCLE into a SQUARE of equal area by using only a ruler and compass. It is a symbol of the attempted penetration of the symbolic meaning of the circle and the square.

SPIRAL: Spiral, presumably as a symbol of life and fertility; Bacha, Sweden; Neolithic period

SPRING: The miraculous spring often appears as a counterpart to St. Peter's denial of Christ. At first sight of the two illustrations, one thinks of the miraculous spring of Moses. Yet the inscription "Petrus" informs us that Moses was only a prefiguration of St. Peter, the prince of the Apostles; from two illustrations on gold glasses in the Vatican (from Schmid's *Musterbuch*)

Squid - The squid is found in ornamental art of the Celts as well as of the Cretans; because of its frequently curled tentacles, it is symbolically associated with the SPIDER and the SPIRAL; as a sea creature that emits clouds of a dark fluid when confronted by enemies, it should perhaps be thought of as a symbol of subterranean powers as well.

Squirrel - In Germanic mythology, the squirrel was sacred to the god of fire and thunder and lived in the world ash tree Yggdrasil (see TREE). —In the symbolic thought of the Middle Ages, it was a symbol of the devil because of its lightning-fast speed and its fiery-red color.

Staff - The staff is a symbol of power and (magical) knowledge, as in the case of the wand; often thought to produce effects through touching, such as the staff of Moses and the miracle of water coming from a rock. —In Greece, the staff of Hermes was thought to be magical and capable of bringing blessings. —Indian deities, specifically the god of death, carry a staff as a sign of power to judge and to punish. —Apotropaic effects were often attributed to the staff; in ancient China, for example, evil powers were driven away with a staff (usually made of peach tree wood or mulberrry tree wood). —In the

Bible or the Apocrypha, there is sometimes mention of a staff that changes into a living being (see SERPENT; budding BRANCH) as a manifestation of divine will (Aaron's staff, Joseph's staff before his betrothal to Mary). —As a sign of their function as messengers, angels often carry a long herald's staff in graphic, and particularly Byzantine, art. —The crook of bishops and abbots developed from the shepherd's staff, which, in Christian art, is associated with Christ, prophets and saints. —Rulers' staves, such as the marshal's baton and the SEPTER, are symbols of legal and often of judicial power. —From a psychoanalytical viewpoint, the staff can also have phallic significance. —The world axis was also sometimes compared with a staff. —The breaking of a staff was an ancient Franconian custom to show the breaking of the rule of law; it was sometimes common at executions as well. See ASCLEPIUS, STAFF OF; KERY-KEION.

Stag - Depictions of stags and of people dressed as stags can be found in caves from the Paleolithic period; they probably served cultic purposes. —The stag was an animal revered world-wide; because of its tall, annually renewed antlers, it was frequently compared with the TREE OF LIFE and was thus also a symbol of fertility, of

SQUARE: Union of a human figure and a square; from a bowl from western Norway, 9th century

SQUARING THE CIRCLE: "Only in threes exist all things, in fours do they rejoice"; from an illustration in Jamsthales's *Viatorium spagyricum*, 1625

(spiritual) growth and of ebb and flow in many cultures and epochs. According to Germanic notions, the stag secured the path to eternal life in the next world for the deceased (see CERNUNNOS). Because of their shape and because of the blood-red color of their cuticles when they wore down in the spring, the stag's antlers seemed to many peoples to be a symbol of light rays and of fire, and the stag thus seemed a sun-like animal or a mediator between the SKY and the EARTH. —For Buddhism, the (golden) stag is (next to the gazelle) a symbol of wisdom and asceticism. —In China, the sun-like aspect of the stag was sometimes interpreted in a negative sense as a symbol of aridity and drought. —Next to the DOE, the stag was also regarded in antiquity as the sacred animal of Artemis; the struggle of the stag with other animals symbolized the struggle between light and darkness. The stag appears as a guide of souls in antiquity and among the Celts (and elsewhere). Antiquity saw the stag as the enemy and killer of SERPENTS, a notion that (mediated by PHYSIOLOGUS) is also encountered in Christian art of the Middle Ages; the identification of the stag with Christ (who tramples the serpent's, i.e. the devil's head under foot) is based in part upon this; the legends of St. Eustace and St.

Hubert tell of the appearance of a stag that carried the crucified Christ between its antlers; the stag's antlers are sometimes compared with Christ, because they can reach up to the sky. In Christian art, the stag is also frequently represented in connection with the water of life (with reference to Psalm 42). —It is sometimes a symbol of melancholia, since it loves solitude. —Because of its striking behavior when in rut, it is also regarded as a symbol of masculine sexual passion.

Staircase - The symbolic meaning of the staircase is essentially co-extensive with that of the LADDER: it is a symbol of emotional and spiritual development, of the gradual acquisition of wisdom and knowledge. In contrast to the ladder, which was thought to lead from bottom to top, i.e., toward the sky, the staircase is occasionally encountered as descending, leading below the earth and into dark regions, thereby symbolizing either descent into the realm of the dead or admittance to occult knowledge or to the subconsciousness. —A white staircase can symbolically refer to clarity and wisdom, a black one to black magic. —The sun religion of the Egyptians thought of the step pyramid as a staircase by means of which the soul rose to heaven; there are also

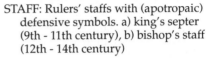

a   SQUID: Decoration on a porphyry
       weight from Knossus, Crete
     STAFF: Aaron before the budding staff;
       bronze door of San Zeno, Verona;
       circa 1100
     STAFF: Rulers' staffs with (apotropaic)
       defensive symbols. a) king's septer
       (9th - 11th century), b) bishop's staff
b   (12th - 14th century)

depictions of barks, in the middle of which are staircases by means of which souls climb toward the light. —The Babylonian ziggurat should probably be understood in a similar sense. —The winding staircase also shares in the symbolism of the SPIRAL.

Stamen - Together with the pistle, it is a popular sexual symbol.

Star - Individual stars usually do not play such a large role in symbolism; when talk is of stars, it is usually planets and comets that are meant. "Star cult" and "star worship" therefore primarily mean "astral cult," and "star mythology" means "astral mythology." —The relative infrequency of star symbols is manifest in the fact that individual stars, in contrast to constellations, particular zodiac images, and combined groups of stars, hardly play a role in astrology. —The earliest representations of stars from the time of Akkad represent symbols of gods: the eight-rayed star is the symbol of the goddess Ishtar (Astarte); the star surrounded by a disk is a symbol of the god Shamash (which means "sun").

Starfish - In Christian symbolism, the starfish is a symbolic name for Mary, who,

pointing out the way over the waves and storms of the world and giving comfort to the faithful, shines forth.

Star of David - See HEXAGRAM.

Stars - As lights in the dark night sky, they are a symbol of spiritual light piercing through the darkness; they can also be a symbol of high or all too high ideals ("to reach for the stars"). —The movement of the stars in regular paths symbolizes the harmonious cooperation of divine powers. —In the mythologies of some peoples, stars in general, or a specific star, are thought of as deceased persons who have gone up to the sky; some American Indian cultures even went so far as to assume that every living creature on the earth was connected with a star. —In late Judaism, there was the notion that every star was guarded by an angel; a star or an angel also guides the Magi from the East to Bethlehem (Star of Bethlehem). —With respect to the great number of stars, the starry sky in the Old Testament symbolizes the promise of the numerous progeny of Abraham, which, according to medieval theologians, is in turn a symbol of the different peoples and races who are spiritually united in the church. —As the Immaculate Virgin, Mary is sometimes portrayed with a crown of stars.

STAG: Doe; detail from an amphora
  painting (7th century B.C.))
STAR: The Holy Virgin with wreath of
  stars; from Speculum humanae
  salvationis; 15th century

Steatopyga - From the Greek. Fatty buttocks, one of the racial characteristics of Hottentot women. During the Middle Paleolithic Age, steatopyga is characteristic of statues of women.

Steer - A symbol of strength, of masculine battle courage, of wildness; because of its activeness, it is symbolically associated with the SUN, and because of its fertility, it is symbolically associated with the MOON (because of their shape, which is reminiscent of a crescent, the horns of the steer and the COW were also a symbol of the Moon). —Among many peoples, the steer was an especially valuable sacrificial animal. —Even Neolithic rock drawings in North Africa show representations of steers carrying images of the sun between their horns. —In Egypt, the fertility god Apis was worshipped in the form of a steer, frequently with a sun disk between his horns; since he was also identified with Osiris, he was a god of death at the same time. The death and burial of the sacred steer that had been declared to be Apis, were always attended with ceremony and ended in a "resurrection" (i.e., the selection of a new steer calf). —In Minoan culture, the steer played an especially important role as a symbol of power and fertility. —Iranian mythology tells (among other things) of the embodiment of cosmic fertility in the form of a primeval steer that was killed by Mithra, after which all plants and animals grew out of its body. Steer sacrifices and baptism with steer's blood in the Mithra cult, from which women were excluded, represent the constantly repeated process of coming to terms with the steer's powers of fertility, death, and resurrection. —In India, the god Shiva was associated with a white steer, the symbol of tamed reproductive energies. —Among various peoples, the steer is also related to storms, RAIN, and WATER due to its fertility. —From a psychoanalytical point of view, the steer corresponds to the animalistic powers and sexuality of humanity; in this regard, steer fights even today probably represent (among other things) the constantly renewed attempt to stave off through visual enactments the inner victory of those powers. —The steer, or Taurus, is the second sign of the zodiac; it corresponds to the second month of spring; the sun passes the sign between April 21 and May 21; the moon is exalted in Taurus; it is the house of Venus; since the time of Hellenic astrology, Mercury, the Moon and Saturn have been its decans; in Indian astrology, Venus, Mercury and Saturn have been its decans. The triplicity of Taurus is earth; Taurus is feminine, negative (passive) and a fixed

STAR: Creation of the sun, Moon and starry skies; from a depiction of a scene from Genesis, mosaic in the Cappella Palatina in Palermo; 2nd half of the 12th century

STAR: Star of Shamash; Star of Ishtar

---

sign. The name of the constellation Taurus was known even in Babylonian sources. —See MINOTAUR; OX.

Steering Wheel - A symbol of responsibility, authority, and higher wisdom.

Steps - As a part of a LADDER or STAIRCASE, steps share in the symbolism of an ascent to higher knowledge, such as the steps leading up to the Philosophers' Stone.

Stilts - In China, the use of stilts (such as in ritual dances) served to identify their user with the CRANE, a symbol of immortality.

Sting - See THORN.

Stone - In most cultures, stone plays a symbolically significant role. The worship of meteorites as "stones fallen from heaven" is especially common the world over; they were thought of as a symbolic manifestation of a connection between heaven (see SKY) and EARTH. —Because of their hardness and immutability, stones are frequently associated with eternal, unchanging, divine powers and are thought of as a manifestation of concentrated energy. Despite their hardness, though, stone are not often seen as something rigid and

dead, but rather as life-giving; in Greek myth, for example, humans arose after the Deluge from stones that Deucalion had strewn about. Many stones, especially meteorites, were thought to grant fertility and to bring rain; for example, they were touched by infertile women who wished to be blessed with children; in the spring or during arid periods, people made sacrifices to them in order to get rain and a rich harvest. —In early antiquity, for example, before the gods were portrayed in human form, an unhewn stone was regarded as a symbol of Hermes or Apollo. —Upright stones as gravestones (see STONE CROSSES) signify protection of the dead from hostile powers; they were also sometimes thought to be the place where the energy or soul of the deceased continued to live. A sacred black stone was part of the cult of the mother goddess Cybele. —The centerpiece in the ritual life of Islam is a black meteoric stone, the Badshar al-aswad in the Kaaba at Mecca. —In the Bible, ROCK and stone are symbols of God's protective strength. —See JEWELS; FLINTSTONE; MENHIR; NAVEL; PHILOSOPHERS' STONE.

Stone Cross - Especially on the British Isles, stones crosses are abundant, often having ornamental motifs from the time

STEER: Zodiacal sign Taurus (from a
medieval woodcut) and the modern
astrological symbol
STEER: Bullfight scene, from F. de
Goya

of the Vikings that reinterpret pagan elements as Christian ones, such as the TREE OF LIFE as a cross-beam around which animals congregate; an example is the 10th century cross of the Isle of Man.

Stonehenge - Located near Salisbury (Wiltshire, England), Stonehenge is a magnificent example of a pre-historic, Stone Age MEGALITH in the shape of a circle as an alignment of MENHIRS. It is very probably related to star symbolism, the solstices, and the paths of the moon. In recent years, Stonehenge has been the center of esoteric circles that have made it a "place of worship."

Stork - In the Bible, it is counted among the unclean animals, yet is otherwise generally revered as a good luck symbol. In the Far East, it is a symbol of long life, since people assumed that the stork itself lived to be very old. Often (such as in Egypt, in antiquity, and among the church fathers), it was regarded as a symbol of child-like gratitude, since it was said that the fledged stork fed its parents. —As a killer of SERPENTS, it was thought of in Christianity as an enemy of the devil and thus as a symbol of Christ. —Since it feeds on animals that live in the ground (and that supposedly assume the souls of de-

ceased persons), it was also sometimes seen as a carrier of souls. —As a migratory bird, it is a symbol of resurrection; it is also probably thought of as a deliverer of children in part because it returns when nature is re-awakening. —Its quiet stance on one leg, which gives it a contemplative aura, made the stork (especially the Marabou species) a symbol of philosophical contemplation.

Storm - Or "thunderstorm." In the religious ideas of many peoples, storms are regarded as a symbol or actual manifestation of the actions of divine powers; junctures in time are also often thought of as catastrophic storms. See LIGHTNING; THUNDER.

Stranger - In all religions that see the hereafter as the true home of man, the stranger is a symbol of the homeless, original state of man on the earth. See PILGRIM.

Strawberry - During the Middle Ages, the strawberry was known only in its small-fruited form. Because of its tripartite leaves, it is a symbol of the Trinity; because it stays short under even the best growing conditions, it is a symbol of noble humility and modesty. The blood-red, hanging fruit was sometimes also interpreted

STEER: Apsis, the sacred steer of the Egyptians, is offered a lotus flower by the goddess Isis; small bronze sculpture

STONE CROSSES: Norman stone crosses from the Isle of Man (10th century); they show the continuation of the motives of the tree of life in the Cross of Christ; the many animals around the cross beams are characteristic

as a symbol for the blood spilled by Christ or by the martyrs, the five-leafed blossom being a symbol of Christ's five wounds. — The ripe fruit could also be interpreted as the readiness of a young women for marriage and motherhood; it is also sometimes encountered as a symbol of worldly desire.

String - Like the CHAIN, string is a symbol of connection, and often especially of that between heaven and earth (also in the sense of the sky's fertilization of the earth, which is why it is sometimes a symbol of RAIN). —According to Buddhist and Hindu thought, Neo-Plato and other world views, man's spirit is connected with his soul or body by an astral, golden string. —For the Freemasons, a string with knots symbolizes the community of all Freemasons.

Stupa - From the Sanskrit, meaning "skull." A sacred structure that developed from the ancient Indian burial mound; stupas are free-standing or located within a chaitya hall. Canonical form: a circular platform, a semi-circular shrine (called an *anda*, which means "egg") above it, a box-like superstructure (called a *harmika*) for relics, and one or more (smaller and smaller) umbrella-like tiers (called *chattravalli* or *chattra* if singular). The site is sur-

rounded by a stone (originally wooden) fence (called a *vedika*) with four gates (called *torana*). The most famous old stupas are those at Sarnath and Sanchih.

Sucellos - A Gallic god, portrayed with a hammer that always hit its mark. Sucellos was regarded as lord over life and death, as a god of abundance, and as the protector of the simple people, who called upon his blessing in particularly great measure.

Suebic Bun - Men's hair buns that are not only decorative, but probably have magical significance. See HAIR.

Sulphur - Next to SALT and quicksilver (see MERCURY), sulphur is one of the philosophical elements and world principles; it represents "that which burns" or the energy and soul (*anima*) of nature; it was sometimes also compared with the SUN. —Folk belief of the Middle Ages reversed the symbolic meaning of sulphur to mean infernal and saw an attribute of the devil in it, its flame and its odor.

Sun - In the geocentric system of ancient astrology and astronomy, the sun is regarded as a normal planet; in the heliocentric system of modern astronomy, the sun is the fixed star closest to the earth and the

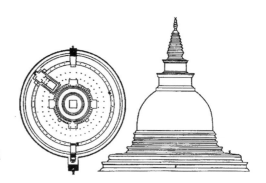

STUPA: Floor plan of an old stupa and
draft of a modern stupa

center of the planetary system. The (apparent) revolution of the sun around the earth was one of the bases of the calendar, i.e., the year, since the beginnings of celestial observations. —In astrology, the sun, like the Moon, is simply called "light." —Among many peoples, it is one of the most important symbols; many primitive peoples and early civilizations worshipped it as a god; it is often represented as the visual embodiment of LIGHT and thus also of the highest cosmic intelligence, of warmth, of FIRE, and of the life-giving principle; its rising and setting, new each day, also made it a symbolic precursor of the resurrection as well as of every new beginning in general. Because the sun shines upon all things with the same light and thereby makes them recognizable, it is also a symbol of justice. —In Egypt, the sun enjoyed particular reverence; it was seen as the embodiment of the sun god Ra (occasionally in connection with or identified with other gods, such as Amun, Chnuum, etc.); Ra had two sun ships with which he drove across the sky. Very common representations of the sun are the SCARAB with a sun sphere or an (often winged) sun DISK with the uraeus SERPENT. —Other sun gods include, for example, the Babylonian Sha-mash, the Greek Helios (with HORSES and sun chari-

ots), the Roman Sol or the late Roman Sol invictus (meaning "the unconquered sun"). Often, such as among the Incas, in Egypt and in Japan, the sun cult was closely associated with the ruler cult. Other gods, although not actual sun gods, are often very closely related to the sun, such as Osiris or Apollo. —The Indian Veda compares Brahma, the absolute, with the spiritual sun. —In China, the sun (in contrast to the MOON) was regarded as a manifestation of the Yang principle (see YIN AND YANG). —Plato saw the sun as the visible representation of the good. —In Christianity, Christ is often compared with the sun (such as in the phrase "sun of justice," which, in early Christian times, was also associated with the late Roman Sol invictus). —Among most peoples, the juxtaposition sun–Moon corresponds to the poles masculine–feminine, yet there are also numerous known examples (such as in Central Asia or in German-speaking lands) having the reverse meaning (whereby the sun is a warming, nourishing, maternal principle). —In alchemy, GOLD, which is also called "the sun of the earth," corresponds to the sun. —Especially in hot lands, though, the sun can also appear in a negative sense as a principle of aridity and drought and thus as an adversary of the fertilizing RAIN. —Some American Indian

SULPHUR: Detail from an illustration in *Musaeum Hermeticum*, Frankfurt, 1677

SUN: Pharoah making a sacrifice to the sun; 18th Dynasty

cultures also have the notion of a black sun, which is a sun that leaves this world during the night in order to shine in another one; it is a symbol of death and calamity and appears in representations on the back of the god of death or in the form of a JAGUAR, for example. —In alchemy, the black sun is a symbol of the *prima materia*. —One occasionally encounters a black sun in modern graphic arts and literature usually as a symbol of metaphysical angst or *melancholia*.

Sun Bride - See MARIGOLD.

Sunflower - Because of the radial arrangement of its petals and its goldish-yellow color as well as its habit of always turning toward the sun, the sunflower is a symbol of the sun and nobility in various cultures. —In Christianity, it is a symbol of God's love, and a symbol of the soul that relentlessly directs its thoughts and feelings to God; to that extent, it is also a symbol of prayer. Because the sunflower was first brought to Europe by Cortez, some of its symbolism is still very recent.

Sun Gate - See DOORS.

Sun Lizard - A term in PHYSIOLOGUS for the LIZARD.

Superbia (Pride) - The female personification of one of the seven deadly sins; she rides upon a lion or a horse. Her symbols include the eagle, the peacock, and the centaur.

Swallow - As a migratory bird, the swallow is often a symbol of spring and thus also of light and fertility. Its nesting on one's house is thought to bring good luck. —During the Middle Ages, it was a resurrection symbol because it returns with the light after winter has run its course and because it was said to enable its young to see by giving them the sap of the CELANDINE (which is why that plant is also called "swallow herb"), just as God enables the dead to see again on Judgment Day. According to PHYSIOLOGUS, the swallow announces the end of winter and wakens sleepers in the morning. The swallow reproduces only once during its lifetime. Interpretation: the Christian Savior was carried once in the womb, born once, crucified once, buried once, and risen once from the dead.—Among black African peoples, it is occasionally a symbol of purity, since it does not sit on the ground and thus does not come into contact with dirt.

Swamp - Or "bog." In Asia, the swamp is sometimes a symbol of quietude and

SUN

As a part of astral cults, the sun is worshipped among many peoples in a sun cult (solarism). This worship of the sun can occur in four ways.

The sun is preferentially worshipped as a physical phenomenon or a personification of a being directed by God. Among these are imperial sun cults that are connected with theocracies, such as in Ancient Egypt, Iran, late Rome (Sol invictus) or in Shinto.

In polytheistic systems, the sun is worshipped next to other gods who stand under the god of heaven; such is the case among most Indo-Germanic peoples (Helios, Sol, Swarog), for example.

The sun can also be merely a manifestation (or hypostasis) of the high god in heaven.

Finally, the sun can be merely a mythically imagined reality that is worshipped only occasionally or sometimes not at all.

Among many peoples, however, there are sun myths without an actual sun cult and sun deities.

Sun symbolism in Christianity is largely determined by the existence of a sun cult among Greeks and Romans as well as in the Mithra cult: Plato called the sun the son of God, the Roman Sol invictus became a "pre-figure" of Christ. We see the most magnificent symbolic representation of the sun in the large rose windows of the Gothic churches and in the sun monstrances. The symbolism of Easter is also closely related to sun symbolism.

Bibliography: J. Jobé (ed.). *Die Sonne, Licht und Leben*. Freiburg, Basel, Wien, 1975.
H.R. Engler. *Die Sonne als Symbol*. Küsnacht, 1962.

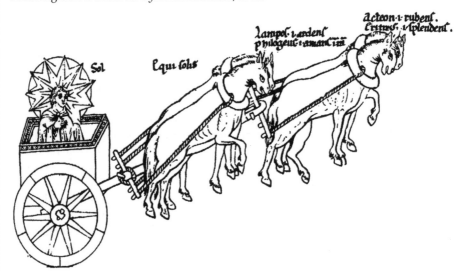

SUN: Christ as Sol invictus in a sun chariot drawn by four horses. An illustration from Herrad von Landsberg's *Hortus Deliciarum*. 12th century

SUN: The falcon-headed Re-Horakhte
with the rising sun; from the grave
of Sennedjem; 20th Dynasty
SUN: Sun as symbol of strength and
fertility; rock drawing from Val
Camonica

contentment. —Among the Sumerians, it was a symbol of undivided matter, of passivity, and of woman. —In ancient Greece, the symbolic meaning of the swamp is closely related to that of the LABYRINTH. —In psychoanalytic dream interpretation, the swamp sometimes appears as a symbol of the unconscious.

Swan - In Asia Minor as in Europe, the white swan is a symbol of light, of purity and of grace (in contrast, the black swan, like the black SUN, is occasionally encountered in occult symbolic contexts); for its part, this symbolism is divided to some extent into feminine and masculine complexes of meaning. Especially among Slavic and Scandinavian peoples and in Asia Minor, the feminine aspect predominates: the swan as a symbol of beauty, of the Holy Virgin (fertilized by water or the earth). In India, China, Japan, Scandinavia and among Arabs and Persians, one encounters the virgin swan as a type of fairy tale figure from the world beyond. In antiquity, on the other hand, the masculine aspect predominated: as a symbol of virility, white swans draw the chariot of Apollo, Zeus draws near to Leda in the form of a swan (although Aphrodite and Artemis are also occasionally accompa-

nied by swans). —According to Greek belief, the swan also possessed the ability to tell fortunes and to herald death. —In the Far East, the swan is a symbol of grace as well as of nobility and courage. — Among the Celts, the swan was thought to be an embodiment of celestial beings; like Hinduism, for example, the Celts did not always distinguish between the symbolic meaning of the swan and the GOOSE, while the goose is thought of as a rather negative counter-image to the swan in many other cultures. —In alchemy, the swan was frequently associated with MERCURY; it was regarded as a symbol of the spirit and of the mediation of WATER and FIRE. —One occasionally encounters the swan egg as a world EGG. —The singing swan, which supposedly begins to sing lugubrious songs before its death (especially when it is trapped in ice), became a symbol of a person's last works or words; in this sense, it is also occasionally a symbol of Christ with respect to His last words on the cross.

Swastika - From the Sanskrit *svasti*, meaning "fortune, happiness." A CROSS passed down through history in various forms. Found on ceramics dating from as early as the 3rd century B.C.; primarily a solar sign. —A cross with four bars of

SUNFLOWER: In Schmid's *Musterbuch*, the sunflower is used to symbolize monastic obedience

SWALLOW: Two swallows in flight. Detail of a mural in a house on Thíra (Santoríni), Mycenaean-Cretan

equal length whose ends are extended at right angles or curved, giving the impression of circular movement; it is also called *crux gammata* because it consists of four (usually reversed) Greek gamma Γ signs. It is a widely common symbol in Asia and Europe and less common in Africa and Central America. It is usually interpreted as being a sun wheel, as intersecting lightning bolts, or (in Nordic lands) as the HAMMER of Thor; it was frequently thought of as a symbol of good luck and healing; among Buddhists, it symbolizes the "key to paradise"; in Romanesque art of the Middle Ages, it often probably had apotropaic significance.

Sweat - In folk belief, sweat was sometimes thought to bear the energies of the person perspiring; it was therefore used in maleficent as well as beneficent magic. —In some American Indian cultures, the body's perspiration was thought to be a sacrifice to the sun god and thus also an atonement and cleansing.

Swing - In Southeast Asia (as well as in parts of Greece and Spain), the swing is related to fertility rites; in such cases, the movement of the swing is apparently associated with the ebb and flow of natural growth; perhaps it is also reminiscent of the wind, which is brought about by rocking and fertilizes the ground. Especially in India, it symbolizes the rising and setting of the SUN, the rhythm of the seasons, the eternal cycle of death and birth, and occasionally the harmonic union of heaven and earth and thus sometimes also the RAINBOW and RAIN.

Sword - Often, the sword is primarily a mere symbol of martial virtues, especially of manly strength and courage; it is thus also a symbol of power and of the SUN (with respect to the active, masculine principle as well as to the darting, sword-like rays of the sun); interpreted in a negative sense, it symbolizes the horrors of war; many gods of war and storm have a sword as an attribute. —It is occasionally a phallic symbol as well. —As a sharp implement for cutting, it is a symbol of decision, of separation into good and evil and thus also a symbol of justice; in many portrayals of the Last Judgment, a double-edged sword extends from the MOUTH of Christ. — According to the medieval two-swords theory, which defines the curial conception of power (primacy of the Church over the state) and the imperial conception of power (equality of both authorities), one sword represents world-ly power and the other represents clerical power. —The flaming

SWASTIKA: Clay tile from Samarra
(Mesopotamian art, 5th millenium
B.C.)

SWASTIKA: Detail of a stone relief
with symbols that bring good luck;
northern India, 1st/2nd century

sword that drove ADAM AND EVE from Eden is also a symbol of power and justice. —The sword can also be a symbol of LIGHTNING, such as in Japan and India, where, for example, the sword of Vedic sacrificial priests is called the lightning of Indra. —A sword tightly tucked into its sheath symbolizes the cardinal virtue of temperance or prudence.

Sycamore - A term for various trees; in Egypt, it especially refers to the sycamore fig, which was regarded as a manifestation of the sky goddess. Its leaves and its shadow were regarded as a symbol of quiet and peace in the next life; the souls of the deceased were sometimes thought of as BIRDS that lived in the branches of the sycamore.

Sycamore Fig - See SYCAMORE.

Symbol - From the Greek *symballein*, meaning "to toss together." In information theory, it is usually a synonym for "sign"; in psychoanalysis, experience and behavior are investigated with an eye to symbolic meanings.

Symbolism - From the Greek. 1) An intended, transcendent meaning represented in a SYMBOL; 2) the practical use or systematic representation of current or historical symbols (such as in color symbolism, typology, architectural symbolism).

Sympathy - Sympathy and CORRELATIVE are pre-scientific concepts that were developed by C.G. Jung and that he sums up with the term "synchronicity." By extension, sympathy in astrology is used in the sense of a hypothetical cause of two events; this is how it was used even in antiquity; the concept "correlative" refers only to a parallelism without a causal connection and does not seek to offer explanations. Sympathy and magic are just as closely related; during the Renaissance, a comprehensive literature arose concerning sympathies and antipathies, stars, minerals, fauna, flora, etc. An example is the "Garden of Sympathies" in J. Ferne's *Blazon of Glory* (1624).

Synagogue - From the Greek, meaning "congregation." 1) The structure serving as a place of Jewish religious prayer and reading, the construction of which is usually patterned on an "O" (Jerusalem) due to requirements of prayer; the ark with the Torah scrolls is at the end opposite the entrance; the NER TAMID and the rostrum are in front of the ark; in the middle of many Orthodox synagogues, there is a

SWORD: Expulsion from the Garden of
Eden with the flaming sword; from
Speculum Humanae Salvationis,
Dutch block book

SWORD: Christ as judge of the world
with a sword in His mouth; from a
miniature, circa 1260

raised platform for the Torah reading. 2)
In Christian art of the Middle Ages, Syna-
gogue was a female personification of the
Jewish religious community. See BLIND-
FOLD; ECCLESIA.

SYCAMORE: The Egyptian sky goddess Nut
in a sycamore tree; middle of the 2nd
millenium B.C.

Tabernacle - In contrast to the stationary CITY, the tabernacle is the abode of wanderers and herdsmen; because it can be easily disassembled, it became a symbol of earthly impermanence and human fallibility; the representation of an open tabernacle in which Mary is standing alone or with the baby Jesus, is regarded as a symbol of the revelation of divine salvation. —Among the Israelites, the ARK OF THE COVENANT is in the Tabernacle of the Covenant.

Table - As a center around which people can assemble, the table is a symbol of common meals, yet also of a select community (such as King Arthur's Round Table). —In Islam, there is the idea of a large table on which God marks peoples' fates.

Tablets of the Law - A symbol of the Old Covenant, on which the Ten Commandments were written.

Taboo - From the Polynesian *tapu*, meaning "that which is strictly prescribed" 1) A magical-religious prohibition that has to do with the sacred (positively charged with higher power and energy) and MANA and that is applicable to persons (priests, chiefs, women in childbed), names (of gods, predatory animals), actions (such as touching kings), objects, times, places, etc. Defilement caused by breaking a taboo is regarded as contagious and requires ritual cleansing. Among primitive peoples, taboos are often involved in the legal securing of property (making fields taboo, etc.); they are often the basis of an entire social order. 2) Generally: something untouchable; something about which one does not speak. See DIETARY TABOO.

Tabula Smaragdina - The smaragd table of the alchemists and astrologers; the mysterious manuscript that seems to exist probably only in legend; is regarded as one of the first written bases of MICROCOSM-MACROCOSM thought.

Tail - The tail is occasionally encountered as a veiled sexual symbol; an example in Romanesque art is the lion's tail, which is often part of ornamentation.

Talisman - From the Arabic *tilasm*, meaning "magic picture." In popular parlance, the talisman is largely identical with the AMULET; occasionally, it is distinguished from the amulet, which was attributed

TETRAMORPH: Tetramorph on two wheels (symbols of the Old and New Testaments); illustration from monastery at Athos, 1213

more with apotropaic traits, as an active bringer of good fortune. In astrology, the talisman was interpreted as being a connecting link to the powers of astral rays, which it was supposed to store within itself.

Tamarisk - A tree or bush that has scale-like leaves and (often) spicate inflorescence. In China, it was regarded as an immortality symbol and its resin was thus used as a drug to prolong life.

Tansy - A member of the Compositae family having a picantly aromatic essential oil; it is an ancient magical and medicinal plant. It is sometimes encountered in medieval art as an attribute of Mary ("leaves of Mary"). At the Assumption of the Blessed Virgin, blessed tansy is supposed to provide protection against sorcerers, witches and the devil.

Tantalus - In Greek myth, he is a king who served the gods his murdered son Pelops as food in order to test their omniscience. As a punishment, he was thrown into Hades and there suffered eternal hunger and thirst: over him hung branches that drew away when he reached for them; he stood with in a lake that disappeared when he wanted to drink. Along with

Sisyphus (see ROCK), Tantalus is regarded as a personification of the unattainability of all human wishes.

Tarot - Appearing first in France, tarot has been a common card game since the Middle Ages; its seventy-eight cards have repeatedly given rise to speculative symbolic interpretations; the sequence of trump cards, in particular, was seen as a symbol of a path of initiation.

Tattoos - From the Samoan *tat(a)u*, meaning "to strike correctly." Often associated with INITIATION; tattoos depict magical or symbolic motifs, and serve as indications of clan membership or position, as well as mere ornamentation; they are one of the more regularly encountered types of body painting throughtout time. Scar tattoos are ancient (having been worn even by Tasmanians); some of them were made by branding, but most were raised segments of scar tissue (proud flesh) produced by repeated scratching of the skin and rubbing of the wounds with ash, lime, and other substances; they are especially common among dark-skinned primitive peoples. Lighter-skinned people (in Indonesia, Oceania, and America) prefer tattoos made by pricking (genuine tattoos), in which dyes are placed under the skin

THORN BUSH, BURNING: Moses at the Burning Thornbush; from a glass painting from the Stiftskirche at Wimpfen im Tal, first half of the 14th century.

by means that include pricking and cutting with thorns or small-toothed hammers (see etymology). Related to this are the drawing of sooty threads through or insertion of amulets under the skin (the former is a more recent practice and occurs in Siberia and in the northwestern and far northern sections of America, the latter occurs among bushmen and in Indo-China); after Cook's return from his trip around the world and exhibition of a tatooed Polynesian, tattoos as a fashion began to appear in English society and spread from there to the widest social circles; today, they are also distinctive marks of members of subcultures.

Tau - The last letter of the Hebrew alphabet. Like the Greek letter OMEGA, it was regarded as a symbol of the end or of completion.

Taurus - The constellation STEER.

Tea - In eastern Asia, it is a symbol of cultivation, often in ritual tea ceremonies as a key part of cult activity, as exemplified by the attitude toward life in the Japanese Way of Zen.

Teeth - A symbol of strength and vitality as well as aggressiveness. Psychoanalysis interprets the loss of one's teeth (in dreams, for example) primarily in connection with the male sex organ and interprets it as a sign of frustration, weakness or castration anxiety. The idea of the *vagina dentata* (a vagina with teeth) is based on a conflation of the genital with the oral and is usually thought of as a projection of male castration anxiety.

Temperantia - Personification of temperance or prudence, one of the four cardinal virtues; frequently represented with a LION, CAMEL, DOVE, ELEPHANT, death's head (see SKULL), HOURGLASS, COMPASSES or a SWORD tightly tucked in its sheath.

Temple - From the Greek and Latin, meaning "separate holy area." The HOUSE of a deity or, in a broader sense, the site of a cult, a consecrated area, an enclosed forest, lone-standing trees, columns.

Tetrakis - The sum of the numbers 1, 2, 3, 4 = 10. Among the Pythagoreans, it was a holy number, the quintessence of perfection; it was personified as the god of harmony. See TEN.

Tetramorph - A term used until the late Middle Ages, encompassing Cherubim

TEN

$$10 = 1 + 9$$
$$= 2 + 8$$
$$= 3 + 7$$
$$= 4 + 6$$
$$= 5 + 5$$

The number ten is the basis of the decimal system and is probably derived from the number of fingers on both hands. Even in antiquity, it was regarded as a sort of perfect number because it contains within itself all numbers between 1 and 9 (see model). For the Pythagoreans, the tetrakis $1 + 2 + 3 + 4 = 10$ made 10 a divine and mysterious number that could also be represented as a figured number (see diagram).

Cardinal numbers in multiples of 10 have a symbolic meaning similar to that of the cardinal numbers themselves. This is especially true for the second and third powers of ten, i.e. $10^2 = 10 \times 10 = 100$ and $10^3 = 10 \times 10 \times 10 = 1,000$; the fourth power of ten, i.e. $10^4 = 10 \times 10 \times 10 \times 10 = 10,000$, is regarded as a symbol of innumerability.

Tetraktys

TEN: The ten stages of a person's life. Single page impression by Abraham Bach

THRONE: Throne of the ruler; from the
Bible of Viviano, 840 A.D.
THYRSUS STAFF: Dionysus priest
with thyrsus staff

(see CHERUB) and symbols of the Evangelists in a single figure having four faces and four or six wings; the idea is derived from a vision, described by St. John in Revelation and by Ezekiel, of four winged creatures that were like a HUMAN, a LION, a STEER, and an EAGLE (in Ezekiel, one creature had a lion's face, another a human's face, another a steer's face, and the last an eagle's face). Originally, tetramorphs were probably a symbol of God's spiritual omnipresence.

Thanatos - In Greek mythology, Thanatos is a symbol and personification of death; portrayed with Hypnos as a winged youth carrying poppy-heads and a small horn, as well as a lowered torch.

Throne - A symbol of rulership and fame in matters temporal and sacred, often raised by a base and having a canopy. The construction and materials of a throne often have additional symbolic significance; in Buddhism, for example, there is the idea of a DIAMOND throne for the Buddha that is supposed to be at the foot of the bodhi tree (see FIG TREE). —Originally, the Egyptian goddess Isis was possibly thought of as the embodiment of the ruler's throne, which was thought to be a divine being; she occasionally has the hieroglyphs for "throne" on her head. —In various religions, the throne of God or of gods was thought to be carried by angels or sacred symbolic animals. —The Koran often speaks of Allah as the "Lord of the Throne" or "Master of the Throne"; in this case, the throne symbolizes the sum of divine wisdom; it is described as being made of an incredibly brilliant shining material and having 70,000 tongues that praise God in all languages; it is said to change its color 70,000 times each day and to contain the prototypical images of all that exists; the distance of each supporting pillar from the others is the distance that a quickly flying bird would travel in 80,000 years. —In Judaism, the throne of the king as well as the entire city of Jerusalem symbolically represented the throne and dominion of Yahweh over His people. In the Old Testament, the throne appears primarily as a symbol of God's judicial authority. —From the Romans, the early Christian church adopted the *cathedra*, a seat with a vaulted back upon which persons of higher position sat while others stood. The church made it into a symbol of spiritual tutelage and accorded it liturgical significance as the seat of the founder of the church or of a bishop. —Early Christian art developed the motif of the symbolic ascension to the throne with respect

THREE

The numerical sign of three

The eye in a triangle as a symbol of God; altar piece

Window with three connected rabbits; Cathedral of Paderborn

3 The basic number of the masculine principle next to 1 (the number of the divine) and 2 (the number of the feminine); water is the element of 3; the triangle is its coordinate geometrical figure. The triangle and water are also associated with one another in alchemist-medical signs. 3 plays an unmistakably fundamental role in all religions. The second and third powers of three are of particular significance, i.e. $3^2 = 3 \times 3 = 9$ and $3^3 = 3 \times 3 \times 3 = 27$, which are regarded as a "strengthening" of the symbolic power of 3. —3 is the basis of numerous systems and ordering schemes; thus, Christianity, for example, has the 3 virtues of faith, love, and hope, and alchemy has the 3 basic principles of SULPHUR, SALT and quicksilver (see MERCURY), etc. Divine triumverates are known in many religions, for example in Egypt (Isis, Osiris, Horus), in Hinduism (Brahma, Vishnu, Shiva), etc. Such divine triumvirates often appear in conjunction with HEAVEN, EARTH and AIR (which binds them together). In contrast to this, Christianity has a triune God who is often envisaged as being a unity of three persons (a trinity). —As the number of fulfillment of a self-contained entirety, 3 is frequently encountered in fairy tales as the number of tests that one must withstand or riddles that one must solve, etc. —In philosophy, the triad or triple-step plays an important role, for example, as the principle of mediation between thinking and being or, as in the case of Hegel, as the principle of dialectical progress (thesis, antithesis, synthesis). See TRIANGLE; TRIDENT.

13 In Christian thought, 13 is thought of as the sum of the Ten Commandments and the Trinity (i.e., 13 = 10 + 3) or as the sum of the Pentatuch (Old Testament) and the resurrection (i.e., the sum of 5 + 8 = 13). According to popular belief, 13 is an unlucky number; tradition interprets it as being Jesus and his 12 Apostles, one of whom was the traitor; it is also unlucky because it exceeds by 1 the symbolic number 12 (which is the number of the signs of the zodiac or the number of the Apostles). In Meso-American lands, 13 seems to have been attributed a special role by astral influences as well: the 20 daily signs of the month are combined with the numbers 1–13, such that the 260 days (13 x 20) of the calendar are clearly determined. —In certain contexts, however, such as in antiquity, 13 was a symbol of strength and sublimity; thus, Zeus, for example, was sometimes described as the thirteenth in a circle of twelve primary gods. —13 is also occasionally encountered in the Old Testament as a number of salvation. —In some American Indian cultures, 13 is a holy number.

30

30 is the number of the perfection of mercy and law, because it is the product of 5 x 6. Yet the number 30 is also associated with order and justice: Moses and Jesus began their ministries at age 30; in the Old Testament (Judges 10:4), the judge Jair had 30 sons, who rode 30 young asses and had 30 towns.

33

The number of perfection: David lived 33 years; Jesus died in his 33rd year; Dante's *Divine Comedy* consists of 3 x 33 + 1 cantos. The Islamic rosary has 33 pearls and thus 1/3 of the most beautiful names of Allah. 3 x 11 = 33 gods are an expression of perfection in Indian mythology.

From a depiction of the Trinity in Hrabanus Maurus's *De origine rerum*

The Trinity as unity, the four-fold based on duality; from *Duodecim* by Valentinus

to the Second Coming of Christ on Judgment Day (see ETIMASIE).

Thema Mundi - Or "horoscope of the world." A separation of the PLANETS at the moment of the creation of the universe, assumed even by Babylonian and ancient Egyptian astrology; it is the basis of speculation about the great Fire and the Flood in Greek tradition. The Babylonian as well as the Egyptian *thema mundi* can never reflect reality (for astronomical reasons). —After the Fourth Lateran Council, it was decided as a matter of dogma what the state of the world, including angels, looked like; approximately one century later, the *thema mundi* enjoyed much popularity in art as a symbol of the divine unity of the world, an example being the work of Sienese painter Giovanni di Paolo (1403–1482).

Third Eye - See EYE.

Thistle - Like many prickly plants, the thistle is a symbol for tribulation and sorrow; in Christian art, it is a symbol for the sufferings of Christ and the martyrs, and is thus a symbol of salvation as well (as is the BROOM). —The prickles, which repel enemies, can also be a symbol of protection. —In China, the thistle was regarded as a symbol of long life, possibly because it keeps its shape even after it has been cut and dried.

Thorn - The thorn is a symbol for tribulation, adversity, and suffering. —For some American Indian cultures, the thorn of the agave was an instrument of self-mortification: the priests used it to scratch their skin in order to sacrifice the flowing blood to the gods. —In Christian graphic arts, a branch of thorns wrapped around a skull is a symbol of eternal damnation. — Christ's crown of thorns is a symbol of pain and derision. In part, the circular tonsure of monks refers symbolically to this. —The thorn bush in the story of Isaac's sacrifice was sometimes regarded as an anticipatory symbol of Christ's cross and crown of thorns. See THORN BUSH, BURNING.

Thorn Bush, Burning - God appeared to Moses in a thorn bush that burned but was not consumed: it is a symbol of the nondestructive power of spiritual FIRE; in Christian art and literature, it is also a symbol of Mary, who became a mother, yet remained a virgin, that is, who "burned," yet remained "unhurt."

Thorn Puller - An ancient bronze sculp-

TOAD: Two toads, dancing in honor of Satan; from an illustration in Collin de Plancy's *Dictionnaire infernal*, 1845

ture of a sitting boy who is pulling a thorn out of his foot; it is a favorite motif especially in Greek and Roman art. In Christian art, it is a symbol of punishment for the person who has strayed from the "right path"; the thorn therefore signifies sickness and vice.

Thousand - See HUNDRED.

Thread - A general symbol of connection. The Upanishads, for example, speak of a thread that binds together this world, the next world, and all beings. Time and life are also frequently compared with a thread (see MOIRAI). In Greek myth, the thread of Ariadne is a ball of yarn that Ariadne, a daughter of king Minos, gave to Theseus and that he used to find his way out of the LABYRINTH. Thread is a proverbial symbol for a principle that guides understanding.

Thread of Life - See MOIRAI.

Threshold - Or "doorstep." Like the DOOR itself, the threshold is a symbol of transition from one place, state, etc. to another or of separation between them. —"To turn someone away at the doorstep" means that one wants to have nothing to do with someone, whereas "to turn up on someone's doorstep" means that one is putting oneself under that person's protection. —The threshold of a temple is thought to be holy in many cultures and thus requires special cleansing before it is crossed (such as taking off one's shoes at the threshold of mosques); among some peoples, the threshold itself may not be stepped upon.

Throat - See MOUTH.

Thumb - The finger whose opposability enables the hand to grasp objects. It is often interpreted as being masculine and creative and is therefore also thought of as a phallus symbol. See FINGER.

Thunder - Like LIGHTNING, thunder is regarded in many cultures as a manifestation and symbol of divine power and thus an attribute of the highest deities. — The ancient Germans thought that thunder was produced when Donar hurled his hammer. —In the Bible, it is a voice, particularly the wrathful voice of God. —The Celts interpreted thunder as an expression of a cosmic disturbance that conjured up the wrath of the elements; it was also seen as a punishment from the gods. —In Siberia and North America, one encounters the idea of a mythic bird that produces

TOMAHAWK: Tomahawks of North American Indians

TORCH: Eye of Horus, holding a torch; from a mural in an Egyptian grave

thunder by flapping its wings; this bird appears as a wild goose or duck, an iron bird, or an EAGLE. —According to the Chinese, thunder was produced by the movements of a celestial DRAGON. —Occasionally, one encounters a one-legged (see ONE-LEGGEDNESS) thunder god, such as in some American Indian cultures. Thunder gods are frequently depicted as having SMITHS as helpers who forge them LIGHTNING, HAMMERS, clubs, etc.

Thunderstorm - See STORM.

Thyrsus - A staff used primarily during antiquity that had PINE branches, was topped with a pine cone, and was wound with IVY and GRAPEVINES (see WINE); it is a symbol of fertility and immortality; it was used in cult ceremonies involving mother deities or in honor of Hermes (Mercury) and as part of the Dionysus mysteries at Eleusis. It is also an attribute of Dionysus and the maenads. —In Christian art, the thyrsus appears as a symbol of plant vitality, yet also of paganism.

Tiger - A symbol of strength and wildness having negative as well as positive significance. In China, the tiger was initially a guardian spirit of hunting, later of farm-

ing. The tiger, living in the dark thicket and characterized primarily by the Yin principle (see YIN AND YANG), sometimes occurs as a good or evil adversary of the DRAGON. The white tiger is a symbol of regal virtues. —In Buddhism, the tiger that finds its way through the jungle is a symbol of spiritual struggle. Since it can orient itself in darkness and during the new moon, the tiger is also a symbol of the inner light or of increase of light and of life after dark and difficult times. —As a rapacious predatory animal, the tiger often symbolizes the dangerous power of uncontrolled urges. —The tiger is the third sign of the Chinese ZODIAC and corresponds to GEMINI.

Toad - As an animal that loves darkness and dampness, the toad is associated in China primarily with the Yin principle (see YIN AND YANG), with the MOON, and with fertility and wealth. —Like the FROG, the toad is related in many cultures to RAIN and rain magic. —In the Occident, it was related to solar symbolism in early times and was later often interpreted ambivalently: on the one hand, as a guardian of treasure and a good house spirit, particularly as an aid at births (since antiquity, the womb has frequently been imagined to be in the shape of a toad); on

TOTEM POLE: ancestral figure
(Bakota) at left, totem pole (Haida)
at right

the other hand, though, as a poisonous witches' animal and often in contrast to the usually positive symbolic significance of the frog. —In Egypt (in Faiyum), the toad was regarded as an animal of death (probably because it preferred to live in the ground), yet, like the frog, was Christianized by the Coptics as a symbol of "personal resurrection" (probably because of the change in form that it undergoes in its development from a tadpole to a mature animal). —In the art of the Middle Ages, the toad appears in representations of death as well as in conjunction with the vices of lust and covetousness.

Tomahawk - From the Algonquin; originally a term for a hammer used as a tool. Refers to various types of clubs; more specifically, it refers to the metal ax (made of iron or brass) that was introduced to the North American Indians by the Europeans in the 16th century and that was initially used as a tool but whose function as a weapon (also for throwing) quickly became known. Because of its multi-purposive use as a weapon—still combined with the tobacco pipe in the 18th century—and as a symbol of war (raised when war was declared), it assumed a significant role in American Indian culture; later, it was simply a term for a battle ax.

Tomato - Because of its red juice as well as its many seeds, it was sometimes associated among black African peoples with blood and fertility. —In Europe, it, like the red APPLE, was sometimes a symbol of love.

Tongue - Because of its shape and agility, it is occasionally identified symbolically with the FLAME. —As the organ that produces speech, the tongue is occasionally interpreted generally with respect to fertility and is thus associated with rain, blood, and sperm.

Tools of the Passion - *Arma Christi*. See PASSION, IMPLEMENTS OF THE.

Top - See HEIGHT.

Torch - As a form of the element FIRE that is both concentrated and reduced to an individual instance, the torch has, to a large extent, the same symbolic meaning as fire. As a symbol of cleansing and illumination, it is commonly used in initiation rites. In antiquity, a lowered torch in the hand of a youth or guardian spirit was a vivid symbol of death as the extinction of life. —In medieval symbolic representations of the deadly sins, the torch sometimes symbolizes anger. —In folk cus-

TOWER: Biblical pictures of the Song of Solomon (Calls of the Laurentian litany), including the tower of David, surround the Holy Virgin as symbols of Mary. Illustration in P. Canisius's *De Maria Virgine*, Ingolstadt, 1577

TOWER: In the Laurentian litany, Mary is called the "tower of David" (from Schmid's *Musterbuch*)

toms, the torch played a role as a fertility symbol, especially during the winter and spring.

Torques - A metal necklace, examples of which exist from as far back as the La Tène period; among the Celts, it was a sign and symbol of a hero.

Totem - See TOTEMISM; TOTEM POLE.

Totemism - From the Algonquin *dodaim* or *ndodem*, meaning "family emblem, guardian spirit." The belief in mystical, familial, cult-like, long-term relationships with a person or that person's lineage ("individual totemism"), or with a social group such as a tribe, clan, etc. ("group totemism") through a "totem" (i.e., animal, plant, other object, natural phenomenon). Individual totemism (especially in northern Asia and northern America) is closely related to shamanism. In Australia, men sometimes have their own specific totem and women theirs (gender totemism). The foundations of totemism lie in the magical, mystical and religious connection to animals among hunting peoples. Nearly mandatory are: exogamy (the prohibition of marriage within the totem group), the meticulous care of the totem, and the prohibition of killing, eat-

ing and touching the totem (which is a guardian, assistant, relative). Totemic features exist among nearly all primitive peoples and in ancient civilizations, including ancient Europe. See MANA; TABOO.

Totem Pole - Usually a tall post with carvings and animal and human figures stacked upon one another (sometimes painted), representing the totem or ancestral legend of a kindred group. They are found among American Indians on the Northwest Coast as well as in Oceania. They are generally found in front of a house as a sign of membership in a respective family.

Touch-Me-Not - See MIMOSA.

Tower - A symbol of power or of transcendence over mediocrity. Because of its shape, it is also a phallus symbol; yet, as a predominately windowless, closed space, it is also a symbol of virginity (Mary, for example, is compared to an ivory tower). As a fortified space that is cut off from the world, the tower can also be a symbol of philosophical thought and meditation (the negative connotation of the IVORY TOWER). —In representations of Chris-

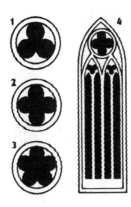

TRACERY: 1) Triple-foiled; 2) quadruple-foiled; 3) quintuple-foiled; 4) Gothic window with triple-foiled and quadruple-foiled tracery

tian art of the Middle Ages, a tower is often a symbol of vigilance; in early Christian times, a tower often symbolized the entire "holy city." Especially at the time of early Christianity, the lighthouse is a symbol of the eternal goal toward which the SHIP of life steers on the waves of this life. —The Babylonian step tower (*ziggurat*) was probably a symbol of the world MOUNTAIN; the individual steps symbolize man's gradual spiritual ascent to heaven. The Tower of BABEL was a ziggurat.

Tracery - A decorative element on Gothic buildings constructed ("measured") with a compass; first used in the arrangement of the panels of arches on windows and in the design of WHEEL WINDOWS and ROSE WINDOWS, they were later used in complicated geometrical patterns as blind windows of walls and panelling of balustrades.

Transmutation - See V.I.T.R.I.O.L.

Transmigration of Souls - Also termed "metempsychosis," "palingenesis," "reincarnation," "rebirth," "reembodiment." It is the belief that the soul alternately enters the bodies of humans, animals, and even lifeless objects. The belief in the transmigration of souls without salvatory import can be found among primitive peoples; however, a particular rebirth is usually thought to be the result of deeds of a previous life. In that case, the transmigration of the soul is a path of purification.

Treasure - Encountered in the mythic imagery of many peoples, especially as a hidden treasure, often guarded by MONSTERS. It is sometimes interpreted as a symbol of esoteric knowledge or, according to the view of psychoanalysis, as a symbol for the goals toward which an individual aspires in his development.

Tree - One of the most significant and wide-spread symbols. As a powerful representation of the plant kingdom, trees were often worshipped ritually as a symbol of divine beings or as the locus of numinous powers. The deciduous tree, with its annually replaced leaves, is primarily a symbol of the rebirth of life vanquishing death ever anew; the evergreen coniferous tree is a symbol of immortality. The shape of a tree, with its roots bound to the earth, its strong, vertically rising trunk, and its crown that often seems to reach for the sky, frequently gave rise to the tree's becoming a symbol of the

TREE

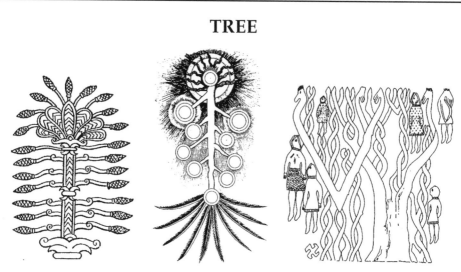

Left: Sacred tree (Mesopotamia, 1500 B.C.); Center: in many cultures, the "inverted" tree plays an important role, such that it can stand next to an altar, for example; in ritual plantings, it is also planted with its roots symbolically pointing toward the sky. Illustration by R. Fludd (1619); Right: Sacrificial tree with hanged men; illustration based on a weaving from the Oseberg excavation.

Left: Palm tree as a symbol of heavenly paradise; from a mosaic in the Church of Saints Cosma e Damiano in Rome (from Schmid's *Musterbuch*); Center: serpent on the Tree of Knowledge, detail from a medieval illuminated manuscript; Right: Tree of Death (from Schmid's *Musterbuch*)

TREE: Round dance about a tree idol; clay model from Cyprus, circa 1000 B.C.

TREE: Trees of life on an Egyptian glass pitcher (one of the oldest in the world); 1500 B.C.

union of the cosmic regions of the subterranean/chthonic, of life on earth, and of heaven. These aspects also play a role in the idea of the world tree, which was thought to be either the support of the world or (more frequently) the embodiment of the WORLD AXIS (such as the evergreen world ash tree YGGDRASIL found in Nordic mythology). The leaves and branches of such trees are frequently inhabited by mythic animals, by the souls of the deceased or the unborn (often in the form of BIRDS), or by the rising and setting sun and Moon. In some mythologies, such as in India and China, one encounters twelve sun birds living in the branches of the world tree, which probably has a symbolic relation to the ZODIAC. Birds living in the crown of the world tree can also be symbols for higher stages of spiritual being and development. Anthropomorphic interpretations of trees are widespread, as trees, like humans, stand upright, grow and pass away. Trees thus appear among different peoples, such as in Central Asia, Japan, Korea and Australia, as mythological forebearers of humans. A further symbolic identification of the tree with humans is the custom, widespread in several regions of India, of marrying a bride to a tree before her wedding in order to increase her fertility; symbolic weddings between two trees, whose vitality is thereby supposedly transferred to a particular pair of humans, are connected with this. —The tree that bears fruit and offers shade and protection is regarded by many peoples as a feminine or maternal symbol, although the upright trunk is usually a phallus symbol. —The association of the tree with FIRE is also common, which probably has to do with the vitality attributed to trees: fire is thought to be hidden in the wood of certain trees, capable of being extracted from the wood by rubbing. —In the Indian tradition, there is an idea of a tree that grows upside down, its roots anchored in the sky and its branches spread out in the earth; this is possibly a symbol (among other things) for the life-giving force of the sun in the physical realm and of spiritual LIGHT in the spiritual realm (see HEIGHT and DEPTH). The Bhagavad Gita also interprets the inverted tree as a symbol for the unfurling of all Being out of a primeval ground: the roots represent the principle of all appearances and the branches represent the concrete and richly specific realization of this principle. The inverted tree is also found in other contexts, such as in the Cabala as a tree of life or in Islam as a tree of happiness. According to Dante's *Divine Comedy* (Purgatorio, Canto

TREE: Tree of Knowledge with Adam and Eve and serpent; from an illustration in *Cod. Vigilanus seu Albeldensis*

TREE CROSS: Personified church with a budding cross; illuminated manuscipt, circa 1180

22), the tree of knowledge that grows from top to bottom cannot be climbed and a voice, recounting instances of temperance, sounds from its branches. —In the Bible, the tree appears primarily in the two-fold form of the Tree of Life and the Tree of Knowledge of good and evil. The Tree of Life symbolizes the original abundance in Eden and is simultaneously a symbol of anticipated fulfillment at the end of the world; the Tree of Knowledge, with its enticing fruits, symbolizes the lure of acting against the divine commandments. Christian art and literature frequently construct a close symbolic relationship between the trees of Eden and the Cross of Christ, which "has returned Eden to us" (see TREE CROSS) and which is the "true Tree of Life." —Psychoanalysis sees the tree as an important symbol that is often interpreted in symbolic relation to the mother, to spiritual-intellectual development, or to death and rebirth. —See APPLE; ARBOR PHILOSOPHICA; ASH; CEDAR TREE; CHRISTMAS TREE; CYPRESS; FIG TREE; LIME; OAK; OLIVE TREE; PEACH TREE; PEAR TREE; PLUM TREE; TREE CROSS; TREE OF LIFE.

Tree Cross - A form of the Cross of Christ encountered especially in Germany and Italy, having leaves, blossoms and fruits

as a symbol of the overcoming of death (see TREE OF LIFE). —A tree that bears leaves or fruits with the Crucified occasionally refers to the paradisal Tree of Knowledge. Examples date back to the 5th century. See BRANCH CROSS.

Tree of Life - 1) Thuja—like all evergreen plants, it is an immortality symbol. 2) In Christian art, the tree of life as a budding and blossoming cross is a symbol of victory over death (in decoration of graves, on portals); as a symbol of heaven at the end of the world, it is usually depicted as being a palm tree or an olive tree; in folk art, it is a symbol of life and a common decorative motif. 3) An Indo-Germanic symbol; in Nordic cultures, the world tree YGGDRASIL. Reinterpreted in the Christian legacy of the ancient Germans and Celts, it became generally thought of as a cross-beam (see STONE CROSS). —See CROSS; TREE.

Trefoil - See LEAF.

Triangle - To a large extent, the triangle shares in the symbolic significance of the number THREE. In antiquity, it was sometimes regarded as a symbol of light. For many peoples, it is a symbol of fire and masculine virility when its tip points up-

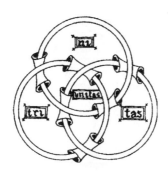

TRIDENT: Trident as an attribute of Neptune

TRINITY: The symbol of the Trinity in the form of three circles; Chartres, 13th century

ward and a symbol of water and the female sex when its tip points downward. —The equilateral triangle is often used as a sign for God or for harmony. In Christianity, it is a symbol of the Trinity (especially since the 17th century, it frequently appears in conjunction with a hand, a head, an eye, or the Hebrew name of God, Yahweh). —According to popular custom, magicians and sorcerers, the triangle is an apotropaic sign. —For the Freemasons, the triangle plays an important role as (among other things) a symbol of God's strength, beauty and wisdom; of the cornerstone of the Freemasons' temple; of the mineral, plant and animal kingdoms; of the three stages of a person's spiritual development (*Separatio*, *Fermentatio* and *Putrefactio*); of correct speech, thought, and action; of birth, maturity and death; and so forth.

Trident - A staff with three prongs, used to catch fish. It is an attribute of ocean deities, particularly of Poseidon; it was also regarded as a symbol for the teeth of sea monsters, for the rays of the sun or for lightning. —In India, it is an attribute of the god Shiva and symbolizes the three-fold nature of time (past, present and future) or the three basic levels or qualities of the empirical world (becoming, being, passing).

Trinity - In Christianity, the trinity is the symbolic representation of God the triune. See VISAGES.

Tripod - From the Greek *tripus*. In antiquity, the tripod was a frame for a container; it was often skilfully made and stood as high as a person. It had sacred and secular functions (as a trophy, votive offering, etc.). The oldest specimens are from Troy and Mycenae. The most famous tripod stood in Delphi as the seat of Pythia, who pronounced oracles. The tripod has been shown to have existed in central and northern Europe at the beginning of the La Tène period as an import from Etruria.

Triskele - Or "triquetra." The division of a circle into three parts; it was used as an ornament even on pre-historic clay pots and as a symbol on coats of arms and coins (of ancient Agrigento, for example); the Christian symbol of the Trinity probably developed from it.

Triumphal Cross - A sculpted representation of the Crucifixion of Christ (in Italy, they are also painted), often with Mary and John; especially in Romanesque churches, they are suspended from triumphal arches or are on wood screens.

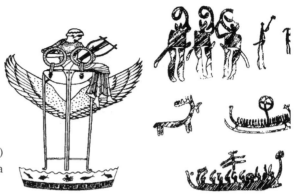

TRIPOD: Apollo on a tripod (Rome, Vatican Museum, 5th century B.C.)
TRUMPET: People blowing lures on a Nordic rock drawing

Trivium - The three paths of learning (grammar, rhetoric and logic); together with the QUADRIVIUM, they constitute the seven liberal ARTS.

Trojaburgs - In a re-interpretation of an erroneously derived etymology of the word "Trälleborg" (Swedish) or "Trøjburg" (Danish) dating from the Age of Humanism, trojaburgs are speculatively associated with hopscotch games in labyrinth-shaped megaliths (see LABYRINTH), sword dances, religious games and naming ceremonies (*Hagen von Tronje*) and connected with many later versions of sagas.

Trowel - A symbol of the Freemasons and part of the so-called work table, derived from the mason's tool.

Trumpet - In Christian symbolism, the trumpet stands for the voice of God, blown by angels as a proclamation of doom or a call to Last Judgment; the trumpet was originally a monotonal signal trumpet that had developed from the ancient Jewish SHOFAR. —Large, curved horns, called LURES, arose during the Nordic Bronze Age and are known from cave drawings and excavation findings.

T-Square - An instrument that is used for drawing rectangles (see SQUARE); it is often a symbol of the earth (with respect to the number FOUR); because only right angles can be drawn with the T-square, it is also a symbol of evenness, uprightness, and lawfulness; in the symbolic thought of the Freemasons, it played a special role. It is symbolically closely related to the COMPASSES.

Tumulus - See GRAVE.

Turban - The wound head covering of Hindus and Muslims that is made of strips of cloth; it exists in various forms, including quite exquisite ones, and is thus often a symbol of high position and power. Muslims use the turban to distinguish themselves from non-believers.

Turkey - Among the Indians of North and Central America, the turkey is a symbol of female fertility and male virility; it is often used as a sacrificial animal in fertility ceremonies.

Turnip - See RADISH.

Turquoise - A gem; it is symbolically associated with the SUN and FIRE in many American Indian cultures.

Turtle - Particularly in the mythologies of

TURBAN: From an depiction of Sultan Selim III

TURTLE: Detail from a Hindu illustration of the creation of the world in which the primeval sea of milk is turned into butter by the periodic churning of the world axis; the world axis stands on a turtle

India, China and Japan, the turtle played a large role. The markings on its back were interpreted in various contexts as patterns of cosmic structures. The turtle itself or its feet are frequently encountered as supports of the universe, of the divine throne, or the primeval waters or also, for example, of the islands of the immortal. In Mongolian myths, there is a golden turtle that carries the central MOUNTAIN of the universe. In accordance with earlier ideas, the arched shell of the turtle's back was sometimes seen as a replica of the heavens, rising over the flat plane of the earth, which is in the shape of the turtle's abdominal shell. In this regard, the turtle appears as a mediary between heaven and earth or also as a symbol of the universe in toto. —Because it lives to be very old, it is also often a symbol of immortality, such as on Chinese graves; therefore, people made elixers, which were supposedly life-prolonging, from its shell and its brain. In Japan (where it was said to live 12,000 years), it was frequently depicted together with the SCOTS PINE and the CRANE, two other immortality symbols. Its old age as well as the mysterious markings on its back, which were thought to be writings, also made it a symbol of wisdom. In Africa as well, where it is sometimes portrayed as having a checkerboard pattern on its back, it is a symbol of wisdom, skill, and power; in addition, its back shell is regarded as a symbol of the vault of heaven. —Because it can withdraw into its shell as though into another world, it is a symbol of concentration and meditation, especially in India. —In China, the turtle also embodies the winter, the north, and water. —In antiquity, it was a fertility symbol and sacred to Aphrodite (Venus) due to its numerous offspring; with respect to the phallic shape of its head, it was also sacred to Pan. Because of its seclusion in its shell, it was also thought of as a symbol of domestic virtues. —The turtle was also thought of as a demonic animal that stood in alliance with dark powers, especially in the Orient and in the Orient-influenced Occident; depictions of the turtle (darkness) in battle with the COCK (light), for example, derive from this. For the church fathers, the (marsh) turtle, which likes to live in the mud, is frequently a symbol of the lowliness of mere sensuality. Because sounding boards of lyres were made of its shell during antiquity, it is sometimes mentioned in Christian literature as a symbol of the moral transformation of the sinful flesh by means of the spirit.

Turtledove - PHYSIOLOGUS extols its

TWO

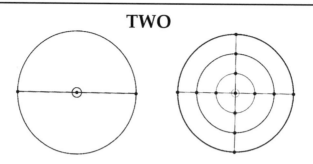

2

The maternal, feminine cardinal number, assigned to the element earth; the exponential numbers $2^2 = 4$ and $2^3 = 8$ extend from the maternal principle to the four-fold enclosed cosmos (see FOUR; EIGHT). —2 is the symbol of duplication, of separation, of discord, of opposition, of conflict, yet also of balance; it symbolizes the movement that initially sets all processes into motion. —Numerous phenomena support a dualistic world view, such as the oppositions of creator and created, LIGHT and SHADOW, male and female, spirit and matter, good and evil, life and death, DAY and NIGHT, heaven (see SKY) and EARTH, land and WATER, active and passive, RIGHT AND LEFT, etc.; YIN AND YANG, the two principles of Chinese philosophy, and Persian Zoroastrianism, with its principles of the good (Ahura Masda) and the evil (Ahriman), represent interpretations of the world that bear especially strong dualistic marks.

12

A cosmic number yielded by multiplying the feminine 4 and the masculine 3 (there are 3 zodiacal signs in each of the 4 quarters of the zodiac!); as a product of 2 (earth) x 2 (earth) x 3 (fire) = 12, it is correlated with the element fire. —In the Bible and in Christian symbolic thought, 12 plays a large role as a symbol of perfection and completeness; it is, among other things, the number of the 12 sons of Jacob and thus of the tribes of Israel, of the 12 jewels on the breast-plate of the Jewish high priest, of the 12 Apostles, and of the 12 gates of Holy Jerusalem (see JERUSALEM, HOLY); the woman in the Book of Revelation wears a crown with 12 stars; the number of the chosen is 12 x 12,000, a number that symbolizes the entirety of all saints.

20

20 has little symbolic value; occasionally seen as the product of 4 (Evangelists) and 5 (books of Moses) = 20.

22

The number of Hebrew letters and thus preserved in Cabalism and tarot: 22 paths connect the 10 sephiroth, the tarot deck has 22 cards.

32

The number of happiness, as in the case of Buddha, who is recognized by 32 primary signs and 80 secondary signs; in Cabalism, it is the sum of the 10 sephiroth and the 22 connecting paths; chess has 32 pieces; there are 32 playing cards for the German card game Skat.

<table>
<tr><td>**42**</td><td>In the Egyptian Book of the Dead, 42 judges pass judgment on 42 sins; during the Middle Ages, it was seen as the product of 6 (days of creation) and 7 (the day of rest on the Sabbath).</td></tr>
</table>

42

In the Egyptian Book of the Dead, 42 judges pass judgment on 42 sins; during the Middle Ages, it was seen as the product of 6 (days of creation) and 7 (the day of rest on the Sabbath).

52

The sum of the important symbolic number 40 + 12 yields the number 52, which is the number of weeks in one year; a 52-year period possibly played a role in pre-Colombian astronomy, resulting from systems based on 13 and 20 (260 days), since the respective starting points of the periods based on 13 and 20 coincide only every 52 years.

72

As a numeral, it shares in the important symbolism of 5 (namely, 360:5 = 72), 6 and 12 (namely, 6 x 12 = 72), and 8 (namely, 2^3) x 9 (namely, 3^3) = 72; the robe of the high priest has 72 little bells; after the Babylonian confusion of languages, there were 72 languages and 72 lands. In China and Central Asia, 72 is the product of 9 (provinces) and 8 (cardinal directions) = 72. This association with the product of 9 x 8 can also be found in Celtic-Germanic lands.

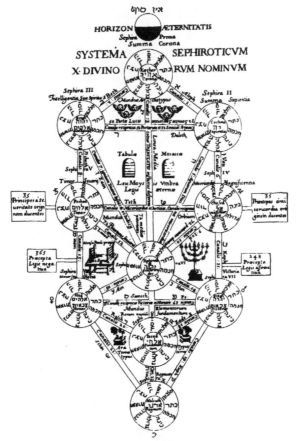

TWO: The sefiroth system as the central glyph of the Cabala: 10 sefiroth as manifestations of God, a total of 22 "true" ways and 32 paths of wisdom. The diagram is from Athanasius Kircher's *Oedipus Aegyptiacus*, Rome, 1652

TWINS: Zodiacal sign of Gemini (from
a medieval woodcut) and the
modern astrological symbol

TWINS: Personification of the zodiacal
sign; from a relief by Agostino de
Duccio Rimini, Templo
Malatestiano; 15th century

secluded life and its solitude and compares it with Christ, who ascended the Mount of Olives, where Moses and Elijiah appeared to him; the most noble servants of Christ are supposed to prefer to go into seclusion. See DOVE.

Twig - The grafted twig is a symbol of penitence, of turning around, and of cultivation.

Twins (Gemini) - They appear in various forms: either of identical appearance and color or one fair and the other dark, the one red, the other blue, the one with its head toward the sky, the other with its head toward the ground, etc. They are a symbol of duality in identity, of man's inner contradictions, of the unity that, from a bird's eye view, exists between day and night, light and darkness, balance and harmony. —In the cosmogonies of various peoples, such as that of the American Indians, there are also twins, one of whom is good, the other evil, one helpful to civilization, the other destructive. —The Twins, or Gemini, is the third sign of the zodiac, corresponding to the last month of spring; the sun passes the sign between May 21 and June 21; it is the house of Mercury; since the times of Hellenic as-

trology, Jupiter (Neptune), Mars and the Sun have been its decans; in Indian astrology, Mercury, Venus and Saturn have been its decans. The triplicity of Gemini is air; Gemini is masculine, positive (active) and a moveable sign. The name of the constellation Gemini can be found even in Babylonian sources.

Tyche - (Blind) Greek goddess of fate; corresponds to the Latin FORTUNA.

Tying and Untying - A common symbolic action among practitioners of magic that is intended to impede or unleash certain forces. See RIBBON; KNOT.

Typology - From the Greek. Theory pertaining to the typical meaning of Biblical writings. It reveals the relationships of types (paradigms) of the Old Testament to their fulfillment (antitypes) in the New Testament (including Christ and church) and thereby ascertains the typical meaning (in contrast to the historical meaning) of the Bible. These typological contexts were the subject of numerous graphic cycles in Christian art of the Middle Ages, especially in small-scale art, illuminated manuscripts and glass painting.

UNICORN: 2 illustrations from Schmid's *Musterbuch*. With three dogs (faith, love, hope), the angel Gabriel (left) shepherds the unicorn into Mary's lap (right)

 **Umbilical Cord** - The umbilical cord is occasionally a symbol of one's continued attachment to one's mother and early childhood.

Umbrella - Usually appears symbolically as a PARASOL.

Unerring Lance - A LANCE owned by the Irish hero Celtchar. The idea of weapons that never miss their target was common not only in antiquity and among the ancient Germans, but among the Celts as well.

Unicorn - A fabulous animal, known to many peoples and popularized in the Christian Occident primarily by PHYSIO-LOGUS, in the form of a ram, ass, rhinoceros, bull or (as was usually the case later) horse with one horn. This one horn can be interpreted as a phallic symbol (compare to the ONAGER), yet, since it protrudes from the forehead, which is the "seat" of the mind, it is also a symbol of the sublimation of sexual energies and therefore became a symbol of virginal purity. —The straight (sometimes spiral) horn that comes to a point is also a symbol of sun rays (see SUN). —In Zoroastrianism, the unicorn was regarded as a symbol of the raw power by which Ahriman is conquered. —In China, it was a symbol of the virtues of rulers. —Christianity sees the unicorn as a symbol of strength and purity. According to legend, it can be caught and tamed only by a virgin into whose lap it flees when hunted. Thus, representations of Mary with the unicorn in her lap are sometimes encountered in Christian art, which refer to Mary's Immaculate Conception (Maria Immaculata). In connection with the allegorical depiction of the prophecy of Christ's birth, Mary is represented in the Hortus conclusus with the unicorn in her lap; during the 16th century, this representation was forbidden in churches because it was increasingly thought of as erotic. —Unicorn powder (from the horn), alleged to heal wounds, and the heart, too, was attributed with curative powers; thus, the unicorn sometimes apppears as a trademark of pharmacies.

Unleavened Bread - See YEAST,

Unveiling - See VEIL.

Uraeus Serpent - See SERPENT.

UNICORN: Virgin with unicorn; from
Defensorium Virginitatis

Urn - See GRAVE.

Uroboros - A SERPENT (or occasionally one or two dragons or—rarely—one or two long-necked birds) biting its own tail; it is a symbol of infinity, of eternal recurrence, of the descent of the spirit into the physical world and its return. In alchemy, it is often a symbol of changing matter.

UROBOROS: Illustration from Horapollo's
Selecta hieroglyphica, 1597

VEIL: "The veil falls from the head of the ancient man", from a miniature, Tours Bible

Valerian - Also called "cats' weed" or "witches' weed." Valerian was already known in antiquity as a medicinal plant. The famous nard-oil with which, for example, Jesus was anointed in Bethany, was produced from Indian nard-valerian. In this regard, the plant appears occasionally on medieval panels, sometimes prominently in the foreground. —According to popular belief in magic, valerian can be used to "smoke out" the devil and drive away witches.

Valley - In contrast to the MOUNTAIN, the valley is a symbol of descent and depth; in a negative sense, it is regarded as a situation involving spiritual-emotional loss; in a positive sense, it is regarded as a deepening of experience and knowledge; in contrast to the rising, masculine mountain, it is also a symbol of the female womb. —In Islam, it is a symbol of the path of spiritual development. —In Taoist literature, one often encounters the valley as a symbol: the wide, open valley symbolizes openness to heavenly influences; as a place to which all waters flow from mountains, it is also a symbol

of mental concentration. —Among various peoples, the green, fertile valley, in contrast to the barren mountains, is also a symbol of abundance and good living.

Vanitas - The vanity, nothingness and impermanence of all earthly things; especially during the Middle Ages, its symbols were LADY WORLD and PRINCE OF THE WORLD as well as the HOURGLASS (and the gear clock) and the death's head.

Vault - See CUPOLA.

Veil - Like the ROBE, the veil is a symbol of concealment and of mystery; in contrast, unveiling is a symbol of revelation, of knowledge, and of initiation. Access to spiritual secrets is sometimes expressed by unveiling the human body. The ritual unveiling of the Egyptian goddess Isis, for example, was a symbol of the appearance of divine light. In this vein, Christ's nakedness on the cross was occasionally interpreted as a sign of the revelation of esoteric secrets. —In Indian philosophy, Maya, the condition of the possibility of all transient appearances, is compared to a veil, since, like a veil, Maya conceals and reveals at the same time: Maya conceals the true basis of all being and thereby provides the richness of the world of appear-

VESSEL: The virgin as a vessel of the divine child; Venetian *Rosario della gloriosa vergine Maria*, 1524

VINE: Illustration from Herrad von Landsberg's *Hortus Deliciarum*

ances with an apparently objective character. —In Islam, the countenance of God is said to be concealed by 70,000 veils of light and shade that tone down the divine splendor in order to make it endurable for human beings; according to some interpretors, however, the veils do not surround God, but rather His creations; only saints are capable of partially lifting these veils. The Koran also speaks of a veil that separates the damned from the chosen. —According to cults and folk custom, a veil serves to ward off enemy demons. —As a sign of awe or fear in the presence of the Holy One, persons making sacrifices frequently wore veils over their faces. —The mourning veil symbolizes mourners' withdrawal; the veil of a bride or a Muslim woman is a symbol of chastity, just as the bridal veil is a sign of being married. The nun's veil has a similar meaning, as nuns considered themselves to be the brides of Christ.

Venus - An ancient Italic goddess of spring and of gardens; later identified with Aphrodite, the goddess of love, she assumed the traits of Aphrodite.

Venus - The Greek "Aphrodite." In ancient mythology, she is primarily a symbol of love and the goddess of love. —In

astronomy and astrology, Venus is a planet that, at the time of its greatest brightness, outshines by far all other planets and fixed stars; it can be observed as the evening star (Hesperus) or as the morning star (Phosphorus). —In alchemy, Venus stands for COPPER; in astrology, it stands for METALS.

Venus Statues - Paleolithic female statues, common from western Europe to Siberia, strikingly naturalistic. They have STEATOPYGA or are stylized in a simplified manner; they probably played a role in fertility cults.

Veronica - See SPEEDWELL.

Vesper - Or "Hesperus." The planet VENUS as the evening star.

Vessel - A symbol of reception and containment, and thus frequently of the woman's womb; Christianity is given to comparing Mary, who received the Holy Spirit into herself, with a vessel. —Vessels, particularly those made of clay, are also a symbol for the body, which is interpreted as the vessel of the soul. —The New Testament compares the faithful with a vessel of mercy. —For some peoples, the pouring of a liquid from one vessel into

VIRGIN: Zodiacal image Virgo (from a medieval woodcut) and the modern astrological symbol

another was a symbol of the reincarnation of the soul. See DRINKING GLASS; CUP.

Vetch - In ancient Egypt, it was a symbol of the tenderness of young girls. —In Christian art of the Middle Ages, it is a symbol of Mary.

Vices - See VIRTUES AND VICES.

Vine - The GRAPEVINE, especially the one bearing edible fruit; also the withered, one-year old shoot of the grape vine that has become wood; its fruits are called grapes.

Vinyard - See GRAPEVINE.

Viola Tricolor - See PANSY.

Violet - A fragrant, short, usually blue-flowered spring plant. At festivals in antiquity, thyrsus staves as well as celebrants were bedecked with violets, in part because it was believed that they protected one from intoxication and headaches. —During the Middle Ages, they were a symbol of righteousness modestly expressed and of humility, and thus also a symbol of Mary. Because of its color (see VIOLET [below]), it is also a symbol of the Passion of Christ.

Violet - Standing between RED and BLUE, violet is a symbol of mediation, of balance between heaven (see SKY) and earth, mind and body, love and wisdom; of measure and of moderation. —In Christian art, violet is often the color of the Passion of Christ (as a symbolic reference to the complete connection of God with humans through Christ's suffering and death); in the Catholic liturgy, violet symbolizes seriousness and readiness to atone and is thus the color of Advent and Holy Week. —In the symbolic thought of folk songs and folk customs, violet sometimes symbolizes fidelity.

Viper - Also called an "adder." An animal mentioned in PHYSIOLOGUS; it is compared with the Pharisees.

Virgin - Or "virginity." A symbol of innocence and of an abundance of possibilities not yet actualized. The Christian mystics also compared the soul of a person ready to receive God with a virgin. —The virgin or Virgo is the sixth sign of the zodiac; it corresponds to the last month of summer; the sun passes the sign between August 23 and September 22; Mercury is exalted in Virgo; Virgo is the house of Mercury; since the times of Hellenic astrology, the sun, Venus, and Mercury have

VULTURE: Vulture as protector of the Egyptian kings

been its decans; in Indian astrology, Mercury, Saturn and Venus are its decans. The triplicity of Virgo is earth; Virgo is feminine, negative (passive) and movable.

Virgo - The constellation VIRGIN.

Virtues and Vices - In Christian art, they are symbolized by female figures (virtues) and male or female figures (vices) that are recognizable from their attributes. In addition to the four cardinal virtues (FORTITUDO, JUSTITIA, PRUDENTIA, TEMPERANTIA), there are the three theological virtues of FIDES, SPES and CARITAS and sometimes humilitas as well. —Juxtaposed to these seven (eight) virtues are the seven deadly sins (vices): SUPERBIA, INVIDIA, GULA, AVARITIA, ACEDIA, IRA and LUXURIA. Representations of virtues and vices are often part of ICONOGRAPHY.

Visages - JANUS as having a head with two faces; the TRINITY as having three faces; and BRAHMA as having four faces.

Vishnu - From the Sanskrit "Vishnu." Probably a pre-Aryan Indian god; Vishnu is a high god (maintainer of the world), next to Brahma and Shiva; he works in the world through his incarnations, especially in Krisna; portrayed as a young man with a blue body, a high mitra, and a yellow robe, sitting on a lotus or on the half-human bird GARUDA.

V.I.T.R.I.O.L. - A symbolic formula of alchemists that has many meanings, often used for the process of transmutation (the transformation of unprecious metals into precious ones, especially GOLD). The letters are usually interpreted as being the initial letters of the formula *Visita Inferiora Terrae Rectificando Invenies Occultum Lapidem* (Seek out the lower reaches of the earth, perfect them, and you will find the hidden stone, i.e., the PHILOSOPHERS' STONE), yet the reading *Visita Inferiorem Terrae Rectificando Invenies Operae Lapidem* was also common. As an esoteric initiation formula, V.I.T.R.I.O.L. should probably be thought of in conjunction with the descent into one's own soul and the search for the deepest part of one's being.

Voodoo - In Benin, the word means "spirit, guardian spirit." Variant spellings are vodoo, voodu, voudon, voudoo, voudou, voudoun, voudu and vaudoux. A secret cult that originated in Benin and that is made up of blacks from Haiti (where it acquired Catholic elements) and their descendents who were brought from there to North America (where it acquired North American Indian elements); the cult maintains belief in spirits and demons. Drumming, singing and dancing to the point of ecstasy are part of the ritual. Animals: snakes, chickens.

Vulture - A symbolic animal in numerous American Indian cultures that is associated with the cleansing and animating power of FIRE and the SUN; among the Mayas, it is also a death symbol. —Because it eats carcasses and transforms them into life energy, the vulture is sometimes thought in Africa to be a creature that knows the secret of the genuine transformation of worthless material into GOLD. —In Egypt, the vulture was the protector of the Pharoahs; Egyptian queens frequently wear a protective "vulture hood," a headdress in the form of a vulture whose wings cover the sides of the wearer's head and whose head protrudes from the wearer's forehead. —Antiquity thought that the flight of the vulture presaged fate; it was sacred to Apollo. —Since the eggs of the female vulture, according to ancient belief, were fertilized by the east wind, the vulture is a symbol of Mary's virginity in Christian symbolism. PHYSIOLOGUS speaks more of the eutocius stone than of the vulture itself; this eutocius stone "is truly that of the Holy Spirit [...], he is arisen from a virgin without human seed."

WASHING, HAND AND FOOT: Foot washing; from a picture by Duccio di Buoninsegna in the Cathedral of Sienna

Wadjet Eye - See EYE.

Wakon - From the Dakotan; also Wah-condah. A Sioux Indian term for vitality, unusual strength. Wakon is the same as the MANA of Oceanic cultures.

Walnut - See NUT.

War Cry - See CRY.

Washing of Hands and Feet - In nearly all religions, one washes oneself, and particularly one's hands, as a sign of ritual purification before sacred ceremonies. — Pontius Pilate washed his hands in order to express symbolically his renunciation of responsibility. —In the Orient, washing the feet of strangers and guests was regarded as a service performed out of love; Christ's washing of his disciples' feet was a demonstration and sign of His servile love; shown to have been a practice in the Catholic liturgy on Holy Thursday since the 7th century. See BATH; BAPTISM.

Washing, Ritual - See BAPTISM.

Water - A symbol with a very complex spectrum of meanings. As an unformed, undifferentiated mass (regardless of whether it is spring, lake, or sea water), it symbolizes the abundance of all possibilities or the primeval beginning of all that exists, *the materia prima*. In this sense, it appears in numerous creation myths: in Indian mythology, for example, it bears the world EGG. The Book of Genesis speaks of the spirit of God that moved over the waters in the beginning. Among various peoples, this is supplemented by the symbolic action of an animal that dives down into the depths and wins a tract of land from the infinite waters. —Water is also a symbol of the power of bodily, emotional and spiritual cleansing and renewal in Islam, Hinduism, Buddhism and Christianity (see BATH; WASHING OF HANDS AND FEET; BAPTISM). Ideas concerning a FOUNTAIN of youth are also part of this context. —In China, water is associated with the Yin principle (see YIN AND YANG); in other cultures as well, water is usually associated with the feminine, with dark depths, and with the MOON. The symbolism of water (see SEA; RAIN), associated with fertility and life, is common all over the world and, in this respect, is occasionally juxtaposed to the desert. Spiritual fertility and the spiritual life are also often symbolized by water (see

WATER: Water as an element of the union of opposites; from an illustration in *Trésor des trésors*, 17th century

WATER-BEARER: The Sumerian god Enki in his water house

SPRING); the Bible, for example, speaks of the water of life in a spiritual sense; water, which cannot be held in one place, also appears in various contexts as a symbol of eternity (the water of eternal life). —As a destructive power, though, water can also have a negative symbolic character, such as in the case of the Flood. —Psychoanalysis sees water primarily as a symbol of the feminine and of the powers of the unconscious. —In alchemy, water is represented by the symbol ∇. —Astrology associates water with the ZODIAC signs Cancer, Scorpio and Pisces.

Waterbearer (Aquarius) - The waterbearer or Aquarius is the eleventh sign of the zodiac; it corresponds to the second month of winter; the sun passes the sign between January 20 and February 18; it is the house of Saturn (Uranus); since the times of Hellenic astrology, Venus, Mercury and the Moon (Neptune) have been its decans; in Indian astrology, Saturn, Mercury and Venus have been its decans. The triplicity of Aquarius is air; Aquarius is masculine, positive (active) and a rigid sign. The image of the waterbearer can be found in Babylonian representations. The Age of Aquarius follows the Age of Pisces and is dominated by Aquarius. The "dawning" of this age, with its anticipated

passionate intellectuality, was forcefully invoked in the Hippie musical *Hair*, for example.

Water Creatures - HYBRID CREATURES of all sorts, usually depicted as having fishtails; MÉLUSINE or the water creatures on the ceiling of the Romanesque church at Zillis (in the Swiss canton of Graubünden) are well known examples.

Waterfall - An important motif of Chinese landscape painting. Its cascading movement is contrasted with the upward movement of the ROCK, its dynamism is contrasted to the quietude of the rock and associated with the opposing pair YIN AND YANG. Its shape, which apparently remains the same while, in reality, its water drops constantly change, is regarded in Buddhism as a symbol of the transience and illusory nature of all earthly things.

Water Lily - See LOTUS.

Waves - Waves must be thought of in close symbolic connection with WATER; yet the nature of their motion, which can assume an impersonal, threatening character, especially when they are in the form of billows, is most important. Waves and billows are thus not only symbols of

WATER

Three-quarters of the globe are covered with water; three-quarters of the body of every plant and animal are water. Water is by far the most common liquid on the earth; it is the only liquid that can constitute oceans. No other substance on earth could replace water. Water is a gift of the earliest stages of the earth's development; along with earth, air and fire, water is one of the four primeval elements.

The learned Jesuit father Athanasius Kircher (1601–1680) believed (see illustration below) that seawater drains into deep caverns in the earth (the swirls in the ocean indicate these locations) and the pressure of the ocean draws the ocean into subterranean veins (shown in black) and high up into the mountain tops. People also believed that steam rose up from the deepest bowels of the earth and formed huge subterranean water reserves by means of condensation—this

> By God is water blessed
> Thirst to quench
> Fish to shelter
> The earth to cover
> — Paracelsus

> All the rivers run into the sea;
> yet the sea is not full;
> unto the place from whence the rivers come,
> thither they return again.
> — Ecclesiastes 1:7

The circulation of water according to Athansius Kircher (1664)

was the explanation for the hot springs that occasionally appeared. Thus, the cycle of water is: springs, rivers, ocean, trickling into the ocean floor due to the formation of whirlpools, subterranean veins, mountains, springs. The reason for precipitation is still missing from this explanation, but was not an explanation for the text found in the Book of Proverbs? - Within the womb, the unborn child floats in the amnion fluid of the placenta; in many cultures, it is said that the child must drink a portion of this water before and during birth in order to become a real human being. Is this not reminiscent of notions about the water of life? - The duality in the symbolism of water can probably be observed in all cultures and at all times: water can be the source of life, yet also the destroyer of life; it can be water from heaven—"sweet" water—as well as water from the depths—"bitter" water; yet the antagonism between water and fire also appears again and again, as does the juxtaposition of water and blood, whereby an analogous dual character is ascribed to blood; as a medium of ritual bathing, baptism, and rebirth or renewal, water appears before us.

Detail from a mural from the grave of
Amen-Nacht (19th/20th Dynasty)

Everything live is water's creation!
Water keeps all things young and vernal!
Ocean, grant us thy rule eternal.
Clouds — were it not for thee sending them,
Nor fertile brooks — expending them,
Rivers — hither and thither bending them,
And streams — not fully tending them,
Then what would be mountains, what plains and earth?
'Tis thou giv'st livingest life its worth.
Thou giv'st livingest life its birth.
 — Thales of Milet to Nereus in *Faust, Part II*
            by J.W. von Goethe

Under heaven nothing is more
    soft and yielding than water.
Yet for attacking the solid and
    strong, nothing is better;
Accomodating to all, it has no
    equal.
The weak can overcome the
    strong;
The supple can overcome the
    stiff.
Under heaven everyone knows
    this,
Yet no one puts it into practice.
    — Lao-tsu in the 78th
    chapter of his *Tao Te Ching*

WATER-BEARER: Zodiacal sign Aquarius (from a medieval woodcut) and the modern astrological symbol

animation and liveliness, but also often symbols for forces that can no longer be controlled.

Weapons - A symbol of power; symbolically equivocal, since they serve for attack as well as for defense and protection; they are attributes of heroes and war-like gods. In the symbolic language of the Bible, Satan as well as Yahweh have "armor and weapons." — Other symbols, such as a raised cross, can also serve as spiritual weapons.

Weasel - According to PHYSIOLOGUS, the weasel is a dirty animal that has sexual intercourse through its snout and, once pregnant, gives birth through its ears; "Now there are people who eat the spiritual bread in the church, but when they leave, they cast out the word of God from their ears," is Physiologus's estimation of the weasel. See ERMINE.

Weather Vane - See COCK.

Weaving - Weavings are often a symbol of the workings of the forces of fate; in Islam, for example, the structure and movement of the entire universe are compared with a weaving. The SPIDER, which "weaves" its web, is also occasionally seen in this regard.

Web - See WEAVING.

Wedding - Or "marriage." In many religions, the wedding is a symbol for the union of divine (usually personified) forces with one another, of man with God or the gods, of the soul with the body, or, especially in alchemy, of the union of opposites. In antiquity, for example, there was the divine couple Jupiter (Zeus) and Juno (Hera), and there were numerous liaisons of the god father with mortal women. —The Old Testament speaks of the marriage between Yahweh and the people of Israel; in the New Testament, there are occasional references to the Christian church as the bride of Christ. The nuns of the Catholic church are given a veil, a garland and a ring upon admittance to the convent as a symbolic expression of their marriage to Christ. —See SACRED PROSTITUTION.

Weeping Willow - See WILLOW.

Werewolf - From the Old High German *wer*, meaning "man"; thus, "man in the form of a wolf." According to folk legends and folk belief, the werewolf is a symbolic figure that is changed into a wolf by putting on a wolf's girdle or shirt and that can assume a wolf's strength and desire to kill.

WEDDING: Symbolic depiction of the union of opposites in alchemy; *Rosarium philosophorum*, 1550

Whale - The whale is occasionally a symbol of abysmal, uncertain darkness; it appears, for example, in the Biblical story of the prophet Jonah, who disobeys God's command to preach in Nineveh, is tossed over board, is swallowed by a giant fish that is usually portrayed as a whale, and is spewed back onto land by the fish (symbolically interpreted as Christ's death, burial and resurrection). PHYSIOLOGUS pays special attention to its extraordinary size, which is "equal to that of an island." —Like other animals (see ELEPHANT; CROCODILE; TURTLE), the whale is also a bearer of the universe in the mythologies of some peoples.

Wheat - The sowing, growth and harvest of grain, especially of wheat, are regarded as a symbol of birth and death or also of death and rebirth. In ancient Greece, the head of wheat, as a fruit of the maternal womb of the earth, also symbolized the fruit of the human body; it was a symbol of Demeter and played a central role in the Eleusian mysteries. —In Egypt, growing wheat was regarded as a symbol of Osiris resurrected from death. —During the Middle Ages, wheat germ was seen as a symbol of Christ, who descended into the underworld and was resurrected. To this day, the Eucharist is symbolized on altar accessories by a head of wheat and a grape. The head of wheat is also a symbol of Mary, as it contains the seeds that yield flour for the Host. Mary (portrayed as a Madonna wearing a dress that has patterns shaped like heads of wheat) is compared with a field in which Christ, as wheat, could grow.

Wheat Head - Even in early civilizations, wheat heads were a symbol of the fertile and life-giving nature of plants. —In Christian art, wheat heads were used in Holy Communion as a Eucharistic symbol of the body (bread) of Christ. See SEVEN races.

Wheel - The wheel combines the symbolic meaning of the CIRCLE with the aspect of movement, becoming and passing that modifies it; aside from the aspect of the wheel's movement, the radial arrangement of its spokes also plays a symbolically important role. In most cultures, the wheel appears as a sun symbol (for example, it is commonly used in some regions even today in customs associated with the winter solstice); the four-spoked wheel sign, which should probably be thought of as being associated with the sun, appeared in many pre-historical European cultures; it first appeared in cen-

WHALE: Jonah climbing out of the jaws of the whale; from an illustration in *Speculum humanae salvationis*, 15th century

WHEAT: Ancient coin with wheat bundle, here symbolizing fertility and prosperity

WHEAT: Madonna in a dress with wheat head pattern; woodcut, 15th century

tral Germany during the Neolithic age. — The rosettes found in many decorations in the Middle East are also possibly associated with the wheel as a sun symbol. — The wheel is a chief symbol in Buddhism; it symbolizes the various forms of being that need salvation as well as the teaching of the Buddha ("Wheel of Life" and "Wheel of the Dharma"). —The wheel can also be a symbol of the entire cosmos with respect to its constant cycles of renewal (such as the *Rota Mundi* of the Rosi-crucians). —The wheel appears on early Christian gravestones as a symbol of God and eternity. The Book of Daniel reports of the vision of flaming wheels around the head of God; Ezekiel reports of wheels that have eyes and that turn yet simultaneously stand still, thereby expressing God's omnipotence. —The ZODIAC is frequently compared with a wheel. —C.G. Jung sees the "wheel" (the center rose window of the facade) of medieval cathedrals as a symbol of unity in multiplicity, a special form of the MANDALA. See WHEEL OF FORTUNE.

Wheel Chandelier - A large, circular CANDLESTICK, often having a rich, ornamental, and often figured shape, such as in the case of the LADY CHANDELIER.

Wheel of Fire - A symbol for LIGHT-

NING and, together with THUNDER, an element of the highest heavenly god of the Celts. Even in the 4th century A.D., there were reports about the Gauls from Agen claiming that the Gauls would annually (as a ritual of the season) let a flaming WHEEL roll out of the temple and back into the temple. The practice of letting such wheels of fire roll downhill (such as in Markgräfler Land, Trier and Luxembourg) is traced back to the worship of the chief Celtic god. See FIRE.

Wheel of Fortune - A special form of the WHEEL symbol that emphasizes fleetingness and constant change. In antiquity, there was a representation of a naked boy on two winged wheels, symbolizing not only ephemeral happiness, but also the fortuity of the moment, the *kairos*. Tyche, the goddess of fortune and fate (see FORTUNA), stands on a wheel. —In art of the Middle Ages, the wheel of fortune is frequently encountered in a more restricted sense: a wheel, often being pushed by Fortuna, to which people or allegorical figures cling; it symbolizes change of fortune, the permanent fluctuation of all that exists, and occasionally the Last Judgment as well.

Wheel Window - A round window hav-

WHEAT HEAD: Fragment from a limestone relief (Mesopotamia, 3rd millenium B.C.)

WHEAT HEAD: "Christ, the Divine Man (A - Ω), offers us (birds) the fruits of His death on the cross (cross) in the Holy Eucharist, which contains His flesh (wheat) and His blood (grapes)" (from Schmid's *Musterbuch*)

ing a spoke-shaped structure, especially in churches of the 12th and 13th centuries. See TRACERY.

Whip - A symbol of power and judicial authority. LIGHTNING is also sometimes compared with a whip. —In the Veda, the sea of MILK at the primeval beginning of the world is turned by whiplashes into BUTTER, the first food of living creatures.

White - White is the color of LIGHT, purity and perfection. Not being a color per se, white, like its opposite, BLACK, has a special place among all other colors (which, taken together, constitute white); it is closely related to the absolute, the beginning and the end, as well as their union and is thus often used in wedding, initiation, and death rites; it is a color of mourning, such as in Slavic lands and in Asia, and sometimes at the court of the French king as well. —White was the preferred color of specially selected sacrificial animals. —Priests often wear white robes because the color symbolizes spirit and light; for the same reason, the angels and the saints in Christianity are often portrayed as wearing white; newly baptized Christians wore white clothes; at the Transfiguration, Christ's robes became "white as snow"; the ceremonial garb of brides, postulants and persons making first Communion signifies innocence and virginity. —In contrast to RED, however, which is a color of life, white is also the color of spirits and ghosts; one occasionally encounters the juxtaposition red = man/white = woman.

Wild Boar - See PIG.

Wild Donkey - In PHYSIOLOGUS as a symbol of and lesson regarding the differing attitudes of the Old and New Testaments toward sexual abstinence and the begetting of children.

Wild People - HYBRID CREATURES of medieval art and poetry; often gigantic and hairy figures clothed with moss or lichen; they still exist in some form as figures appearing in Alemannic carnival celebrations on the day before the start of Lent; wild people are often depicted in 15th century Upper Rhenish tapestries.

Wild Thyme - Formerly in Bavaria, it was carried in processions celebrating Corpus Christi. It is regarded as an apotropaic herb. In Christian tradition, fragrant wild thyme is regarded as a Marian plant and is referred to regionally as "Mary's bed straw."

WHEEL: Picture from the sun temple Konarak, India

WHEEL: The wheels of Ezekiel; detail from a miniature in the Evangeliar of the library at Aschaffenburg, 13th century

Willow - A tree or bush. In antiquity, it was thought to be infertile and sometimes appears in that sense, even during the Middle Ages, as a symbol of chastity. Because one can prune its branches and they always grow back, the willow was compared with the Bible as an inexhaustible source of wisdom. —According to folk belief, the willow can vicariously take diseases upon itself through magic; it is supposed to be a preferred abode of spirits and witches; on Palm Sunday, blessed willow branches were thought to offer protection from lightning, storms and evil influences. —Because of its shape, which is poised toward the ground and reminiscent of streams of tears, the weeping willow is often a symbol of mourning.

Willow Fetters - In places where Germanic cults existed, willow fetters were used to tie up the sacrificial object that was to be killed.

Wind - Because it is intangible and often changes direction abruptly, wind is a symbol of fleetingness, instability and nothingness; as a storm, it is also a symbol of divine powers or human passions; as a breath, it is a symbol of the workings of or manifestation of the divine spirit; winds, like angels, can thus also be thought of as messengers of the gods. — In Persia, the idea of the wind as a support of the world and as the guarantor of cosmic and moral balance, played a role. —In Islam, the wind bears the primeval waters, which, in turn, bear the divine THRONE.

Wind Heads - Symbols of the winds, which have been personified since antiquity.

Window - Windows sometimes symbolize receptivity and openness to external influences. —The stained glass windows of Gothic churches frequently symbolize the colorful abundance of Holy Jerusalem. —In visual arts of the Middle Ages, a window that does not emit light but allows sunlight to shine through, sometimes signifies Mary, Mother of God, who chastely and humbly bore the Son of God.

Wine - Because of its color and the fact that it is made from the grape vine's "vital fluids," wine is frequently a symbol of blood (the Greeks regarded it as the blood of Dionysus). It was often thought to be an elixir of life and an immortality potion (such as among the Semitic peoples and the Greeks and in Taoism). In Greece, sacrifices of wine to gods of the underworld

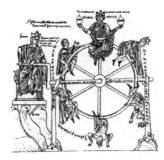

WHEEL OF FORTUNE: Miniature from Herrad von Landsberg's *Hortus Deliciarum*, end of the 12th century

WHEEL OF FORTUNE: Illustration from Petrarca's *Von der Artzney beyder Glück*, 1532

were forbidden, since wine was the drink of the living. Because of its intoxicating effect, it was also sometimes regarded as a means for acquiring esoteric knowledge. —In Islam, wine is, among other things, a drink of divine love, a symbol of spiritual knowledge and of eternity's fullness of being; in Sufism, the existence of the soul before the creation of the world was thus thought to be surrounded by the wine of immortality. —According to Biblical tradition, it is a symbol of joy and of the abundance of God's gifts. In Christianity, wine acquired its holiest and most profound significance as the blood of Christ in the eucharistic transubstantiation.

Winepress, Mystical - Medieval allegory and metaphorical symbol of Christ, who is stomping grapes in a winepress and is Himself being squeezed down by a winepress bar. The passage Isaiah 63:3 was interpreted by the church fathers as being an allusion to the Passion of Christ. See MILL, MYSTICAL.

Wings - See BIRDS.

Witches - A generic term, based in part on popular belief in magic and ghosts, for human beings (usually women, rather seldomly men) who are supposedly in league with the devil and are thereby supposed to possess magic powers, such as the ability to fly through the air (witches' ride to the witches' Sabbath); witch hunts (evinced even in antiquity) culminated in the ecclesiastical-secular trials from the 14th century until the Enlightenment; "convicted" witches were punished with death by fire. See CAULDRON.

Witches' Weed - See VALERIAN.

Wolf - The wolf appears as an ambivalent symbolic animal in a negative, wild and diabolical vein and in a positive, spirit-like vein. Since it can see well in the dark, it was known as a symbol of light, especially in Northern Europe and Greece; it can occasionally appear as an attendant of Apollo (Apollo Lyceius), for example. — The Chinese and Mongolians had the idea of a sacred wolf; for the Mongolians, it was the ancestor of Genghis Khan; for the Chinese, it was the guard of the Heavenly Palace. The legendary she-wolf who nourished the abandoned twins Romulus and Remus and became the symbol of Rome, appears in a positive vein, namely, as a symbol of helpful animal or chthonic powers. —Like the DOG, the wolf occasionally appears as a guide of souls. —In

WIND HEADS: The Wind of the West and the Wind of the East from the world map in Gregor Reisch's *Margarita Philosophica*

Germanic mythology, the rapacious, voracious wolf appears as a dangerous demon that proclaims the end of the world (among other things) by its howling. —In Hinduism, the wolf is an attendant of terrible deities. —Among many peoples, it appears as a symbol of war or aggression. —Antiquity also associated the wolf with the underworld; Hades, for example, wears a mantle made from a wolf's pelt. —Christian symbolism refers primarily to the wolf-lamb relation, whereby the LAMB symbolizes the faithful and the wolf the powers that threaten the faith. A wolf that is biting through the throat of a lamb can also be a symbol for the death of Christ. Among the seven deadly sins, the wolf symbolizes gluttony as well as covetousness. —Medieval folk belief saw the wolf as a menacing, demonic animal; magicians, witches or the devil appear in the shape of a wolf; in many sagas and fairy tales, as well, the wolf appears in a similarly negative vein. —The proverbial "wolf in a sheep's skin" is a symbol of feigned innocuity.

Woman - A grown female human being, ordered to man as man is to her. She has assumed a varying position at various times and among various peoples according to local customary, religious and cultural views. Ever since the family and family-based economic activities (farming, handicrafts) have receded as the primary locus of women's activity in modern times, the social position and responsibility of women have steadily increased, especially since the 19th century (women's movement). —In Judaism, the woman is regarded as a symbolic figure for Israel, Jerusalem or "Zion"; by extension, the concept of woman also applies to daughter and bride.

Women's Wiles - See LOVE SLAVES.

Womb - A symbol for fertility, sheltering protection, and, finally, for mysterious, hidden powers in general. The alchemists' ovens, in which important physical, mystical and moral transformations took place, were frequently compared with the womb. See INITIATION; YONI.

Wood - As one of the oldest and most important materials of man, it was often equated with matter in general or with *materia prima*. Thus, it also is closely related symbolically with the complex of meanings "life force," "motherliness" and "carrying and containing." —In China, wood, as one of the five ELEMENTS, corresponded symbolically to the east and to spring.

WINE: Grape harvest, painting in the grave of Nacht, Egypt, 18th Dynasty

Woodcock - A symbol of Christ, since it is thought of as a killer of serpents; the STORK or HEDGEHOG, for example, have a similar meaning.

Woodpecker - Many peoples regard the green woodpecker, in particular, as a bringer of protection and good fortune and some people believe that it can also tell the future and presage weather. Among the ancient Germans, it was also thought of as a symbol of lightning (possibly because it penetrates tree bark with its beak) and of thunder (because of its pecking). —In Christianity, the woodpecker also became a symbol of unrelenting prayer due to its constant pecking. Since it kills worms (see WORM), it was also thought to be the enemy of the devil and was thus sometimes a symbol of Christ. —The black woodpecker can be regarded as a symbol of the devil because it "taps at the hearts of people and sees whether moral vermin are present and, if possible, makes its nest there" (according to a version of PHYSIOLOGUS).

Word - See LANGUAGE.

Work - An important symbolic concept in Freemasonry, primarily signifying any gathering of Freemasons for any purpose of Freemasonry. In a more restricted sense, it signifies the work table, the teaching table, the so-called carpet, and the drawing board.

World Axis - Many peoples have the notion of a world axis that connects heaven (see SKY) and EARTH or the underworld, earth and heaven; it is a symbol of the interrelationship of all levels or areas of the cosmos known to man and the center around which they are arranged. The world axis has been envisionedin many forms; among the most common ones are the COLUMN, the pole, rising columns of smoke, the TREE, the tall MOUNTAIN, the STAFF, and the LANCE; the Indian LINGA is also often associated with the world axis. —The world axis was also sometimes associated with the symbolism of LIGHT; according to Plato, for example, it is made of a self-luminescent diamond. —Christian literature also sometimes compares the Cross of Christ with the world axis. —Tantrism sees the spine as a symbol of the world axis.

World Egg - See EGG.

Worm - As an animal that lives in dirt and under the earth, the worm is for some peoples a symbol of life newly awakening from darkness and death.

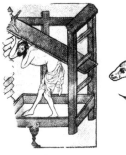

WINEPRESS, MYSTICAL: Mystical winepress
WITCHES: Ride of witches to witches' sabbath. Woodcut, circa 1489

Wormwood - A type of mugwort (Compositae family) that grows up to one meter in height in the warmer regions of Eurasia; used for seasoning and medicinal purposes. Its bitter taste made it a symbol of pain and of bitterness.

Wrapping - Since time immemorial, wrapping in China has often followed certain rules that depend not upon the shape of the object to be wrapped, but rather upon association with the symbolism of the number FIVE, which is sacred in China; the object, flanked by the four corners and sides of a piece of paper, cloth, etc., symbolizes the number five and is thus, at that time, analogous to the center of the world.

Wreath - Differentiated from the CROWN primarily on the basis of the material from which it is made (usually leaves and flowers), the wreath in antiquity served as an ornament, a prize and a sign of the divinely blessed at competitions, festivals and sacrifices (sacrificial animals also wore wreaths). People believed that they could protect themselves from drunkenness by wearing wreaths (which were originally made of ivy and later often of herbs). —The Bible speaks of wreaths of honor, joy and victory (largely synonymous with the notion of the crown). —In Christianity, the victory wreath of antiquity came to designate a sign of attained salvation; it also appears in this sense on gravestones, etc., occasionally in conjunction with the CHRIST MONOGRAM or with the DOVE or LAMB. —During antiquity, the Middle Ages, and modern times, rulers and victors were frequently portrayed with LAUREL wreaths. Since the Age of Humanism, the laurel wreath (borrowing from antiquity) has also been a favorite mark of distinction of particularly outstanding artists, poets and scholars. —The Advent wreath, which is made of evergreen branches and has four candles as a symbol of preparation and hope, is particular to German-speaking lands and did not appear until after the First World War.

WOLF: The Capitoline she-wolf
WOODPECKER: The woodpecker as an image of the devil (from Schmid's *Musterbuch*)

334

**Yantra** - A symbolic graphic depiction, common in Hinduism, of a deity or divine force, especially of the goddess Shri as Shakti; it is a symbolic visual rendition of the primeval, undifferentiated unity with Brahma that developed into the multiplicity of the empirical world; it is common as a meditation sign, but also as an amulet.

Yeast - Even in early Judaism, yeast was occasionally a symbol of decomposition, of spiritual ruin, and of impurity. Sacrificial breads thus always had to be unleavened. During the Exodus of the people of Israel from Egypt, which occured at night and in haste, unleavened bread dough was taken along since there was no more time to wait for the process of fermentation; thus, during the Jews' flight, unleavened bread was eaten; the annual Jewish festival of Passover, which is also called the "feast of unleavened bread," is the symbolic recapitulation of the Exodus from Egypt, which, for its part, is a symbol of God's promise.

Yellow - A very bright color closely related to the symbolic meaning of GOLD, LIGHT, and the SUN; like gold, it is sometimes a symbol of eternity and transformation. —As the color of autumn, yellow is also occasionally encountered as a color of maturity. —In China, yellow was opposed to BLACK, yet, as its complement, was closely tied to it, which corresponds to the manifold relations of the two principles Yang (yellow) and Yin (black); see YIN AND YANG. Yellow thus arises from black in a manner similar to how earth arises from the primeval waters. Since yellow designates the center of the universe, it is also the color of the emperor. —Sometimes a clear distinction is drawn between different shades of yellow, for example, golden yellow indicates "good, bright" and sulphurous yellow indicates "evil, devilish." In Islam, golden yellow signifies wisdom and good advice, where-as pale yellow signifies treachery and deception. —During the Middle Ages, negative interpretations predominated: yellow as the color of envy (as also in ancient Egypt) or disgrace (as in the clothes of Jews, heretics and prostitutes). It is encountered in a positive context on medieval panels, especially as a substitute for gold.

Yew Tree - As an evergreen tree and because of the fact that it grows to be very

YIN AND YANG: Chinese, temple of the lama

old, the yew tree is a symbol of immortality. Because its needles and seeds are poisonous, it was also thought to be lethal and was thus sometimes regarded as a symbol of death and resurrection as well. —In the Middle Ages, it was thought to offer defense against enchantment.

Yggdrasil - Or Ygdrasil. The evergreen world ash tree, the most sacred tree of the ancient Germans. According to ancient Germanic thought, its branches extend over heaven and earth; its roots, from which three springs sprang, connect Midgard, Utgard and Niflheim. An eagle sat on top of Yggdrasil and observed the world, and enthroned between its eyes was a hawk, which was the weather maker. The Norns lived near Yggdrasil and guarded it; verdicts were also pronounced near Yggdrasil. The final withering of the tree, which otherwise always blossomed anew, was supposed to mark the beginning of the Götterdämmerung, the twilight of the gods. —In connection with Christian ideas, Yggdrasil became conflated with the "heaven-high tree of life" around which the animals gathered, as in the case of English STONE CROSS.

Yin and Yang - The two contrary cosmological basic principles of Chinese philosophy to which all things, beings, events and time periods are ordered. Corresponding to the Yin principle are the negative, the feminine, darkness, the earth, passivity, wetness, and the broken line; corresponding to the Yang principle are the positive, the masculine, brightness, the sky, activity, dryness, and the unbroken line. The two principles represent the polarisation into which the unity of the primeval beginning separated. They are visually represented as a circle that is divided symmetrically by a serpentine line; of the two areas thereby produced, one is dark, the other light; in the middle of each area, however, there is a spot that is the color of the other area, which is a sign of the mutual dependency of both principles; the powers of Yin and Yang are never fundamentally opposed to one another; rather, they constantly influence one another and alternatingly wax or wane periodically in definite periods of time.

Ymir - Ymir is an ancient giant in Germanic mythology that reproduces asexually. This is how the frost or hoarfrost giant came to be.

YONI

Yoke - A common symbol of oppression and forced heavy burdens, also in the sense of an unhappy union of two individuals or sets of circumstances, such as "the yoke of marriage." —For the religions of India, on the other hand, the yoke positively symbolizes subordination to spiritual principles and self-discipline encompassing body and mind (the German word for yoke, *yoch*, is derived from the Indo-European root *yug*, as is the word *yoga*).

Yoni - The female counterpart to LINGA; a symbol of the maternal womb and fertility. Usually represented together with the linga as its pedestal. The graphic sign for the yoni is a TRIANGLE standing on its tip.

ZODIAC: Depiction of the relationships between man and zodiac; woodcut from a German calendar, Augsburg, 1490

Zero - A symbol of nothingness and worthlessness; with respect to series of numbers beginning with zero, it is also a symbol of beginning.

Ziggurat - See STAIRCASE; TOWER.

Zodiac - The zone on either side of the ecliptic that is (apparently) traversed each year by the sun; it is approximately eighteen degrees wide and is coursed by the planets and the Moon; it is divided according to the stars into twelve constellations or corresponding signs of the zodiac; it appears the same from all points on the earth, yet has been portrayed by various peoples either in different images (which nevertheless nearly always numbered twelve) or by different names (whereby the same division of images was maintained). Thus, what we know as Capricorn corresponded to the Babylonian goatfish; among the Chinese, the cat corresponded to our Cancer, etc. Because of precession of the equinoxes, the starting point of the zodiac is constantly shifting such that there is a difference between the zodiacal sign and the constellation. In astrology, the individual signs of the zodiac correspond to various life forms. There are many speculations about the motifs for the association of constellations with particular characters and types (such as the Virgo type, the Aquarius type). It is assumed, for example, that the character of a season influenced by a particular sign of the zodiac was symbolically associated with the character of the animal for which the constellation was named. —In many details, the connection between astrology and alchemy took place through signs of the zodiac; in medicine from the Middle Ages into the 18th century, the zodiac as a macrocosmic system of signs was reflected in the microcosm, such that the cosmic signs of the zodiac had their counterparts in the human organism (visually portrayed as ADERLASSMÄNNCHEN). —In the idea of the cosmic WHEEL, the zodiac is linked with the symbol of the CIRCLE. —In Christian art of the Middle Ages, one often encounters representations of the zodiac (often in conjunction with images depicting tasks typically performed in any given month) as symbols of fleeting time, yet also of divine immutability beyond all change, and, additionally, as a symbol of the heavenly spheres. Individually, the signs of the zodiac sometimes referred to the twelve Apostles or to various Christian subjects, although frequently with differing meanings; for example, Aries was interpreted as a symbol of the Lamb of God, Gemini as the Old and New Testaments, Leo, which conquers Scorpio (the symbol of the serpent), as a symbol of the Resurrection, Pisces as Jews and pagans who are saved by the baptismal water that is poured by Christ, who is Aquarius, and so forth.

Meaning of the zodiacal symbols according to Agrippa von Nettesheim and J.J. Scaliger:	NAME	SYMBOL	EXPLANATION
	Aries	♈	ram's head
	Taurus	♉	ox's head
	Gemini	♊	2 people, arms and legs tied together
	Cancer	♋	claws of a crab (or symbol of crab's forward and backward movement)

Constellations of the zodiac and the associated planets:	Leo	♌	tail of a lion
Signs of the Spring	Virgo	♍	wings of a virgin
Aries (Mars)	Libra	♎	2 balance beams
Taurus (Venus)	Scorpio	♏	scorpion with raised tail
Gemini (Mercury)	Sagittarius	♐	arrow resting on a bowstring
Signs of the Summer	Capricorn	♑	the wound tail of a goat-fish
Cancer (Moon)	Aquarius	♒	stream of water
Leo* (Sun)	Pisces	♓	2 fishes, backs facing one another and tied together with a band
Virgo* (Mercury)			

Signs of the Autumn
Libra* (Venus)
Scorpio* (Mars)
Sagittarius (Jupiter)
Signs of the Winter
Capricorn* (Saturn)
Aquarius (Saturn or Uranus)
Pisces (Jupiter or Neptune)
* = "day houses" of the planets, the others being "night houses"

Christian interpretation: God as the sun, the 12 zodiacal signs as the 12 Apostles and the 12 Minor Prophets (from Schmid's "Musterbuch")

ZODIAC

The term "zodiac" is actually an incorrect translation of the Greco-Latin word *zodiacus*; indeed, it has nothing to do with the Greek root word for "animal," but rather is derived from the Greek radical for "animate creatures." Thus, the zodiac derives from the very early phases of the development of civilization, when people thought that the heavenly bodies were inhabited by an astral spirit, an intelligent mind or a soul. The effect of the planets (which moved within the zodiac and *never* left it) and the astral spirit thought of as acting in them, were seen as present in all organic substances (people, animals, plants) and inorganic substances (metals, minerals, precious stones): "Everything in the world is subject to the astral spirits according to its individual planetary value and sovereignty." This idea is one of the crucial links in microcosm-macrocosm thought and reached its zenith and culmination in the magical speculations of the late Middle Ages and at the advent of modernity.

The canon of zodiac pictures has been established for more than 3,000 years; it possibly already existed in Mesopotamia and then disseminated more and more in the course of a "transfer of knowledge," constantly adapting to regional circumstances (Egypt, China, Greece, Islam). The number of zodiac pictures is not necessarily twelve; determined by factors of historical development, it can vary between eight and fifteen; a primitive calendar characterized by agriculture probably had a retroactive effect or the two influenced one another; it is even possible

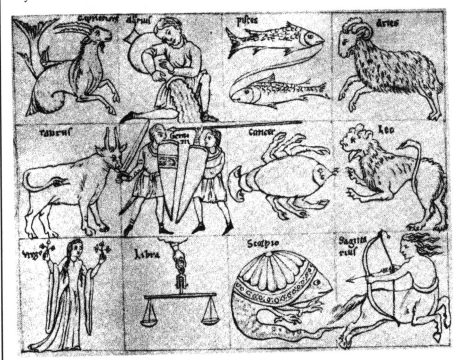

Illustration of the pictures of the zodiac in Herrad von Landsberg's *Hortus Deliciarum*, 12th century

Right: Association of the zodiac and the seasonally determined tasks of peasants. The extension of this notion led to the series of pictures depicting scenes typical of individual months (French woodcut of 1504). Center: An ancient Indian depiction of the zodiac: the twelve zodiacal signs correspond largely to those known to us; the Sun with its planets is depicted in the center. Below: The 12-part Chinese zodiac; the outer figures represent the circle of animals, the scripted writings in the center designate the "12 earthly tribes" upon which a rigid subdivision into 30 days was based.

that the subdivision of the zodiac was originally determined in part by the ancient system of the winds.

The development and the history of the astrological symbols is largely unknown. It seems that they appear for the first time in Greek manuscripts of the late Middle Ages; on the other hand, they are a further development of the first and last letters of the respective Greek terms for the zodiacal signs; in the case of some other astrological signs, one can assume that they are related to Egyptian hieroglyphics or are simply marks. The numerous speculations regarding the zodiac that are based on the number 12 (4 x 3), were hardly known to, or hardly used in, ancient astrology; nearly all are products of the modern age. On the other hand, the notion of a power working in the individual signs of the zodiac (which, in today's terms, are 30-degree ecliptical segments), has persisted to the present day with hardly any change. There is hardly any phenomenon of the sublunar world that has not been associated with the zodiac, such as animals and plants, foods, perfumes, cities and countries, the tribes of Israel and the Apostles. These associations are always made according to a

In A. Kircher's *Oedipus Aegyptiacus* of 1653, the complicated history of the zodiac becomes clear: Egyptian, Roman and Greek influences are apparent in the illustrations. The system is surrounded by the 36 decans.

scheme whereby an object (plant, stone, etc.) is controlled by a sign when certain connections can be made in the astrological tradition (see PLANETS). Associations with the zodiac can even be found in Ptolemy.

Archimedes standing on the flat earth, surrounded by water, air and fire and the heavenly spheres; the zodiacal signs are depicted as a sort of procession, led by the sign Pisces.

Finis coronat: Final page from Jacob Cat's (1577-1660, Dutch statesman and poet) auto-biographical work about his 82-year life; the woodcut was printed by Jan van der Deyster in Leyden (1732). "Finis coronat" means "the conclusion crowns the work."

BIBLIOGRAPHY

Aurenhammer, H. *Encyclopedia of Christian Iconography* [Lexikon der christlichen Ikonographie], 1969-1977.

Becker, U. (compiler) *Encyclopedia of Astrology* [Lexikon der Astrologie], 1981.

Behling, L. *The Plant World of Medieval Cathedrals* [Die Planzenwelt der mittelalterlichen Kathedralen], 1964.

Beigbeder, O. *La symbolique*, 1961

Beigbeder, O. *Lexique des symboles (La nuit des temps)*, 1969

Biedermann, H. *Knaur's Encyclopedia of Symbols* [Knaurs Lexikon der Symbole], 1989

Biedermann, H. *Pictorial Symbols of Prehistorical Times* [Bildsymbole der Vorzeit], 1977

Biedermann, H. *Pocket Encyclopedia of Magical Arts* [Handlexikon der magischen Künste], 1976

Cairo, G. *Dizionario ragionato dei simboli*, 1967

Chevalier, J. and Gheerbrant, A. *Dictionario des symboles*, 1974

Clébert, J.P. *Bestiaire Fabuleux*, 1971.

Dieckmann, H. *Fairy Tales and Symbols* [Märchen und Symbole], 1990

Endres, F.C. and Schimmel, A. *The Mystery of Numbers* [Das Mysterium der Zahl], 1984

Ferguson, G. *Signs and Symbols in Christian Art*, 1961

Forstner, D. *The World of Symbols* [Die Welt der Symbole], 1977

Forstner, D and Becker R. *New Encyclopedia of Christian Symbols* [Neues Lexikon christlicher Symbole], 1991

Grotjahn, M. *The Language of Symbols* [Die Sprache des Symbols], 1977

Heinz-Mohr, G. *Encyclopedia of Symbols, Images and Signs in Christian Art* [Lexikon der Symbole, Bilder und Zeichen der christlichen Kunst], 1991

Herder Encylopedia of Biblical Figures [Herder Lexikon Biblischer Gestalten]. Compiled by Ohler, A., 1981

Herder Encyclopedia of Enthnology [Herder Lexikon Ethnologie]. Compiled by Grohs-Paul, W. and Paul, M., 1981

Herder Encyclopedia of Germanic and Celtic Mythology [Herder Lexikon Germanische und Keltische Mythologie]. Compiled by Coenen, D. and Holzapfel, O., 1990

Herder Encyclopedia of Greek and Roman Mythology [Herder Lexikon Griechische und Römische Mythologie]. Compiled by Coenen, D., 1990

Herder Encyclopedia of Art [Herder Lexikon Kunst]. Compiled by Böing-Häusgen, U., 1977

Herder Encyclopedia of Symbols [Herder Lexikon Symbole]. Compiled by Oesterreicher-Mollwo, M., 1990

Jung, C.G. *Man and His Symbols* [Der Mensch und seine Symbole], 1986

Kirchgässner, A. *The World as Symbol* [Welt als Symbol]. 1968

Lauf, D.-I. *Symbols, Diversity and Unity in Eastern and Western Culture* [Symbole, Verschiedenheit und Einheit in der östlichen und westlichen Kultur], 1976

Encyclopedia of Christian Iconography (8 Volumes) [Lexikon der christlichen Ikonographie, 8 Bände]. Edited by E. Kirschbaum, 1968-1976

Lipffert, K. *A Primer of Symbols* [Symbol-Fibel], 1975

Lurker, M. *Bibliography of Symbolism* (3 Volumes) [Bibliographie der Symbolkunde, 3 Bände], 1964-1968

Lurker, M. *Bibliography of Symbolism, Iconography and Mythology* [Bibliographie der Symbolik, Ikonographie und Mythologie], 1968ff.

Lurker, M. *Dictionary of Biblical Images and Symbols* [Wörterbuch biblischer Bilder und Symbole], 1990

Maier, J. and Schäfer, P. *Small Encyclopedia of Jewry* [Kleines Lexikon des Judentums], 1981

Mode, H. *Fabulous Animals and Demons: The Fantastic World of Hybrid Creatures* [Fabeltiere und Dämonen: Die phantastische Welt der Mischwesen], 1977

De Osa, V. *The Animal as Symbol* [Das Tier als Symbol], 1968

Von Rabbow, A. *Encyclopedia of Political Symbols* [Lexikon politscher Symbole], 1970

Randall, R.A. *A Cloister Bestiary*, 1960

Rech, Ph. *Essence of the Cosmos* [Inbild des Kosmos], 1960

Sachs, H., Badstübner, E., and Neumann, H. *Index of Christian Iconography* [Christliche Ikonographie in Stichworten], 1973

Sauer, J. *The Symbolism of Church Construction* [Symbolik des Kirchengebäudes], 1924, reprinted 1964

Schiller, G. *Encyclopedia of Christian Iconography* [Lexikon der christlichen Ikonographie], 1966-1976

Schmid, A. *Christian Symbols* [Christliche Symbole], 1909 (cited as "Schmid's 'Book of Patterns'")

Schwarz-Winklhofer, I. and Biedermann, H. *The Book of Signs and Symbols* [Das Buch der Zeichen und Symbole], 1975

Seel, O. *Physiologus* [Physiologus], 1960

Seibert, J. (compiler) *Encyclopedia of Christian Art* [Lexikon christlicher Kunst], 1989

Spitzing, G. *Encyclopedia of Byzantine Christian Symbols* [Lexikon byzantinisch christlicher Symbole], 1989

Symbolism of the Religions: A Religious Studies Series (25 Volumes) [Symbolik der Religionen, eine religionswissenschaftliche Reihe, 25 Bände), 1958ff.

Treu, U. *Physiologus* [Physiologus], 1981

Urech, E. *Encyclopedia of Christian Symbols* [Lexikon christlicher Symbole], 1976

De Vries, A. *Dictionary of Symbols and Imagery*, 1976